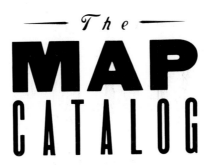

The

MAP
CATALOG

Also from Vintage Books/Random House and Tilden Press:

The Air & Space Catalog
The Complete Sourcebook to Everything in the Universe

The Nature Catalog
From Arboreta to Zoos, From Astronomy to Wildflowers, From Oceans to Deserts, an Encyclopedic Sourcebook—Everything You Need to Know About the Natural World

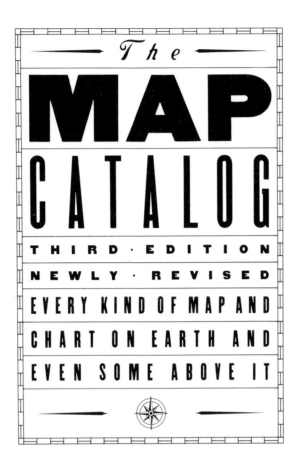

The MAP CATALOG

THIRD · EDITION
NEWLY · REVISED

EVERY KIND OF MAP AND CHART ON EARTH AND EVEN SOME ABOVE IT

Joel Makower
Editor

A Tilden Press Book

VINTAGE BOOKS
A division of Random House, Inc. New York

A Vintage Original, October 1992
Third Edition

LIBRARY OF CONGRESS CATALOGING-IN-PUBLICATION DATA

The Map catalog: every kind of map and chart on earth and even some above it / Joel
    Makower, editor— 3rd ed., rev.
    p. cm.
    "A Tilden Press book."
    ISBN 0-679-74257-3 (pbk.): $18
    1. Maps—Catalogs. I. Makower, Joel, 1952– .
Z6028.M23 1992
[GA105.3]
912'.0294—dc20   92-53582
                                                             CIP

Typesetting by MacSachel Imagesetting, Wheaton, MD.
Manufactured in the United States of America

10 9 8 7 6 5 4 3

Much of the information on pages 270-273 was excerpted from "Globes: A Librarian's Guide to Selection and Purchase," by James Coombs, from the March 1981 issue of the *Wilson Library Bulletin*. Reprinted with permission.

About This Book

The world is changing fast—and so are the maps that must keep up with it.

Recent years have seen dramatic changes in national boundaries, with countries breaking apart, merging, or just changing names. (See "As the World Turns," page 13, for details.) The world's cartographers struggle to keep their maps and charts current, a feat that always seems more a dream than a reality.

As this book goes to press, the map world seems to be on the verge of an explosion of new maps, globes, and atlases of Eastern Europe, the result of the breakup of the former Soviet Union as well as ongoing turmoil in Yugoslavia. Many of those new publications and products are listed in these pages. Others, unfortunately, will be too late for this edition. Still, this edition reflects the current crop of maps on a wide range of subjects, from the discovery of the New World to the creation of a new world order.

A book containing a list of every map published, or even every map presently available, should such a book be possible to compile, would be of little use to most people. In this book, we have attempted to provide information about the many types of maps available, the major sources of each map type, and descriptions or examples of the map products available from each source.

Much like a good map itself, The Map Catalog is a reference tool, a portrait of the cartographic landscape. Like a map, it shows you possible destinations, but not always the exact directions by which to reach them. Ultimately, it is up to the reader to determine how the tool may best be used. Like a map, this book may be browsed and enjoyed for the pure pursuit of knowledge; or it may serve as a source for acquiring specific maps for specific needs.

We have divided the maps and charts in this book into several sections: "Travel Maps," "Maps of Specific Areas," "Boundary Maps," "Scientific Maps," "History Through Maps," "Utility and Service Maps," "Water Maps," "Sky Maps," "Images as Maps," "Atlases and Globes," and "Et Cetera," with each section itself divided into several chapters. The delineations are, admittedly, arbitrary at times. A map of U.S. forests, for example, could reasonably be listed under "Agriculture Maps," "Energy Maps," "Land-Use Maps," "Natural Resource Maps," "Tourism Maps," "United States Maps," or "Wildlife Maps"; we have chosen to list them under "Recreation Maps." To minimize confusion, there are cross-references within each subsection and a thorough index at the end of the book.

Most addresses of map sources appear within their respective listings. Addresses of most map-producing government agencies, however, are contained in the book's appendixes, to avoid repeating the same addresses many times throughout the book. The appendixes, moreover, contain addresses of map sources not necessarily referred to in the text—of selected map stores, for example, and major map libraries.

This third edition of The Map Catalog expands the first two editions, with additional chapters and product categories. We have been grateful for the comments and contributions of readers and reviewers and continue to welcome them, which we will incorporate in subsequent editions of this book. Please send them to The Map Catalog, c/o Tilden Press Inc., 1526 Connecticut Ave. NW, Washington, DC 20036.

Contents

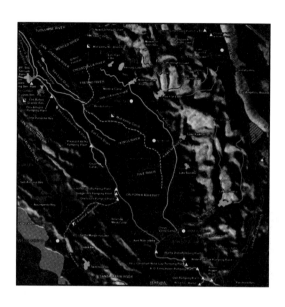

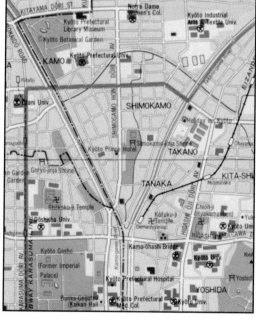

Acknowledgments

Alan Green played a major role in updating and expanding this edition of *The Map Catalog*, for which he deserves recognition and thanks. He was ably assisted by the efforts of the staff at Tilden Press, Inc., including Kerry Fitzmaurice, Alex Friend, Anna Mulrine, and Nancy Tienvieri. Thanks also to the following individuals and organizations who provided valuable support to this project:

Robert T. Aangeenbrug, Association of
  American Geographers
Dr. Paul S. Anderson, Department of Geogra-
  phy-Geology, Illinois State University
Marty Asher, Vintage Books
Ron Beck, EROS Data Center
André Caron, Canada Map Office
Alice Chen, Maps Alberta
June Crowe
Jack Dodd, Tennessee Valley Authority
Melvin Dunaway, Defense Mapping Agency
Joyce Hodel, Rand McNally
David C. Jolly, David C. Jolly Publishers
Jesse Levine, Laguna Sales
Edward W. Lollis and Schera Chadwick,
  GeoVisual Business Systems

Barbara Marcus
Sally Meyers, Association of American
  Geographers
James O. Minton
Eric Riback, DeLorme Mapping Co.
Dr. Arthur H. Robinson
Linda Rosenberg, Vintage Books
Randy J. Rosenberg
Shayna P. Rosenberg
David Sacks, MacSachel Imagesetting
Robert Sims, National Geographic Society
John P. Snyder, American Cartographic
  Association
Norman Strasma, International Map Dealers
  Association
Betty Tinsley, U.S. Geological Survey

A WORLD OF MAPS

State of the Art

We have become a world awash in maps.

For more than five centuries, we have measured and documented virtually every square foot of our planet, not to mention the oceans and the heavens. And we have recorded our findings with astounding accuracy in graphic representations—in black and white and in glorious color—called "maps." We have maps of everything from airports to zip codes, from highways to hurricanes to hidden treasures.

Maps are so much a part of our everyday lives that we may think of them as being more real than the "real world" itself. Consider Huck Finn and Tom Sawyer, soaring high above the Midwest in a balloon in Mark Twain's *Tom Sawyer Abroad*. Estimating their present location, Huck claims they're still over Illinois; Tom thinks they've floated into Indiana. "I know by the color," says Huck. "And you can see for yourself that Indiana ain't in sight."

"What's color got to do with it?" asks Tom.

"It's got everything to do with it," explains Huck. "Illinois is green, Indiana is pink. You show me any pink down here, if you can."

"Indiana pink? Why, what a lie!"

"It ain't no lie; I've seen it on the map, and it's pink."

This is a sentiment that's been expressed by others even more worldly than Messrs. Sawyer and Finn. Astronaut John Glenn, approaching splashdown near the end of his historic 1962 Mercury space flight, informed Mission Control, "I can see the whole state of Florida, just laid out like on a map."

Maps have become a way of life. How many maps are there? No one knows for sure, but some data from the federal government, the world's most skilled and prolific cartographer, are revealing. According to Uncle Sam, there are some 39 federal agencies involved in map-making. Together, they have produced nearly a quarter-million separate maps. In a typical year, the 12 largest map-making agencies alone distribute more than 161 million copies of their maps at a cost of just over a half-billion dollars. All 39 agencies expend about 13,000 worker-years of effort annually carrying out their map-making responsibilities. That's just the tip of the cartographic iceberg. Each year, Rand McNally, the world's largest nongovernment map-maker, sells about 400 million maps, through its 2,500 or so sheet maps, atlases, and globes. The 33-million-member American Automobile Association distributes about 55 million state, regional, and city maps a year, along with another 255 million strip maps. There are road maps galore from oil companies, state and local tourism offices, foreign embassies, and other sources. And there are countless other map-makers around the world, producing anywhere from a handful to several hundred different maps each year for general or highly specific audiences. Some of these maps end up in collections. While literally hundreds of private and public libraries have map collections, the 70 largest collections contain nearly 20 million maps and about 22 million aerial photographs.

It's safe to say that the output of maps, globes, atlases, and related products is well over a half-billion copies a year in this country alone.

And such variety! The types of information being mapped these days seem nearly as endless as the world itself. If you doubt this, take a browse through *New Mexico in Maps, 2nd ed.*, a 409-page reference book ($7.95 paperback) edited by Jerry L. Williams and published by the University of New Mexico Press (Albuquerque, NM 87131; 505-277-7564). The book, containing only government-produced maps of the state, features (unfortunately, in black and white) maps on some 131 different topics, from "Vacation Facilities" to "Vulnerable Aquifers," "Housing Characteristics" to "Horse Shows." Keep in mind that, except for the Rio Grande on its southern border, New Mexico is a landlocked state; given a substantial body of water, the number of map types available for the state might double.

There's good reason for this veritable map mania. In our information society, maps play an important role. A mere three-foot-square map can contain thousands of pieces of information on an endless number of topics, making maps highly efficient information-storage devices. But it is for more than just data that we turn to maps. For some, maps make fascinating reading. It's not unreasonable to curl up with a good map to try to put things into perspective, to determine where you are, where you're going (or would like to go), or where you've been. For many, maps are works of art, worthy of display on a wall, perhaps even framed. Indeed, some antique maps truly are works of art, with price tags that may ascend into the thousands of dollars.

The pages that follow reveal the vast and varied world of maps, atlases, globes, and related products—who makes them, how they're compiled, how they're used, and where they can be found. All told, this information represents something more than a mere celebration of maps. Understanding the nature of, say, a topographic map can provide insight into our planet's structure and beauty. Even a colorless census map can speak volumes about the myriad forces that shape society. From the earliest sketches to the latest in digital imaging, maps tell the story of our world and our lives in ways that words can't even begin to describe.

So, anybody need a map?

The Map Unfolds

The history of maps dates back to man's first realization that a picture really is worth a thousand words. Archaeologists and other social scientists have often marveled at early man's almost instinctive ability to produce rough but amazingly accurate sketches of his surroundings. Throughout the world's civilizations—from African tribesmen to Arctic Inuits—there are examples of these early maps, drawn in the earth or on stones or animal skins, showing the relative positions and distances of landmarks and localities. The Babylonians, more than 2,000 years before Christ, surveyed land holdings on clay tablets. Known as cadastral maps, they represent one of the earliest forms of graphic expression. Those ancient surveys later became the basis for map-making in Europe during the Middle Ages and, four millenia later, for land plats produced by the U.S. government.

The modern-day craft of making maps can be traced to western Europe in the 13th century. The regional and local maps of the day represented radical changes from the drawings that preceded them: rather than being derived from literary sources and mythology, they were based on observation and measurements—the first maps intended for practical use by travelers on land or sea. The second half of the 13th century produced the earliest surviving nautical charts and post-Roman road maps.

It was in the waters of the Mediterranean and Black seas that map-making made great strides. The development of the mariner's compass permitted angular measurement, enabling a level of accuracy in nautical charts that wouldn't be seen in land maps for several hundred years. Among these first efforts were the Italian portolan charts, which were sets of sailing instructions created on parchment around 1250 by a community of Italian draftsmen just becoming familiar with

mathematics and measurement. Many of the early European cartographers were recruited from the ranks of painters, miniaturists, and other artists, whose introduction to the profession consisted largely of copying and decorating existing maps. Later, they were able to compile their own. Italy, especially Florence, was a center of cartographic activity for several centuries. Here, a succession of explorers, artists, and mathematicians created new pictures that expressed an expanding world view.

The era of Christopher Columbus was another time of great map-making advances. The year 1492, in fact, saw the creation of the first modern terrestrial globe, the work of Germans Martin Behaim, a cosmographer, and Georg Holzschuher, a miniaturist. The 20-inch-wide globe showed the equator, the two tropics, and the Arctic and Antarctic circles. Another key innovation was the copperplate, which proved a far more effective medium for map reproduction than the woodcut and helped launch a booming map trade throughout Europe. By the early 1600s, the governments of Spain, Portugal, and England were among those recognizing the importance of maps, using them for property assessment, taxation, military planning, and to inventory national resources.

Mapping underwent radical changes in 17th-century France, due largely to an unquenchable thirst for maps and nautical charts. Such innovations as the telescope, the pendulum clock, and logarithm tables permitted accurate astronomical observations and the measurement of arcs on the Earth's surface. Both contributed to major advances in cartography. New standards of precision, in turn, led to other advancements, such as the creation of the bubble level, the aneroid barometer, and the theodolite, all of which resulted in great leaps forward in plotting

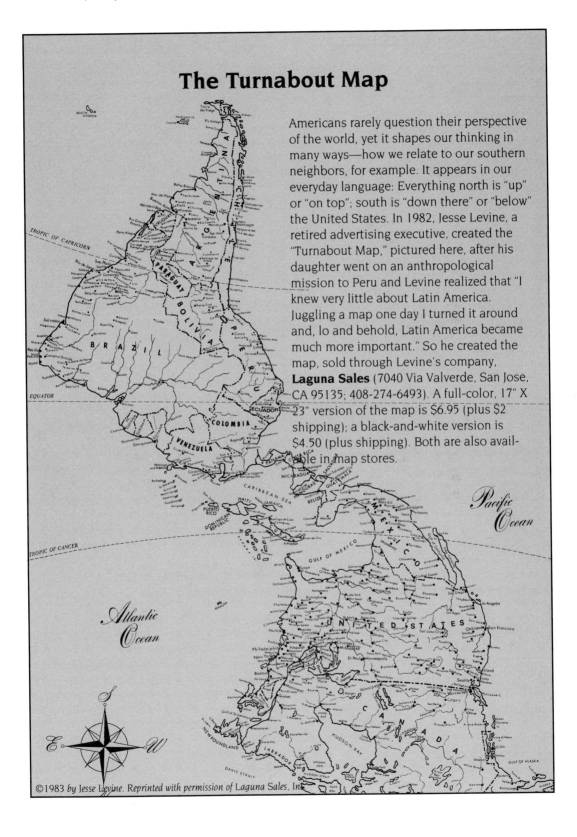

The Turnabout Map

Americans rarely question their perspective of the world, yet it shapes our thinking in many ways—how we relate to our southern neighbors, for example. It appears in our everyday language: Everything north is "up" or "on top"; south is "down there" or "below" the United States. In 1982, Jesse Levine, a retired advertising executive, created the "Turnabout Map," pictured here, after his daughter went on an anthropological mission to Peru and Levine realized that "I knew very little about Latin America. Juggling a map one day I turned it around and, lo and behold, Latin America became much more important." So he created the map, sold through Levine's company, **Laguna Sales** (7040 Via Valverde, San Jose, CA 95135; 408-274-6493). A full-color, 17" X 23" version of the map is $6.95 (plus $2 shipping); a black-and-white version is $4.50 (plus shipping). Both are also available in map stores.

Chinese woodcut world map first published in Korea sometime during the late 17th or early 18th century. Courtesy American Geographical Society.

topographic measurements and absolute altitudes. The 18th century brought several advancements in printing, not the least of which was the introduction of chromolithography—the ability to print several colors at once—which enabled map-makers to enhance their works with color detail. All of these advances aided the creation of such early cartographic masterpieces as Jacques Cassini's remarkable *Déscription géometrique de la France*. Published in 1783, it consisted of 182

engraved maps showing an entire nation in unprecedented detail—everything from canyons to channels to churches.

Meanwhile, in the newly formed United States of America, efforts were being made to take inventory of the burgeoning nation. As early as 1777, George Washington appointed a geographer and surveyor to the Continental Army to "take sketches of the country." This marked the first time that the U.S. government became involved in cartography. The first official large-scale surveying and map-ping program was proposed by Thomas Jefferson and his congressional Committee on Public Land in 1784. This led to the creation of the General Land Office, which produced a mountain of township plats and accompany-ing field notes. As president, Jefferson was concerned with the lack of information available about the newly acquired land west of the Mississippi River. During the War of 1812, his concerns led to creation by the War Department of an elite Bureau of Topographic Engineers, later the Army Corps of Engineers, which played a vital role in surveying and documenting the nation's lands and waters. Jefferson is further credited with the creation of the Survey of the Coast, later the Coast and Geodetic Survey.

During the 19th century, while government surveyors measured and subdivided regions that were relatively well known, the War Department sent exploring parties into largely unmapped territory. Many of the documents that emerged were vital in building the roads, canals, and railroads needed to accommodate a prospering populace. The topographic surveying and mapping programs conducted by the U.S. Geological Survey (USGS) from its inception in 1879 were based on a complex system set up by the Coast and Geodetic Survey, the leading scientific agency in the federal government during the last century.

Prior to the Civil War, government surveys were limited to the vast Midwest. The west-ward migration that followed the war created an urgent need for detailed information about the resources and natural features of the western United States. By the beginning of the 20th century, the USGS was undertaking a 20-year program to map nearly every inch of the nation in rigorous scientific detail.

Map-making excelled during World War I, when many USGS topographers were commis-sioned by the Army Corps of Engineers. Some played key roles in developing aerial-photog-raphy techniques used for military intelli-gence. Returning after the war, these topogra-phers applied their new skills to cartography. Throughout the 1920s, experimenting with the new science of photogrammetry—the ability to take measurements from photographs—they succeeded in making maps from aerial photos. This development would change map-making forever.

A great surge in the application of photo-grammetry came with the establishment in 1933 of the Tennessee Valley Authority. One of TVA's first needs was map coverage of the entire valley. Working with USGS, surveyors prepared planimetric maps of the area using state-of-the-art, five-lens aerial photographs and innovative radial-line plotting tech-niques. Their efforts began a revolutionary swing away from field methods as the basis of map-making, establishing aerial photos as the basis for all the maps that would follow.

After World War II, map-making innova-tions were rampant. Combining a variety of sophisticated measuring instruments with emerging computers, cartographers produced a treasure trove of new map types and products. The advent of space imagery and electronic imaging, along with the digitization of map data in computers, produced yet another revolution in map-making. And there would be more revolutions to come.

Mapping the Future

There are many who predict the demise of the map as we know it, the elimination of those familiar, hard-to-refold sheets of paper upon which we depend for so many things. Along with other technofuturistic predictions—that the computer will replace the printed book, for example, or that newspapers will someday appear only on video screens—this will never be completely true. Which is not to say that maps, and map-making, are not changing in dramatic ways. Or that the map of tomorrow won't appear in some rather innovative forms. But there will always be paper maps, although maybe not as many of them.

As it has with so many other things, the computer has revolutionized the world of mapping in myriad ways. Computerization has introduced an impressive list of new carto-graphic tools and techniques, such as elec-tronic distance-measuring, inertial navigation, remote sensing, digital imaging, space science, and geographic-information systems. We are just beginning to learn how to use these tools. A new generation of cartogra-phers is using computers' digital technology to make and modify maps. In the new high-tech cartography, map data are no longer entered by skilled draftsmen working on light tables but are created using satellite images by cartographers at keyboards. Map data are entered on computer tapes and floppy disks, among other things, which in turn generate visual displays for editing, or which can be printed out to use in producing conventional paper maps.

With map data in a computer, cartogra-phers can easily modify maps, enlarge them, change their scale, isolate segments for use with other maps, and make them, or any part of them, instantly available to other cartogra-phers and map users who can call up digital information on their computer screens around the world. Among the many benefits of computerization is speed: combined with

other map-making techniques, computers can shorten considerably the four to five years it once took to produce a printed map from an aerial photograph or satellite image. Today, it can be done in a matter of days.

Two of the most ambitious digital-mapping programs come from the U.S. Geological Survey's Office of Geographic and Carto-graphic Research. The agency, which bud-geted almost nothing on digitized mapping a decade ago, is now spending $13 million a year on it. By the year 2000, USGS expects to complete the National Digital Cartographic Data Base, which will include all the informa-tion that now appears on the agency's maps. When completed, users will be able to illustrate almost instantly the relationships among such features as population density, water supplies, power lines, land-use pat-terns, and the presence of various natural resources. Moreover, USGS teamed up with the U.S. Bureau of the Census to produce a cartographic data base called TIGER, for "Topologically Integrated Geographic Encod-ing and Referencing" system. Created for the 1990 census, TIGER shows every river, lake, highway, and railroad track in the United States as well as displaying a wide range of census data. Now these data bases are accessible to individuals and businesses, which use them to create still other maps and computer products.

Other digital-mapping technology comes from the Defense Mapping Agency, which uses map data to guide "smart" missile systems. The process involves loading data about routes to potential targets into a missile, then instructing the missile, before launch, on which route to take. DMA has reduced the entire world map to digits and made it available on computer disk and tape. (See "World Maps" for information on DMA's "Digital Chart of the World.")

There are many other computerized-

As the World Turns
Names of New Countries/Name Changes Since 1990

Old Names	New Names
East Germany West Germany	Germany
Southwest Africa	Namibia
USSR	Armenia Azerbaijan Byelarus Estonia Georgia Kazakhstan Kyrgyzstan Latvia Lithuania Moldova Russia Tajikistan Turkmenistan Ukraine Uzbekistan
Yemen Arab Republic People's Democratic Republic of Yemen	Republic of Yemen
Yugoslavia	Yugoslavia Bosnia and Hercegovina Croatia Slovenia

Source: U.S. Department of State

mapping programs and geographic data bases, some of which are available for use on personal computers; see "Map Software" elsewhere in this book.

ON THE ROAD WITHOUT A MAP

Ultimately, all this high-tech wizardry is expected to become available to individuals through what may well be standard equipment on the cars of the late 1990s. With dashboard navigation systems—simplified, inexpensive versions of the systems that allow airline pilots and ship's captains to know exactly where they are even in cloudy weather—drivers in the not-too-distant future may be able to choose the best route to a destination (even taking into account an accident or construction project), or more easily negotiate unfamiliar territory.

While automakers have talked for years about such sophisticated tracking systems, they are finally becoming available, albeit in limited numbers. In 1992, an experiment began in Florida that may pave the way for computerized maps in cars. A collaboration of

The dashboard computer of a "smart car." Courtesy TravTek.

microcomputers, each with a 40-megabyte hard drive. Each car also features a strange-looking white cone on the trunk that is a transponder that communicates with a system of global positioning satellites.

Inside the car is a color-coded video display screen mounted on the dashboard. The car's exact position is shown on the screen by way of the transponders. Using something called a global positioning system (GPS), they send radio waves to the satellites, which bounce them back in a microsecond, helping the car to orient itself. The result is a white triangle that appears on the on-screen map.

The computer screen also offers from a menu of options that you select by touching the screen. Among them are: "Where to Stay," "Things to See and Do," "Where to Eat," "Other Services," and "City Facts." Selecting a topic yields still more options from which to choose. When you enter your desired destination, the computer plots a course. The computer also has a voice, which has been likened to that of a Swedish male. It tells you when to turn right or left to reach your intended destination. It also offers such helpful and timely advice as "Traffic is moderately congested on Interstate 4 East."

the Federal Highway Administration, the American Automobile Association (AAA), General Motors, the state of Florida, and the city of Orlando, the experiment begins at the Orlando airport, where Avis is renting so-called "smart cars" to AAA members for $29 a day. There are 100 Oldsmobile Toronados in the experiment that are packed with twin 386

As useful as it all sounds, the system still leaves a lot to be desired. Early test drives

Maps for the Visually Impaired
by Dale Gasteiger

People who have experienced sight loss use maps in many ways. Tactile maps can provide instruction, direction, mobility assistance, room and area descriptions, campus layouts, bus and train routes, and many other kinds of important information. The Americans with Disabilities Act (ADA), which went into effect in 1992, accents the need for reliable, portable tactile maps for blind users. Even though the ADA may cause the installation of wall plaques and signage in braille or large print, these are only useful once a blind person has been given directions to the available signs or maps. But since memorizing such signs and maps is inconvenient and unreliable, there remains a need for good portable maps that can be easily referred to when necessary.

Braille Institute is a private, nonprofit organization that offers many services and programs to help blind and visually impaired people achieve independence. The Braille Institute Press is attempting to fill a serious void in the lives of blind people by producing tactile maps at no greater cost than those produced for sighted users.

Until recently, tactile map-making at Braille Institute was a slow, tedious process involving paper, string, glue, and other items used to provide various textures and shapes. Tactile maps of this sort are fragile, expensive to construct, and inconvenient to use. We have been experimenting with two new techniques for producing portable, durable, and easy-to-use tactile maps using computer-assisted methods.

One method involves the Howtek Pixelmaster, a 240-dots-per-inch color ink-jet printer attached to a Macintosh computer. We are using the Pixelmaster to produce maps for individual use and for braille social studies and geography textbooks. It can also be used to make floor plans of hotels, office buildings, and museums; diagrams of paths and walkways for school campuses and individual orientation; and mobility maps for personal use.

Another method involves the use of "nyloplates" to print paper maps, graphs, and illustration outlines that can be mass-produced for use in braille publications. The nyloplate process is simple, easy to use, and requires standard ink-printing procedures. A special negative is produced from camera-ready art, then burned into a nyloplate. One difference from ink printing is the need for a second plate to complete the embossing process. The technique has been used to produce the graphic illustrations that appear in our annual braille anthology of children's stories, *Expectations*, which is distributed free worldwide to English-speaking blind children, their parents, and the institutions that serve them. Initial reactions to the new method of solid raised outlines—as opposed to the old process, which utilized raised dots—have been very favorable.

In the past, technological limits and prohibitive costs made it impossible for blind and visually impaired people to own tactile maps, atlases, and globes. Now, Braille Institute has the technical ability to give blind people useful tools for mobility and independence. We urge interested members of the map-making community to contact us with suggestions on how we might further improve our cartographic processes.

Dale Gasteiger is director of Braille Institute Press. For more information, contact the press at 741 N. Vermont Ave., Los Angeles, CA 90029; 213-663-1111.

revealed that these "smart cars" weren't always as smart as they were cracked up to be. After all, they are only as reliable as the technology behind them. Should a computer fail or the navigation system go on the blink, the system may shut down and the hapless driver could be quickly lost in a strange city.

The bugs will inevitably be worked out. And we will likely find ourselves with a strange new friend on our automobile dashboards—a friend who not only knows where to go, but will tell us how to get there.

Eventually, say those on the cutting edge of map-making technology, instead of stopping at a service station for directions, we may be able to punch our destinations into the service station's computer and obtain (for a fee, of course) a made-to-order map, complete with a detailed list of restaurants, motels, and attractions along the way.

But that's far from all we can expect in the brave new world of maps. Already, there are 3-D maps that are displayed on computer screens from compact videodiscs; hand-held GPS units used by hikers, soldiers, and others to help locate themselves on a map (and to let others find them too); video animation showing geologic sequences, as well as environmental and political changes; and compact discs packed with maps and animated "flybys" of terrain. In the not-too-distant future we'll see holographic maps showing such things as changes in weather and environment.

The possibilities go on and on. Thanks to computers and other technologies, they are virtually endless. From city planning to coastal management, commuting to armchair travel, digital and other high-tech mapping techniques are increasingly finding their way into our lives, making the world around us a bit more manageable and, perhaps, a little easier to understand.

How to Choose a Map

Finding a map on just about anything is relatively easy: you simply consult your local map store, or contact one of the hundreds of other resources listed in this book.

Finding a *good* map is another matter. There are maps that will suit your purpose, and maps that won't. Choosing from among the many available products requires a bit of insight into what makes a good map.

Selecting the right map can be somewhat like selecting a car: there are so many to choose from that the ultimate decision boils down to a combination of what's available and what suits your taste. But like cars, maps have a number of features (albeit far less technologically sophisticated) that you should consider when making a selection.

Among the things to consider are how the map will be used. A travel map, for example, must show sufficient detail to allow you to traverse unknown roads. If it shows only major highways, it will be of little use once you exit the main road in search of your destination. However, if all you plan to do is drive through an area on your way to some-place else, a highway map may do just fine.

Here are some additional considerations when choosing a map:

■ **Format.** Does the area covered require several sheets? This may make it more difficult to use while driving. On the other hand, a very large region—Los Angeles, for example—may be best suited to several less-comprehensive maps. If several maps are required, are they contained in one publica-tion, or will you have to switch back and forth between several maps or books? If it is a folding map, can you easily refold it?

■ **Media.** Most people are used to maps printed on paper. But other media are sometimes appropriate. Some map collec-tions or series are available on computer disk or on microfiche, for example, allowing for easy access to a great many map images with a minimum of storage.

■ **Materials.** A flimsy map can be used only under scrupulous conditions. Ideally, a map should be printed on good-quality paper that is resistant to aging and tearing. If a map is intended for heavy use outside of a home, office, or library—in a car, on a trail, in a boat—it should be made of a water- and tear-resistant material (Tyvek is one such material), and perhaps be laminated to protect it from the elements. Lamination, however, makes it impossible to fold a map, which may be impractical. A good alternative is a protective spray that you can apply yourself; map covers and cases may also be helpful (see "Map Accessories").

■ **Design.** Are words and symbols large enough to read? Are they sufficiently distinct from their backgrounds and from one another to be easily seen and interpreted? Are colors, contrast, and patterns used to enhance the information, or do they make it cluttered and confusing?

■ **Currency.** A good map should be up to date. Keep in mind, however, that some maps—topographic maps, for example—don't go out of date very quickly. Most road maps, on the other hand, are of little use when not current. And aeronautical and nautical charts go out of date within a few weeks or months, making them dangerous (and often illegal) to use after they have become outmoded. Publication date alone is only one factor: a 1990 map will be of limited use if it is based on 1970 population data. Keep in mind that some maps are created on a one-time basis (due, usually, to a one-time appropriation of resources for this purpose).

■ **Scale.** Map scale is one of the most important aspects of any map, but one of the least considered by many map buyers. Scale, simply put, expresses the ratio of distance on the map to actual distance on the ground (or air or sea, for an aeronautical or nautical chart). So a map with a scale of 1:1 would be life-size, literally: every inch of the map would represent one inch of land. That's not feasible, of course, and defeats the whole purpose of maps—to represent a vast area in a relatively small space.

Map scales range widely, from 1:1,000 to 1:100,000,000 and smaller; the larger the second number, the smaller the scale. (Scale is sometimes expressed with a slash instead of a colon, as in 1/100,000.) Topographic maps range from about 1:20,000 to 1:1,000,000; the former are large-scale maps, commonly used by campers and hikers, the latter might be used for a topographic map of the world. (See "Topographic Maps" for more on this.) City street maps fall in the 1:10,000 range. Some of the largest-scale maps, at 1:1,000 or even 1:500, are used by city governments for tax-collecting and property-assessing purposes.

To convert scale to actual size, use 1:60,000 as a rough base. At that scale, one inch on the map equals approximately one mile on land. (The exact ratio is 1:63,360.) So, on a 1:125,000 map, a mile would be covered in about a half-inch; a 1:500,000 map would cover about eight miles per inch.

MAP PROJECTIONS

For centuries, map-makers have grappled with the problem of how to depict a round world on a flat surface. Despite advancements in geometry and the creation of complex mathematical models, there remains controversy over the optimum method of producing maps of the world without distorting one or more sections of the Earth's surface.

For more than 400 years, the traditional view of the world was based on the models produced by Gerhardus Mercator, considered the leading cartographer of the 16th century. His grid system of cartography—revealed in his 1569 map of the world—became the classic expression of cartography and has dictated our geographical world concept ever since. His map was revolutionary; among other things, the spherical nature of the globe, proved by Ferdinand Magellan's circumnavigation of the world, was clearly expressed in it.

But the Mercator projection has its problems—and its critics. For one thing, the polar regions appear grossly enlarged, as land masses and bodies of water are spread to fill the lines of latitude and longitude. Another problem is that the equator appears below the midpoint of the map, thereby enlarging the continents north of the equator.

Mercator's projection of the globe has been followed by many others. All told, more than 200 world-map projections have been produced, with about 100 receiving significant

Gall-Peters

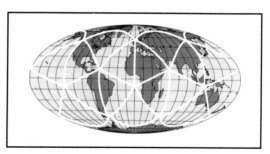

Mollweide

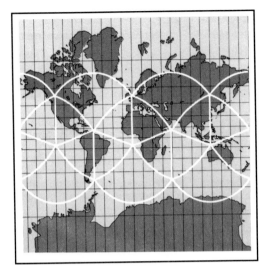

Mercator

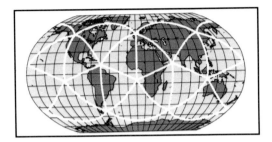

Robinson

Goode Homolosine

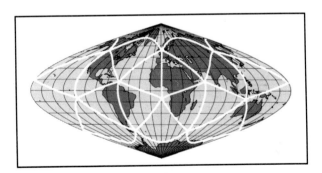

Sinusoidal

Six examples of map projection systems, courtesy American Congress on Surveying and Mapping.

use. About a dozen projections have gained widespread use in the late 20th century. But until recently, the Mercator projection reigned supreme.

While there have been campaigns waged for decades to supplant the Mercator projection with other, more accurate versions, the movement reached a new peak in 1988 when the National Geographic Society, after reviewing nearly 20 proposals, unanimously chose the Robinson projection as its new official view of the world. Since 1922, the society had used maps that relied on a system developed by American engineer Alphons van der Grinten. But that projection, much like Mercator's, depicted Greenland 554 percent larger than it is. The Soviet Union was depicted 223 percent larger, and the United States 68 percent larger.

The Robinson projection, created by Arthur H. Robinson, professor emeritus of cartography and geography at the University of Wisconsin–Madison, was completed in 1963. Robinson had directed the U.S. Office of Strategic Services' map division during World War II and decided to devise a new projection system after encountering many problems in mapping a worldwide war.

The Robinson projection gained even greater official acceptance in 1989, when the American Cartographic Association and five major geographical organizations passed a resolution condemning the widespread use of rectangular maps of the world—such as Mercator's—and endorsed the Robinson version. In the resolution, which began "Whereas, the earth is round . . . ," the cartographers urged book and map publishers, the news media, and government agencies to stop using rectangular maps.

Such official endorsements notwithstanding, there remain other projections that have garnered attention—and controversy—among cartographers. A map created in 1974 by German historian Arno Peters, for example, attempts to correct Mercator's distortions,

which Peters says distort the shape of continents to overemphasize Caucasian countries in temperate regions. As a result, North America and Eurasia appear considerably larger than South America and Africa. Peters' notions, while not generally accepted by geographers and cartographers, caught the attention of the United Nations, which helped fund development of a detailed 51" X 35" color world map based on the Peters projection. Copies of the world map are available for $9.95 (includes shipping) from **Friendship Press** (P.O. Box 37844, Cincinnati, OH 45237; 513-948-8733).

Another intriguing model is the Fuller projection, created by Buckminster Fuller, the self-described "engineer, inventor, mathematician, architect, cartographer, philosopher, poet, cosmologist, comprehensive designer, and choreographer." Fuller's projection shows our planet without any visible distortion of relative shapes and sizes of the land and sea areas, and without any breaks in the continental contours. The map is available in a variety of forms, from flat maps to T-shirts, from the **Buckminster Fuller Institute** (1743 S. La Cienega Blvd., Los Angeles, CA 90035; 310-837-7710), which offers a free catalog (see "World Maps" and "Map Stuff" for descriptions of Dymaxion maps and products).

The best sources for further reading on the subject of map projections are three publications by the Committee on Map Projections of the American Cartographic Association: *Which Map Is Best? Projections for World Maps*; *Choosing a World Map—Attributes, Distortions, Classes, Aspects*; and *Matching the Map Projection to the Need*. They are available from the **American Congress on Surveying and Mapping** (5410 Grosvenor Ln., Ste. 100, Bethesda, MD 20814; 301-493-0200). The price for either of the first two is $10 for ACSM members ($12 for others), while the third book in the series is $15 for ACSM members and $20 for others. A complete catalog of publications is available from ACSM upon request.

Learning About Map Skills

by Dr. Paul S. Anderson

A "Peanuts" cartoon strip from a few years ago features Lucy posing a question to Snoopy, who is reclining, as always, on the roof of his doghouse.

"Can you read a map?" she asks.

"Of course!" responds the dog.

"If you're going to visit your brother in Needles, you'll need a map," she says, offering Snoopy a folded road map.

Snoopy, sitting up and perusing Lucy's offering, reflects, "I'm good at reading maps. I just don't know what all those squares and dots and lines and colors and numbers and names mean."

Like Snoopy, most people consider themselves to be good map readers. But when they hold a map in their hands, the map's message is often lost or only partially understood. There are three reasons for this:

■ **The subject matter.** Many topics, such as topography, geology, census data, and tidal currents, cannot be fully absorbed from even a simple map if the basic concepts of the subject matter are not understood. Fortunately, maps themselves can help us learn some of the things we need to know.

■ **Lack of experience.** After grade school, few Americans have formal education with maps. At age 16, when one typically obtains a driver's license, there is a certain newfound interest in road maps, but even that diminishes over the years, thanks to well-marked interstate highways, with their big green-and-white signs.

■ **The "language" of maps.** Maps are *graphical* expressions of spatial relationships. They are different from books that are read from left to right, top to bottom, page by page, from beginning to end, with words made from combinations of 26 letters. Maps, in contrast, have no uniform starting point, no verbs, relatively few nouns, and hundreds of shapes and colors. Even the size of the symbols can have meaning on maps, and the spacings between objects are crucial bits of information. Without formal guidance or explanation of this language, each map user learns only a few basic expressions, something akin to speaking German with a vocabulary consisting of *Achtung, auf Wiedersehen, Bratwurst,* and *Volkswagen.*

Fortunately, the language of maps is easier to learn than German—or any other foreign language—and there are several sources for help. Concise, well-written explanations of map projections, scale, and basic symbols for small-scale (atlas-type) maps are commonly found in the introductory pages of most atlases. Map legends, often called "keys," serve as translators to explain what the diverse symbols represent. If the legend is not printed on a map (such as a topographic map), one is usually available separately from the publisher.

A readily available source of information on the use of large-scale (which describe small areas in great detail) topographic maps is the Boy Scouts of America. The main *Boy Scout Handbook* features about 10 pages on scales, symbols, directions, and general map use. In addition, the *Merit Badge Pamphlet for Orienteering* gives 32 pages that are useful for anyone planning to take a hike ($1.85; available from **Boy Scouts of America**, P.O. Box 909, Pineville, NC 28134; 800-323-0732).

For those who desire to learn greater map skills, four books offer excellent how-to explanations:

■ *Map Reading and Land Navigation* (Government Printing Office, S/N 008-020-00156-2; $6.50) is a U.S. Army field manual (FM 21-26) available for public use. Its illustrations are excellent, albeit with a military perspective.

■ *Map Use: Reading, Analysis, and Interpretation*, *2nd ed.* ($30; JP Publications, P.O. Box 44173, Madison, WI 53744; 608-231-2373) is the first college-level text on the subject. Its author, Philip Muehrcke, has put together an appropriate mixture of technical explanations, quality illustrations, and comic wit.

■ *Map Use and Analysis*, by John Campbell ($39.87; William C. Brown Publishers, 2460 Kerper Blvd., Dubuque, IA 52001; 319-588-1451), has an easy-to-read, straightforward presentation of the full range of map-reading topics.

■ *The Language of Maps*, by Phillip Gershmel ($15), has been published by the National Council for Geographic Education (16A Leonard Hall, Indiana Univ. of Pennsylvania, Indiana, PA 15705; 412-357-6290). Although intended to be used as a university text, this book is highly relevant as a tool for teachers in primary and secondary schools as well as for members of the general public interested in understanding maps.

Two other books focus on map appreciation (and less on skills) but may also be helpful:

■ *Map Appreciation*, by Mark Monmonier and George A. Schnell ($46.67; Prentice Hall, 200 Old Tappan Rd., Old Tappan, NJ 07675; 201-767-4970; 800-223-2348), is a well-illustrated text organized by map themes such as landscape, population, and politics.

■ *Interpretation of Topographic Maps*, by Victor Miller and Mary Westerback ($36; Macmillan Publishing Co., 866 Third Ave., New York, NY 10022; 800-428-3750), is devoted strictly to understanding physical landscapes using contour lines on topographic maps.

Another interesting aspect of maps is knowing how they are made. The profession of cartography (map-making) is highly skilled and well developed around the world, as shown in the multitude of map products discussed in this book. For a thorough explanation of the art and science of cartography, consult the following books:

■ *Elements of Cartography*, *5th ed.* ($19.95; John Wiley & Sons, 605 Third Ave., New York, NY 10158; 212-850-6000). This classic by Arthur Robinson has been continually updated by him and his coauthors Sale, Morrison, and Muehrcke. It remains the leading college-level textbook on the subject.

■ *Introductory Cartography*, *2nd ed.*, by John Campbell ($46.40; William C. Brown Publishers, 2460 Kerper Blvd., Dubuque, IA 52001; 319-588-1451), is a well-written overview of the field of cartography. This book is shorter and less technically oriented than Robinson's book, and so appeals to a larger audience.

Learning how to use maps is a very worthy objective. You are encouraged to contact your local college or university about map-related courses, usually offered by the geography faculty. Schoolteachers and education-minded parents can also bring the benefits of map skills to students using some of these publications.

Dr. Anderson is an associate professor of geography in the Department of Geography-Geology at Illinois State University in Normal, Illinois.

Having a Map Made

Map-maker, map-maker, make me a map.

You've looked everywhere, through every atlas and library and map store, and still you can't find just what you're looking for. Where do you go?

Getting a custom map made is sort of like shopping for a custom-tailored suit. You can find someone who'll make you what you want, but it'll cost you.

The options for custom maps fall into three basic categories:

■ You can go to a company that specializes in making maps, a few of which are listed below. This is the high-end option; it will generally cost about $75 an hour, but the chances are excellent you will get what you want.

■ A number of universities around the country have cartography labs that will do outside work for a fee, ranging from $10 to $35 an hour. Here you'll find individuals who are up on the latest technology and are trained to make maps, although they may not offer the design flair of some of the professional commercial firms.

■ You can call a local drafting or graphic-design firm and inquire about custom maps. While these individuals don't generally have traditional cartographic training, you're at least likely to get a finished product that looks good. This would be a good option for a small-scale map—that is, a map showing a fairly large area without a great deal of detailed information.

The cost of a custom-made map can vary greatly, from hundreds to thousands of dollars, depending on what's being mapped, how much information needs to be included, and the map's complexity, color, and size. If you want more than one copy, you'll have to pay printing costs, which vary widely, based on the number of colors, the size of the map, the type of paper used, the quantity you're printing, and any special features, such as folding, binding, or packaging.

There's certain information you should have in hand when going to a map-maker. First are the data to be represented on the map; most map-makers don't do research. Bring as much information as possible—the more the better. You should also have answers to a few basic questions: Is the map to be reproduced on a photocopy machine or on a printing press? Do you want it in hard-copy form or as a digital (computerized) file? That will make a big difference in the way the map is constructed.

In other words, you should have a very clear understanding of what you are going to do with the map once it is finished: who the audience is, what it will be used for, and so on. The more information you can provide, the better the map-maker will be able to help you. If the map is intended to accompany a text, such as an article or book, you should provide the map-maker with that information as well.

While most map-makers won't go out and survey land or take aerial photographs, you don't always have to know everything. Because cartographers are usually aware of the kinds of information available, the map-maker may be helpful in obtaining the information you need.

If you are using or modifying a map that somebody else has done, you must consider rights or permissions. You cannot simply use someone else's map, even if you make changes on it. To do so could result in copyright violations, and you could be liable for damages. (See "Copying Maps? Beware!" on page 25 for more information.)

Custom Map-Makers

There are hundreds of organizations and individuals who make maps professionally. Here are just a few examples:

Dewberry & Davis (8401 Arlington Blvd., Fairfax VA 22031; 703-849-0100) is an engineering, drafting, and surveying firm that offers a wide range of custom mapping services, including survey work and digitized mapping. The company does very small-scale mapping and very large-scale work up to a scale of 1 inch=10 feet. The firm has done flood insurance maps for the Federal Emergency Management Agency and also takes on smaller clients. Prices vary from as little as a few hundred dollars to several million for large data bases.

R. R. Donnelley Mapping Services (P.O. Box 3261, Lancaster, PA 17604; 717-393-9707) claims to be the nation's largest custom map provider. It offers full-service map-making, including in-house photography and typesetting capabilities. Donnelley does maps for atlases and atlas sections, antique and historical maps for Bibles, and maps for college and high school textbooks and encyclopedias as well as book publishers and travel companies. They also make maps for telephone books. The firm's final product is usually printing-plate-ready film, color-separated and touched up, with a color proof.

Eureka Cartography (2030 Addison St., Ste. 200, Berkeley CA 94704; 510-845-MAPS) specializes in custom-designed and -produced maps. The firm's clients range from the University of California Press to Fodor's travel guides. The firm also makes maps for telephone directories. Most of Eureka's work is done on Macintosh computers. The finished product is a plate-ready film negative.

GeoVisual Business Products (12700 Virginia Manor Rd., Beltsville, MD 20705; 301-470-0100) offers map-making and consulting services for companies and individuals. In addition to map-making, GeoVisual offers on-site training on a variety of map-making computer software packages, as well as consulting on geographic information systems.

Global Graphics (2819 Greentop St., Lakewood, CA 90712; 310-429-8880) is a smaller custom map firm that publishes street maps, road maps, topographic maps, and relief maps. The firm also makes thematic maps and charts.

Magellan Geographix (109 S. LaCumbre Ln., Santa Barbara, CA 93105; 805-967-3131) began creating electronic map graphics for the newspaper industry, but has extended its services to others. The company provides custom computer cartography to varying industries, including the film industry, magazines, government agencies, and textbook publishers. Magellan also offers an on-line mapping service, in which editable maps are available through an electronic bulletin board system.

Mapping Specialists, Ltd. (1319 Applegate Rd., Madison, WI 53713; 608-274-4004) is a full-service cartographic firm that specializes in thematic maps and other kinds of maps, and also works for book and encyclopedia publishers. The company will assist with research, and produces camera-ready film or data on computer disk.

Maryland Cartographics (9241 Rumsey Rd., Columbia, MD 21045; 410-740-4820) produces maps of all kinds, including oblique-view maps that "disappear" over the edge of the horizon and geologic maps that show different strata. The average four-color map for a textbook costs $250, but maps can range from $100 to $800. The firm uses Macintosh computers and delivers camera-ready film.

Meridian Maps (8103 Timber Valley Ct., Dunn Loring, VA 22027; 703-698-7141) can make reference maps, tourist guides, and maps showing market areas, statistics, and news

Copying Maps? Beware!

Need to make a map? Creating one from scratch is easier these days than it used to be, thanks to "desktop mapping" programs for personal computers (see "Map Software"). But for many individuals, companies, and associations the temptation to copy an existing map is overwhelming.

Copying many maps is illegal. The same copyright laws that prohibit you from stealing other writers' words or artists' images protect map-makers as well. Simply put, according to the International Map Dealers Association, "It is illegal for any firm or individual to reproduce copyrighted works, in whole or in part, regardless of the final purpose of the reproduction, without permission of the copyright owner." Technically, even a single photocopy of a map is a copyright violation.

There are two exceptions. Maps produced by federal or state government agencies usually are in the public domain and may be reproduced without restriction. And copyright-free maps are available from several companies, notably Facts on File, which produces a set of photocopyable boundary maps called "Maps on File" (see "Boundary Maps" for details).

Some map publishers, seeking to thwart those who illegally reprint their maps, have taken to adding "sham" streets and other landmarks to their maps. Usually, these are innocuous, half-block-long alleys, sometimes bearing the names of the map-makers (or their friends and relatives). When those streets show up on other maps, there is no question that the map was "stolen" from its creator.

The fact is, obtaining permission to reprint all or part of a copyrighted map usually is relatively simple and inexpensive. The alternative—the penalties allowed under federal copyright law for unauthorized use of copyrighted material—can be severe, and may include payment of triple royalties, damages, court costs, and attorney's fees.

For a free brochure, *Questions and Answers About Map Copyrights*, send a stamped, self-addressed legal-size envelope to the **International Map Dealers Association**, P.O. Box 1789, Kankakee, IL 60901.

events. The firm also does political maps showing cultural, economic, environmental, and social relationships. Meridian has done work for the Audubon Society, the White House, and other government agencies and consulting firms. Meridian does not use computerized mapping techniques.

Thomas Nast, Cartographer (12 Vera Pl., Montclair, NJ 07042; 201-746-1047) specializes in black-and-white maps that illustrate books, articles, and the like.

Williams & Heintz Map Corp. (8119 Central Ave., Capitol Heights, MD 20743; 301-336-1144) is a full-service custom map firm with its own in-house printing presses and photo labs.

It will print maps, draft maps from a customer's rough sketch, and will teach map drafting to customers. Among its customers are the National Parks Service and Michelin.

Cartographic Labs, United States

University Cartography Laboratories
Laboratory for Geographic & Spatial Analysis
306 Carroll Hall
University of Akron
Akron, OH 44325
216-972-7620

Cartographic Lab
Dept. of Geography
University of Alabama
Tuscaloosa, AL 35847
205-348-1536

Cartography Lab
Dept. of Geography
Arizona State University
Tempe, AZ 85287
602-965-7449

Staff Cartographer
Dept. of Geography
Ball State University
Muncie, IN 47306
317-285-1760

Dept. Cartographer
Dept. of Geography
501 Earth Sciences Bldg.
University of California, Berkeley
Berkeley, CA 94720
510-642-3903

Digital Cartographic Production Class
Dept. of Geography
3611 Ellison Hall
University of California, Santa Barbara
Santa Barbara, CA 93106
805-893-3663

Cartographic Services Unit
University of Chicago
5828 S. University Ave., Ofc. 307
Chicago, IL 60637
312-702-8305

Manager, Cartography Lab
Graduate School of Geography
Clark University
950 Main St.
Worcester, MA 01610
508-793-7367

Cartographer
Dept. of Geography
216 Newark Hall
University of Delaware
Newark, DE 19716
302-831-2294

Cartography Lab
Florida Resources & Environmental
    Analysis Center
Rm. 361, Bellamy Bldg.
Florida State University
Tallahassee, FL 32306
904-644-2883

Cartography Research Laboratory
Dept. of Geography
Georgia State University
Atlanta, GA 30303
404-651-3232

Cartographic Services
Dept. of Geography-Geology
Schroeder Rm. 110
Illinois State University
Normal, IL 61761
309-438-8403

University of Kansas Cartographic Service
Dept. of Geography
214A Lindley Hall
University of Kansas
Lawrence, KS 66045
913-864-5147

Computer Cartographic Laboratory
Dept. of Geography
Kent State University
P.O. Box 5190
Kent, OH 44242
216-672-3226

Cartographic Laboratory
Dept. of Geography
University of Kentucky
Lexington, KY 40506
606-257-4745

Resource Information Management & Spatial
    Analysis Laboratory
College of Forest Resources
252 Nutty Hall
University of Maine
Orono, ME 04469
207-581-2852

Cartography Laboratory
Dept. of Geography, MSU Box 2
Mankato State University
Mankato, MN 56002
507-389-2617

Cartographic Laboratory
Dept. of Geology/Geography
Morrill Science Center
University of Massachusetts
Amherst, MA 01003
413-545-2078

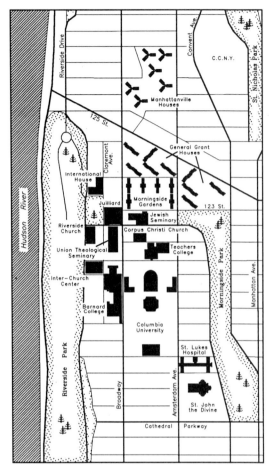

Map showing urban redevelopment in the Morningside Heights neighborhood of Manhattan, circa 1954, by Thomas Nast, Cartographer.

Cartographic Services Laboratory
Dept. of Geography
Johnson Hall, Rm. 216
Memphis State University
Memphis, TN 38152
901-678-2387

GIS Lab
Dept. of Geography
217 Shidler Hall
Miami University
Oxford, OH 45056
513-529-5010

Center for Cartographic Research &
    Spatial Analysis
Dept. of Geography
Michigan State University
East Lansing, MI 48824
517-355-4658

Cartography Lab
Dept. of Geography
410 Blegen Hall
University of Minnesota
Minneapolis, MN 55455
612-625-0892

Geographic Information & Analysis Laboratory
Dept. of Geography
105 Wilkeson Quad
State University of New York, Buffalo
Buffalo, NY 14261
716-636-2722

GIS Lab
Dept. of Geography
203 Saunders Hall
University of North Carolina
Chapel Hill, NC 27599
919-962-8901

Cartography Lab
Dept. of Geography & Earth Sciences
University of North Carolina, Charlotte
UNCC Station, Hwy. 49
Charlotte, NC 26223
704-547-4265

Cartography Lab
Dept. of Geography
Box 8274
University of North Dakota
Grand Forks, ND 58502
701-777-4246

Laboratory for Cartographic
    & Spatial Analysis
Dept. of Geography
Davis Hall, Rm. 115
Northern Illinois University
DeKalb, IL 60115
815-753-6830

Production Cartographic Lab
Dept. of Geography
University of Northern Iowa
Cedar Falls, IA 50613
319-273-6948

Cartographic Laboratory
Dept. of Geography
Northern Michigan University
Marquette, MI 49855
906-227-2636

Ohio University Cartographic
  Center
104 Clippinger Laboratories
Ohio University
Athens, OH 45701
614-593-1150

Cartography Service
Dept. of Geography
203A HEE
Oklahoma State University
Stillwater, OK 74708
405-744-7344

Dept. of Geosciences Cartographic Service
Wilkinson Hall 104
Oregon State University
Corvallis, OR 97331
503-737-1222

Informational Graphics Laboratory
Dept. of Geography
University of Oregon
Eugene, OR 97403
503-346-4970

Deasy GeoGraphics Laboratory
302 Walker Bldg.
Pennsylvania State University
University Park, PA 16802
814-863-4562

Tideman Cartographic Center
Dept. of Geography
St. Cloud State University
St. Cloud, MN 56301
612-255-3019

Cartography Laboratory
Dept. of Geography
Callcott, Rm. 101
University of South Carolina
Columbia, SC 29208
803-777-6746

Syracuse University Cartographic Laboratory
343 H.B. Crouse Hall
Syracuse, NY 13244
315-443-3937

Cartographic Laboratory
Dept. of Geography & Urban Studies
Temple University
12th & Berks
Philadelphia, PA 19122
215-787-4748

Cartographic Services Laboratory
Dept. of Geography
408 Geology & Geography Bldg.
University of Tennessee
Knoxville, TN 37996
615-974-2418

Cartographics
Dept. of Geography
O & M Bldg., Rm. 712
Texas A & M University
College Station, TX 77843
409-845-7144

Digit Lab
Dept. of Geography
270 Orson Spencer
University of Utah
Salt Lake City, UT 84112
801-581-3612

Director, Cartographic Laboratory
Dept. of Geography
Villanova University
Villanova, PA 19085
215-645-7435

Cartographic Laboratory Manager
Dept. of Geography
Weber State University
Ogden, UT 84408
801-626-6197

Cartographic Services
Dept. of Geography
317 Wood Hall
Western Michigan University
Kalamazoo, MI 49008
616-387-3410

Carto Graphic Section
Social Science Center
University of Western Ontario
London, Ontario N6A 5C2
519-661-3425

TRAVEL MAPS

Bicycle Route Maps

Over the years, biking has grown from a Sunday pastime to a full-blown sport, complete with high-tech equipment, designed racing gear, and detailed route maps. Whether you're looking for a morning glide through a neighborhood park or a cross-country endurance test, there are maps to keep you on track.

The quality of bike route maps varies among publishers. Some maps are simply road maps with a line drawn to indicate a bike route. Other maps provide detailed information about weather conditions, repair or supply services available, and points of interest.

State highway departments or bureaus of tourism often produce bike route maps that are free or inexpensive. Write to the appropriate office (see Appendix A), or get in touch with a local bicycling group. Many groups publish their own maps and most know the best sources for maps in their area. If no bicycling group is listed in a local phone book, try one of the following national organizations, whose publications often cover biking activities and map products.

NATIONAL BICYCLE ORGANIZATIONS

Bicycle Federation of America (1818 R St. NW, Washington, DC 20009; 202-332-6986) is a nonprofit organization that publishes a monthly newsletter, *ProBike News* ($30 a year, higher outside U.S.), including reports on mapping and bicycle organizations.

League of American Wheelmen, 190 W. Ostend St., Ste. 120, Baltimore, MD 21230; 410-539-3399; 800-288-BIKE for membership) is a bicycle advocacy membership organization that produces a variety of bicycling advocacy and educational publications, including *Bicycle* USA, a magazine that covers a myriad of bicycling subjects. The magazine's annual Almanac issue contains a state-by-state listing of biking information, including organizations, mapping

and travel services, and tourism departments. The TourFinder issue lists more than 100 bicycle touring companies, as well as a description of the tours they offer. Membership is $25 for individuals, $30 for families.

BikeCentennial (P.O. Box 8308, Missoula, MT 59807; 406-721-1776) publishes a touring magazine, *BikeReport*, nine times a year and provides member discounts on maps. BikeCentennial produces a route network series of state-of-the-art bike maps covering the U.S. The maps, printed on water-resistant paper, are sized to fit in handlebar map cases. Illustrated in shades of blue and green, the maps are drawn to a scale of about 1:250,000. They provide such information as local bike laws, weather, stopovers, and special attractions. The maps feature detailed riding information and matchlines that enable bikers to move effortlessly from one route map to the next. Write for a free catalog.

MAPS OF DOMESTIC BIKE ROUTES

There are thousands of maps created by hundreds of local bike groups and publishers. Below are producers of maps or books containing maps for a variety of routes throughout the U.S.:

ADC The Map People (6440 General Green Way, Alexandria, VA 22312; 703-750-0510; 800-ADC-MAPS) produces bicycling maps for Delaware, Maryland, North Carolina, Pennsylvania, South Carolina, and Virginia. A free list of products is available.

American Youth Hostels (P.O. Box 37613, Washington, DC 20013; 202-783-6161). Local AYH branches sometimes produce bike route maps for their areas. Write to AYH to obtain a list of local AYH offices.

The Butterworth Co., Cape Cod (291 Main St., W. Dennis, MA 02670; 508-760-2000) publishes a

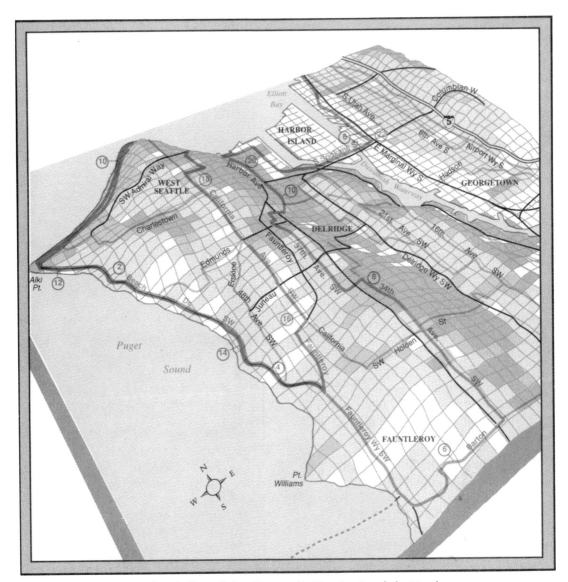

Bicycle route map of West Seattle and Alki Beach, from Terragraphics' Touring Seattle by Bicycle.

"Rail-Trail Map" ($2.95) detailing points of interest along the trail from Dennis to Eastham. (See Rails-to-Trails Conservancy below for more on rail-trails.)

CTM/Zia Maps (P.O. Box 4982, Boulder, CO 80306; 303-444-1670) produces "Boulder County Mountain Bike Map," a unique two-dimensional and three-dimensional representation of mountain bike riding trails in the

Boulder, Colorado, area. One side is a 1:50,000 USGS topographic map with all routes and historical information. The flip side is a 3-D mesh view showing the same area, along with cross sections and helpful riding points. Folded version is $8.50 plus $4 shipping; flat version, 25" X 38" is $10 plus shipping. The company also produces the "Marin-Sonoma Mountain & Road Bike Map," which uses the same format, but is based on a scale of 1:100,000. The 3-D side is a striking image encompassing a majority of the San Francisco Bay area and showing the Sierra Nevada mountain range on the horizon. Price is $8 folded, $10 flat.

DeLorme Mapping Co. (P.O. Box 298, Freeport, ME 04032; 207-865-4171) produces "Bicycling" ($3.95), a handlebar-bag-size booklet of full-color maps covering the Maine coast and inland trips.

Globe Pequot Press (10 Denlar Dr., Chester, CT 06412; 203-526-9571; 800-243-0495; 800-962-0973 in Conn.) sells the Short Bike Rides series ($8.95 to $14.95). These guides offer maps of different rides of varying length and difficulty. Guides available are "Cape Cod/Nantucket/The Vineyard," "Connecticut," "Greater Boston/Central Massachusetts," "New Jersey," "New York City," "Long Island," and "Rhode Island."

Gulf Publishing Co. (P.O. Box 2608, Houston, TX 77252; 713-529-4301) distributes *Bicycling in Texas* ($9.95), a 104-page map-laden guide to scenic routes between major cities as well as "spot tours" of special areas not centered in the cities.

Mountaineers Books (1011 SW Klickitat Way, Seattle, WA 98134; 206-223-6303) publishes *Washington's Rail-Trails* ($10.95). The 160-page guide, which features 35 maps, describes 40 rail-trails in Washington State open to cyclists and others. Other titles include

three books by Erin and Bill Woods, who logged more than 20,000 miles on their bikes researching the trilogy: *Bicycling the Backroads Around Puget Sound*, 3rd ed. ($12.95); *Bicycling the Backroads of Southwest Washington*, 2nd ed. ($12.95); and *Bicycling the Backroads of Northwest Washington*, 3rd ed. ($12.95), a 208-page guide filled with 56 maps that includes 39 tours.

Pantheon Books (201 E. 50th St., New York, NY 10022; 212-872-8238; 800-638-6460) publishes *Bicycle Touring in the Western United States* ($11.95). Authors Karen and Gary Hawkins provide maps for tours covering 7,500 miles of terrain through Arizona, California, Colorado, Idaho, Montana, Nevada, New Mexico, Oregon, Utah, and Wyoming. Also included is information about weather conditions, places to stay, repair and supply sources, and topographic details.

The Rails-to-Trails Conservancy (1400 16th St. NW, Ste. 300, Washington, DC 20036; 202-797-5400) publishes guidebooks to the various rail-trails, abandoned railway routes converted into recreation paths, many of which are good bike paths. Its *Guide to America's Rail-Trails* is a directory of existing rail-trails in the U.S. In addition to other useful information, the guide lists trail length, type of surfacing, and suitable uses ($5 members, $6.50 nonmembers). *Sampler of America's Rail Trails* ($2) features maps and descriptions of 12 of the nation's best rail-trails. Also included is information on types of trail use and places to eat and sleep along the trails.

Section of BikeCentennial's Virginia-to-Florida Bicycle Route, showing the Santee River area in South Carolina. Reprinted with permission of BikeCentennial, the Bicycle Travel Associaiton.

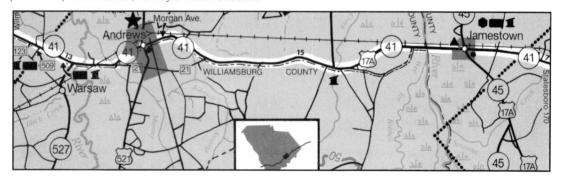

Sunbelt Publications (8630 Argent, Ste. C, Santee, CA 92071; 619-258-4911) distributes three books with mapped bike routes published by the Southwest Trails Association. *Southwest American Bicycle Route* ($9.95) is a 140-page book with several maps that trace a 1,748-mile route from Oceanside, California, to Larned, Kansas, including travel and topographic information. *Bicycling Baja* ($12.95) has 260 pages with 17 maps that detail bike routes in Baja, Mexico. Sunbelt Publications also offers an extensive bike book list from other sources, with many of the books containing detailed bike maps.

Terragraphics (P.O. Box 1025, Eugene, OR 97440; 503-343-7115) publishes unique bicycle touring guidebooks that use three-dimensional maps, so bikers can easily see what terrain lies ahead. Titles available include: *Touring the Islands: Bicycling in the San Juan, Gulf and Vancouver Islands; Touring Seattle by Bicycle; Touring the San Francisco Bay Area by Bicycle; Touring California Wine Country by Bicycle; Touring the Washington, D.C. Area by Bicycle; Touring New England by Bicycle; Touring the Los Angeles Area by Bicycle;* and *Touring Pennsylvania's Countryside by Bicycle.*

Maps of Foreign Bike Routes

Information about bike routes through foreign countries is often available from the tourist boards of those countries. Some additional organizations that publish foreign maps are:

Gulf Publishing (300 Raritan Center Pkwy., Edison, NJ 08818; 201-225-1900) distributes the PAN/Ordnance Survey's "Cycling Britain" ($14.95), a comprehensive guide to cycling routes in England, Scotland, and Wales, which includes more than 200 two-color maps.

Omni Resources (1238 Anthony Rd., P.O. Box 2096, Burlington, NC 27216; 919-227-8300; 800-742-2677) distributes Kümmerly & Frey's cycling maps of Switzerland. These maps provide information on such things as scenic routes, road gradients, and road surfaces. The set of 15 cycling maps covers western Switzerland from the German to the French border ($15.95 each).

Mass Transit Maps

Transit maps reflect where we are—and where we're going. Even a simple bus or subway map can reveal the changing patterns of a region: the newest communities, the growth of suburb-to-suburb commuting, the rebirth of downtown. But more likely, the purpose of such maps is considerably more utilitarian. By helping you to understand a city's bus or subway system at a glance, they can make arrival in a major city far less forbidding. They may even make life in your own hometown a bit easier.

Bus and subway maps are far more attractive than they used to be. Many of the graphic innovations in cartography have been pioneered at the local level, in attempts to overhaul and simplify maps of public-transit systems, many of which are far from simple. As energy and environmental matters have breathed new life into public transportation—even car-worshiping Los Angeles is getting a subway—map-makers have strived harder to reduce citizen resistance to learning these new or renewed systems by creating easy-to-understand maps.

While many transit systems have system maps readily available from bus drivers or subway attendants, you needn't come into town empty-handed. Here are addresses and ordering information for obtaining transit maps for major U.S. cities. They are free unless otherwise indicated.

Atlanta, GA
Metro Atlanta Rapid Transit Authority (MARTA). Numerous maps for Atlanta's rail and bus systems are available, including a systemwide map, individual rail route schedule/maps, individual bus route maps, the "85-Cent Enjoy Ride" book, and "Guide to MARTA." They can be picked up at the MARTA Ride Store (5 Points Rail Station) or obtained by writing or calling MARTA, Customer Service, 2424 Piedmont Rd. NE, Atlanta, GA 30324; 404-848-5077.

Baltimore, MD
Maryland DOT/Mass Transit Administration. "Ride Guides," featuring system maps of bus and subway routes, as well as timetables, are available in Metro stations and pass sales outlets, or can be requested by writing the Mass Transit Administration (Customer Service Dept., 300 W. Lexington St., Baltimore, MD 21201) or by calling Customer Service: 301-539-5000.

Boston, MA
Massachusetts Bay Transportation Authority (MBTA). Boston's bus and subway routes are shown on a system map, a wallet card, and individual bus schedule/maps. They can be picked up at the Park Street Station Information Booth (Park St. & Tremont St.), or requested by writing or calling MBTA Marketing Dept., Attn.: Map & Scheduling Information, 120 Boylston St., 3rd fl., Boston, MA 02116; 617-722-5740; 617-722-5146 for the hearing impaired; 800-392-6100 in New England.

Buffalo, NY
Niagara Frontier Transportation Authority (NFTA). Various route maps are available for Buffalo, including a systemwide map, a rail system map, a downtown rail map, and individual bus route schedule/maps. Maps can be picked up at NFTA offices (Main fl., 181 Ellicott St.) or obtained by sending a self-addressed, stamped envelope to NFTA, Attn.: Metro Public Relations, 181 Ellicott St., Buffalo, NY 14202. For more information call 716-855-7211.

Chicago, IL
Chicago Transit Authority. Various route maps are available from CTA: a "CTA Map," showing bus and subway routes in the city; an "RTA Map," illustrating bus and train routes in the city and suburbs; and maps for some individual bus routes. They can be picked up at CTA headquarters (Merchandise Mart Plaza, Chicago) or at the RTA (Regional Transit Authority)

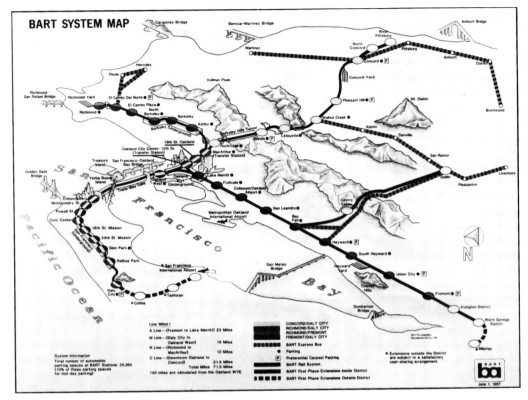

System map of BART, the Bay Area Rapid Transit system, in the San Francisco Bay area.

office (1 N. Dearborn St., 11th fl.). Information and maps can also be obtained by calling 312-836-7000 or 800-972-7000 (in Illinois).

Cincinnati, OH
Southwest Ohio Regional Transit Authority.
"RideGuide" bus schedules feature route maps. Information and RideGuides can be found at "METROCenter" (122 W. 5th St.), 7:30 a.m. to 5 p.m., Monday through Friday. Call 513-621-4455 for information.

Cleveland, OH
Greater Cleveland Regional Transportation Authority. System maps and individual route schedules/maps of buses in the Cleveland area can be obtained from the Customer Service Center (315 Euclid Ave.) or by writing or calling the Greater Cleveland Regional Transportation Authority, Attn.: Communications Dept., 615

Superior Ave. NW, Cleveland, OH 44113; 216-621-9500.

Dallas, TX
Dallas Area Rapid Transit (DART). Maps showing bus and rail routes can be picked up at or ordered by mail from the DART Action Center (1701 N. Market St., Ste. 302 W., Dallas, TX 75202), or obtained by calling 214-573-8500.

Denver, CO
Regional Transportation District. A system map of Denver's 149 bus routes, as well as individual timetables featuring route maps, can be obtained at the Market Street Station (Market St. and 16th), the Civic Center Station (Colfax and Broadway), or at area K marts, Waldenbooks, and Vickers gas stations. They can also be obtained by mail by writing the Regional Transportation District (Customer

Service, 1600 Blake St., Denver, CO 80202), or by calling the Customer Service Telephone Information Center, 303-628-9000.

Detroit, MI
Detroit Dept. of Transportation. Detroit's bus system is described on individual route maps and a system map. They can be found in the Cadillac Square Information Center (Cadillac St. between Woodward & Bates), or requested by writing or calling the Dept. of Transportation, Bus Schedules, 1301 E. Warren, Detroit, MI 48207; 313-933-1300.

Ft. Lauderdale, FL
Broward County Transit. Ft. Lauderdale's bus system is revealed on a system map that includes points of interest; individual route maps are also available. They can be picked up at area libraries, chambers of commerce, or the main government center, or ordered through the mail by writing or calling Broward Co. Transit, Attn.: Marketing, 3201 W. Copans Rd., Pompano Beach, FL 33069; 305-357-8400.

Houston, TX
Metro Transportation Authority of Harris County. Systemwide individual route maps are available at Metro offices (1201 Louisiana St.), or can be requested by writing or calling Marketing, P.O. Box 61429, Houston, TX 77208; 713-739-4000.

Indianapolis, IN
Indianapolis Public Transportation Corp. Single copies of system maps and individual route maps of Indianapolis's buses can be picked up at Indianapolis Public Transportation Corp. (Customer Service Center, 36 N. Delaware St.) or requested by writing or calling Marketing Dept., P.O. Box 2383, Indianapolis, IN 46206; 317-635-3344.

Kansas City, MO
Kansas City Area Transportation Authority. System maps and schedules of buses can be picked up in downtown stores, libraries, and churches, or can be requested by writing or

calling the Kansas City Area Transportation Authority, Information Services, 1200 E. 18th St., Kansas City, MO 64108; 816-221-0660.

Los Angeles, CA
Orange County Transit District. A system map and individual route schedules and maps can be found in area stores, banks, post offices, libraries, and malls, or requested by writing or calling Public Information, 11222 Acacia Pkwy., Garden Grove, CA 92642; 714-636-7433.

Southern California Rapid Transit District (RTD). A system map and sector maps—available for San Fernando Valley, San Gabriel Valley, South Bay, Western Region, Mid-Cities, South Central, Downtown L.A., East L.A., and Burbank/Glendale/Pasadena—can be picked up at any of 10 service centers (call for nearest location), or requested by writing RTD, Customer Relations, 425 S. Main St., Los Angeles, CA 90013; 213-972-6000.

Miami, FL
Metro-Dade Transit Authority. Miami's bus system is illustrated on a systemwide map; maps of individual bus routes are also available. Pick them up at the Metro Rail Station or the Government Center Station, call Maps by Mail (305-638-6137), or write Metro-Dade Transit Authority, Marketing Div., 111 NW 1st St., Ste. 910, Miami, FL 33128.

Milwaukee, WI
Milwaukee County Transit System. Systemwide maps and route maps of Milwaukee's transit system can be found in area libraries, banks, and shopping centers, or requested by writing or calling Milwaukee County Transit System, 1942 N. 17th St., Milwaukee, WI 53205; 414-344-6711.

Minneapolis/St. Paul, MN
Metropolitan Transportation Commission. Maps of transit routes in the Minneapolis/St. Paul metropolitan area are available at the MTC Transit Store (719 Marquette Ave., on Baker Block in Minneapolis) or American

National Bank (Skyway Level, St. Paul), or can be requested by writing or calling MTC, Attn.: Schedule Information, 560 6th Ave. N., Minneapolis, MN 55411; 612-827-7733.

New Orleans, LA

Regional Transit Authority. A systemwide map is available for streetcar and bus routes in New Orleans, as well as individual schedules, which include map sketches. They can be picked up at the RTA office (101 Dauphine St., New Orleans) or obtained by calling (504-569-2700) or writing RTA RideLine, 101 Dauphine St., New Orleans, LA 70112.

New York, NY, and Vicinity

Metropolitan Suburban Bus Authority. A system route map and individual timetables are available for suburban New York areas by writing or calling Metro Suburban Bus Authority, Public Affairs, 700 Commercial Ave., Garden City, NY 11530; 516-766-6722. They can also be found in local libraries or on the buses.

NJ Transit. A comprehensive bus and rail map for Hudson County, New Jersey, with information in both English and Spanish, is available from NJ Transit, 2 Journal Sq. Plaza, 8th fl., Jersey City, NJ 07306.

New York City Transit Authority. A bus system map is available for each borough; a map showing the subway system is also available. The maps can be found in libraries, hotels, token booths, tourist information centers, and the information booths at Penn Station and Grand Central Station. They can be mailordered by writing or calling the NYC Transit Authority, Consumer Information, 370 Jay St., Rm. 875, Brooklyn, NY 11201; 718-330-8757.

Port Authority Trans-Hudson. A free "PATH Map Guide" is available by calling 800-234-PATH.

Philadelphia, PA

Southeastern Pennsylvania Transportation Authority (SEPTA). A city map and a regional map showing transit system routes can be picked up at the SEPTA office (Concourse, 15th & Market sts.) or obtained by writing or calling SEPTA, Customer Service Dept., 841 Chestnut St., Philadelphia, PA 19107; 215-580-7852. If you include your Philadelphia itinerary, SEPTA will send all relevant route maps.

Phoenix, AZ

Phoenix Transit System. A "Busbook," which includes a tear-out systemwide map and is packed with information on the Phoenix transit system, can be obtained by writing Phoenix Transit System, Attn.: Marketing, P.O. Box 4275, Phoenix, AZ 85030; 602-253-5000.

Pittsburgh, PA

Port Authority Transit. A county-wide rail and bus route map, with an inset map of the downtown area, can be obtained at the Port Authority Transit Service Center (534 Smithfield St., Mellon Square) or by writing or calling Port Authority Transit, Marketing Dept., Beaver Ave., Pittsburgh, PA 15233; 412-237-7139.

Portland, OR

Tri-County Metropolitan District of Oregon (Tri-Met). Systemwide maps of bus and light-rail routes can be found at the Tri-Met Customer Assistance Office (#1 Pioneer Courthouse Square, Portland; or call 503-238-4982); or write to Tri-Met Consumer Programs, 4012 SE 17th Ave., Portland, OR 97202. A Tri-Met guide with map is $2 (add 50 cents postage if requesting by mail).

San Antonio, TX

VIA Metropolitan Transit System. A system map of San Antonio's bus routes and individual schedule/maps can be purchased at VIA Information Center (112 N. Soledad) or obtained by writing or calling VIA Metropolitan Transit System, Customer Service, 800 W. Myrtle, San Antonio, TX 78212; 512-227-2020.

San Diego, CA

Metropolitan Transit Development Board. A regional transit map of San Diego, as well as

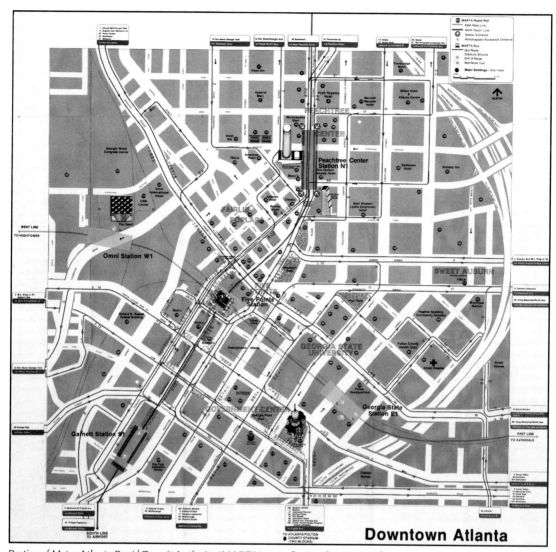

Portion of Metro Atlanta Rapid Transit Authority (MARTA) map showing downtown Atlanta.

maps of individual bus and trolley routes, can be picked up at The Transit Store (449 Broadway, downtown San Diego) or requested by contacting MTDB, 1255 Imperial Ave., Ste. 1000, San Diego, CA 92101; 619-233-3004.

San Francisco, CA
Bay Area Rapid Transit District (BART). A system map of BART and bus routes in San Francisco is available by writing or calling BART, Attn.: Public Information, 800 Madison, Oakland, CA 94607; 510-464-7115.

Alameda-Contra Costa Transit District. Maps of the East Bay bus system, as well as individual route schedules with route maps, are available by calling, writing, or stopping by AC Transit, Customer Relations, 1600 Franklin St., Oakland, CA 94612; 510-839-2882.

San Francisco Municipal Railway. A "Muni Map," San Francisco's official street and transit map, shows Muni bus, streetcar, and cable car lines, BART and CalTrain stations, and routes of other transit agencies that serve San

Francisco. It also includes an index to streets and points of interest. The map is available for $2, payable by check or money order, from Muni Map, 949 Presidio Ave., Rm. 238, San Francisco, CA 94115. The map can also be obtained at many Bay Area bookstores and newsstands for $1.50.

San Jose, CA
Santa Clara County Transportation Agency. A system map of San Jose bus routes and individual route timetables with schematic maps are available at the agency's downtown office (4 N. 2nd St.), or can be obtained by writing S.C.C. Transit (Customer Service, P.O. Box 611900, San Jose, CA 95161) or calling the Telephone Information Center, 408-287-4210.

Washington, DC
Montgomery County Transit Ride-On. A system map and individual bus route maps for the bus system in the suburban Washington, D.C., area are available in local libraries and government service centers, or can be requested by calling 301-217-7433 (301-217-2222 for the hearing impaired).

Washington Metro Area Transit Association (WMATA). A posterlike, full-color "All About Metro" system map of subway routes in the Washington, D.C., area can be obtained by stopping at ($10) or writing ($13) to: Metro Headquarters, 600 5th St. NW, Washington, DC 20001.

Railroad Maps

The railroads of America crisscross the country, connecting coast with coast and small town with metropolis. For 150 years they have carried settlers to the West and presidents to the White House. Maps of railroad lines are mirrors of America's past and, in some cases, projections for its future. Railroad maps are also useful tools for travelers, engineers, planners, military strategists, transportation buffs, and historians.

The Baltimore & Ohio Railroad was under construction—and surveyance—by 1830, opening 14 miles of track before the end of that year. Dozens of other railroads soon followed, as rail travel for passengers and freight became popular in the expanding nation. The first American railroad map was probably an 1809 survey of the Leiper Railroad in Pennsylvania. The original didn't survive, but a long-winded reproduction, "Draft Exhibiting...the Railway Contemplated by John Leiper Esq. from His Stone Sawmill and Quarries...to His Landing on Ridley Creek," can be found in an 1866 book, *A Short Account of the First Permanent Tramway in America*, by Robert P. Robins. The book itself is part of the **Library of Congress** collection.

Railroad maps are available from a variety of sources, including the federal government, commercial map publishers, the railroad lines themselves, and as reproductions from libraries and map collections. Some are made specifically for or about a railroad, while others are general-use maps that include railroad lines.

GOVERNMENT SOURCES, UNITED STATES

The **U.S. Geological Survey** publishes a number of maps that depict the U.S. rail system. Topographic maps of the states include past and present railroads (see "Topographic Maps"). The rails are depicted according to the condition and use of the tracks rather than by type of train travel: mainline tracks are drawn as solid lines-and-crossties; those under

construction are shown as dashed lines; abandoned but still-intact tracks appear as double crossties; and dismantled tracks are indicated by a dashed trail symbol and the legend "Old Railroad Grade." The maps also distinguish between standard- and narrow-gauge tracks and single- and multirail routes. One advantage of topographic maps is that you can see at a glance the past and present railroads that run along a specific section of land.

Railroads are also depicted on other USGS maps. For example, "U.S. Base Map" ($3.10; 10-AO; 24" X 36") includes markings for railroads along with other standard features such as roads, parks, and cities; "U.S. General Reference" ($3.10; 19" X 28") is a colorful, single-sheet map from the National Atlas depicting major features, including railroad lines.

The **Tennessee Valley Authority (TVA)** has a topographic map of the region that includes railroad routes. The map ($10, plus $3 for mailing tube and handling; 48" X 62"), a 1979-80 full-color edition of TVA's principal base map, is also available with an overprint of an index to the maps available in the region. Also available through TVA is a blueline print of a map published in 1864, "Railroad and County Map of Tennessee" ($.50; 453 D 754-7).

The **Government Printing Office** distributes two books on railroad maps produced by the Library of Congress. *Railroad Maps of North America: The First 100 Years* ($28; 1984; S/N 030-004-00021-3) is a 207-page history of American railroad maps, beautifully illustrated and containing full-color as well as black-and-white map reproductions, as engrossing to scan as it is to study. *Railroad Maps of the United States: A Selected Annotated Bibliography of Original Maps in the Geography and Map Division of the Library of Congress* ($5.50; 1975; S/N 030-004-0014-1) is a 117-page paperbound volume presenting a concise history of railroad maps held in the Library of Congress, with commentaries on

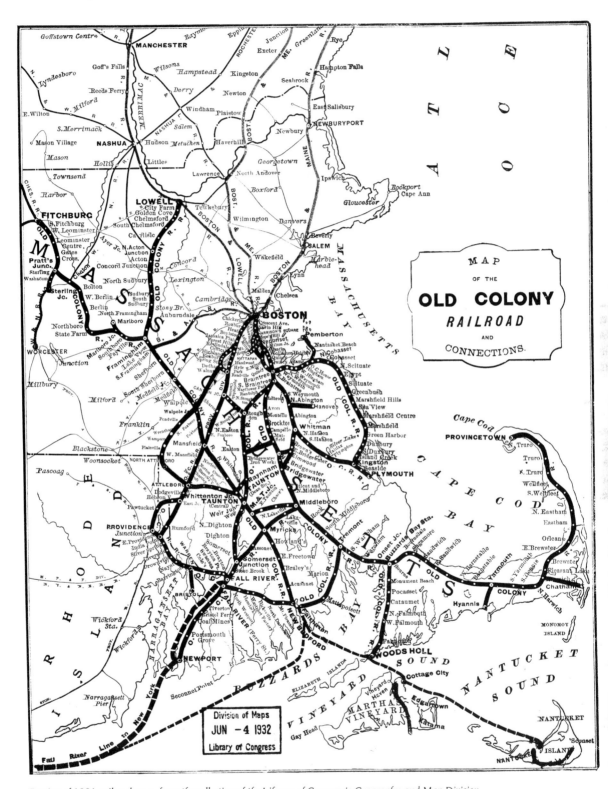

Portion of 1891 railroad map, from the collection of the Library of Congress's Geography and Map Division.

many. The illustrations are in black and white.

Like the Library of Congress, the **National Archives** holds thousands of railroad maps in its collection of maps and charts that trace the history of transportation in America as surveyed by the government. The first railroad to request and receive federal assistance for mapping its line was the B & O in the early 1830s, quickly followed by numerous eastern railroads vying for government surveyors. The federal government also became involved in mapping railroads to show right-of-way privileges and land grants in the booming West. These and other railroad-related maps (including maps of postal routes that used the railroads to carry mail and railroad routes through Indian reservations) are stored in the Archives' collections.

Central Intelligence Agency. The CIA produces maps of foreign countries, some depicting transportation systems. Examples are the now-historic "USSR Railroads" ($11.50; PB 82-927925), "Senegal/Gambia, Israel, and West Berlin, Transportation Systems" ($11.50; PB 82-928044) and "China: Cities, Transportation and Administrative Divisions" ($10; PB 88-928315).

GOVERNMENT SOURCES, CANADA

Canada Map Office (615 Booth St., Ottawa, Ontario K1A 0E9; 613-952-7000) distributes "Canada in Motion" ($16.55 Canadian), a package of four maps from *The National Atlas of Canada* that supply fascinating information on Canada's network of rail, road, air, and water routes, along with text on transportation geography.

Maps Alberta (Land Information Services Div., Main fl., Brittania Bldg., 703 6th Ave. SW, Calgary, Alberta T2P 0T9; 403-297-7389) publishes the *Alberta Resource and Economic Atlas* ($30 Canadian; code 930), a series of generalized thematic maps, including (as part of the "Service and Recreational Facilities" series) "Airlines, 1984" (D21) and "Transportation" (D24). The maps are 99 cents each Canadian;

some are outdated, so inquire first. Also available is a series of historical road maps of Alberta, spanning the years 1923 to 1961. The nine maps (code 253), which vary in size and scale, cost $2.97 Canadian each. Maps Alberta also produces "Railway Networks" (code 418 MCR 4070), a $37\frac{1}{2}$" X 71" map showing railway lines, operators, and stations in Alberta ($9.30 Canadian).

COMMERCIAL SOURCES

The following companies publish railroad maps in various forms. Some are contained in trade publications; others are history-teaching tools; still others are designed as business or travel maps. All are available directly from the publisher, although a few may also be found in book, travel, or map stores.

George F. Cram Co. (P.O. Box 426, Indianapolis, IN 46206; 317-635-5564; 800-227-4199) publishes a series of 19 52" X 40" American history maps (set no. 50) for classroom use, including two colorful depictions of the growth of the American railway network: "Transportation, Early Railroad Period, 1840-1880" and "Transportation, Principal Railroads Since 1880" ($320 for the set).

Forsyth Travel Library (9154 W. 57th St., P.O. Box 2975, Shawnee Mission, KS 66201; 913-384-3440; 800-367-7984) is a travel book and map store, as well as a nationwide mail-order company that offers a free catalog of travel books and maps for most of the world. It is distributor of the "Thomas Cook Rail Map of Europe" ($9.95, plus $2 shipping), a detailed map of European passenger railways as far east as Moscow and the Black Sea. The map includes insets of local areas with intense levels of rail service, such as the Netherlands and Germany. The company is also exclusive distributor of the "Visitor's Rail Map of Great Britain & Ireland" ($9.95, plus $2 shipping), which includes the main passenger networks of British Rail and Irish Rail covering all of Great Britain, Northern Ireland, and the Republic of

Ireland. Newly mapped for 1992 to show most major tourist attractions, it boasts a special information feature on the top 200 locations.

Hunter Publishing (300 Raritan Center Pkwy., Edison, NJ 08818; 908-225-1900) distributes several rail maps, including "Thomas Cook Rail Map of Europe" ($9.95; 27" X 36"); "Thomas Cook Rail Map of Great Britain & Ireland" ($8.95; 27" X 36"); Kümmerly & Frey's "Rail Map of Europe" ($8.95) at a scale of 1:2,500,000; and *Trans-Siberian Rail Guide, 2nd ed.* ($15.95), a 207-page book with city and route maps as well as information on this romantic rail journey between Europe and Asia.

Interurban Press (P.O. Box 6444, Glendale, CA 91225; 818-240-9130) publishes a variety of books on railroad history; many include maps. Especially noteworthy for their maps are: *Rails Through the Orange Groves* (Vol. I, $31.95; Vol. II, $34.95), tracing the history of railroad development in Orange County, California; and *Forty Feet Below* ($13.95). A catalog is available.

K-III Information Company, Inc. (424 W. 33rd St., New York, NY 10117; 212-714-3100; 800-221-5488) publishes a series of books for the travel and freight industries. The books may be purchased through subscription or on a single-copy basis. The maps in the books are utilitarian, black-and-white line drawings of specific routes. Three books include railroad maps: *The Official Railway Guide* (Freight Service Edition: six issues, $110; single copy, $40); each of the six issues concentrates on a single freight line, with locator and route maps for all areas of the country serviced by freight railroads.*The Official Railway Guide* (Travel Edition, four issues, $90;

single copy, $40) is updated four times a year to provide the latest pricing and departure information from major passenger carriers—including Amtrak, National Railways of Mexico, and VIA Rail Canada—as well as partial listings for a number of international carriers. *Railway Line Clearances* (1992-93 issues, $72) covers rail clearance and weight limitations across America. The maps identify routes and correspond to information in the accompanying charts and tables.

Nystrom (3333 N. Elston Ave., Chicago, IL 60618; 312-463-1144; 800-621-8086) publishes an American history map series, which includes "Transportation Unites the Nation," a series of four maps illustrating railroads, waterways, and major highways, air routes, and oil and gas pipelines. Prices range from $47 to $72, depending on mounting.

Rail Line (P.O. Box 4671, Dept. M, Chicago, IL 60680; no phone) distributes diagrams and maps of various U.S. railroads, such as "Amtrak's 14th Street Coach Yard" ($11.50), "Illinois Central's Central Station Operating Diagram" ($11.95), and "St. Paul Union Depot Trackage" ($5.85). A free catalog is available.

John Szwajkart (P.O. Box 163, Brookfield, IL 60513; 708-485-1222) produces "Train Watcher's Guides" to Chicago, St. Louis, and Kansas City, which include maps and photos of rail lines. The *Train Watcher's Guide and Map to Chicago* is $15.50; the *Train Watcher's Guide and Map to St. Louis* is $11.50; and the *Train Watcher's Guide and Map to Kansas City* is $15.25. Extra maps are $2.50.

■ **See also: "Mass Transit Maps."**

Recreation Maps

Whether you're out for a Sunday in the park or a month in the mountains, recreation maps can help find the best route to a nearby or faraway hiking trail, swimming hole, campsite, or amusement park—or they may reveal a new and exciting "discovery" you weren't expecting. Water-recreation maps can point the way to the best fishing or the fastest boating.

Federal, state, and provincial agencies are a good source for recreation maps, as are tourist boards and organizations devoted to the preservation and enjoyment of the wilderness, such as the Sierra Club. Finding a recreation map can be as easy as walking into a local sporting goods store. Many retailers, especially chains such as Herman's World of Sports, Eddie Bauer, and REI, sell maps along with their canoes, skis, and parkas. Other sources include the many outdoors, conservation, and sports organizations that provide maps to members and the public, sometimes to promote their activities. Name a sport, hobby, or pastime, and chances are there's a map to match.

GOVERNMENT SOURCES, UNITED STATES

Army Corps of Engineers, created in 1838 and responsible for mapping a lot of the Wild West, now spends much of its time preserving and mapping the water and natural resources under its jurisdiction. There are district offices all over the country (see Appendix B), and each has free or inexpensive maps and guides to the lakes, rivers, and beaches it maintains for public recreation and enjoyment.

Bureau of Land Management (BLM) administers nearly 450 million acres of public land known as the National Land Reserve. Most of BLM's holdings are in the West, although there are small sections in the South and North that fall under its jurisdiction. There are more than 3,600 miles of marked trails in BLM territory, as well as more than 3,000 federal recreation areas open to the public. BLM maps for these trails and recreation areas can be obtained from BLM offices (see Appendix B).

Fish and Wildlife Service administers the National Wildlife Refuge System, which encompasses more than 90 million acres of land and miles of waterways in the United States. Over 470 National Wildlife Refuges provide habitat for more than 60 endangered species of birds, mammals, amphibians, reptiles, fish, and plants. Approximately 330 refuges offer recreational opportunities including hiking, auto-tour routes, wildlife observation, fishing, and nature study. The U.S. Geological Survey's series of maps show the boundaries of all the National Wildlife Refuges. "A Visitor's Guide to National Wildlife Refuges" is a fold-out map showing the locations of more than 300 refuges and the recreational opportunities they offer to the public. This brochure is available from the Government Printing Office for $1, or free from the Fish and Wildlife Service at its refuges, Washington headquarters, or regional offices.

National Ocean Service (NOS), part of the Commerce Department's **National Oceanic and Atmospheric Administration**, has sailing and boating maps covering most of the nation's water recreation areas. The NOS sailing and boating maps and charts are drawn at various scales and show sailing routes, flows of tides and currents, danger zones, and other important sailing and boating information for all craft sizes, from yachts to canoes. Free nautical catalogs show the sailing and boating maps and charts available from NOS (see "Nautical Charts and Maps"). Also available from NOS are bathymetric fishing maps for most known fishing regions along U.S. coastlines. These are topographic depictions of the sea floor designed for use by recreational or

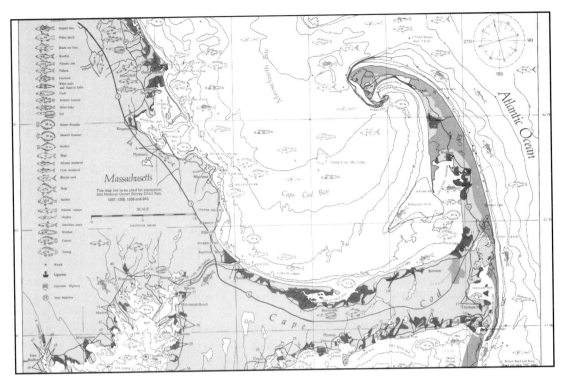

Fishing map of Cape Cod showing species and known locations of indigenous fish, from GPO's Angler's Guide to the U. S. Atlantic Coast: Fish, Fishing Grounds and Facilities: Nantucket Shoals to Long Island Sound.

commercial fishermen. The maps, which cost $4, illustrate and identify the distribution of bottom sediment and obstructions that may give clues to the location of fishing grounds. The NOS series is drawn to a scale of 1:100,000 and is described in a free catalog available from NOAA.

Names and addresses of retailers of water-recreation maps that sell government maps are printed in NOAA catalogs. There are thousands of boating and tackle shops around the country that distribute maps for their regions, and these are the best overall sources for finding local maps.

National Park Service administers millions of acres of parkland, as well as nine national seashores and four national lakeshores. There are schematic and topographic maps available for most of these parks, as well as recreational and historic site maps. Nearly all national parks have free brochures containing maps and information, available either at the individual park headquarters or through the Public Inquiries Office of the National Park Service (see Appendix B). GPO publishes and sells several Park Service guides, including "Map and Guide: National Parks of the United States" (single copies free from Park Service, $1.25 from GPO) and "The National Parks: Lesser-Known Areas" ($1.50). The National Park Service also has maps for the National Wild and Scenic River System.

Tennessee Valley Authority (TVA) produces multicolored pocket-size recreation maps of TVA lakes, showing highways, roads, mileages, cities and rural communities, public access areas, commercial recreation areas, boat docks, private clubs, group camps, public parks, wildlife-management areas, boat-launching sites, and lands open to public use. Maps (no charge) are available for Cherokee/Douglas/Nolichucky Lakes, Chickamauga Lake, Fontana

Lake, Fort Loudon Lake, Guntersville Lake, Kentucky Lake, Melton Hill Lake, Nickajack Lake, Norris Lake, Pickwick Lake, Tims Ford Lake, Upper Hiwassee Lakes (Blue Ridge, Chatuge, Hiwassee and Nottely), Wheeler and Wilson Lakes, Watts Bar Lake, Upper Holston Lakes (South Holston, Watauga, Boone, and Fort Patrick Henry), Normandy Lake, and Tellico Lake.

U.S. Forest Service (USFS) maintains 155 national forests and has maps for all of them. The Forest Service produces various types of maps for its lands, such as forest visitors' guides and maps, wilderness area maps, and Special Designated Area maps. Maps can be ordered through the USFS regional and national offices, and selected maps are available through GPO. Requests for maps should, if possible, include a note about which parts of a particular forest interest you, because many of the larger forests are set out on several maps, divided by ranger stations. USFS can be most helpful in selecting appropriate maps if you indicate what activities are planned for a given area; there are different maps for hikers, campers, and geologists.

U.S. Geological Survey (USGS) is the government's largest mapping agency, as well as its most complex. Maps depicting the topography, geology, and recreational use of national forests, parks, and refuges are available from USGS for a small fee, usually less than $4. Depending on the size and importance of the public-recreation area, details of these lands may be included in larger-scale maps that cover the area around the park. Detailed boundaries of these areas are usually shown if they are of substantial size. Smaller patches of public land may not be shown, but wildlife refuges and game preserves always appear on USGS maps.

USGS produces a "National Wilderness Preservation System" map ($3.10; 1987), showing locations and boundaries of wilderness areas administered by the U.S. Forest Service, the Bureau of Land Management, the Fish and Wildlife Service, and the National Park Service.

An "Index to USGS Topographic Map Coverage of the National Park System" is available free from USGS Earth Science Information Centers and Map Distribution Centers (see Appendix B).

GOVERNMENT SOURCES, CANADA

Canada Map Office (615 Booth St., Ottawa, Ontario K1A 0E9; 613-952-7000) distributes the Canadian National Park Maps series. The multicolor maps range in price from $5.15 to $9.30 Canadian, and are available for the following parks: Banff, Kootenay, and Yoho (MCR 0220), Fundy (MCR 0215), Jasper (MCR 0221), Mount Revelstoke & Glacier (MCR 0219), Prince Albert (MCR 0210SR), Riding Mountain (MCR 0207), Terra Nova (MCR 0214), Waterton Lakes (MCR 0222), Pacific Rim National Park (MCR 0223), and Elk Island National Park (MCR 0224). Maps of numerous areas in other Canadian national parks are also available; a map index/price list is available upon request.

The Canada Map Office also distributes National Topographic Series maps, which contain information vital to canoeists, hikers, and others. The maps illustrate in detail geographic and hydrographic features of the land, as well as population centers, road and rail networks, trails, and other notable information. Complete coverage of Canada is available at a scale of 1:50,000; these maps are recommended for wilderness canoeists. The Canada Map Office also distributes a pamphlet, "Maps and Wilderness Canoeing," produced by the Ministry of Energy, Mines and Resources, which provides useful information for canoeists, as well as guidelines on obtaining the appropriate maps for a canoe trip.

Canadian Hydrographic Service (Dept. of Fisheries and Oceans, 1675 Russell Rd., P.O. Box 8080, Ottawa, Ontario K1G 3H6; 613-998-4931) produces hydrographic charts of the coast and major navigable waterways and lakes of Canada, which are often useful for canoeists and water recreationists. Chart catalogs and price lists are available upon request.

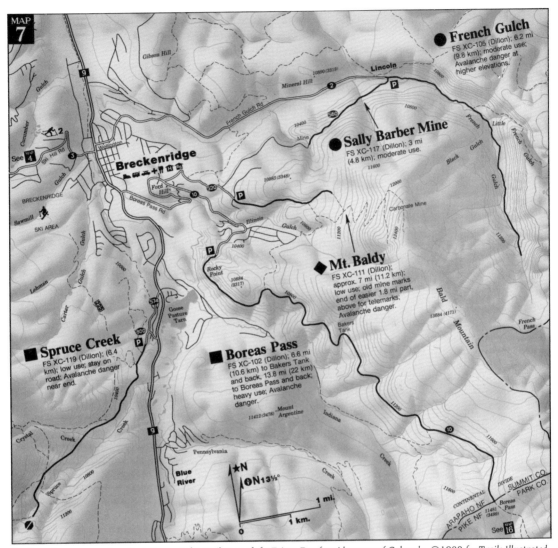

Portion of a cross-country skier's topographic trail map of the Frisco-Breckenridge area of Colorado. ©1988 by Trails Illustrated.

Manitoba Natural Resources (Surveys and Mapping Branch, 1007 Century St., Winnipeg, Manitoba R3H 0W4; 204-945-6666) produces lake-depth charts of Manitoba lakes designed for use by anglers. The maps are not intended for use in navigation as they do not show navigational aids or underwater structures; they do, however, illustrate lake depths and contours to offer some clues as to where fish can be found. The charts are available in "Angling Packages," which include the Manitoba Angling Map, showing a listing of the major sport-fishing lakes in Manitoba and the species of

fish found in each lake. Angling Packages are available for the following regions: Duck Mountain, Flin Flon/The Pas, Grass River, Nopiming, Northern Whiteshell, Southern Whiteshell, Thompson/Split Lake, and Western Manitoba. The Manitoba Angling Map is also available separately.

The Surveys and Mapping Branch also publishes a series of Canoe Route Maps, created by Manitoba artist Real Berard. The illustrated, information-laden maps are not intended for navigational purposes, but they provide an excellent aid in planning a trip or learning about the natural and cultural history of an area. Maps are available for the following waterways: Assiniboine, Grass River, Kautunigan, Land of the Little Sticks, Little Grand Rapids, Middle Track/Hayes River, Mistik Creed, Oiseau, Riviere aux Rats, Sasaginnigak Canoe Country, Waterhen Country, Whitemouth River, and Winnipeg River.

Maps Alberta (Land Information Services Div., Main fl., Brittania Bldg., 703 6th Ave. SW, Calgary, Alberta T2P 0T9; 403-297-7389) distributes many of the Canadian National Park series maps ($9.30 Canadian each; code 418). It also distributes two maps of unique areas within the national parks: Columbia Icefields ($5.85 Canadian; code 440 1WD 1011) and Peyto Glacier ($5.85 Canadian; code 440 1WD 1010). The maps illustrate a variety of glacial features and include additional information on the physical environment and

hiking trails in the areas.

Ontario Ministry of Natural Resources
(Public Information Centre, 99 Wellesley St. W., Rm. 1640, Toronto, Ontario M7A 1W3; 416-314-1666) publishes small- and medium-scale maps of many recreational areas in the province. Map types vary but may include hiking trails, canoe routes, portages, and campsites. Available maps are: Algonquin Provincial Park Canoe Routes ($2.55 Canadian); Algonquin Provincial Park Backpacking Trails/Topographic ($1.39 Canadian); Killarney Provincial Park/Topographic ($3.01 Canadian); Lake Superior Provincial Park ($2.80 Canadian); Leslie M. Frost Natural Resources Centre ($3.47 Canadian); Sleeping Giant Provincial Park/Topographic ($4.63 Canadian); and Quetico Provincial Park ($9 Canadian, printed on waterproof paper). A catalog of maps available through the ministry is furnished upon request.

Portion of "Map of Yosemite Valley," published by Tom Harrison Cartography. ©1988 *by* Tom Harrison.

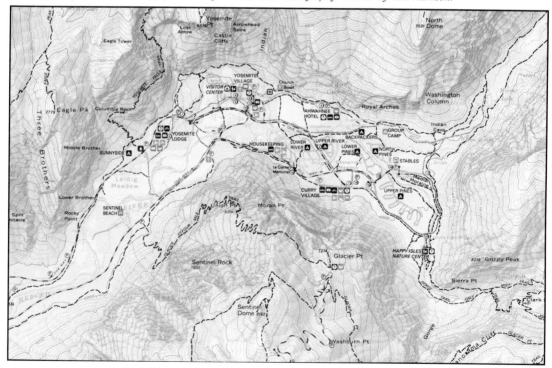

COMMERCIAL SOURCES

There are a vast number of companies producing maps for recreational use; a sampling is below. For maps of bicycle routes, see "Bicycle Route Maps"; topographic maps can be found in "Topographic Maps."

Other sources include publishers of maps for business promotional use. These are often free or inexpensive and are created to illustrate the recreational or tourist facilities of a certain region. One such map-producing company is **The National Survey** (Chester, VT 05143; 802-875-2121), which produces a variety of recreation maps for state and local governments and retailers. One example is National Survey's free, ad-filled "Eastern Ski Map," showing ski and winter recreation resorts around the eastern United States.

Other sources include:

ADC The Map People (6440 General Green Way, Alexandria, VA 22312; 703-750-0510; 800-ADC-MAPS) produces recreational maps (navigational, fishing and boating, and bicycling) for Delaware, Maryland, North Carolina, Pennsylvania, South Carolina, and Virginia. A free listing of products is available.

Adirondack Mountain Club Books (RR 3, Box 3055, Lake George, NY 12845; 518-668-4447) has two books of maps for canoeing in the waters of the Adirondack's rivers: *Adirondack Canoe Waters—North Flow* ($15.95), with 49 maps; and *Adirondack Canoe Waters—South and West Flow* ($12.95), with 70 maps and 20 charts.

A.I.D. Associates, Inc. (4378 Spring Valley Rd., Dallas, TX 75244; 214-386-6277; 800-243-6277) publishes quality custom city maps and regularly revised contoured depth aerial maps depicting underwater features of lakes and rivers, navigational markers, road systems, access points, and public areas. Maps are available for Arkansas, Louisiana, Mexico, Mississippi, Missouri, Oklahoma, and Texas ($3.45 each).

Appalachian Mountain Club (5 Joy St., Boston,

MA 02108; 617-523-0636; 800-262-4455) produces maps and guides to recreation areas throughout the East, including the AMC *White Mountain Guide* ($16.95, 672 pages), an up-to-date guide with seven full-color maps in a back pocket; "Map of Mount Washington and the Heart of the Presidential Range" ($8.95; 27$\frac{1}{2}$" X 40"), a seven-color map drawn to a scale of 1:20,000; and the AMC Trail Guide series, recognized as a reliable and comprehensive source of trail information. The guides, which include maps, trail directions, and distances, are available for "Maine Mountains," "Mount Desert Island and Acadia National Park," "Mount Washington and the Presidential Range," "Massachusetts/Rhode Island," "West Virginia," and "North Carolina." Maps contained in the guidebooks are also available separately, in paper ($2.95 each) or on waterproof, tearproof Tyvek ($4.95 each).

The Butterworth Co., Cape Cod (291 Main St., W. Dennis, MA 02670; 508-760-2000) publishes a four-color "Fresh Water Fishing Map" ($3.95; 20" X 28") showing fish types, water depth, contours, access roads, boat ramps, fishing tips, and pond locations for 110 Cape Cod and Plymouth lakes.

Clarkson Map Co. (1225 Delanglade St., P.O. Box 218, Kaukauna, WI 54130; 414-766-3000) distributes Canadian Boundary Waters maps ($13 each), including maps for Kabetogama Lake, Rainy Lake, and Lake of the Woods. It also sells lake maps for most lakes in Minnesota, Upper Michigan, and Wisconsin (prices vary); canoe charts for Wisconsin lakes ($4 each); Lake Michigan Marine Maps ($11.95), a complete set of maps showing shorelines, harbors, and offshore depths; and Wisconsin Trout Waters ($12.95), a collection of Wisconsin county maps showing the best trout streams.

Compass Maps, Inc. (P.O. Box 4369, Modesto, CA 95352; 209-529-5017) publishes several recreation maps for California and Nevada, including "Redwood Coast," "Ski Map of California and Nevada," "Tahoe Recreation

Map," and "Wine Tasting Guide Map." A brochure is available upon request.

Countryman Press (Maxham Meadow, Rte. 4 East, P.O. Box 175, Woodstock, VT 05901; 802-457-1049) publishes a Walks and Rambles series, complete with maps, for the Delmarva Peninsula, the Upper Connecticut River Valley, and three other areas in the Northeast ($9.95 each). Countryman Press also distributes canoeing and cross-country skiing guides for New England; in addition, there is the "Fifty Hikes" series for New England, New York, the Mid-Atlantic, and the Midwest ($10.95 to $12.95 each). All are 6" X 9" books with photos and maps. In addition, there is a bicycle tour series of books for the same regions, all with maps. Included are such titles as 25 *Bicycle Tours in Vermont* ($9.95) and 25 *Bicycle Tours in Ohio's Wesern Reserve* ($11.95).

DeLorme Mapping Co. (P.O. Box 298, Freeport, ME 04032; 207-865-4171) publishes a variety of recreation maps for Maine, including topographic maps of many state and national parks. Examples are "Moosehead Lake Map & Guide," "Trail Map & Guide to the White Mountain National Forest," and "Baxter State Park and Katahdin Map & Guide" ($4.95 each); Fishing Depth Maps ($3.95 each), 17 volumes of 1,700 Maine lakes and ponds, illustrating depths and fish species in each water; Maine Fishing Maps ($10.95 each), containing large-scale maps and descriptions of Maine's best fishing spots (Volume I focuses on lakes and ponds, while Volume II features rivers and streams); *New Hampshire Fishing Maps* ($10.95), a 112-page guide to the Granite State's rivers, streams, lakes, and ponds; and *Canoeing* ($3.95 each), a set of three 48-page guides to canoeing in Maine.

Earthwalk Press (2239 Union St., Eureka, CA 95501; 707-442-0503) produces more than a dozen topographic hiking and recreation maps. The one-sided maps—including "Mount Rainier National Park," "Grand Teton National Park," and "Lassen Volcanic National Park"—are $2.95

(paper) or $5.95 (waterproof); two-sided maps—including "Yellowstone National Park," "Capitol Reef National Park," and "Sawtooth Wilderness"—are $3.95 (paper) or $6.95 (waterproof). Other recent maps include the seven-color "California's North Coast Recreation Map" ($3.95 paper, $6.95 waterproof), which covers California's north coast from Clam Beach County Park to the Oregon border, and the eight-color "Hawai'i Volcanoes National Park Recreation Map" ($3.95 paper, $6.95 waterproof).

Globe Pequot Press (10 Denlar Dr., Chester, CT 06412; 203-526-9571; 800-243-0495; 800-962-0973 in Conn.) sells *Sixty Selected Short Walks in Connecticut* ($8.95; 184 pages) and *Short Nature Walks on Long Island* ($8.95; 144 pages), guides to walks in and around the woods, mountains, lakes, waterfalls, and flower sanctuaries.

Gulf Publishing Co. (P.O. Box 2608, Houston, TX 77252; 713-520-4301) publishes a number of recreation guidebooks that include maps. A sampling is: *Camper's Guide to Texas Parks, Lakes, and Forests* ($9.95; 148 pages); *Camper's Guide to British Columbia Parks, Lakes ,and Forests ,Vol. 1: Vancouver, Lower Mainland, Cariboo-Shuswap-Okanagan* ($16.95; 152 pages); *Camper's Guide to British Columbia Parks, Lakes ,and Forests ,Vol. 2: Kootenay and Northern British Columbia* ($16.95; 152 pages); *Camper's Guide to Michigan Parks, Lakes, and Forests* ($15.95; 162 pages); *Camper's Guide to California Parks, Lakes, Forests & Beaches, Vol. 1, Northern California* ($12.95; 176 pages); *Camper's Guide to California Parks, Lakes, Forests & Beaches, Vol. 2, Southern California* ($12.95; 176 pages); *Camper's Guide to Colorado Parks, Lakes, and Forests* ($14.95; 156 pages); *Camper's Guide to Florida Parks, Trails, Rivers, and Beaches* ($12.95; 176 pages); *Camper's Guide to Minnesota Parks, Lakes, Forests, and Trails* ($12.95; 160 pages); *Camper's Guide to Texas Parks, Lakes, and Forests* ($14.95; 160 pages); *Hiking and Backpacking Trails of Texas* ($9.95; 148 pages); *A Guide to Texas Rivers and Streams* ($9.95; 120 pages); *Rock Hunting in Texas* ($9.95; 90 pages); and *Fishing in Texas* ($9.95; 128 pages).

Tom Harrison Cartography (333 Bellam Blvd., San Rafael, CA 94901; 415-456-7940) produces six-color shaded-relief topographic maps of state and national parks, forests, and wilderness areas, all in California. Twenty maps are available ($5.95 each), including: "Angeles High Country," "Desolation Wilderness," "Kings Canyon High Country," "Mt. Rainier National Park," "Mt. Whitney High Country," "San Diego Backcountry," "Santa Monica Mountains" (Central, East, and West in separate maps), "Sequoia & Kings Canyon National Park," "Yosemite National Park," and "Yosemite Valley."

High Tech Caribbean Ltd. (P.O. Box 325, Road Town, Tortola, British Virgin Islands; 809-494-3811) publishes a colorful "Sail/Dive the Virgin Islands," a two-sided, 24" X 18" chart illustrating choice diving spots ($5.95). Also available is "The Chartsman's Guide to the Virgin islands," a two-sided 38" X 25" map reproduced from Admiralty charts that features anchorage and tourist advice for both the British Virgin Islands and the U.S. Virgin Islands.

Hubbard Scientific, Inc. (P.O. Box 760, Chippewa Falls, WI 54729; 800-323-8368) produces more than 225 raised-relief maps of the country's mountainous areas—everything west of the Rocky Mountains, including the Hawaiian Islands, and portions of the eastern U.S., from Alabama to Maine. Hubbard's maps are not as colorful as those of other companies, but they include high-quality detail. Maps vary in size, but are generally 21" square and represent approximately 110 X 70 miles. Prices are $16.95 unframed, $42.95 framed.

Kingfisher Maps, Inc. (P.O. Box 1604, Seneca, SC 29679; 803-882-5840) publishes topographic-vicinity and lake-contour maps for anglers and boaters printed on waterproof paper ($7.99 each). Maps are available for a variety of lakes in Alabama, Arkansas, Florida, Georgia, Illinois, Indiana, Iowa,

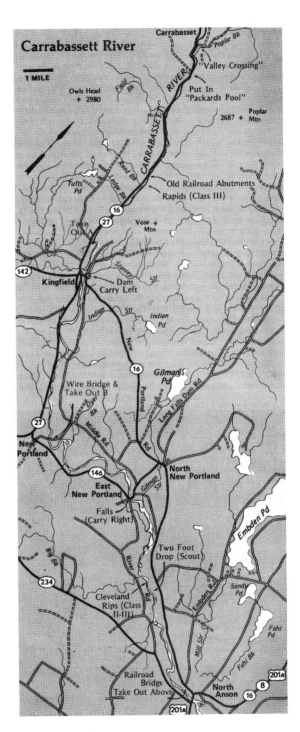

Canoeing map of the Carrabassett River in western Maine, showing rapids and other landmarks, from Maine Geographic Canoeing, Volume 2: Western Rivers. Copyright DeLorme Mapping Company. Reproduced with permission.

Kansas, Kentucky, Mississippi. Missouri, Nebraska, North Carolina, Ohio, Oklahoma, Pennsylvania, South Carolina, Tennessee, Texas, Virginia, and West Virginia.

Latitudes Map and Travel Publishers (P.O. Box 80688, Minneapolis, MN 55408; 612-825-8117) publishes "The Minneapolis Lakes District" map ($4.95), which includes information on biking, sports, parks, and festivals in and around Cedar Lake, Lake of the Isles, Lake Calhoun, and Lake Harriet.

Mountaineers Books (1011 SW Klickitat Way, Seattle, WA 98134; 206-223-6303) sells outdoor recreation guides, many containing useful maps. Examples are: *The High Sierra: Peaks, Passes and Trails* ($19.95; 368 pages); *Trekking in Nepal: A Traveler's Guide* ($16.95; 446 pages); and *Bicycle Touring in Australia* ($17.95; 176 pages).

New England Cartographics (P.O. Box 369, Amherst, MA 01004; 413-253-7415) produces topographic maps of recreational areas in New England; titles available include "Mt. Greylock Trail Map" ($2.95), "Holyoke Range East" ($2.95), "Quabbin Reservation Guide" ($2.95), and "Connecticut River Guide" ($5). Guides include *Hiking the Pioneer Valley*, *Metacomet-Mondanock Trail Guide*, and *Guide to the Taconic Trail System* ($5). Maps are available laminated or on waterproof paper.

Northern Cartographics (P.O. Box 133, Burlington, VT 05402; 802-860-2886) publishes *Access America* ($89.95), an atlas and guide to the 37 national parks for disabled visitors. Detailed, full-color maps, regional maps illustrating selected support services within a 100-mile radius of the park; and information on paths of travel, accessible parking, restroom evaluations, road elevations, medical services, lodging, dining, and campgrounds are provided. It also distributes *The Atlas of Vermont Trout Ponds* ($11.95; 176 pages) and *Vermont Trout Streams* ($19.95; 128 pages), with six folded maps inside.

Omni Resources (1238 Anthony Rd., P.O. Box 2096, Burlington, NC 27216; 919-227-8300) distributes Kümmerly & Frey's hiking maps of Switzerland. These provide information on the national trail system, way stations, hikers' huts, and scenic routes. The set of 64 hiking maps ($12.95 each) covers most of Switzerland. Also available are government-produced maps of U.S. and Canadian national parks, as well as many of the Italian hiking map series by Kompass and Tobacco.

Pacific Historical Maps (P.O. Box 201 [CHRB], Saipan, Mariana Islands 96950) publishes a "Dive Map of the Ghost Fleet of Truk Lagoon" ($3.50), a pictorial map describing the U.S. Navy Task Force 58's aircraft-carrier raid on the Japanese fleet in 1944. The map is available from the **Truk Visitor's Bureau**, P.O. Box FQ, Moen, Truk, F.S.M. 96942.

Pelican Publishing Co. (1101 Monroe St., Gretna, LA 70053; 504-368-1175) distributes *The Frank Davis Fishing Guide to Lake Pontchartrain and Lake Borgne* ($8.95), a 160-page guide to these southern Louisiana lakes that is supplemented with detailed maps, and the *Cruising Guide to Eastern Florida* and the *Cruising Guide to the Northern Gulf Coast: Florida, Alabama, Mississippi, Louisiana* ($24.95 each), which include pertinent navigational information supplemented with maps.

Pierson Graphics Corp. (899 Broadway, Denver, CO 80203; 303-623-4299) publishes "Colorado Deluxe Road and Recreation Map" ($4.95), a 32" X 42" shaded-relief map with insets of major cities and national parks.

Pittmon Map Co. (732 SE Hawthorne Blvd., Portland, OR 97214; 503-232-1161; 800-547-3576 in western states) produces Pittmon Recreational County Maps ($2.99 each), indexed maps created for use by hunters, fishermen, four-wheelers, prospectors, and other recreationists. Available for most counties in Oregon and Washington. Pittmon also

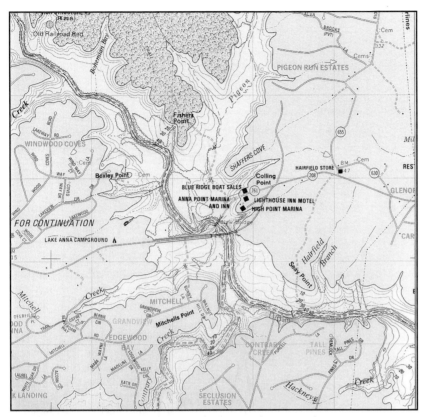

Portion of recreation map of Lake Anna, VA, from ADC, The Map People.

PhotoMaps ($4.95 each), groups of photos taken from the land and the air with written descriptions, along with a general map sketch of the area. PhotoMaps are available for Lake Powell, the San Juan/Escalante River Arm, and the Grand Canyon. These maps are not useful for finding your way around in these areas but can help you to identify the areas you are seeing.

Sierra Club Books (distributed by Random House, 201 E. 50th St., New York, NY 10022; 301-

distributes Wilderness Maps for areas in the Pacific Northwest, as well as USGS topographic and National Forest maps for areas in Oregon.

The Rails-to-Trails Conservancy (1400 16th St. NW, Washington, DC 20036; 202-797-5400) publishes guidebooks to rail-trails, abandoned railway routes converted into recreation paths. *America's Rail-Trails* is a directory of 360 existing rail-trails in the U.S. Among other useful data, the guide lists trail length, type of surfacing, and suitable uses ($6 members, $8 nonmembers). The "Sampler of America's Rail-Trails" ($2) features maps and detailed descriptions of 12 of the nation's best rail-trails. Also included is information on types of trail use and places to eat and sleep along the trails.

Rainbow Gold, Inc. (P.O. Box 21681, Salt Lake City, UT 84121; 801-943-0298) produces

848-1900; 800-726-0600) publishes a series of paperback guides to parks and natural recreation areas, which include between 10 and 18 full-color maps per title. There are two series: Sierra Club Guides to Natural Areas of the U.S. (with separate titles for California; Colorado and Utah; Idaho, Montana, and Wyoming; New Mexico, Arizona, and Nevada; and Oregon and Washington) and Sierra Club Guides to the National Parks (with separate titles for parks of the desert Southwest; the East and Midwest; the Pacific Northwest and Alaska; the Pacific Southwest and Hawaii; and the Rocky Mountains). Another series, Sierra Club Totebooks, features hikers' guides that contain maps for a variety of wilderness areas, including the Great Smoky Mountains, the Grand Canyon, the North Cascades, the Wind River Mountains, the High Sierras, the Swiss Alps, the John Muir Trail, the Great Basin, Bigfoot

Country, and Yellowstone backcountry.

Square One Map Co. (P.O. Box 1312, Woodinville, WA 98072; 206-485-1511) publishes various maps, most including park/campground charts, of Washington state's recreation areas. Titles include "San Juan Islands Map and Recreation Guide" ($4.95), "Mount Rainier—Central Cascades" ($3.98), "The Okanogan—Central Washington" ($3.98), "Mt. Baker—Northwest Washington" ($3.98), "Olympic Peninsula" ($3.98), and "Alpine Lakes Wilderness & Surrounding Area" ($7.95).

Sunbelt Publications (P.O. Box 191126, San Diego, CA 92119; 619-258-4911, 800-626-6579) distributes several map series focusing on recreation areas of California and the Southwest. Of special interest is its Off-road Map series, showing off-road vehicle maps of canyon and mountain areas. A free catalog is available.

Trails Illustrated (P.O. Box 3610, Evergreen, CO 80439; 303-670-3457) publishes more than 100 topographic maps of recreational areas in Colorado, Utah, and more than 40 national parks. The waterproof, tearproof maps are updated annually and are available in retail stores or can be ordered directly. A catalog and price list are available. Trails Illustrated produces the following series:

■ Colorado Series ($7.95 each), including maps for Flat Tops, Indian Peaks, Kebler Pass West, Maroon Bells, Steamboat Springs, Tarryall Mountains, and Weminuche/Chicago Basin.
■ National Park and Recreation Areas Series ($7.95 each), including Dinosaur National Monument, Glacier/Waterton National Park, Grand Canyon National Park, Rocky Mountain National Park, Sequoia/Kings Canyon National Park, and nearly 40 more.
■ Cross Country Series ($5.95 each), maps for Aspen-Carbondale, Frisco-Breckenridge, Nederland-Georgetown, and Vail-Leadville.
■ Mountain Bike Series ($5.95 each), including maps for Moab Area, Winter Park, and Durango.

■ Utah Series ($7.95 each), including Timpanogos Peak, Dark Canyon, Fish Lake, and Grand Gulch.
■ Specialty Series ($5.95 each), including Triple David Peak, Old Faithful, Mammoth Hot Springs, and Yellowstone Lake.

University of Hawaii Press (2840 Kolowalu St., Honolulu, HI 96822; 808-956-8255) publishes *On the Na Pali Coast: A Guide for Hikers and Boaters* ($10.95; 112 pages), designed as a guide for both land and sea, containing detailed maps and narrative text.

Wilderness Press (2440 Bancroft Way, Berkeley, CA 94704; 510-843-8080) publishes many map-filled guides to recreational areas in California and the western U.S. A sampling is: *Arizona Trails: 100 Hikes in Canyon and Sierra* ($14.95; 320 pages); *Yosemite National Park* ($19.95; 290 pages); *Afoot and Afield in San Diego County* ($16.95; 306 pages); *Kauai Trails: Walks, Strolls and Treks on the Garden isle* ($12.95; 234 pages). It also distributes "Point Reyes National Seashore Map" ($5.95), a 24" X 36" "pictorial landform" map that gives an aerial perspective of the Point Reyes Peninsula, and numerous topographic maps of California wilderness areas (see "Topographic Maps").

WILDERNESS CLUBS

Below is a listing of outdoor groups that offer maps for hikers, bikers, campers, and nature lovers. There may be some restrictions on the availability of maps, especially to non-members of some membership organizations.

■ **Adirondack Mountain Club** (RR 3, Box 3055, Lake George, NY 12845; 518-668-4447) has maps of New York's Adirondack Mountains.
■ **Appalachian Mountain Club** (5 Joy St., Boston, MA 02108; 617-523-0636) sells a wide range of guidebooks and maps.
■ **Appalachian Trail Conference** (P.O. Box 807, Harpers Ferry, WV 25425; 304-535-6331) has maps of the Appalachian Trail's 14-state route.
■ **Buckeye Trail Association Inc.** (P.O. Box 254, Worthington, OH 43085) sells maps and

trail guides of Ohio's 1,200-mile Buckeye Trail.
■ **Canadian Orienteering Federation** (1600 James Naismith Dr., Ste. 713, Gloucester, Ontario K1B 5N4; 613-748-5649) sells orienteering maps for areas in Canada, published and distributed by individual clubs; a list of clubs is available.
■ **Colorado Mountain Club** (2530 W. Alameda St., Denver, CO 80219; 303-922-8315) has several topographic and trail maps of Colorado mountains, as well as hikers' guides to various wilderness areas in Colorado.
■ **Finger Lakes Trail Conference, Inc.** (P.O. Box 18048, Rochester, NY 14618) sells maps and guides for the 800-mile Finger Lakes trail system across the southern tier of New York State. Maps are 85 cents each; a complete set of 45 is $15. Guides range from $2.25 to $6.75.
■ **Florida Trail Association** (P.O. Box 13708, Gainesville, FL 32604; 904-378-8823) has trail maps of 43 sections of the Florida Trail, which expands from the Big Cypress National Preserve in the south to the Gulf Island Seashore near Pensacola. It also publishes *Florida Hiking*

Trails: The Official Guide to the Florida Trail on Public Lands ($11.95, plus $3 postage).
■ **Green Mountain Club** (RR 1, Box 650, Rte. 100, Waterbury Center, VT 05677; 802-244-7037) offers maps of Vermont's 265-mile "Long Trail," as well as maps of day hiking trails throughout the state.
■ **Potomac Appalachian Trail Club** (118 Park St. SE, Vienna, VA 22180; 703-242-0315) has maps of trails in Washington, D.C., Maryland, Pennsylvania, and Virginia, as well as circuit hike books and two local guide books.
■ **United States Orienteering Federation** (P.O. Box 1444, Forest Park, GA 30051; no phone) has orienteering maps, sold through individual clubs; a list of clubs and associate groups is available.

■ **See also: "Agriculture Maps," "Bicycle Route Maps," "Land-Use Maps," "Natural Resource Maps," "Nautical Charts and Maps," "River, Lake, and Waterway Maps," "Topographic Maps," "Tourism Maps and Guides," and "Wildlife Maps."**

Tourism Maps and Guides

The boom in travel maps mirrors the recent boom in travel. It wasn't long ago that choosing a touring map meant selecting between one or two potential products; often only one was readily available, making the "choice" somewhat easier. No more. Today there are dozens of maps for some popular parts of the globe, many of which may be found at a well-stocked map or travel store.

Such competition has resulted in an overall improvement of tourism maps. Striving to distinguish themselves, the current crop of travel maps includes some impressive entries, which feature valuable travel information that goes beyond mere street names and landmarks. Color and detail on some maps are nothing short of spectacular. A few are printed in the country's native language, allowing you to make sense more easily of road signs along the way. There are laminated, pocket-size maps; pop-up maps; and maps that automatically fold themselves.

Equally impressive is the degree of special-ization of some of today's maps; the themes range from the ridiculous to the sublime. There are a half-dozen or so maps of wine-making regions around the United States, as well as shopping maps, literary maps—even a jazz map. There is a map dedicated to the habitat of the Loch Ness monster, a whiskey map of Scotland, and a map of Shakespeare's England.

A note about maps of Eastern Europe and especially the countries that were once part of the former Soviet Union: as this book went to press, many publishers were planning to publish new maps of the region. Several of them are included in this chapter, but there will likely be many more to come. You are encouraged to ask your local map retailer for the latest editions.

The maps below are organized by continent. At the beginning of each section are listings of map publishers whose products cover the entire continent or several countries. Following that are descriptions of maps that relate to specific countries in each region.

AFRICA

American Map Corp. (46-35 54th Rd., Maspeth, NY 11378; 718-784-0055; 800-432-6277) distributes a map of Morocco ($9.95).

Central Intelligence Agency. The CIA produces numerous city and tourist-related maps, including "Senegal/Gambia, Israel Transportation Systems" ($11.50; PB 82-928044) and the ever-useful "Standard Time Zones of the World" ($8.95; PB 88-928358). CIA maps can be ordered from the National Technical Information Service (see Appendix B).

Hammond, Inc. (515 Valley St., Maplewood, NJ 07040; 201-763-6000; 800-526-4953) distributes Bartholomew's World Travel Map series ($10.95 each), featuring full-color reference maps for most countries of the world. The maps, in a variety of sizes and scales, are of frameable quality. Map titles include: "Africa," "Central and Southern Africa," "East Africa," "West Africa," "Egypt," and "Kenya."

Hunter Publishing (300 Raritan Center Pkwy., Edison, NJ 08818; 908-225-1900) distributes Kümmerly & Frey's World Travel Maps ($7.95 to $9.95), fully indexed maps that are updated annually. Maps are available for Africa and North and West Africa. Hunter also distributes Hildebrand Travel Maps ($8.95), which contain travel information on climate, customs, currency, shopping, and more in the margins, as well as detailed city maps. They are available for East Africa, Egypt, Morocco, South Africa, the Seychelles, Tenerife, Tunisia, and other countries.

Michelin Travel Publications (P.O. Box 19001, Greenville, SC 29602; 803-458-6458; 800-423-0485) publishes Main Roads maps of Africa ($7.95 each), including "North & West," "Northeast, including Egypt & Arabia," "Central & South Madagascar," "Morocco," "Algeria-Tunisia," and "Ivory Coast."

Rand McNally (P.O. Box 7600, Chicago, IL 60680; 312-673-9100) publishes the Cosmopolitan map series ($1.95 to $3.50) for Africa. It also publishes the International map series, 52" X 34" maps of the United States and maps of the world ($3.50).

The Talman Co., Inc. (150 Fifth Ave., New York, NY 10011; 212-620-3182) distributes Ravenstein Verlag's International Road Map series of detailed, large-scale maps ($8.95 each) that depict topographic features, roads, towns, picturesque locales, cultural sights, and camping grounds, with legends in four to six languages. Available African titles are: "Morocco," "East Africa," "Africa," "South Africa," and "Egypt."

THE AMERICAS

Allmaps Canada, Ltd. (390 Steelcase Rd. E., Markham, Ontario, L3R 1G2, Canada; 416-477-8480) publishes and distributes maps and StreetFinder Map Books for all the cities and regions of Canada, including all the provinces and the cities of Vancouver, Calgary, Edmonton, Saskatoon, Regina, Winnipeg, Windsor, London, Kitchener, Greater Toronto, Montreal, Quebec, and Halifax.

American Map Corp. (46-35 54th Rd., Maspeth, NY 11378; 718-784-0055; 800-432-6277) publishes an annual road atlas, *United States Highway Atlas*, that covers the U.S.,

Mexico, and Canada. The 242-page book details interstate highways and major state and county roads; also included are metropolitan area maps detailing major streets in 55 leading cities. AMC also publishes a *City to City Atlas* designed for the business traveler, and seven state maps—Illinois, Indiana, Kentucky, Michigan, Missouri, Ohio, Wisconsin—that include a travel guide designed for planning vacations and weekend getaways.

Coastal Cruise Tour Guides (158 Thomas St., Ste. 11, Seattle, WA 98109; 206-448-4488) publishes three different guides for people taking cruises and tours of Alaska/Canada's Inside Passage, Western Mexico, or the Eastern Caribbean. The six-foot guides feature fold-out, five-color shaded relief maps showing points of interest, resort locations, roads, airports, and other geographical features. The guides also contain illustrations, photos, and descriptive text and information on the culture, politics, religions, and arts of each area. Each guide comes in a sturdy vinyl envelope. Visa and MasterCard orders are taken at the $14.95 price, which includes shipping and handling. Quantity discounts are available.

Hammond, Inc. (515 Valley St., Maplewood, NJ 07040; 201-763-6000; 800-526-4953) distributes Bartholomew's World Travel Map series ($10.95 each), featuring full-color reference maps for most countries of the world. The well-documented maps, in a variety of sizes and scales, are of frameable quality. Map titles include "North America," "South America," "Argentina/Chile/Paraguay/Uruguay," "Brazil/Bolivia," "Canada," "Mexico," "Peru/Colombia/Venezuela/Ecuador," "Western U.S.A.," and "Eastern U.S.A."

Hippocrene Books (171 Madison Ave., New York, NY 10016; 718-454-2366) is North American distributor of Falk City Maps, including "New York" ($9.95), and Falk Country Road Maps, including "USA Atlas" ($9.95).

Hunter Publishing (300 Raritan Center Pkwy., Edison, NJ 08818; 908-225-1900) distributes

Kümmerly & Frey's World Travel Maps ($7.95 to $9.95), fully indexed maps that are updated annually. Maps are available for Canada and South America, as are world political and world physical maps. Hunter also distributes Hildebrand Travel Maps ($8.95), which contain information on climate, customs, currency, shopping, and more, as well as detailed city maps. Titles include "California," "The Caribbean," "Hispaniola," "Jamaica," "Mexico," "Puerto Rico," "The Southern Rockies," "Eastern U.S.," "Western U.S.," and "The U.S."

National Geographic Society (17th & M sts. NW, Washington, DC 20036; 301-921-1200) produces a Close-Up series of plastic-coated maps showing places and events—festivals, historic sites, wilderness areas, resort areas, museums, etc.—including a mileage/kilometer guide for estimating driving time. Each Close-Up map comes with a 208-page index/guide.

The maps make for good supplements to road maps. Close-Up maps ($4 each) are available for all regions in the U.S. and all Canadian provinces.

National Geographic offers various other maps of the Americas, such as:

■ "Canada Political/Vacationlands" ($7.95; 20007), a 23" X 34" map printed on both sides.
■ "Heart of the Grand Canyon" ($7.95; 02803), a 35" X 36" topographic map depicting trails, roads, campgrounds, cliffs, and contours.
■ "West Indies/Tourist Islands" ($7.95; 02841), a 34" X 23" map printed on both sides.
■ "South America" ($7.95; 02014; 23" X 31").

Prentice Hall (200 Old Tappan Rd., Old Tappan, NJ 07675; 201-767-4970; 800-223-2348) sells Baedeker Road Maps ($9.95 each), the cream of the crop of international driving maps.

"The Islands of Hawaii," published by Travel Graphics International

Roadside attractions, motels, scenic routes, and speed limits are all detailed. Titles include "Caribbean" and "Mexico."

Rand McNally (P.O. Box 7600, Chicago, IL 60680; 312-673-9100) publishes the Cosmopolitan map series ($1.95 to $3.50) for Canada, Mexico, South America, the West Indies/Caribbean, and Alaska. It also publishes the International map series, 52" X 34" maps of the U.S. and the world ($3.50). In addition, Rand McNally creates many travel and road atlases that are updated regularly and filled with maps and information to enhance any trip. Titles include: *Road Atlas* ($7.95), a road and highway guide good for planning and taking vacations or business trips; *Road Atlas & Vacation Guide* ($17.95), an annual containing the full-color road and city maps of the *Road Atlas*, plus descriptions of 1,900 places of interest, ideal for family vacation planning; *Business Traveler's Road Atlas* ($16.95), an annual publication with full-color road and city maps, as well as major city information for business people; *Motor Carriers' Road Atlas* ($16.95; laminated deluxe edition, $75), a road and highway atlas for truckers. Also available is "The City Map Collection" ($34.95), a set of 36 Rand McNally city road maps covering all parts of North America, and "The State Map Collection" ($34.95), a set of 50 state maps.

Sunset Publishing Co. (80 Willow Rd., Menlo Park, CA 94025; 800-227-7346; 800-321-0372 in California) publishes a series of 19 travel guides for locations around the world, including 11 in the United States. Destinations include Alaska, Arizona, Hawaii, Washington, Oregon, New England, Southern California, and Northern California ($10.95 to $12.95 each). Also publishes *Gold Rush Country*, a 128-page guide to California's Mother Lode area that includes locator maps ($8.99).

The Talman Co., Inc. (150 Fifth Ave., New York, NY 10011; 212-620-3182) distributes Ravenstein Verlag's International Road Map series of detailed, large-scale maps ($8.95

each) depicting topographic features, roads, towns, picturesque locales, cultural sights, and camping grounds, with legends in four to six languages. Maps of South America and North America are among the more than 50 titles available.

Travel Graphics International (1118 S. Cedar Lake Rd., Minneapolis, MN 55405; 612-377-1080) produces colorfully illustrated map/posters of popular vacation areas. The 17" X 23" Pocket Maps ($2.95 each, including shipping), simplified maps showing tourist points of interest, are available for "The Islands of Hawaii," "Oahu," "Maui," "Hawaii," "Acapulco," "Mexico City," "Cancun/Cozumel," "Puerto Vallarta," "San Francisco," "Dallas," "Las Vegas," and "Minnesota." Functional Pocket Maps (17" X 23"), showing major roads and buildings in metropolitan areas, are available for Rochester, Minneapolis/St. Paul, St. Louis, San Francisco, and Indianapolis ($2.95 each, including shipping). Colorful posters, although not useful as road or street guides, illustrate activities and things to see. Titles available are "The Islands of Hawaii," "Oahu," "Hawaii," "Maui," "Kauai," "Mexico," "The Caribbean," "Las Vegas," "Florida," and "Minnesota" ($6.50 each; 22" X 28" to 25" X 38"). Prices are discounted for orders of more than one map or poster.

Treaty Oak (P.O. Box 50295, Austin, TX 78763; 512-326-4141) distributes maps from 27 publishers in 16 countries and specializes in maps of Latin America. Among them are maps published by Hfet, Sigsa, Guia Roji, and Cartur.

INDIVIDUAL COUNTRY MAPS

CANADA

MapArt/Peter Heiler, Ltd. (72 Bloor St. E., Oshawa, Ontario, L1H 3M2; 416-668-6677) publishes dozens of travel/road maps and guides for Canadian provinces and cities (many in the $1.95 to $2.95 range). New maps include "Saskatchewan" ($1.95), "Quebec and Ville de Quebec Guide" ($7.95), "Toronto and Ontario

Overview map from "San Francisco and Bay Area Illustrated Pocket Map," published by Travel Graphics International.

Highway Guide" ($7.95), and "Ontario Street Guide" ($6.95). All prices are Canadian dollars.

MEXICO

designWorks! (949 Apollo Way, Incline Village, NV 89451; 702-832-2205) produces *Gringo's Guide to Baja California, Mexico,* offering complete coverage of the peninsula on a topographic map, along with information on the culture, land, people, restaurants, hotels, and camping areas. The guide is available as a laminated wall mural ($17.95; 24" X 36") or in an accordion-folded version that fits into a Ziploc travel pouch ($8.95). Add $2 for shiping.

Treaty Oak (P.O. Box 50295, Austin, TX 78763; 512-326-4141) distributes state maps and city plans by Hfet; Pronto maps of Mexican cities and states; and state and city maps by Guia Roji, including four atlases. Also available are Mexican topographic maps, nautical charts, and a laminated wall map of the entire country.

Warren Communications (P.O. Box 620635, San Diego, CA 92162; 619-236-0984) distributes

topographic maps of Mexico published by the Mexican government at scales of 1:50,000 and 1:250,000. The titles available vary; it's best to inquire. Individual copies of maps that Warren Communications imports can be ordered from **The Map Centre**, 2611 University Ave., San Diego, CA 92104; 619-291-3830.

UNITED STATES

Basin Street Press (20460 Will Rd., Abita Springs, LA 70420; 504-893-1130) produces a "Jazz Map of New Orleans" ($6.50, including postage) by Dr. Karl Koenig, which pinpoints the city's existing jazz clubs; the accompanying 30-page booklet outlines a driving tour of Storyville, the French Quarter, and St. Charles Street, tracing the rich history of jazz in New Orleans. Also available is *Just a Closer Walk* ($6.50), a guidebook to a walking jazz tour of the French Quarter, with street maps through-out.

The Butterworth Co., Cape Cod (291 Main St., W. Dennis, MA 02670; 508-760-2000) publishes helpful street maps of the Cape Cod area.

"Cape Cod Map & Guide" ($2.95) shows highways and roads along with beaches, golf courses, historic sites, and other points of interest; *Cape Cod & Islands Atlas and Guide Book* ($13.95) includes detailed street maps for every town, as well as information on points of interest, Cape Cod living, outdoor recreation activities, and fishing maps of 80 Cape Cod lakes and ponds; and *Eastern Massachusetts Atlas* ($12.95) contains maps of 173 communities in the eastern part of the state. Butterworth also produces pocket street maps for Cape Cod, the islands, and southeastern Massachusetts areas ($2.95 each).

DeLorme Mapping Co. (P.O. Box 298, Freeport, ME 04032; 207-865-4171) produces an Atlas & Gazetteer series of full-color, large-scale, well-detailed and accurate atlases. Back roads, as well as major roads and highways, are shown, along with geographic features such as forests, mountains, lakes, ponds, rivers, and trails. Each 11" X 15" atlas includes a detailed place-name index. The gazetteer sections of the atlases list hundreds of places to go and things to do, from hiking, canoeing, and fishing spots to museums, historic sites, and golf courses. DeLorme Atlas & Gazetteers are available for Alaska, Colorado, Florida, Idaho, Illinois, Michigan, Minnesota, New York State, North Carolina, Northern California, Ohio, Oregon, Pennsylvania, Southern California, Tennessee, Virginia, Washington, and Wisconsin ($14.95 each), and Maine, New Hampshire, and Vermont ($11.95 each). DeLorme also publishes the "Maine Map and Guide" ($1.95), a state highway map including a mileage chart and listings of travel and recreational services, as well as inset maps of major cities and towns, and Upstate New York City Street Maps, which includes coverage of 53 cities, from Newburgh to the south to Plattsburgh to the north to Niagara Falls and Buffalo to the west ($9.95)

Ferry Tale Productions (P.O. Box 1004, Friday Harbor, WA 98250; 206-378-2648) produces a ferry guide and map of Washington State's San Juan Islands ($2.50), showing ferry routes and

Portion of "Wineries of the Napa Valley," published by Napa Valley Vintners Association.

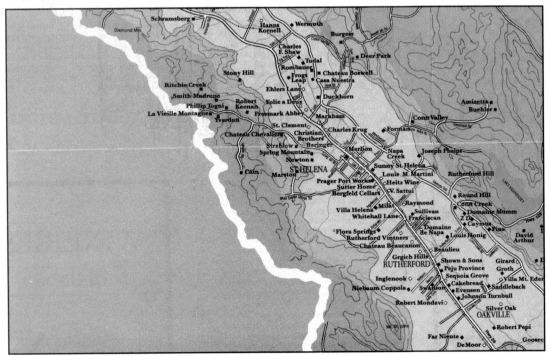

giving descriptions of each island. The map is available on the ferries, in local stores, or by mail (add $1 postage).

Funmap, Inc. (705 W. 6th Ave., Ste. 209, Anchorage, AK 99501; 907-892-7356) publishes colorful two-sided tourist maps of areas in Alaska. One side is a general overview map of the area; on the reverse is a pictorial street map of the metro region. The maps ($1.99 each, available through local retail outlets or directly from Funmap) have the added bonus of folding easily to fit in their paperback-book-size cover. Maps are available for Anchorage, Seward, Fairbanks, Juneau, Ketchikan, Sitka, Homer, Kodiak, Nome, and the entire state.

Global Graphics (2819 Greentop St., Lakewood, CA 90712; 310-429-8880) publishes street, freeway, and road maps for several California and Nevada locations, including "San Francisco Street Map," "San Francisco Transit Map," "Los Angeles Freeway Map," "Los Angeles Street Map," "San Diego," "Las Vegas," and "California." Most maps feature tourist information, relief shading, and easy-to-read cartography. A complete list is available. Most maps are $2.95; some are $2.50.

Government Printing Office. GPO distributes "United States Road Symbol Signs" ($2.25; S/N 050-000-00152-1), a useful supplement to highway maps and atlases. The folder illustrates different kinds of symbol signs, colors, shapes, and highway route markers for each state. GPO also has a small sampling of maps and guides for tourism in the United States, including:

■ "Welcome to Washington" (S/N 024-005-00823-3), maps of downtown Washington, D.C., and the metropolitan Washington area, with information on possible day trips, available only in quantities of 100 for $42.
■ "Devils Tower" ($4.25; S/N 024-005-00899-3), a history and travel guide that includes maps and tourist information for the famous volcanic rock tower in the Black Hills of Wyoming.

Graphic Concepts (1148 State Farm Dr., Santa Rosa, CA 95403; 707-545-5751) publishes a full-color "Wine Country Tour Map" ($2) of 138 wineries in the Napa, Sonoma, Mendocino, and Lake counties of California. The reverse side of the map lists addresses, phone numbers, hours, and activities available at each winery.

H. M. Gousha (15 Columbus Cir., 15th fl., New York, NY 10023; 800-421-7308) publishes the 50 Maps series, which captures the essence and spirit of each place through a mix of facts and fantasy, with 50 maps on everything from Boston's Ivy League campuses to the Palm Beach social whirl. Other titles cover San Francisco and Washington, D.C.

Kooros Maps (P.O. Box 3780, Washington, DC 20007; 703-521-3213) distributes a 20" X 38" aerial view map of the Mall in Washington, D.C., showing the monuments and federal buildings in color.

Map Art/Peter Heiler, Ltd. (72 Bloor St. E., Oshawa, Ontario, L1H 3M2; 416-668-6677) distributes many Gousha state and city maps of the U.S. and Canada. Call or write for an index.

Napa Valley Vintners Association (P.O. Box 141, St. Helena, CA 94574; 707-963-0148) distributes a "Wineries of the Napa Valley" map, available as a rolled poster or as a folded map/brochure (one copy free).

Pelican Publishing Co. (1101 Monroe St., Gretna, LA 70053; 504-368-1175) publishes "Plantations on the Mississippi River: From Natchez to New Orleans," a full-color engraved map showing ownership of plantations along the Mississippi in 1858 ($25; 32" X 54").

Phillip A. Schneider, Cartographer (2109 Plymouth Dr., Champaign, IL 61821) produces "U.S. Virgin Islands," a full-color shaded relief tourist map of St. Thomas, St. John, and St. Croix ($6.95).

Prentice Hall (200 Old Tappan Rd., Old Tappan, NJ 07675; 201-767-4970; 800-223-2348) distributes Gousha Fastmaps, four-panel city maps that fold to a convenient $5\frac{1}{4}$" X 11". On the reverse is an enlarged inset of the downtown area and a street index. Fastmaps are laminated, so routes, directions, and notes can be written on and wiped off later. Fastmaps ($4.95 to $6.95 each) are available for more than 50 destinations.

Raven Maps & Images (34 N. Central, Medford, OR 97501; 503-773-1436; 800-237-0798) produces the "Vineyards & Wineries Map of California" ($35; $65 laminated), a 41" X 52" colorful map of California wine country, with a detailed inset focusing on the Napa-Sonoma region. The map illustrates all bonded wineries and production levels and includes a second inset showing the state's 56 wine-making regions.

Tennessee Valley Authority. TVA publishes several lake recreation maps, available free. Also available from TVA is an 1838 lithograph of an "Aboriginal Tourist Map of Tennessee" ($1; 453 G 77), which shows steamboat routes, towns, county outlines, and drainage. The print measures 15" X 21".

U.S. Geological Survey. Many USGS map products, especially topographic and general reference maps, include major highways and roads. These aren't necessarily the best to take on a driving trip, but they can help in planning one. The USGS National Atlas map "Highways" (1987), shows the complete interstate system, with route markers, and selected other major highways ($3.10; US05630-38077-AZ-NA-07M-00). See "Topographic Maps" for more information on other USGS maps depicting highways.

University of Hawaii Press (University of Hawaii at Manoa, 2840 Kolowalu St., Honolulu, HI 96822; 808-956-8255) publishes "Reference Maps of the Islands of Hawai'i" ($2.95 each). The topographic shaded-relief maps are available for "Hawai'i," "Kaua'i," "Maui," "Moloka'i/Lana'i," and "O'ahu."

Wide World of Maps, Inc. (2626 W. Indian School Rd., Phoenix, AZ 85017; 602-279-2323) publishes the "Metro Phoenix Recreation & Shopping Map" ($2.25; 25" X 18"), locating more than 225 recreation and shopping opportunities, including golf courses, parks, riding stables, shopping centers, and other points of interest.

World Impressions (P.O. Box 460, Tracyton, WA 98393; 800-255-3627) publishes colorfully illustrated sports and travel theme maps, called ArtMaps, principally of North America and the United States. Available as postcards ($.50 each, 10 minimum), laminated in flexible polyvinyl ($19.95 each), or as ready-to-hang wall plaques ($59.95 each). Many are available as jigsaw puzzles (550 pieces, $12.95, or 1,200-piece Expert puzzle, $15.95).

Newest products include:

■ The "History of Basketball ArtMap," produced for the celebration of the 100th anniversary of the sport, contains illustrations of classic scenes from basketball's early days right up to today's high-powered, above-the-rim game of Michael "Air" Jordan. Also available as postcard, laminated map, jigsaw puzzle, and wall plaque.
■ The "Endangered Species of the World ArtMap," a 24" X 36" illustrated tableau of 50 of the world's most threatened species. Also available as a 1,200-piece jigsaw puzzle.

Other sports titles are:

■ "The Official Major League Baseball ArtMap" (24" X 36") features colorful baseball scenes, all American and National League team logos and stadiums, along with lots of baseball trivia. Also available as a 550-piece jigsaw puzzle.
■ "Famous Motorsport Raceways of North America" (24" X 36") features more than 100 tracks and racing events of all types, with sanctioning bodies, official logos, track descriptions, phone numbers, and historical trivia. Also available as postcard, jigsaw puzzle, and wall plaque.

■ "Golf of North America, Hawaii and the British Isles" has illustrated golf scenes with more than 200 golf resorts, clubs, and logos, with a border of 18 of the toughest holes in golf. Also available as jigsaw puzzle and wall plaque.

Travel and non-sport titles include:

■ "Washington...," "Oregon..." (16" X 24"), and "California Adventure" (24" X 36") feature hundreds of attractions, events, natural wonders, and points of interests.
■ "Yosemite Adventure" (16" X 24") colorfully celebrates Yosemite's 100th anniversary, with a detailed trail and services map on the reverse.
■ "San Francisco" (24" X 35"), a 63-color, hand-painted ArtMap, illustrates the architectural charm of more than 50 San Francisco neighborhoods. Also available as a 1,200-piece Expert jigsaw puzzle, postcard, and wall plaque.

ASIA

American Map Corp. (46-35 54th Rd., Maspeth, NY 11378; 718-784-0055; 800-432-6277) distributes World City Maps ($8.95 each) for such cities as Bangkok, Hong Kong, Kuala Lumpur, Singapore, and Tokyo; and World Maps ($9.95 each) for Indonesia, Philippines, and Southeast Asia.

Central Intelligence Agency. The CIA produces a surprising number of city and tourist-related maps. Selections include "Moscow, Downtown" ($8.95; PB 88-928355), "Moscow Street Guide" ($18.95; PB 88-928332), "Clothing Recommendations for Travel in China" ($10; PB 86-928343), "Shanghai Street Guide" ($15.50; PB 87-928303), "Beijing Street Guide" ($21.50; PB 86-928305), "Leningrad, Downtown" ($10; PB 86-928363), and the ever-useful "Standard Time Zones of the World" ($8.95; PB 88-928358). All can be ordered through the National Technical Information Service (see Appendix B).

Hammond, Inc. (515 Valley St., Maplewood, NJ 07040; 201-763-6000; 800-526-4953) distributes

Bartholomew's World Travel Map series ($10.95 each), featuring full-color reference maps for most countries of the world. The maps come in a variety of sizes and scales. Titles include "Southeast Asia," "China/Mongolia," "The Indian Subcontinent," "Israel/Jordan," "Japan," "Singapore/Malaysia," "Thailand," and "Eurasia."

Hunter Publishing (300 Raritan Center Pkwy., Edison, NJ 08818; 908-225-1900) distributes Kümmerly & Frey's World Travel Maps ($7.95 to $9.95), fully indexed maps that are updated annually. Maps are available for Asia, China, the Middle East, and Turkey. Hunter also distributes Hildebrand Travel Maps ($6.96 to $7.95), which contain in the margins travel information on climate, customs, currency, shopping, and more, as well as detailed city maps. Titles available are "China," "Hong Kong," "India," "Israel," "Korea," "Philippines," "Sri Lanka," "Taiwan," "Thailand/Burma/Malaysia," and "Turkey."

National Geographic Society (17th & M sts. NW, Washington, DC 20036; 301-921-1200) offers several maps of Asian countries, including:

■ "Middle East" ($7.95; 02296; 37" X 23").
■ "Japan and Korea" ($7.95; 20022; 23" X 30").
■ "Mount Everest/Heart of the Himalayas" ($7.95; 20033; 23" X 35").
■ "South Asia" ($7.95; 02294; 28" X 23").

Omni Resources (1238 Anthony Rd., P.O. Box 2096, Burlington, NC 27216; 919-227-8300) distributes maps made by dozens of Asian publishers and government agencies. A free catalog is available.

The Talman Co., Inc. (150 Fifth Ave., New York, NY 10011; 212-620-3182) distributes Ravenstein Verlag's International Road Map series of detailed, large-scale maps ($8.95 each), depicting topographic features, roads, towns, picturesque locales, cultural sights, and camping grounds, with legends in four to six languages. "South & East Asia," "Western Soviet Union," "Mideast," "Israel," "Turkey," "Eastern Mediterranean," and "Near East" are among the more than 50 titles available.

INDIVIDUAL COUNTRY MAPS

China

Interarts, Ltd. (15 Mt. Auburn St., Cambridge, MA 02138; 617-354-4655) distributes a "China Map" ($18.95 folded, $25 flat, $85 laminated) drawn to a scale of 1:4,000,000 and measuring 46" X 62".

Japan

Prentice Hall (200 Old Tappan Rd., Old Tappan, NJ 07675; 201-767-4970; 800-223-2348) sells a Baedeker Road Map of Japan ($9.95), depicting roadside attractions, motels, scenic routes, and speed limits, among other useful items of information.

Teikoku-Shoin Co., Ltd. (29 Kanda, Jimbocho 3-chome, Chiyoda-ku, Tokyo 101, Japan) publishes maps and atlases of Japan, such as the *Complete Atlas of Japan*, *Atlas Japan*, and the "Map of Japan." Its maps are available in the U.S. through **Map Link**, 25 E. Mason St., Santa Barbara, CA 93101; 805-965-4402.

EUROPE

American Map Corp. (46-35 54th Rd., Maspeth, NY 11378; 718-784-0055; 800-432-6277) publishes the perfect-bound Travel Atlas series, with each atlas featuring full-color, detailed, large-scale driving maps of Europe. Atlas titles include "Austria," "France, with Belgium, Luxembourg, and The Netherlands," "Germany," "Italy," "Spain/Portugal," "Switzerland," and "Turkey" ($9.95 each). American Map Corp. also distributes other series, including:

■ Pocket Atlases ($9.95 each) for Europe and Great Britain/Ireland.
■ Europe City Maps ($8.95 each) for 31 different cities, including Athens, Barcelona, Flo-rence, Istanbul, Moscow, Munich, Paris, Prague, Warsaw, and Vienna.
■ Euro-Cart Country Maps ($9.95 each) for 20 different locales, including the Alps, Denmark, Greece, Hungary, Norway, Portugal, Switzerland, and Yugoslavia.
■ Euro-Cart Regional Maps ($9.95 each), a series of maps detailing 13 different regions in France, Great Britain, Greece, Italy, Spain, and Yugoslavia. Locales include Loire Valley, Aegean Islands, Tuscany, Canary Islands, and Adriatic Coast.
■ Holiday Maps ($9.95 each) for five resort areas: Costa Brava, Costa del Sol, Gran Canaria/Fuerteventura, Mallorca, and Tenerife.

Europe Map Service/OTD, Ltd. (1 Pinewood Rd., Hopewell Junction, NY 12533; 914-221-0208) distributes a European topographic map series in various scales, including 1:25,000 and 1:1,000,000. The series consists of travel and recreation maps, hydrographic maps, water-resources maps, and administrative maps for Austria, Belgium, Denmark, Finland, France, Germany, Ireland, Luxembourg, the Netherlands, Norway, Sweden, and Switzerland. Also available are reproductions of official administrative World War II maps showing borders of the Third Reich from 1937 to May 1945.

Gabelli U.S. (1228 West Ave. #711, Miami Beach, FL 33139; 305-532-6956) publishes maps of France using its patented Montiscolor process, which shows in three dimensions the actual relief of the Earth's surface in fine detail. Maps include "Cultural France," "Leisure in France," and "Regions of France." In addition, the company produces relief maps of France and Corsica.

Hammond, Inc. (515 Valley St., Maplewood, NJ 07040; 201-763-6000; 800-526-4953) distributes Bartholomew maps, including:

■ World Travel Map series ($10.95 each), featuring full-color reference maps for most countries of the world. The maps, in a variety of sizes and scales, are of frameable quality. Map

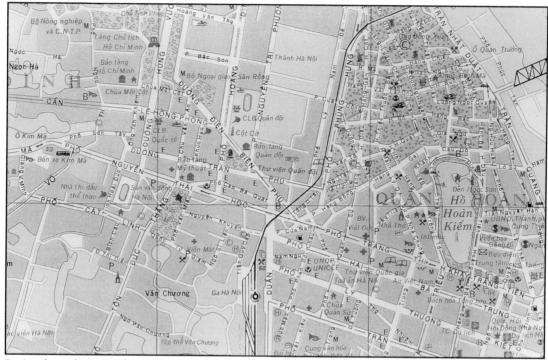

Portion of central Hanoi, with text in Vietnamese, from a map published by Vietnam's State Department of Geodesy and Cartography and distributed by Omni Resources.

titles include "British Isles," "Central Europe," "Eastern Europe," "Western Europe," "France," "Germany," "Italy," "Scandinavia," and "Spain/ Portugal."

■ Tourist Route Maps ($9.50 each), showing roadways, service areas, golf courses, beaches, scenic spots, and other points of interest. Titles include "England North," "England South," "Scotland," "Britain," "Ireland," and "Europe."

■ Holiday Route Planner series ($12.95 each), showing all types of transportation routes and including tourist information. Titles include "Belgium/Luxembourg," "Holland," "Channel Ports to the Hull," and "Europe."

Hippocrene Books (171 Madison Ave., New York, NY 10016; 718-454-2366) is the North American distributor of Falk City Maps, whose European titles include "Amsterdam," "Brussels," "The Hague," and "Rotterdam" ($9.95 each), as well as "Barcelona," "Budapest," "Dublin," "Florence," "Helsinki," "Lisbon," "Paris," and "Stockholm" ($8.95 each).

Hunter Publishing (300 Raritan Center Pkwy., Edison, NJ 08818; 908-225-1900) distributes Kümmerly & Frey's World Travel Maps ($7.95 to $9.95), fully indexed maps that are updated annually. Maps are available for most countries and regions, including "Austria," "Finland," "Greece," "Hungary," "Rumania/Bulgaria," and "Yugoslavia." Also, Kümmerly & Frey's *Euro-Atlas*, a 174-page atlas of road maps from Britain to Moscow, is available for $16.95. Hunter also distributes Hildebrand Travel Maps ($6.96 to $7.95), which contain travel information on climate, customs, currency, shopping, and more in the margins, as well as detailed city maps. Among the European titles available are "Algarve," "Balearic Islands," "Corsica," "Crete," "Gran Canaria," "Majorca," "Peloponnese," "Sardinia," "Tenerife," "Yugoslav Coast North," and "Yugoslav Coast South."

Interarts, Ltd. (15 Mt. Auburn St., Cambridge, MA 02138; 617-354-4655) distributes vibrant GLA Kartor (formerly Esselte) maps of

Scandinavia, including a "Sweden Map" ($19.95), measuring 24" X 46" and drawn to a scale of 1:1,500,000, and Scandinavia Folded Maps ($8.95 each), which include "Stockholm Map and Guide," "Scandinavia," and "Sweden Tourist Maps" (eight individual regional maps).

Kooros Maps (P.O. Box 3780, Washington, DC 20007; 703-521-3213) offers colorful aerial view drawings of London, Paris, and Rome ($19.95 each), as well as two specialized maps of France: "The Gardens of Claude Monet at Giverny" and "The Chateaus of the Loire" ($19.95).

Michelin Travel Publications (P.O. Box 19001, Greenville, SC 29602; 803-458-6458; 800-423-0485) publishes Main Roads maps ($7.95 each), including "Europe" (1:3,000,000 scale), "Greece" (1:700,000), "Germany" (1:750,000) "Scandinavia/Finland" (1:1,500,000 scale), and, at a scale of 1:1,000,000, "Great Britain & Ireland," "Germany, Austria, Benelux," "Italy," "France," "Spain & Portugal," and "Yugoslavia" (1:1,000,000 scale). Also available are *Road Atlas of Europe* ($19.95), *Road Atlas of Great Britain & Ireland* ($19.95), and *Road Atlas of France* (19.95).

National Geographic Society (17th & M sts. NW, Washington, DC 20036; 301-921-1200) offers maps of European countries, including:

■ "British Isles" ($7.95; 02022; 23" X 20").
■ "Germany" ($7.95; 02814; 23" X 29").
■ "Historical France" ($7.95; 20041; 22" X 33").
■ "Traveler's Map of Germany" ($7.95; 20058; 20" X 26"), decorative with descriptive text.

Omni Resources (1238 Anthony Rd., P.O. Box 2096, Burlington, NC 27216; 919-227-8300) distributes maps made by dozens of European publishers and government agencies. A free catalog is available.

Passport Books (4255 W. Touhy Ave., Lincolnwood, IL 60646; 312-679-5500; 800-323-4900) publishes travel maps and guides, including:

■ *Passport's European Atlas for Travelers* ($16.95), containing comprehensive maps of European roads, along with codes for road conditions, points of interest, and detailed city maps. Each map is in the language of the country to correspond with road signs.
■ Passport Maps ($9.95), showing all highways and secondary road systems, with scenic routes highlighted. Available for Scandinavia, Italy, Britain, France, Germany, Benelux, Spain/ Portugal, and Switzerland/Austria/The Alps.

Prentice Hall (200 Old Tappan Rd., Old Tappan, NJ 07675; 201-767-4970; 800-223-2348) sells Baedeker Road Maps ($9.95 each), the cream of the crop of international driving maps. Roadside attractions, motels, scenic routes, and speed limits are all detailed. Titles include "Alps," "Austria," "Belgium," "Denmark," "Europe," "France," "Germany," "Great Britain," "Italy," "Spain/Portugal," "Switzerland," and "Yugoslavia."

Rand McNally (P.O. Box 7600, Chicago, IL 60680; 312-673-9100) publishes the Cosmopolitan map series ($1.95 to $3.50) for Europe. It also publishes the International map series, 52" X 34" maps of the U.S. and the world ($3.50).

The Talman Co., Inc. (150 Fifth Ave., New York, NY 10011; 212-620-3182) distributes Ravenstein Verlag's International Road Map series of detailed, large-scale maps ($8.95 each), depicting topographic features, roads, towns, picturesque locales, cultural sights, and camping grounds, with legends in four to six languages. Maps for Norway, Czechoslovakia, Greece, Ireland, and the Benelux countries are among the more than 50 titles available. The Talman Co. also distributes Ravenstein Verlag's European Pocket Map series of full-color detailed maps of more than 20 European countries. The topographic maps show cities and towns, railroad routes, scenic routes, campsites, tourist sights, and other points of interest. Titles include "Europe," "Austria," "Italy," "Yugoslavia," "Hun-

A Guide to the Guides

Travel guides are a fast-growing part of the book-publishing business. Whereas there used to be only a couple of guidebooks from which to choose for a given area, there now can be a dozen or more for some tourist hotspots. And just as the quality of these books' writing and information varies widely, so, too, do the maps they contain. Astonishingly, some books have no maps at all—or at least no detailed ones. The importance of detailed, translated maps was underscored by the results of a 1988 survey by Berlitz Guides U.S.A. Respondents called good maps of "dire importance" and "absolutely essential" when selecting a travel guide.

To help you wend your way through the guidebook jungle, here are some guides that contain good maps:

Howard W. Sams & Co. (Box 7092, Indianapolis, IN 46206; 317-298-5400; 800-428-7267) distributes Berlitz travel guides. Among its many guides, two are notable for

their full-color road atlases—the Blueprint series and the More for the Dollar series. Blueprint Guides, available for France and Italy, contain 1:1,000,000-scale, 30-page Hallwag road atlases, as well as 40 itineraries with route maps. The illustrated guides are packed with information on what to see and do, how to get around, restaurant and hotel recommendations, and a brief history of the country ($16.95 each). More for the Dollar hotel and restaurant guides to France and Italy ($19.95 each) also have 30-page Hallwag road atlases, and feature hotel and restaurant coupons worth more than $5,000.

Langenscheidt Publishers, Inc. (46-35 54th Rd., Maspeth, NY 11378; 718-784-0055; 800-432-6277) produces the Self-Guided series of guidebooks that emphasize touring information, with detailed maps for driving and walking tours. Each book contains more than 100 maps, photos, and illustrations. Self-Guided titles are available for Florida ($8.95),

gary," "France," "Poland," and "Rumania/ Bulgaria" ($3.95 each).

VLE Limited (P.O. Box 444, Fort Lee, NJ 07024; 201-585-5080) publishes Walks Through, a series of European city maps designed especially for "map illiterates." Visitors start reading at the bottom of the page and walk straight ahead, following a dotted line to the top of the page, turning where indicated. Photos or drawings of landmarks are positioned along the dotted line, as they appear along the route, and short descriptions of each site are also included. (In addition to such landmarks as cathedrals and museums, the maps also highlight everything from cafés, banks, and American Express offices to benches, telephones, and restrooms.) Walks Through maps ($3 each) are available for Paris, Rome, Vienna,

Zurich, Munich, Brussels, Amsterdam, Stuttgart, Madrid, Barcelona, Seville, and London. VLE Limited also produces EURoad, *The Complete Guide to Motoring in Europe* ($6.95), a 64-page guide to motoring in Europe that includes everything from trip-planning information to ferry routes to vocabulary assistance.

INDIVIDUAL COUNTRY MAPS

France
Michelin Travel Publications (P.O. Box 19001, Greenville, SC 29602; 803-458-6458; 800-423-0485) publishes Detailed Maps, a series of nearly 50 road maps drawn to a 1:200,000 scale, which cover all regions in France ($5.95 each), as well as Benelux and Switzerland/Northern Italy ($4.95); Regional Maps, road maps drawn to a 1:200,000 scale for all French regions ($6.95

Alaska ($9.95), Berlin ($9.95), Canada, Egypt, England, European Cities, France, Italy, and Mexico ($12.95 each).

Prentice Hall (200 Old Tappan Rd., Old Tappan, NJ 07675; 201-767-4970; 800-223-2348) distributes American Express Pocket Guides, pocket-size guides featuring a section of full-color highway maps, general maps of major cities in the area, and general two-color Orientation Maps, showing towns and major roads. The handy guides include travel advice, hotel and restaurant recommendations, and a calendar of interesting events. Titles available ($8.95 to $13 each) are "California," "England/Wales," "Florence/Tuscany," "Greece," "Hong Kong/Singapore/Bangkok," "London," "Mexico," "New York," "Paris," "Rome," "Spain," "Venice," and "Washington, D.C."

It also publishes Baedeker's Guides, well-known for their map coverage. Each guide features a large fold-out map of the entire area, street maps of cities, small area maps inset in the text, and layout illustrations of museums, galleries, and monuments. The guides are full of information on history, population, religion, transportation, culture, and commerce and industry, and include listings of hotels and restaurants. Among the 37 country and regional titles available ($12.95 to $23 each) are "Caribbean," "Egypt," "Germany," "Israel," "Japan," "Mediterranean," "Mexico," "Provence/Cote d'Azur," "The Rhine," "Scandinavia," and "Yugoslavia." There are also 23 titles available in the city-specific Baedeker Guides, including "Athens," "Bangkok," "Copenhagen," "Hong Kong," "Jerusalem," "Moscow," "New York," "Paris," "Tokyo," and "Vienna" ($17 each).

Prentice Hall also distributes Mobil Travel Guides, including full-color, fold-out city maps, with walking tours shown on smaller maps, along with information on sightseeing, transit systems, shopping and entertainment, and restaurants. Regional titles ($14 to $15 each) include "California & The West," "Great Lakes," "Northeast," "Northwest & Great Plains," "Southeast," "Southwest & South Central," "Major Cities." Five city guides are available: Boston, Chicago, New York, San Francisco, and Washington, D.C. ($5.95 each).

each); and various maps of Paris, including a *Paris Atlas* ($10.95), arranged by *arrondissements* (neighborhoods), and "Paris Transportation" ($4.95), showing bus, Métro, and rail routes, as well as major roads. Michelin also publishes the Road of History series, including "Valley of Kings" ($7.95) and "Treasure Houses of the Sun King" ($7.95), and "Euro Disney" ($2.95).

Germany
Central Intelligence Agency. Among the numerous city and tourist-related maps the CIA produces are the historic "West Berlin, Transportation Systems" ($11.50; PB 82-928044) and the ever-useful "Standard Time Zones of the World" ($8.95; PB 88-928358). CIA maps can be ordered through the National Technical Information Service (see Appendix B).

Europe Map Service/OTD Ltd. (1 Pinewood Rd., Hopewell Junction, NY 12053) distributes a *Gazetteer of the Federal Republic of Germany*, a now-historic publication packed with information on geographical names and features, official map series and their numbers, and various administrative offices ($88; 794 pages).

Omni Resources (P.O. Box 2096, Burlington, NC 27216; 919-227-8300) has available numerous maps from a variety of publishers, including a number of travel maps of unified Germany.

United Kingdom
Hammond, Inc. (515 Valley St., Maplewood, NJ 07040; 201-763-6000; 800-526-4953) distributes Bartholomew maps, including:

■ Leisure Maps ($9.95 each), large-scale maps

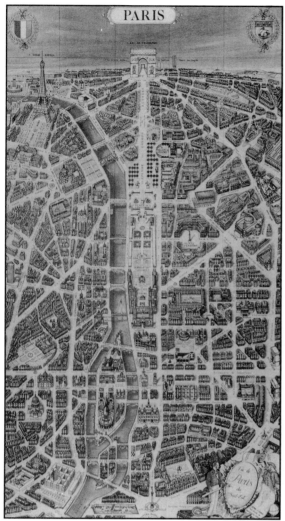

Aerial view of Paris, from Kooros Maps.

- "Cathedrals and Abbeys" ($9.95).
- "London Big Ben" ($4.95), a pocket-size map showing tube stations, bus routes, theaters, cinemas, shops, hotels, and restaurants.

Scotland
- "Scotland Touring Map" ($9.50), a driving map with an index to places of interest, such as castles, historical houses, golf courses, and picnic spots.
- "Scottish Kitchen Map" ($9.95), with recipes.
- "Tartan Map" ($9.95).
- "Whiskey Map" ($9.95).
- "Loch Ness and the Monster Map" ($9.95).
- "Scotland Motorways and Main Roads" ($7.95).
- "Historical Clan Map" ($9.95).
- "The Clans of Scotland" ($9.95), a wall map describing the events and development of Scotland's culture and its clans.
- City plans and street guides for major metropolitan areas in Scotland.

Ireland
- "Historical Map of Ireland" ($9.95).
- "Irish Family Names Map" ($9.95).
- "Irish Kitchen Map" ($9.95), with recipes.

Hunter Publishing (300 Raritan Center Pkwy., Edison, NJ 08818; 201-225-1900) distributes numerous tourist maps, including:

- *London A-Z* ($9.95; 288 pages), a street atlas of London with full-color, highly detailed maps. Underground stations, railway lines and stations, hospitals, fire and police stations, and post offices are also shown.
- *A-Z Great Britain Road Atlas* ($14.95; 128 pages), full-color road maps covering all of Britain, followed by maps of every major town.

Ordnance Survey (Export Sales Branch, Rm. C456, Romsey Rd., Southampton, England SO9 4DH) publishes hundreds of maps and guidebooks, many of which are distributed in the U.S. by **International Specialized Book Services**

with layer contouring, an index of leisure activities available in each area, and marked points of interest, such as historic houses, ancient monuments, nature reserves, museums, and sailing and fishing areas. Maps are available for most areas in the U.K.
- Handy Maps ($8.95 each), color-coded maps for London, Britain/Ireland, Ireland, North England, Scotland, and South England.

England/Wales
- "Tourist Map of Britain" ($8.95), showing every tourist information center and describing each one's services.

World Status Map

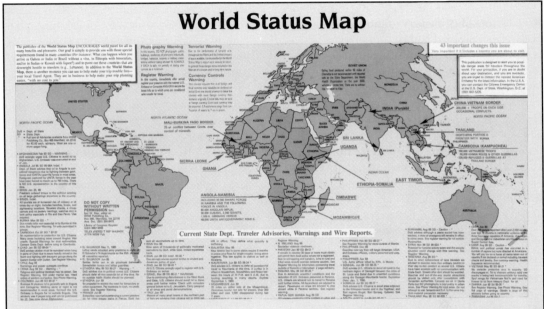

Current State Dept. Traveler Advisories, Warnings and Wire Reports.

Going somewhere? Want to be prepared for just about anything?

Pinkerton Risk Assessment Services (1600 Wilson Blvd., Ste. 901, Arlington, VA 22209; 703-525-6111) publishes the "Pinkerton World Status Map," a bimonthly product loaded with useful advisories for international travelers. Pinkerton gathers information from a multitude of sources, including the U.S. Department of State, World Health Organization, the United Nations, the news media, the Centers for Disease Control, the federal and foreign governments, and private sources of information. The map, highlighting danger areas for travelers, includes travel advisories and warnings as well as passport, visa, and vaccination requirements. It also provides valuable information on the special requirements the traveler may encounter in many Third World countries. A single copy of the map is $6, and a one-year subscription is $36.

Pinkerton also offers "Eye on Travel," a computer-disk-based data base that is updated monthly. More detailed travel advisories are available for every country in the world, along with currency exchange rates, holidays, travel tips, and special-interest articles. Disks can be ordered in either $5\frac{1}{4}$-inch or $3\frac{1}{2}$-inch formats for use on IBM-compatible computers. Annual subscription is $129.

Inc. (see page 72). New products include *Motoring Atlas of Great Britain* 1992 and County Street Atlases for Buckinghamshire, East Kent, West Kent, East Sussex, and West Sussex. Other maps and atlases available are:

■ RouteMaster Maps, a series of nine maps, available folded or flat and suitable for mounting, that help motorists find the shortest or most scenic routes between cities; special features include a table of distances between major towns.
■ Landranger Guidebooks, a series of 11, 144-page pocket-size guidebooks that include a detailed gazetteer of places of interest, suggested car tours, walks, and town plans.
■ Leisure Guides, larger-format guidebooks that give local information about such things as history and landscape. Among the most recent issues are "Cornwall," "Cotswolds,"

"Northumbria," and "Scottish Highlands."
■ Touring Map and Guides, 15 maps that cover popular holiday and tourist areas at various scales. Many have a colorful, illustrated guide to the area, with car tours and gazetteer on the reverse side. Titles include "North York Moors," "Scotland," and "Dartmoor."
■ Outdoor Leisure Maps, a series of more than 30 maps drawn at a 1:25,000 scale that cover popular leisure and recreation areas, including information on youth hostels, camping sites, picnic areas, footpaths, and viewpoints.
■ Pathfinder Maps, more than 1,300 maps, drawn to a 1:25,000 scale, produced for walkers. All the maps show rights-of-way and networks of footpaths that cross the countryside.

International Specialized Book Services, Inc. (5602 NE Hassalo St., Portland, OR 97213; 503-287-3093; 800-547-7734) distributes the British government's Ordnance Survey maps ($8.95 each), including Landranger Maps, popular "all-purpose" maps for driving, walking, and cycling tours in England; Motorway Maps, showing major roadways in and around cities, with a gazetteer of place names (available are "M25 & London/Manchester," "Sheffield," "Leeds," and "York"); "Great Britain Routeplanner Map," covering the British Isles, with inset maps of major towns and park areas; RouteMaster Maps, nine maps covering Britain, showing ground relief, road distances, and tourist information; and "Town & City: London Central," including transportation systems, car parks, cinemas, sports grounds, and other points of interest.

Travel Graphics International (1118 S. Cedar Lake Rd., Minneapolis, MN 55405; 612-377-1080) produces colorfully illustrated maps and posters of popular vacation areas. The 17" X 23" "Pocket Maps of London" ($2.95, including shipping) is a simplified set of maps showing tourist points of interest. Colorful posters ($6.50 each), although not useful as road or street guides, illustrate activities and things to see; they are available for London and Britain (including England, Scotland, Wales, and

Ireland). Prices are discounted for orders of more than one map or poster.

TripBuilder (30 Park Ave., Ste. 5-O, New York, NY 10016; 212-679-6419; 800-525-9745) produces an England TripBuilder ($29.95), a 100-page guide custom-designed according to the buyer's interest. Pick 10 categories of interest from a list of 22 (including "Literary England," "Historic Castles," "Royalty Watching," "Long Walks & Country Rambles," and "Imbiber's England"), and you'll receive a loose-leaf book with a base map of England and a transparent overlay for each category with corresponding information sheets on sites of interest. Other TripBuilder destinations include Scotland, France, the Netherlands, Portugal, and Belgium.

EASTERN EUROPE

American Map Corp. (46-35 54th Rd., Maspeth, NY 11378; 718-784-0055; 800-432-MAPS) publishes a "Commonwealth of Independent States Map" ($2.95) that reflects changes in the former Soviet Union.

GeoLearning Corp. (P.O. Box 2042, Sheridan, WY 82801; 800-843-6436) sells the "Magnetic Globe Puzzle," a 15-inch diameter metal sphere with 470 magnetized puzzle pieces. The map pieces are supplied on flat sheets, and when assembled on the globe they give an accurate to-scale representation of the world. As the world changes, so does the puzzle: replacement pieces, showing new geographic boundaries, become available for $3, plus shipping. Price of the complete unit is $150.

Interarts, Ltd. (15 Mt. Auburn St., Cambridge, MA 02138; 617-354-4655) sells a detailed world Tyvek map that includes many of the recent changes in the new world order. The former Soviet republics are now shown as independently colored and named entities, including: Bylarus, Ukraine, Russia, Moldova, Georgia, Armenia, Azerbaijan, Turkmenistan, Uzbekistan, Kazakhstan, Kyrgyzstan, and Tajikistan. Also

Map of "Post-Soviet Russia," published by Rand McNally.

changed are many of the city names, such as St. Petersburg for Leningrad, Vyatka for Kirov, Mensk for Minsk, and Nizhnij Novgorod for Gorky. Further west, the names of Yugoslavian republics have been added, with Slovenia and Croatia screened apart from the other republics. In addition , the map also includes other recent changes from around the world. In addition to the Tyvek map, the "Wearin' the World" Map Jacket Interarts sells incorporates all these changes.

Magna Carta (4608 Davenport St. NW, Washington, DC 20016; 202-244-0506) offers a 45" X 28", 14-color map of the former Soviet Union in its original Cyrillic lettering. Price is $19 postpaid.

Omni Resources (1238 Anthony Rd., P.O. Box 2096, Burlington, NC 27216; 919-227-8300) sells a wide variety of topographic, thematic, and historical maps of the Baltic Republics. In particular, there is an excellent selection of

Estonian maps, due to the work of the new map company Regio, based in Tallinn. The Soviets systematically destroyed Estonian maps and atlases, and Regio has borrowed originals from European libraries as the basis of their publications. Titles include:

■ "Estonia—Road Atlas" ($9.95) includes 74 pages of maps produced by the Estonian Road Administration.
■ "Estonia—Road Map" ($9.95) is based on Russian and Estonia data, and is the first accurate map showing roads, towns, villages, rivers, and so on.
■ "Estonia—City Street Map" ($9.95) is a multilingual map that includes bus routes.
■ "Latvia—Topographic Quadrangle Maps" ($15) are from the set of current Soviet military topographic maps covering the Baltic Republics. Coverage is relatively complete; the maps for Estonia (also $15) are the most comprehensive.
■ "Latvia—Riga City Map" ($9.95) is a multilingual map with index.

■ "Lithuania—Road Map" ($10.95) shows roads, distances between junctions, vegetated areas, towns and villages. The bilingual map is one sheet, folded.
■ "Lithuania—Vilnius City Map" ($9.95) has an inset of the city center, an index of street names, and a listing of theaters, restaurants, museums, etc. In Lithuanian.
■ "Lithuania—Vilnius Region Topographic Map ($12.95) shows excellent detail of the region surrounding Vilnius.

Rand McNally (P.O. Box 7600, Chicago, IL 60680; 708-673-9100) has a number of new up-to-date products, including:

■ *Today's World Atlas,* an entirely new 200-page reference atlas that shows the latest world political situation. Price is $24.95 through 1992, $29.95 thereafter.
■ *Reader's Digest Atlas of the World* ($39.95) includes 125 pages of up-to-date maps that use a combination of tints and shading to achieve a three-dimensional effect. The 1992 edition has been updated to include changes in Eurasia.
■ *The New Cosmopolitan World Atlas* ($60)includes maps that reflect the changes in Europe.
■ *Traveler's World Atlas & Guide* ($7.95) includes 64 pages of maps showing the latest changes in Europe, the former Soviet Union.
■ *Quick Reference World Atlas* ($4.95) includes 46 pages of full-color maps that detail the most up-to-date changes in Europe and Asia.
■ Distributes Hallwag International Road Maps. Country maps ($9.95 each) include Germany and the former Yugoslavia; political reference maps ($10.95 each) include the world, Europe, and the former Soviet Union.

OCEANIA

Hammond, Inc. (515 Valley St., Maplewood, NJ 07040; 201-763-6000; 800-526-4953) distributes Bartholomew's World Travel Map series featuring full-color reference maps for most countries of the world. The maps, in a variety of sizes and scales, are of frameable quality. Maps available are: "Australia" and "The Pacific," including inset maps of the islands ($10.95 each).

Hunter Publishing (300 Raritan Center Pkwy., Edison, NJ 08818; 908-225-1900) distributes Hildebrand Travel Maps ($8.95), with travel information on climate, customs, currency, and shopping in the margins, as well as inset detailed city maps. A Hildebrand Travel Map is available for Western Indonesia.

National Geographic Society (17th & M sts. NW, Washington, DC 20036; 301-921-1200) offers "Australia" ($7.95; 20002; 24" X 30").

Pacific Historical Maps (P.O. Box 201 [CHRB], Saipan, Mariana Islands 96950) publishes books and maps of the Micronesian Islands, including a map of Rota ($3), a little-known island in the Marianas archipelago, with notes and sketches on the ocean and sealife, as well as the mysterious stone mushroom-capped pillars known as "Latte Stones." Available from Roy Alexander, **Alexander Real Estate**, P.O. Box 1969, Saipan, M.P. 96950. Also publishes a "Tourist Map of Belau" ($4.50) that describes the history, geography, and culture of the last remaining Trust Territory created after World War II. Available from **Western Caroline Trading Co.**, P.O. Box 280, Koror, Palau, W.C.I. 96940.

The Talman Co., Inc. (150 Fifth Ave., New York, NY 10011; 212-620-3182) distributes Ravenstein Verlag's International Road Map series of detailed, large-scale maps ($8.95 each), depicting topographic features, roads, towns, cultural sights, and camping grounds, with legends in four to six languages. Maps for New Zealand and Australia are available.

■ See also: "Business Maps," "County Maps," "Foreign Country Maps," "Recreation Maps," "Selected Atlases," "United States Maps," and "Urban Maps and City Plans."

MAPS OF SPECIFIC AREAS

County Maps

William Faulkner's Yoknapatawpha County may have been fictional, but it embodied the regional distinctiveness and closely knit culture many American counties possess. County maps are both useful and fascinating reflections of these national dividing lines that are smaller than states but bigger than cities.

The boundaries of U.S. counties are usually subdivided into townships, cities, and villages. There are some states, especially those in the West, that do things a bit differently, however: New Mexico's counties are divided into election precincts and two Indian reservations, for example, and Wyoming's counties are divided into election districts, although a large portion of the state is given over to Yellowstone Park, which has no county affiliation. Louisiana has no counties at all; it is divided into parishes.

Some counties have personalities of their own. New York's Westchester County, for example, is known as one of the richest in the nation. California's ultra-hip Marin County has been parodied in the movie *Serial*. Harlan County, Kentucky, was the title and subject of a well-known documentary film about coal miners. As a microcosm of American life, the county often represents a portrait of its region or the resources around which it has grown.

County maps both illustrate and mirror the variety of county life and land in America. There are basic county maps showing the subdivisions, highways, parks, and industrial areas. County census maps show a myriad of demographic characteristics. County congressional district maps provide a political reference for an area. County recreational maps show rivers, lakes, parks, and forests open for public use.

The federal government creates a number of topographic, agricultural, geologic, and recreational maps of counties. State and county governments also create county maps, many of which are distributed free to the public. County and regional historical societies and map collections are good places to find older county maps for research purposes. And there are several commercial map companies specializing in the production of county and regional maps.

GOVERNMENT SOURCES

Census Bureau. The Census Bureau creates maps of counties from statistics it gathers during its surveys. For more information on these maps, see "Census Maps."

Tennessee Valley Authority. TVA produces inexpensive blueline and lithographic prints of both contemporary and historical maps of the region, several of which detail counties and county outlines. Handling charges apply; a price catalog is available at no cost.

■ "Railroad and County Maps of Tennessee" (50 cents; 453 D 754-7), a blueline print of a map published by E. Meoendenhall in 1864.
■ "County Map of Virginia and North Carolina" ($1.25), a lithographic reproduction from a mid-1800s atlas that includes some counties in West Virginia.
■ "County Map of Kentucky and Tennessee" ($1.25), a reproduction from the same atlas as the above map.
■ "Map of Tennessee" ($1; 453 K 315), a blueline print of an 1824 map showing county outlines and county seats.

U.S. Geological Survey. USGS has an ongoing program to produce county-formatted topographic maps at scales of 1:50,000 or 1:100,000. Published maps vary in size and are available in a limited number of states at this time ($4).

COMMERCIAL SOURCES

The "City Maps" chapter lists companies specializing in local and regional maps. Most of the companies listed also produce county maps. Others include:

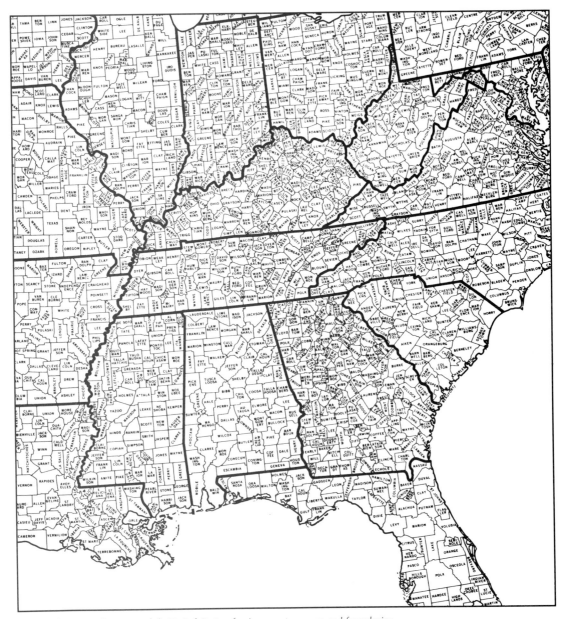

Portion of a USGS base map of the United States showing county names and boundaries.

ADC The Map People (6440 General Green Way, Alexandria, VA 22312; 703-750-0510; 800-ADC-MAPS) publishes street map books for counties and metropolitan areas in southeastern Pennsylvania, Maryland, Delaware, Virginia, the Raleigh-Durham, North Carolina area, and Atlanta. The newest line of products is state road atlases of Maryland-Delaware, Pennsylvania, Virginia, New York, and New Jersey. Price for most books is $8.95. A free list is available.

Alfred B. Patton, Inc. (Swamp Rd. & Center St., Doylestown, PA 18901; 215-345-0700) publishes county road maps and atlases for Pennsylvania and New Jersey counties. Prices vary; a catalog is available upon request.

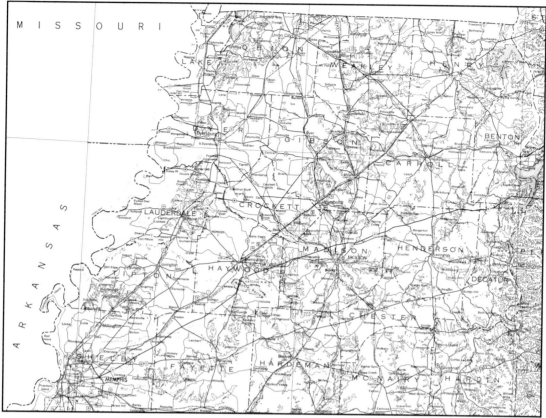

Portion of Tennessee Valley Authority county map of Tennessee.

Champion Map Corp. (200 Fentress Blvd., Daytona Beach, FL 32014; 800-874-7010; 800-342-1072 in Fla.) produces City/County Wall Maps, detailed maps showing county boundaries as well as roads and highways, subdivisions, schools, parks, cemeteries, etc. Maps are available for most counties in most states.

Clarkson Map Co. (1225 Delanglade St., P.O. Box 218, Kaukauna, WI 54130; 414-766-3000) sells the *Wisconsin County Map Book* ($12.95), featuring county maps that show roads, wildlife information, public hunting-ground locations, and lake size, depth, and fish types. It also distributes individual maps for Wisconsin counties.

Compass Maps, Inc. (P.O. Box 4369, Modesto, CA 95352; 209-529-5017) produces street and road maps for nearly all counties in California.

Dolph Map Co., Inc. (430 N. Federal Hwy., Ft. Lauderdale, FL 33301; 305-763-4732) publishes county maps for most parts of Florida. Dolph also publishes county street atlases for Broward County, Dade County, Palm Beach County, and Martin/St. Lucie/Indian River counties.

Geographia Map Co. (231 Hackensack Plank Rd., Weehawken, NJ 07087; 201-867-4700; 212-695-6585) distributes county road maps of New York, New Jersey, and Pennsylvania.

Marshall-Penn-York Co., Inc. (538 Erie Blvd. W., Syracuse, NY 13204; 315-422-2162) publishes city, county, and state maps for the northeastern United States.

Map Works (2125 Buffalo Rd., Ste. 112, Rochester, NY 14624; 716-426-3880; 800-822-

6277 in New York) produces four-color city and regional maps of New York State ($2.50 to $3.95). City titles include Rochester, Buffalo, Syracuse, Capital District, Jamestown, Binghamton, Poughkeepsie, Ithaca, Oswego/Fulton, and Corning/Elmira. Numerous smaller cities/villages in New York are also shown on Map Works Regional Maps. These maps are large, full-color sheets, and include Finger Lakes, Western Region, North County, and Central Leatherstocking. The company also publishes its own atlases of Rochester ($11.95) and Buffalo ($9.95), a New York State map and maps of several New York counties, and maps of Erie, Pennsylvania, and Toledo, Ohio.

Pittmon Map Co. (732 SE Hawthorne Blvd., Portland, OR 97214; 503-232-1161; 800-547-3576 in Western states) publishes Pittmon Book Maps of counties in the Pacific Northwest ($15 to $19.95), as well as Pittmon Recreational County Maps for all counties in Oregon and Washington ($2.99 each).

Rockford Map Publishers (P.O. Box 6126, Rockford, IL 61125; 815-399-4614) has been producing county plat books since 1944, with more than 600 County Land Atlases and Plat Books currently in publication. The Land Atlas and Plat Books measure $8^1/_2$" X 11" and are wire-bound, with black-and-white maps of cities and population centers, as well as a black, red, and white county highway map in the center of the volumes. Rockford has County Land and Plat Books available for counties in Alabama, Florida, Idaho, Illinois, Indiana, Iowa, Michigan, Minnesota, Mississippi, Missouri, New York, Oklahoma, Pennsylvania, South Dakota, West Virginia, and Wisconsin. Prices range from $15 to $35. Also now available are Plat Books in a digital format.

Square One Map Co. (P.O. Box 1312, Woodinville, WA 98072; 206-485-1511) produces the following four-color maps: "Western Snohomish County" ($2.50) and "Western Whatcom County" ($1.75).

Thomas Bros. Maps (17731 Cowan, Irvine, CA 92714; 714-863-1984; 800-899-6277) publishes Thomas Guides—detailed street guides with easy-to-read, multicolored maps and complete index—for Northern and Southern California and counties in Washington, Arizona, and Oregon ($11.95 to $33.95).

Wide World of Maps, Inc. (2626 W. Indian School Rd., Phoenix, AZ 85017; 602-279-2323) produces maps for Arizona communities and counties, including Maricopa, Pinal, Yavapai, Mohave, and Yuma counties. They also publish a series of central Arizona lake maps called Desert Charts, as well as a wall map of Albuquerque and several maps of Las Vegas.

■ **See also: "Business Maps," "Census Maps," "Congressional District Maps," "Topographic Maps," and "Urban Maps and City Plans."**

Foreign Country Maps

Not all maps of other lands were designed to get you from here to there. Some maps of foreign countries are intended for use by students, scientists—or spies. While most foreign country maps can be found under "Tourism Maps," here is a selection of both general and specialized maps of our neighbors around the globe. For more specialized maps of specific countries—geologic or energy maps, for example—you should contact the appropriate government agencies of those countries directly (see Appendix C). Maps may also be available from countries' tourism offices or from their embassies or consulates.

GOVERNMENT SOURCES

Central Intelligence Agency. The CIA, one of the federal government's more prolific mapmakers, has more than 100 maps of foreign countries available to the public. Some are not very detailed, so it's best to get a description of each map before ordering. Examples of CIA foreign country maps, available through the National Technical Information Service, are:

■ "Africa" ($8.95; PB 88-928359).
■ "Bolivia" ($12; PB 86-928325).
■ "Terrain Map of Iceland" ($10; PB 88-928312).
■ "Kuwait" ($12; PB 91-928316).
■ "Mainland Southeast Asia" ($8.95; PB 88-928359).
■ "United Arab Emirates" ($11; PB 88-928317).
■ "Uruguay" ($11; PB 88-928319).

Defense Mapping Agency. DMA produces topographic, hydrographic, and related maps and charts of foreign countries. DMA map series of foreign countries include the following (stock numbers for individual sheets in multisheet series are listed in DMA's "Public Sales Catalog"; see Appendix B):

■ Area Outline Maps ($6.25 per sheet; Series 1105), a series of black-and-white planimetric maps, drawn to a scale of 1:20,000,000, that delineate international and major subdivision boundaries, national capital cities of major importance, and water drainage patterns. The entire world is covered in this series of 27 sheets, each of which is about 14" X 11".
■ Europe ($6.25 per sheet; Series 1209), based on a British topographic map of Europe created by the British Mapping and Charting Establishment Royal Engineers. This series of six sheets shows international boundaries, major civil subdivisions and administrative boundaries, city and town populations, road classifications, operable railways and airports, and other key topographic features. The six 42" X 58" sheets are drawn to a scale of 1:2,000,000, and are designed to fit together to form a 5' X 12' wall map.
■ "Middle East Briefing Map" ($6.25; Series 1308; 1308XMEBRMAP), measuring 34" X 38" and drawn to a scale of 1:1,500,000. This multicolored physical map shows armistice demarcation lines and international boundaries, populations of significant towns, roads, railways, airfields, and oil pipelines.
■ Africa ($6.25 per sheet; Series 2201), a multicolored topographic map series comprised of 36 sheets drawn to a scale of 1:2,000,000. Shown are international and major administrative boundaries and prominent topographic features, including cities, towns, transportation routes, and vegetation. The average size of each sheet is 29" X 26".
■ "Administrative Areas of the USSR" ($6.25; Series 5103; 5103XADMAUSSR) is a multicolored, planimetric, political administrative map showing boundaries, towns, transportation and hydrographic features, and pipelines. A glossary and administrative list with abbreviations are also included in this now-historical map.

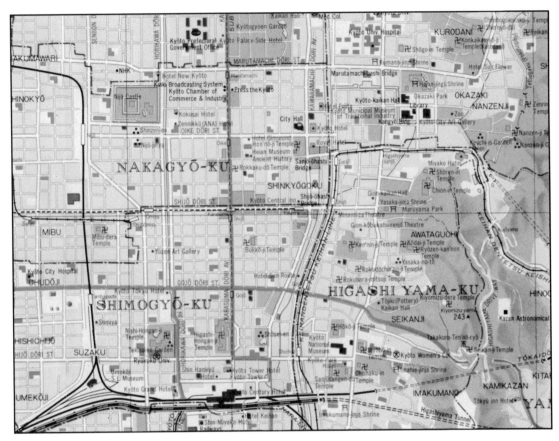

Portion of map of Kyoto, from Teikoku–Shoin Co. Ltd.'s Complete Atlas of Japan.

A description of DMA's hydrographic products can be found under "Nautical Charts."

Government Printing Office. The State Department's Bureau of Public Affairs produces several atlases of foreign countries, available from GPO, including:

■ *Atlas of the Caribbean Basin* ($1.50; S/N 044-000-02022-0), with maps and charts illustrating the Caribbean Basin's economic and political features.
■ *Atlas of United States Foreign Relations* ($5; S/N 044-000-02102-1), a 1985 atlas containing basic information about U.S. foreign relations that is divided into six sections. There are 90 maps and charts.

COMMERCIAL SOURCES

Many publishers of tourist and road maps of foreign countries can be found in "Tourism Maps." A sampling includes:

Europe Map Service/OTD, Ltd. (1 Pinewood Rd., Hopewell Junction, NY 12533; 914-221-0208) distributes a European topographic map series in various scales, including 1:25,000 and 1:1,000,000. The series consists of travel and recreation maps, hydrographic maps, water-resources maps, and administrative maps for Austria, Belgium, Denmark, Finland, France, Germany, Ireland, Luxembourg, the Netherlands, Norway, Sweden, and Switzerland. Also available are reproductions of the official administrative World War II maps showing the borders of the Third Reich from 1937 to May 1945.

Gabelli U.S. (1228 West Ave. #711, Miami Beach, FL 33139; 305-532-6956) distributes the brightly colored French-made *Editions Geographiques et Touristiques* Gabelli maps. Their vivid Montiscolor Picture of the Earth maps, showing the depths of the oceans and geographic relief of the land, are available for each continent. The maps are printed on either paper or flexible plastic, with sizes and prices varying from $7.95 to $55. Titles include "Europe," "Africa," "Asia," "Oceania," "North America," and "South America," and "The United States."

Hippocrene Books (171 Madison Ave., New York, NY 10016; 718-454-2366) is North American distributor for Falk County Road Maps. Titles include "Austria," "Benelux," "France Atlas," "Germany Atlas," "Italy," "South Scandinavia," "Spain and Portugal," "Switzerland," and "Yugoslavia" ($9.95 each).Hippocrene also sells maps for other countries and cities (see "Tourism Maps").

Hunter Publishing (300 Raritan Center Pkwy., Edison, NJ 08818; 201-225-1900) distributes Kümmerly & Frey's World Travel Maps ($7.95 to $9.95), fully indexed maps that are updated annually. Maps are available for most countries and regions, including "Austria," "Canada," "Finland," "Greece," "Hungary," "Rumania/ Bulgaria," "South America," and "Yugoslavia," as well as world political and world physical maps. Also available are Recta/Foldex International Maps for Florence ($6.95 each).

Interarts, Ltd. (15 Mt. Auburn St., Cambridge, MA 02138; 617-354-4655) distributes a "China Map" ($18.95 folded, $25 flat) drawn to a scale of 1:4,000,000 and measuring 46" X 62". It also distributes GLA Kartor (formerly Esselte) maps of Scandinavia, including a "Sweden Map" ($19.95), measuring 24" X 46" and drawn to a scale of 1:1,500,000, and "Scandinavia Folded Maps" ($8.95 each), which include "Stockholm Map and Guide," "Scandinavia," and "Sweden Tourist Map" (eight individual regional maps).

International Map Services Ltd. (P.O. Box 2187, Grand Cayman, Cayman Islands, British

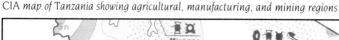

CIA *map of Tanzania showing agricultural, manufacturing, and mining regions.*

West Indies; 809-949-4700) produces maps of the Caribbean and Central America. Prices vary.

National Geographic Society (17th & M sts. NW, Washington, DC 20036; 301-921-1200) offers several full-color maps of foreign countries, including:

- "Australia" ($7.95; 20002; 24" X 30").
- "Mexico" ($7.95; 02391; 34" X 23").
- "China" ($7.95; 20057; 22" X 29").
- "Japan and Korea" ($7.95; 20022; 23" X 30").

Omni Resources (1238 Anthony Rd., P.O. Box 2096, Burlington, NC 27216; 919-227-8300) sells a wide variety of foreign-country maps, from topographic to geologic to tourist maps. A catalog is available.

Ordnance Survey (Export Sales Branch, Rm. C456, Romsey Rd., Southampton, England SO9 4DH) publishes European Community Maps, a series of four flat or folded maps (political, farming, forests, and population); and Ordnance Survey Worldmaps, a series of colorful tourist maps of some of the more exotic of the world's destinations, including Kilimanjaro, Mount Kenya, Cayman Islands, Belize, and Saint Lucia.

Rand McNally (P.O. Box 7600, Chicago, IL 60680; 312-673-9100) publishes the Cosmopolitan map series ($1.95 to $3.50) for Canada, Mexico, Europe, South America, Africa, West Indies/Caribbean, and Alaska. It also publishes the International map series, 52" X 34" maps of the U.S. and the world ($3.50).

Teikoku-Shoin Co., Ltd. (29 Kanda, Jimbocho 3-chome, Chiyoda-ku, Tokyo 101, Japan)

publishes maps and atlases of Japan, such as the *Complete Atlas of Japan*, *Atlas Japan*, and the "Map of Japan." Its maps are available in the U.S. through **Map Link**, 25 E. Mason St., Santa Barbara, CA 93101; 805-965-4402.

Travel Genie (3714 Lincolnway, Ames, IA 50010; 515-232-1070) stocks most of the 1:50,000-scale sectional maps of Norway and Denmark ($7.95, plus $1.50 postage). It takes more than 700 of these to cover all of Norway and more than 100 to cover Denmark. They are widely used by people doing family history work, since they show the locations of many individual farms by name. They also show topographical detail.

Warren Communications (P.O. Box 620635, San Diego, CA 92162; 619-236-0984) distributes topographic maps of Mexico published by the Mexican government at scales of 1:50,000, 1:250,000, and 1:1,000,000, as well as bathymetric maps drawn to a scale of 1:1,000,000. Coverage includes most of the country; individual copies of maps Warren Communications imports can be ordered from **The Map Centre**, 2611 University Ave., San Diego, CA 92104; 619-291-3830.

World Eagle, Inc. (64 Washburn Ave., Wellesley, MA 02181; 800-634-3805) sells "Would You Believe?" a 24" X 31" outline map of Africa that shows the superimposed boundaries of Argentina, China, Europe, India, New Zealand, and the U.S., fitting within the continental borders of Africa. Laminated and grommeted; $9.95, plus $3.95 shipping.

- **See also: "Political Maps," "Tourism Maps and Guides," and "World Maps."**

Native American Land Maps

A legacy of government mapping was born in 1804, when Thomas Jefferson sent Meriwether Lewis and William Clark in search of the mysteries of what later became the western part of the United States. And so began the federally recorded history of the absorption of Indian territory into the body of the fledgling country. Within a short time, the mapping of Indian lands became routine.

The Lewis and Clark maps showed general locations of Indian tribes, bands, and villages, as well as the number of tents, lodges, and "souls." Later maps reflected the growing conflict between Indians and whites: They stated the number of warriors in a tribe, for example, or the favorite haunts of raiding parties. Although the War Department was charged with duties that included those "relative to Indian affairs," Uncle Sam learned quickly that burying the hatchet was a better tactic in winning land from Indians. So, in 1824, the Bureau of Indian Affairs was established within the War Department to handle the nonmilitary aspects of Indian affairs. The Bureau (transferred to the Department of the Interior in 1849), with its various divisions covering everything from Indian forestry to population statistics, created the need for maps of Indian land and life.

Still more maps were produced to redefine boundaries each time a treaty was drawn up between the government and an Indian tribe or nation. Westward expansion and development led to the creation of specialized maps of Indian lands, showing railroad rights-of-way across Indian territories and hydroelectric facilities near reservations, among other things.

Sometimes the process of mapping itself spurred the erosion of Indian land ownership. The General Allotment Act of 1887 charged the government with surveying Indian reservations to establish land values for agricultural purposes. If agricultural worth was significant, the land was allotted to qualifying Indians, the catch being that any surplus allotted lands were usually bought up by the government. Legislation in the 1930s prohibited future sales of Indian land, but by that time the Indians had lost some 100 million acres of treatied land to the government's allotment program.

Aside from depicting the steady loss of territory over the years, Indian land maps can be helpful in studying irrigation, crop rotation, and other land use, as well as the social structure and community planning of various tribes. Although the major wave of Indian-land mapping abated at the beginning of the 20th century, the federal government includes reservations in many of its overall mapping projects (census, topography, and utilities, for example), and several thousand earlier maps have been carefully preserved in map libraries. Indian maps are also produced by a number of map companies as American history teaching tools and by organizations involved in the study of Native American cultures.

GOVERNMENT SOURCES, UNITED STATES

Bureau of the Census. The decennial census of 1860 was the first to treat the Indian population as a separate race, but it wasn't until 1890 that the census counted the number of Indians living in their own territories or on reservations. (The Bureau of Indian Affairs Statistics Division, abolished in 1947, surveyed the Indian population long before the Census Bureau got around to the task.) Some BIA population maps are included in the holdings of the National Archives, as are early census maps (see "Census Maps").

Tennessee Valley Authority. Not only does the TVA produce power from its battery of transmission stations, but it is also one of Uncle Sam's more prolific map-makers. The TVA has two Indian-related maps available:

■ "A Draft of the Cherokee Country" (50 cents plus postage; 11" X 17"). This print of Henry Timberlake's 1762 map shows the Little Tennessee River, Indian governors, Indian villages, and forts.
■ "Cherokee 'Nation' of Indians 1884" ($1.50 plus postage; 23" X 32").

U.S. Geological Survey. USGS, part of the Interior Department, produces maps that include BIA information. USGS topographic and other maps depicting boundaries illustrate Indian lands according to BIA categorization: tribal lands (reservations owned by an entire tribe that are subject to tribal laws and are intact); Indian lands allotted in part (reservations, including both tribal lands and tracts of land allotted to individual Indians); and allotted and open (reservations with individually owned land tracts, other tracts to the public, and any remaining tribal lands). Former Indian reservations are generally not noted.

As part of the National Atlas Program, the USGS also produces a general map of Indian lands, titled "Early Indian Tribes, Culture Areas, and Linguistic Stock" ($3.10). This multicolored map, created in 1967, includes explanatory text on the back.

Library of Congress and **National Archives.** The map collections of both the Library of Congress and the National Archives are full of old Indian land maps. The maps in the Library's Geography and Mapping Division date back to the colonial explorers, who set out to diagram the wilds of the New World for their sovereign nations. Most of these maps are general exploration studies that note Indian villages and territories along with other interesting features of the land.

More comprehensive and specific is the enormous collection of Indian maps in the Cartographic and Architectural Branch of the National Archives, composed of several collections from various federal mapping agencies. Maps of Indian lands and life made by the BIA, the Census Bureau, the Corps of Topographic Engineers, and the War

Portion of "Guide to Indian Country," showing reservations in southern New Mexico. The map is available from the Southwest Parks and Monuments Association. ©1989 by the Automobile Club of Southern California. Reproduced by permission.

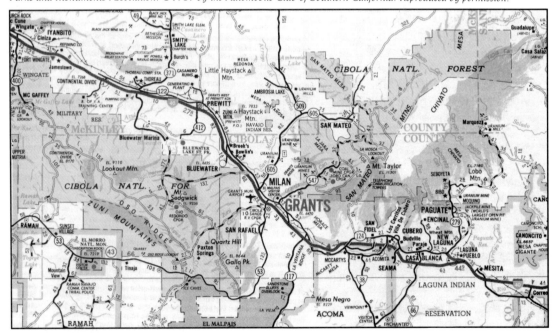

Department's Office of Explorations and Surveys, to name a few, are included in the Archives holdings. Some maps are as recent as 1950, although most date from 1781 to 1883. Included in the collections are such maps as:

■ "Sectional Map From the Coast of Maryland, Virginia, and North Carolina From Cape Henlopen." This 1781 map was drawn by John Purcell under the instructions of Lt. Col. Thomas Brown, Superintendent of Indian Affairs in the Southern District. The map is in six sections and measures $73\frac{1}{2}$" X 75".

■ "A Map of Lewis and Clark's Tract Across the Western Portion of North America, From the Mississippi to the Pacific Ocean, by Order of the Executive of the United States in 1804, 5 & 6." This map, in manuscript on tracing paper, was copied by Samuel Lewis from the original drawing of William Clark. The map includes the positions of numerous Indian tribes, villages, and bands, as well as some population information.

■ "Map Illustrative of the Route of H.R. Schoolcraft Ind[ian] A[gent] between L. Superior & Mississippi R. in the Summer of 1831. By D. Houghton, Surgeon 7 Nat[uralist] to the Exp[edition]." This map illustrates parts of the Chippewa, Sioux, Menominee, and Winnebago territories, including names of Indian chiefs and population numbers for Indian villages along the route and on area lakes and rivers.

■ "Map of the Indian Reservations Within the Limits of the United States." This 1883 map, drawn by Paul Brodie, shows Indian reservations by color and includes population figures.

Reproductions of maps from both the National Archives and Library of Congress may be obtained through the reproduction services of each collection. For further information, see "Uncle Sam's Treasure Chest."

GOVERNMENT SOURCES, CANADA

Canada Map Office (615 Booth St., Ottawa, Ontario K1A 0E9; 613-952-7000) distributes

Canadian Indian land maps as part of the *National Atlas of Canada, 5th ed.*, published in 1980 ($5.50 Canadian each). Maps available are "Indian and Inuit Communities and Languages" (MCR 4001), "Indian and Inuit Population Distribution" (MCR 4031), and "Native Peoples of Canada, 1630" (MCR 4054). Indian land maps from the *National Atlas of Canada, 4th ed.*, published in 1973, are also available ($2 Canadian each), including "Indian Lands and Languages" (MCR 1170) and "Indian and Eskimo Population" (MCR 1171). All maps from the *National Atlas* are available with either English or French text.

Maps Alberta (Land Information Services Div., Main fl., Brittania Bldg., 703 6th Ave. SW, Calgary, Alberta T2P 0T9; 403-297-7389) also distributes the above maps from the *National Atlas of Canada, 5th ed.*, as well as "Indian and Inuit Communities" for various provinces ($9.30 Canadian each, code 418).

COMMERCIAL SOURCES

Modern School (1609 E. Kercher Rd., Goshen, IL 46526; 219-533-3111; 800-431-5929) produces 13 history maps for classroom use, including "Indian Tribes & Cultures," "Early Exploration," and "Territorial Expansion to 1848—The Mexican War." The series is available in two different mountings, ranging from $303 to $395. The "Indian Tribes and Cultures" map illustrates the locations, migrations, and languages of Indian tribes at the time of Columbus's arrival in the northern Americas.

Nystrom (3333 N. Elston Ave., Chicago, IL 60618; 312-463-1144; 800-621-8086) produces a set of colorful American history maps as part of its social studies series. Two relate to Indians: "Indian Tribes and Settlements in the New World 1500-1700," which illustrates the locations of natural resources and Indian cultures, as well as Cortés's conquest of Mexico and Pizarro's conquest of Peru; and "The Roots of American Culture: Westward to the Mississippi," which depicts the Old Southwest and

Northwest and shows sites of major Indian battles. Each 50" X 38" map is $47 folded and equipped with eyelets for hanging, or $72 on a spring roller.

Rand McNally (P.O. Box 7600, Chicago, IL 60680; 312-673-9100) produces two series of American history maps for schools that include Native American maps: in the American History Maps for Intermediate Grades, there is "Home-lands of the American Indians—North America" ($49 to $69; 50" X 50"), a brightly colored markable and tear-resistant map depicting the homelands of the major Indian nations before the arrival of Columbus; and in the Our America Series, there is "Early Indians and Their Culture" ($49 to $69; 44" X 38"), a full-color map showing seven major and 18 other linguistic areas, as well as pictorials of food sources, products, habitats, and culture.

Other producers of Indian maps and charts include:

Automobile Club of Southern California (P.O. Box 2890, Los Angeles, CA 90051) produces "Guide to Indian Country," an annually revised map featuring the Four Corners region—Arizona, New Mexico, Colorado, and Utah—and highlighting the region's Indian reservations, national parks, and monuments. It also con-tains detailed information on points of interest in the region, local tribes and events, recre-ational opportunities, wilderness trips, and campgrounds. The guide is available at most national parks and monuments in the area, or by mail ($3.95, plus $1 postage) from **South-**

west Parks and Monuments Association, 157 Cedar St., Globe, AZ 85502; 602-622-1999.

Celestial Arts (P.O. Box 7327, Berkeley, CA 94707; 510-845-8414; 800-841-2665) sells a wall chart, "The Aztec Cosmos" ($9.95, plus $2 shipping and $.65 tax for Calif. residents), illustrating the cultural and artistic accomplish-ments of the Aztec civilization and religion. A 32-page explanatory booklet is included.

Facts On File, Inc. (460 Park Ave. S., New York, NY 10016; 212-683-2244; 800-322-8755; 800-443-8323 in Canada) publishes *Atlas of the North American Indian* ($16.95 paperback; $29.95 hardcover), a 288-page atlas by Carl Waldman that covers the history, culture, and location of Native Americans from ancient times to the present, with more than 120 maps.

National Geographic Society (17th & M sts. NW, Washington, DC 20036; 301-921-1200) produces "Indians of North America" ($7.95; 02816; 33" X 38½"), a full-color ethnological map created in 1982, and a 1991 map, "A Visitors Guide to Native American Heritage" ($7.95; 20059; 29" X 29").

Wide World of Maps, Inc. (2626 W. Indian School Rd., Phoenix, AZ 85017; 602-279-2323) offers an Arizona topographic map showing, among other things, Indian reservations in the state ($8.95 paper, $32.95 laminated; 48" X 54").

■ **See also: "Boundary Maps," "Census Maps," "Land-Ownership Maps," and "Topographic Maps."**

State and Provincial Maps

Like national and county maps, state and provincial maps encompass much of the cartographic spectrum. In addition to state road maps and tourism maps, there are land plat maps, geologic maps, topographic maps, recreation maps, boundary maps, and many other charts, surveys, and maps depicting resources or features. All are described in their respective chapters elsewhere in this book.

The wide variety of available state and provincial maps is reflected in the number of producing companies and agencies. Among the many kinds of state maps that Uncle Sam creates are the **U.S. Geological Survey**'s topographic, geologic, and natural resource investigations maps; the **National Oceanic and Atmospheric Administration**'s hydrologic maps; aerial photomaps available from the USGS Earth Science Information Center offices and **EROS Data Center**; and the **Census Bureau**'s demographic maps.

For purposes of getting from here to there, the best source of free, up-to-date road maps are state tourism offices (see Appendix A). Most are straightforward road maps, although a few are spiced with interesting graphics or themes. (Indiana, for example, distributes an illustrated "Adventure Map," with state activities and attractions geared toward entertaining and educating children.) But that's just the beginning of maps published by state governments. Most states produce and distribute one or more of the following: geologic maps, soil maps, natural resource maps, recreation maps, and maps related to travel, land use, and industry within their borders. Local commercial publishers produce state atlases, road maps, travel guides, recreational and business maps, and basic wall maps for use in schools and businesses.

Older state maps can be found in the collections of the **National Archives** and the **Library of Congress**. A 1794 map of Maryland,

created by Dennis Griffith, and an 1851 map, "A New Constructed and Improved Map of the State of California," by J. B. Tassin, can be found in the Archives. Another source for older state maps are the holdings of state, county, and local historical societies or agencies.

Here are selected sources of state maps:

GOVERNMENT SOURCES

The federal government produces many types of state maps, all covered more fully in other chapters of this book:

■ The **U.S. Geological Survey** produces a series of state topographic maps, covering an entire state or specific areas; scales vary by coverage. Other USGS products that encompass state maps include the National Atlas Program, geologic and energy investigations maps, seismicity maps, and Bureau of Land Management land plat maps for public lands (see "Emergency Information Maps," "Energy Maps," "Geologic Maps," "Land-Ownership Maps," "Natural Resource Maps," "Selected Atlases," and "Topographic Maps").

■ The **Census Bureau**'s *Congressional District Atlas* ($33), regularly updated, contains state-by-state maps of congressional districts. The Census Bureau also publishes a wide range of other maps (see "Business Maps," "Census Maps," and "Congressional District Maps").

■ The **National Oceanic and Atmospheric Administration** creates numerous state maps related to lakes, rivers, and waterways, as well as aeronautical charts that cover certain states (see "Aeronautical Charts," "River, Lake, and Waterway Maps," and "Recreation Maps").

■ The **Defense Department** produces an annual *Atlas/State Data Abstract for the United States* ($9), available from the Government Printing Office, containing state-by-state maps and information on military bases, personnel, and

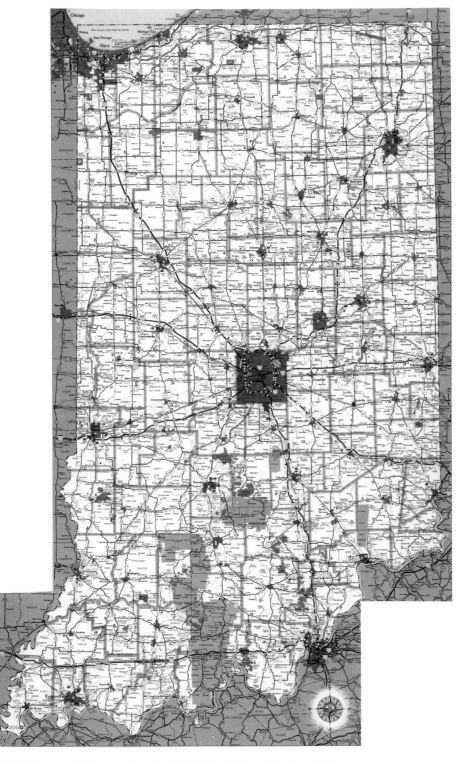

Official state map of Indiana, courtesy Tourism Division, Indiana Department of Commerce.

defense contracts (see "Military Maps").

■ The **Tennessee Valley Authority** has topographic, geologic, and utilities maps for states in its region (see "Energy Maps," "Geologic Maps," "Natural Resource Maps," "Topographic Maps," and "Utilities Maps").

■ The **Federal Emergency Management Agency**'s Flood Insurance Administration publishes state maps of flood plains (see "Emergency Information Maps").

COMMERCIAL SOURCES

Virtually every major map company produces some kind of state or provincial map. Any map store and most bookstores carry state maps, at least local ones. Other sources include most of the publishers listed under "Urban Maps and City Plans," as well as those listed in Appendix D. Here are some examples:

American Automobile Association (1000 AAA Drive, Heathrow, FL 32746; 407-444-7000) has free state travel maps available to AAA members only. The maps may not be ordered through the mail, but must be obtained at local AAA offices.

Facts On File, Inc. (460 Park Ave. S., New York, NY 10016; 212-683-2244; 800-322-8755; 800-443-8323 in Canada) produces "State Maps on File," a seven-volume loose-leaf compendium of reproducible state maps ($75 each; $345/ set). There are an average of 20 different maps for each state, including political, historical, environmental, cultural, economic, and natural resources maps.

Peter Heiler, Ltd. (72 Bloor St. E., Oshawa, Ontario, Canada L1H 3M2; 416-668-6677) distributes numerous maps of the Canadian provinces.

Kistler (4000 Dahlia St., Denver, CO 80216; 303-399-0900, 800-523-5485) produces raised-relief maps of several states, most of which are 22" X 17". Relief maps are available for Alaska, California, Colorado, Hawaii, Idaho, Montana,

New Mexico, Oregon, Texas, Utah, Washington, and Wyoming.

The Map Place (3545 Arctic Blvd., Olympic Center, Anchorage, AK 99503; 907-562-4700) sells a number of maps of Alaska, including one of the state superimposed over the U.S., illustrating its true size. Interesting facts and details are included on the map.

Rand McNally (P.O. Box 7600, Chicago, IL 60680; 312-673-9100) produces a series of state road maps ($1.50 each), as well as a set of mural wall maps of 28 states ($59.95 each).

Raven Maps & Images (34 N. Central, Medford, OR 97501; 503-773-1436; 800-237-0798) produces 20 shaded-relief maps of states in the Western U.S. and the Northeast. The maps ($20 paper; $45 laminated) show towns, roads, and railroads, as well as geographical features. Maps are available for Alaska, Arizona, California, Colorado, Hawaii, Idaho, Maine, Massachusetts/Connecticut/Rhode Island, Montana, Nevada, New York, New Mexico, Ohio, Oregon, Pennsylvania/New Jersey, Utah, Vermont/New Hampshire, Washington, and Wyoming.

University of Hawaii Press (Univ. of Hawaii at Manoa, 2840 Kolowalu St., Honolulu, HI 96822; 808-956-8255) publishes "Reference Maps of the Islands of Hawai'i" ($2.95 each).

University of New Mexico Press (Albuquerque, NM 87131; 505-277-7564) publishes *New Mexico in Maps*, a 409-page book featuring maps and accompanying essays, graphs, tables, and charts on 131 topics such as "Groundwater Pollution," "Mining and Stagecoaching, 1846-1912," "Physician Distribution," "Ranching and Rangeland," "Alternative Communities," and "Presidential Elections." This impressive book is a good source of otherwise hard-to-find facts on the state ($7.95; 2nd ed. published 1986).

■ **See also: "Tourism Maps and Guides."**

United States Maps

"It was wonderful to find America, but it would have been more wonderful to miss it," wrote Mark Twain in *Pudd'nhead Wilson's Calendar*. For many, finding America—in all its many cartographic forms—is nearly a national pastime. From tourists to teachers, biologists to bus drivers, nearly everyone uses maps of the United States in their quest to find America. And there's a U.S. map for nearly everyone, too.

When Thomas Jefferson authorized the purchase of the Louisiana Territory from Napoleon in 1803, the size of America more than doubled overnight. Little was known about the new land, and even less was known about the trails and passages that were purported to exist throughout this vast wilderness. There was believed to be a single, small mountain range running across the center of the territory, through which passage to the Pacific Coast could be easily maneuvered. But when the Lewis and Clark expedition, ordered by Jefferson to find this "Pacific Passage," discovered instead the nearly impenetrable Rocky Mountains, the mysteries of the new territory became evident.

The Lewis and Clark team brought back maps that illustrated everything from the number of "souls" in Indian villages to the placement of tributaries along the West's major rivers. It would take many subsequent explorations before the extent, treachery, and wealth of the land was fully understood and mapped.

Today, the spectrum of U.S. maps is vast and comprehensive. The agencies of the federal government produce hundreds of maps, ranging from general reference works to specific thematic maps of U.S. history, resources, transportation, agricultural, industrial, military, and recreational areas—and anything else that can be mapped. Commercial map-makers also produce thousands of general and thematic

U.S. maps, in forms ranging from atlases to classroom wall maps to small, pocket-size road maps.

The vaults of map libraries, historical societies, and local land offices hold a wealth of U.S. maps within their protective care. Although the originals of some of these maps may be examined only on the premises, the national collections—the **Library of Congress** and the **National Archives**—as well as many of the smaller ones, provide reproduction services for a fee (see "Uncle Sam's Treasure Chests").

Whether one is seeking maps of America's soil or soul, its parks or pipelines, they likely exist in abundance. Most chapters of this book contain some kind of U.S. map, although there are others that defy simple classification. Here is a sampling of U.S. maps not included elsewhere in this book:

GOVERNMENT SOURCES

Every map-producing agency of the federal government creates maps of the United States in one form or another. The National Archives and the Library of Congress have extensive collections of U.S. maps that are available to the public for study or reproduction through the collections' facilities (see "Uncle Sam's Treasure Chests"). Most sources of U.S. maps fall under other headings in this book. Other federal sources include:

Tennessee Valley Authority. TVA has several inexpensive blueline and lithographic reproductions of aboriginal and historical maps of the United States, including:

■ "Aboriginal Map of Eastern U.S." ($1; G MD-453 G 552), a lithoprint of a 17" X 22" map made by a Frenchman in 1718 that shows towns and drainage.

■ "Map of Eastern U.S. Made to Accompany 'History of American Revolution'" ($1.50; G MD 453 K 701), a blueline print from a map reprinted in 1811.

■ "North West Section of Map of the United States" ($1.50; 453 K 274), a blueline print of a 1784 map.

■ "United States and Mexico" ($2; G MD 453 P 754-4), a blueline print of an 1860 map by Colonel Butterfield.

There's a $1 handling charge for orders up to $10; additional charges apply for maps shipped in mailing tubes.

U.S. Geological Survey. USGS produces and distributes many U.S. maps, far too many to list in detail here; a free brochure, "Catalog of Maps," is available. A sampling of USGS maps includes:

■ National Atlas Program's "U.S. General Reference Map" ($3.10; 00438, code 38077-AA-NA-07M-00), an all-purpose map suitable for use as a basic reference tool. The map measures 19" X 28" and is drawn to a scale of 1:17,000,000. Several thematic U.S. maps are also available from the National Atlas Program, many of which are mentioned elsewhere in this book.

■ "An Emerging Nation" ($4), a full-color reproduction of a 1784 U.S. map on one side and 14 territorial growth maps, drawn to various scales, on the other.

■ Base, contour, outline, and physical-division maps of the United States, available in various scales, colors, and sheet sizes. Prices range from 70 cents to $6.10. Many of these are mentioned in other chapters; see "Geologic Maps," "Natural Resource Maps," and "Topographic Maps."

COMMERCIAL SOURCES

There are hundreds of U.S. map and atlas publishers. All major companies produce maps of the U.S. for a wide range of purposes, from business maps to travel maps, general reference maps, and historical maps, among many others. Most of these are mentioned elsewhere

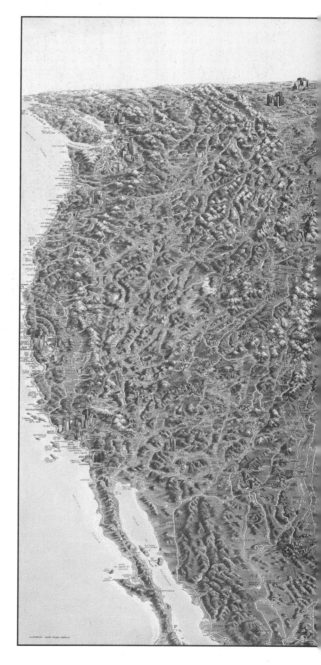

Right: "Portrait USA," illustrating attractions and skylines of major cities. © Meridian Graphics.

in the book. Here are a few more intended for general reference use:

American Automobile Association (1000 AAA Drive, Heathrow, FL 32746; 407-444-7000) produces road maps of the United States, Canada, Mexico, and Central and South

America that are free to AAA members but are not for sale to the general public. The maps may be obtained at local AAA offices.

The Chart House Travel Map Co., Inc. (5222 Venice Blvd., Los Angeles, CA 90029; 213-965-9380; 800-322-1866) produces Personalized

Travel Maps, designed to record one's travels. The legend of the map has space for personalizing. Each comes with a Charting Kit, consisting of map pins, a route-charting ruler, and a pen for drawing routes. The full-color maps come in three sizes: standard (30" X 20"), deluxe (33" X 22"), and king (51" X 33"). They range in price from $38 to $99.50 and are drawn on the Mercator projection centered on the Americas.

Cypress Book (U.S.) Co., **Inc.** (Paramus Place, Ste. 225, 205 Robin Rd., Paramus, NJ 07652; 201-967-7820) distributes a novel "Map of the United States," published in the Republic of China, with text in both Chinese and Roman characters ($2.95).

Kistler (4000 Dahlia St., Denver, CO 80216; 303-399-0900, 800-523-5485) produces raised-relief maps of the United States in three sizes: 26" X 17", 34" X 22", and 42" X 28". The 26" X 17" map is also available in a natural oak frame.

Meridian Graphics (5446 Peachtree Industrial Blvd., Ste. 200, Atlanta, GA 30341; 404-454-6280) publishes "Portrait USA," which shows full-color aerial perspectives of landmark buildings, attractions, topographical features, and major roads. In addition, Meridian publishes Portrait Series maps of several major U.S. cities.

National Geographic Society (17th & M sts. NW, Washington, DC 20036; 301-921-1200) has several maps and atlases of the U.S., including:

■ "United States Political" ($7.95; 02003),a full-color 43" X 30" map. An index is available ($2; 02004). The map is also available enlarged to 70" X 49" ($9.95; 02008).
■ "United States Physical" ($7.95; 20040), measuring 25" X 36".
■ "United States/Territorial Growth" ($7.95; 20025), measuring 43" X 30".

Rand McNally (P.O. Box 7600, Chicago, IL 60680; 312-673-9100) produces a "United States Map" ($3.50; 52" X 34"), part of the Cosmopolitan map series. The map is finely detailed and subtly colored, suitable for decorating an office or boardroom. Rand McNally publishes another "United States Map" ($3.50; 52" X 34"), which shows physical features in graphic detail. Both are available laminated for $16.95 each.

■ **See also: "Agriculture Maps," "Antique Maps," "Boundary Maps," "Business Maps," "Census Maps," "Congressional District Maps," "Energy Maps," "Geologic Maps," "History Maps," "Military Maps," "Native American Land Maps," "Natural Resource Maps," "Railroad Maps," "Recreation Maps," "Space Imagery," "Topographic Maps," "Tourism Maps and Guides," and "Wildlife Maps."**

Urban Maps and City Plans

"All cities are mad: but the madness is gallant. All cities are beautiful: but the beauty is grim," writes Christopher Morley in *Where the Blue Begins*. All cities are confusing, he might have added, which can be both maddening and grim. Getting lost at least once in a new city is almost a given, but it needn't become habit. A good map can be a valuable guide to the gallant madness and grim beauty of any modern metropolis. City maps are as useful to the native urbanite as they are to the urban neophyte; some cities can take a lifetime to learn.

Basic city maps come in a variety of sizes, shapes, forms, and detail. There are simple pocket and glove-compartment maps showing major roads and official buildings; there are wall maps showing most streets; there are indexed atlases with detailed maps of every neighborhood and district. There's more: land plats showing the location and use of buildings and parks, tourism maps pinpointing locations of award-winning eateries. There are even aerial and satellite photomaps of most American cities.

Large cities like New York or Los Angeles appear on countless maps by both national and local map-makers, while many smaller cities and towns have been mapped only by a local chamber of commerce, city hall, or bank. There are probably hundreds of city maps made for internal use by local, state, and federal governments, from sewer maps to taxation maps, but these usually aren't helpful to the typical visitor. The number, type, and quality of maps available for any city are usually directly related to the size of its tourist trade.

Hundreds of commercial map-makers specialize in creating city maps for a particular region or state. Many such companies do not sell directly to the public, but sell promotional maps that banks, Realtors, and other businesses distribute to customers. There are also companies specializing in certain kinds of city maps. **Historic Urban Plans** (P.O. Box 276, Ithaca, NY 14850; 607-272-MAPS), for example, produces full-color and black-and-white reproductions of more than 400 maps from the 15th to 19th centuries showing American and European cities.

The best sources for free city maps are the local tourist bureau, chamber of commerce, or city planning office. State and county governments produce general tourism and highway maps of their regions; morever, they can often advise you on where to find local maps. Although the federal government includes city outlines on some of its general-use maps, it does not produce detailed, street-by-street maps of American cities. (The CIA does, however, produce maps and guides to various foreign cities; see "Foreign Country Maps.")

More detailed street maps and atlases, or specialized theme maps, will probably be more expensive. They may be purchased at a local bookstore, travel store, or through the producing companies themselves. Many aerial and Landsat photomaps of cities are available from the federal government through its **EROS Data Center** and other distributing agencies. There are also several commercial producers of Landsat images and numerous commercial aerial photo companies that can provide photomaps of cities (see "Aerial Photographs" and "Space Imagery").

For older or antique city maps, the best national resources are the map collections of the **Library of Congress** and the **National Archives**. The Archives collection includes city plans and plats mapped by the government up to 1950. The Library of Congress maps include thousands of commercial city maps, as well as those made by federal, state, county, and local governments. One of the Library's most prized possessions is its set of Sanborn city fire insurance maps, which trace the history of hundreds of American towns from the mid-19th century (see "Emergency Information Maps"). Also in the Library of Congress is a large collection of panoramic city views.

Local map collections, university libraries, and historical societies are also good resources for finding older city maps and plans.

GOVERNMENT SOURCES, UNITED STATES

Tennessee Valley Authority. TVA has a series of inexpensive lithographic reproductions of pictorial historical maps for four cities in its region. The lithographs, made from artists' sketches of the cities from an oblique aerial view, are suitable for framing. Available lithographs include:

■ "Pictorial Map of Knoxville" ($1.25; 455 K 94; 22" X 29").
■ "Pictorial Map of Chattanooga" ($1.25; G MD 455 K 558; 23" X 30").
■ "Pictorial Map of Nashville in the 1880s" ($1.25; 24" X 41").

■ "Pictorial Map of Memphis" ($1.25; 16" X 23").

Local, county, and state boards of tourism and chambers of commerce are other good resources for finding city maps.

COMMERCIAL SOURCES

Allmaps Canada, Ltd. (390 Steelcase Rd. E., Markham, Ontario, L3R 1G2, Canada; 416-477-8480) publishes and distributes maps and StreetFinder Map Books for all cities and regions of Canada, including all provinces and Vancouver, Calgary, Edmonton, Saskatoon, Regina, Winnipeg, Windsor, London, Kitchener, Greater Toronto, Montreal, Québec, and Halifax.

American Map Corp. (46-35 54th Rd., Maspeth, NY 11378; 718-784-0055; 800-432-6277) distributes Europe City Maps ($8.95 each) for 31 different cities, including

Three views of New York City: Portion of "New York City and Region," from Unique Media (below), ©1989, Unique Media Inc., Box 4400, Don Mills, Ontario M3C 2T9; 416-924-0644; "Streetwise Manhattan," from Streetwise Maps, Inc. (opposite page, top); and portion of "Aerial View of Lower Manhattan," from David Fox (opposite page, bottom), © David Fox, 1986.

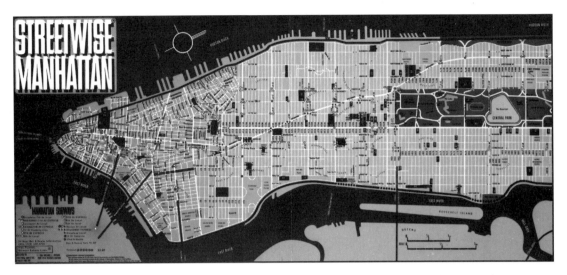

Amsterdam, Berlin, Budapest, Copenhagen, Innsbruck, Leipzig, Madrid, Milan, Paris, Rome, Seville, Venice, and Warsaw.

Arrow Map, Inc. (Myles Standish Industrial Park, 25 Constitution Dr., Taunton, MA 02780; 508-880-2880; 800-343-7500) produces maps for cities in Massachusetts, New Hampshire, Rhode Island, Maine, Connecticut, Georgia,

Delaware, and Virginia, and many other states. Also publishes road maps of the New England states, as well as the Arrow *Zip Code Directory*.

Creative Sales Corp. (1350 Michael Dr., Wood Dale, IL 60191; 312-350-0770) publishes the *Chicagoland Atlas* ($39.95 paper; $79.95 laminated), a fully indexed, spiral-bound street atlas of the Chicago area. Also available are 16

different Chicago-area street maps (25" X 36"; $2.95 each) that include lakes, forest preserves, golf courses, parks, and other points of interest.

David Fox (P.O. Box 533, Narberth, PA 19072; 215-667-2136) produces four-color axonometric maps of Boston (1983), Chicago (1982), New Orleans (1984), Philadelphia (1981), and Washington, D.C. (1985). Each 25" X 38" map is $20 postpaid. Also available for $24 each: "Aerial Views of Lower Manhattan" (1986), "Boston Financial District" (1987), as well as St. Louis (1990) and Philadelphia (1990).

Dolph Map Co., Inc. (430 N. Federal Hwy., Ft. Lauderdale, FL 33301; 305-763-4732) publishes city maps for most metropolitan areas in Florida, as well as Alabama, Georgia, Kansas, Louisiana, Maryland, Mississippi, New Mexico, Ohio, Pennsylvania, South Carolina, Tennessee, Texas, and Virginia.

Era-Maptec, Ltd. (5 S. Leinster St., Dublin 2, Ireland; 353-1-766266) produces maps, atlases, and guidebooks. Specializes in Apple Macintosh maps, and has maps of many major cities in digital format. The company patented the integration of cartography and satellite imagery, and recently completed an eight-volume (700 pages), 1:100,000-scale *Road Atlas of Japan*.

Geographia Map Company (231 Hackensack Plank Rd., Weehawken, NJ 07087; 201-867-4700; 212-695-6585) publishes street maps and atlases for New York City, Buffalo, Chicago, Cincinnati, Gary, Pittsburgh, and Rochester. Geographia also distributes Streetwise city maps and DeLorme maps and atlases, among other brands.

Hagstrom Map Co. (46-35 54th Rd., Maspeth, NY 11378; 718-784-0055; 800-432-6277) sells pocket maps for various eastern cities, including New York, Stamford, Bridgeport, Philadelphia/Camden, Rochester, and Boston/Cambridge. Prices range from $2.25 to $3.95.

Hammond, Inc. (515 Valley St., Maplewood, NJ 07040; 201-763-6000) distributes Bartholomew's Easy Fold World City Plans ($8.95) for Athens, which gives 11 different "spreads" of the city. Also distributes "London Big Ben" ($4.95), a pocket-size map of central London that shows tube stations, bus routes, theaters, cinemas, and so on.

Hippocrene Books (171 Madison Ave., New York, NY 10016; 718-454-2366) is the North American distributor of Falk City Maps for more than 50 major cities worldwide ($5.95 to $9.95 each), including Antwerp, Belgrade, Bucharest, Innsbruck, Istanbul, Leipzig, New York, Oslo, Peking/Eastern China, Rio de Janeiro, Thessaloníki, Tokyo, and Warsaw.

Latitudes Map and Travel Publishers (P.O. Box 80688, Minneapolis, MN 55408; 612-825-8117) publishes two-sided, laminated pocket maps of Minneapolis and St. Paul ($3.95 each) that show downtown points of interest and, on the reverse, an area map; each is indexed with downtown streets, area towns, cultural points of interest, and major buildings, businesses, and government offices.

Marshall-Penn-York Co., Inc. (538 Erie Blvd. W., Syracuse, NY 13204; 315-422-2162) publishes city maps and atlases of New York, Pennsylvania, Virginia, West Virginia, and Southern New England under the Visual Encyclopedia trademark.

Meridian Graphics (5446 Peachtree Industrial Blvd., Ste. 200, Atlanta, GA 30341; 404-454-6280) publishes Portrait Series maps that show full-color aerial perspectives of landmark buildings, attractions, topographical features, and major roads. Titles include "Portrait Atlanta," "Portrait Orlando," "Portrait Miami," "Portrait Dallas," and "Portrait Tampa Bay," with other titles added regularly. There is also "Portrait USA," with a bird's-eye view of the entire country.

Metro Graphic Arts, Inc. (P.O. Box 7035, Grand Rapids, MI 49510; 616-245-2271) produces wall

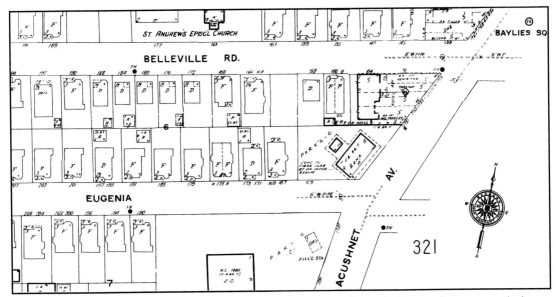

Portion of Sanborn Map Company's land plat of New Bedford, Massachusetts, showing building numbers, streets, and other specific features of the city.

maps, street guides, and pocket maps of various cities in Alabama, Georgia, Indiana, Iowa, Kentucky, Michigan, Missouri, Nebraska, Ohio, Tennessee, Texas, West Virginia, and Wisconsin.

Omni Resources (1238 Anthony Rd., P.O. Box 2096, Burlington, NC 27216; 919-227-8300) distributes maps for more than 3,000 cities worldwide. Geoscience Resources stocks more than 500 foreign city maps and has access to more than 2,500 other city maps through affiliated foreign publishers, including maps for the most capital cities, most tourist-oriented cities, as well as hard-to-find maps of cities in developing countries. Prices vary.

Ozark Map Co. (Hwy. 135, Rte. 2, Box 324-B, Gravois Mills, MO 65037; 314-374-6553) produces city maps of Kansas City, St. Louis, Springfield, Columbia/Jefferson City, and Branson, MO; and Lincoln, NE ($1.75 to $2.25 each). Also produces a *Greater Kansas City Street Atlas* ($9.95).

Pierson Graphics Corp. (899 Broadway, Denver, CO 80203; 303-623-4299) publishes the Bird's-Eye View series of four-color axonometric maps;

and Visitors Guide maps of New York, Chicago, Dallas, Denver, Houston, and the West Loop of Houston ($2.95 to $27.95). Also available are 4" X 9" street maps of Colorado metropolitan areas ($1.95 to $3.95), and David Fox Studios axonometric maps of other cities.

Pittmon Map Co. (732 SE Hawthorne Blvd., Portland, OR 97214; 503-232-1161; 800-547-3576 in Western states) sells city maps for most cities in the Pacific Northwest ($2.25).

Prentice Hall (200 Old Tappan Rd., Old Tappan, NJ 07675; 800-223-2348) distributes Gousha city maps ($2.25 each) for more than 200 American cities, including Akron, Albuquerque, Baton Rouge, Cleveland, Gainesville, Las Vegas, Little Rock, Oklahoma City, Pensacola, Salt Lake City, and Winston-Salem. Gousha's Metro Maps each show a major city and its suburbs, with inset maps of downtown areas. They are available for 16 metropolitan areas in the U.S.

Random House (201 E. 50th St., New York, NY 10022; 212-751-2600; 800-726-0600) distributes Flashmaps ($5.95), 80-page, single-subject guides to various cities in the U.S. and abroad. Included in the London guide are maps of "Historical Sites," "National Trust Houses," "Literary England," "Architectural Highlights," "Major Shopping Areas," "Royal Residences," "Blue Plaque Houses," "Treasures," "Art Galleries," "Antiques," "Transportation," and "Museums." Flashmaps are also available for Boston, Los Angeles, New York, Philadelphia, and Washington, D.C.

Square One Map Co. (P.O. Box 1312, Woodinville, WA 98072; 206-485-1511) publishes the "Greater Seattle Map" ($1.95) and the "Downtown Seattle Map" ($1.25).

Streetwise Maps, Inc. (P.O. Box 2219, Amagansett, NY 11930; 516-267-8617) produces handy-size, laminated city maps that fold to fit into a pocket or purse. Maps of New York City include "Address Map" ($1.95), "Central Park" ($1.95), "Bus/Subway" ($1.95), "Manhattan" ($3.95), "Mid-Manhattan" ($4.95), "Downtown Manhattan" ($2.95), "Transitwise N.Y., New Jersey, Connecticut" ($4.95), and "Welcome to New York" (in six languages, $5.95). Also available are Streetwise maps ($3.95 to $4.95 each) for Boston, Chicago, London, Los Angeles, New Orleans, Paris, Philadelphia, Rome, San Francisco, and Washington, D.C. In addition, a Streetwise series called Artwise ($4.95 each) details information about museums and cultural institutions, including admission costs, opening hours, museum contents, and so on. Twelve cities are included: Amsterdam, Boston, Florence, Los Angeles, London, New York (Manhattan), Munich, Paris, Rome, Venice, Vienna, and Washington, D.C.

T. R. Map Co. (16403 W. 126th Terr., Olathe, KS 66062; 913-782-6168) publishes wall maps of metropolitan areas in Arkansas, Iowa, Kansas, Missouri, Nebraska, and Oklahoma. Products include full-color, 38" X 50" maps of Lincoln ($69.50, gloss; $89.50, laminated) and Tulsa ($79.50, gloss; $99.50, laminated).

Unique Media, Inc. (Box 4400, Don Mills,

Ontario, Canada M3C 2T9; 416-924-0644) publishes pictorial maps featuring a bird's-eye perspective of the physical terrain, landmarks, and individual buildings of urban areas in Canada and the U.S. ($6 each, or $16 for flat, laminated copies). They include "Greater Los Angeles," "San Francisco," "San Diego," "San Antonio," "Pittsburgh," "New York City," "Metro Toronto," "Downtown Toronto," "Niagara Region," "State of California & Nevada," "Las Vegas & Region," "North York," "Canada" (Ottawa on the reverse), "Canada" (Vancouver, B.C. on the reverse), and "United States of America."

VanDam, Inc. (430 W. 14th St., New York, NY 10014; 212-929-0416; 800-321-6277) publishes a series of pop-open city maps in the award-winning UNFOLDS format. These maps open to 18 times their original size, then refold automatically. They hold U.S. and global patents and a copyright as kinetic sculpture. Maps in the World Unfolds series include Amsterdam, Berlin, Boston, Chicago, Cologne, Dallas, Detroit, Hamburg, Hawaii, Hong Kong, London, Los Angeles, Miami, Munich, New Orleans, New York City, NYC Subway, Paris, Rome, San Francisco, Stuttgart, Tokyo, Vienna, Washington, D.C., and Zurich ($6.95 each). Licensors of VanDam's folding technology include Putnam (America Unfolds), Langenscheidt USA (Smartmaps), and Bertelsmann (Eurostar). The company also publishes a new book series called "That VanDam Book" that combines a 158-page book with three fully indexed pop-up street maps. Books in the series include *New York City*, *London*, and *Paris* ($9.95 each).

COMMERCIAL SOURCES

Other sources for cities in their regions include:

Alaska
Funmap, Inc.
705 W. 6th Ave.
Anchorage, AK 99501
907-892-7356

The Map Place
3545 Arctic Blvd., Olympic Center
Anchorage, AK 99503
907-561-7335

Arizona
Wide World of Maps
2626 W. Indian School Rd.
Phoenix, AZ 85017
602-279-2323

California
Global Graphics
2819 Greentop St.
Lakewood, CA 90712
213-429-8880

Connecticut
Mail-a-Map Street Maps
P.O. Box 1945
New Haven, CT 06509
203-773-3267

District of Columbia
Mino Publications
9009 Paddock Ln.
Potomac, MD 20854
301-294-9514

Florida
Trakker Maps
12027 SW 117th Ct.
Miami, FL 33186
305-255-4485

Louisiana
New Orleans Map Co., Inc.
3130 Paris Ave.
New Orleans, LA 70119
504-943-0878

Maine
DeLorme Mapping Co.
P.O. Box 298
Freeport, ME 04032
207-865-4171

Massachusetts
Butterworth Co. of Cape Cod, Inc.
703 Main St.
Harwich, MA 02645
508-432-8200

Nevada
Front Boy Service Co.
3340 Sirius Ave.
Las Vegas, NV 89102
702-876-7822

New York
Map Works, Inc.
2125 Buffalo Rd., Ste. 112
Rochester, NY 14624
716-426-3880; 800-822-6277

Oregon
Pittmon Map Co.
732 SE Hawthorne Blvd.
Portland, OR 97214
503-232-1161; 800-547-3576

Washington
Square One Map Co.
P.O. Box 1312
Woodinville, WA 98072
206-485-1511

Canada
Perly Toronto, Inc.
1050 Eglinton Ave. W.
Toronto, Ontario M6C 2C5
416-785-6277

World Maps

It's simply not possible to count the number of world maps that exist—even just those currently available. There are thousands of maps, dating from the birth of map-making. There are maps of the world when only one continent was known to exist and maps of the world today, with every inch of the globe plotted with astounding accuracy. There are maps of world vegetation, rainfall, mineral reserves, soil types, and industrial strongholds. There are, in short, as many maps as there are ways to interpret and comprehend the modern world.

The uses of world maps are as varied as the maps themselves. Geologic maps of the world are vital to the work of earth scientists; maps showing the amount of annual sunshine that falls on various spots around the world are key to planning energy resources. Maps showing the growth of socialism, the decline in arable land, the shifts of industrial wealth, and the flows of maritime commerce all have their respective professional constituencies.

World maps are created by most cartographic government agencies and private companies. The federal government publishes several general, as well as specific, world maps, ranging from "mosaics" of Landsat images to a map of illegal drug-growing regions and smuggling routes.

Commercial companies also make a vast range of world maps, as do various geographic, political, and earth science societies around the world.

Some of the most beautiful world maps are also the oldest, drawn in the days when artists moonlighted as map illustrators. Sources for antique world maps include the collections of the **Library of Congress** and the **National Archives**, as well as a number of dealers in antique maps, globes, and atlases specializing in world maps; some may be willing to search for a particular map (see "Uncle Sam's Treasure Chests" and "Antique Maps").

Here is a sampling of what's available:

Government Sources, United States

Central Intelligence Agency. The CIA has several world maps, available through the National Technical Information Service, including:

■ "Political Wall Map—World" ($11; PB 88-928323).
■ "World Map" ($11.95; PB 88-928325).
■ "Standard Time Zones of the World" ($8.95; PB 88-928358).
■ "U.S. Foreign Service Post and Department of State Jurisdictions" ($10; PB 84-928009), published in 1984, so information may now be slightly out of date.

National Geophysical Data Center. The NGDC, part of the National Oceanic and Atmospheric Administration, produces a three-sheet set of world maps, "Relief of the Earth's Surface." The set includes two color maps and one black-and-white ($25 rolled).

U.S. Geological Survey. USGS has several large world maps available, including the "International Map of the World" ($4), a multicolor reference Mercator projection map showing borders, capital cities, elevation tints and shaded relief, and other key features to delineate the nations of the world.

Also available from USGS are:

■ "World Seismicity Map" ($3.10), showing different areas of seismic activity on an international level, using a Mercator projection centered on the Americas.
■ "Political Map of the World" ($3.10), which shows nations, dependencies, and island groups, drawn with the Miller Cylindrical

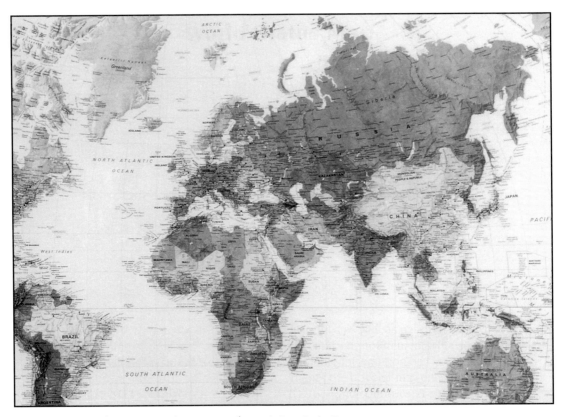

Portion of world map from Interarts, showing recent changes in Post-Soviet Europe.

projection centered on the Prime Meridian.
■ "Outline Map of the World," based on the
Van der Grinten projection centered on the
Americas, a two-color map showing political
boundaries, country names, capitals, and
selected cities, available in two sizes: 48" X 33"
($3.10) and 25" X 18" ($1.70, with no cities
named).

GOVERNMENT SOURCES, CANADA

Maps Alberta (Land Information Services Div.,
Main fl., Brittania Bldg., 703 6th Ave. SW,
Calgary, Alberta T2P 0T9; 403-297-7389)
publishes "Alberta in the World (Political)"
($3.38 Canadian; 28" X 30"; code 273), an
azimuthal projection of the world from a
perspective above Edmonton, showing political
boundaries in eight colors. The map is no
longer in print, but a blueline copy is available.

COMMERCIAL SOURCES

World maps used to be the backbone of many
map companies—the standard maps that
"never go out of style." With all the uncertainty
of national names and borders in some parts of
the world, that expression is no longer as true
as before. Still, finding a map of the world is
generally as easy as walking into a local travel,
book, or map store. There are thousands of
world maps available; many of a thematic
nature are listed elsewhere in this book. Here is
a small sampling of available world maps:

American Geographical Society (156 Fifth
Ave., Ste. 600, New York, NY 10010; 212-242-
0214) distributes two world maps: "World Map"
($4; 14" X 14"), reproduced from the small *Under
Heaven Map Book*, published in Korea in the late
17th or early 18th century; and "The World" ($11
per sheet), a 17-sheet series using the Miller

oblated stereographic projection system, showing land and water physical features, bathymetry, political boundaries, towns, roads, railroads, airports, and other features. Seven sheets, drawn to a 1:5,000,000 scale, are available from the AGS; size varies.

The Chart House Travel Map Co., Inc. (5222 Venice Blvd., Los Angeles, CA 90029; 213-965-9380; 800-322-1866) produces Personalized Travel Maps, designed to record one's travels. The legend of the map has space for personalizing. Each map comes with a Charting Kit, consisting of map pins, a route-charting ruler, and a pen for drawing routes. The full-color maps come in three sizes, standard (30" X 20"), deluxe (33" X 22"), and king (51" X 33"). They range in price from $38 to $99.50 and are drawn on the Mercator projection centered on the Americas. Personalized U.S. maps are also available (see "United States Maps").

Environmental Graphics, Inc. (11571 K Tel Dr., Minnetonka Blvd., Minnetonka, MN 55343; 612-938-1300; 800-328-3869) produces an 8'8" X 13' World Map Photomural ($59.95), a colorful map drawn with the Mercator projection.

Buckminster Fuller Institute (1743 S. La Cienega Blvd., Los Angeles, CA 90035; 310-837-7710) sells copies of the Dymaxion map in several forms: "Fuller Projection/Dymaxion Air-Ocean World" ($12.95), a 38" X 25" wall map; "Spaceship Earth Greeting Card" ($15 for a pack of 10), a formal-size card with a full-color Dymaxion map on the cover and quotes from Fuller inside; "Raleigh Edition Dymaxion Map" ($6.95), a reprint of Fuller's first edition of the Dymaxion map, in very subtle colors; "Dymaxion Sky-Ocean Globe" ($5), a 22" X 14$\frac{1}{2}$" map on heavy stock that folds into a 5$\frac{1}{2}$" icosahedron; and postcards ($1.95 each for 10).

Gabelli U.S. (1228 West Ave. #711, Miami Beach, FL 33139; 305-532-6956) distributes two vibrant French-made Gabelli maps (drawn with the Mercator projection centered on Africa):

■ "World Political," available in paper or flexible plastic, or laminated, in a number of sizes.
■ "World Montiscolor," showing the continents and oceans in colorful relief, also available in a number of sizes.

Gabelli U.S. world maps are also available on notebooks, folders, pencil holders, and traveling bags (see "Map Stuff").

Geochron Enterprises, Inc. (899 Arguello St., Redwood City, CA 94063; 415-361-1771; 800-342-1661) manufactures the Geochron World Time Indicator, a back-lighted, electromechanical map/clock of the world. Its Mercator projection (updated and available each year) displays all the legal time zones in the world. The map moves at a rate of one inch per hour, reflecting the Earth's rotation, while a stationary time scale at the top of the map displays the correct time for each zone. In conjunction with the time, Geochron accurately depicts the moment of sunrise and sunset, anywhere in the world; the duration of sunlight changes automatically with the seasons. Four models are available, with prices ranging from $1,265 to $2,465.

Hansen Planetarium (1098 S. 200 W., Salt Lake City, UT 84101; 800-321-2369) sells "Earth-At-Night" ($6.50, $14.50 laminated), a map from a montage of satellite images showing what the Earth looks like at night. It reveals gas flares in the Middle East, slash-and-burn agriculture in Southeast Asia, and urbanization in Europe, Japan, and North America. This fascinating map measures 23" X 35" and comes with a reference guide.

Peter Heiler, Ltd. (72 Bloor St. E., Oshawa, Ontario L1H 3M2; 416-668-6677) publishes a 24" X 36" political/physical world map, drawn with the Peters projection ($4.95 paper, $12.95 laminated).

Interarts, Ltd. (15 Mt. Auburn St., Cambridge, MA 02138; 617-354-4655) distributes a number of GLA Kartor maps, including:

The World Game Map

Imagine that you are 2,000 miles tall, standing on the Earth looking down. The space shuttle would be in orbit at your ankles, the sun would seem to be a mere 47 miles away, the length of your foot would stretch 300 miles. It would take four human steps to traverse the United States. Assuming you took one step per second, your speed would reach the equivalent of 2.5 million miles per hour. At this speed, you could circumnavigate the Earth 109 times per hour.

Clearly, you would be viewing the planet Earth from a whole new perspective.

Those are precisely the intentions of The World Game, an innovative playground of learning created by the nonprofit **World Game Institute** (University City Science Ctr., 3508 Market St., Philadelphia, PA 19104; 215-387-0220), which describes itself as "a peace research and education organization developing tools and solutions for global and local problems."

The World Game features what its creators call "the world's largest and most accurate map of the whole earth," a 40-by-70-foot map (its creators have dubbed it the "Big Map") painted onto the asphalt or concrete of a playground, parking lot, or neighborhood plaza. The map, at a scale of 1:2,000,000, is based on Buckminster Fuller's Dymaxion projection (see "Map Projections"). This gigantic map becomes the basis for a variety of presentations, games, and workshops that focus on such issues as economics, hunger, energy, population, nuclear war, education, resources, technology—and, of course, geography. For example, in the World Game Sessions, a two- to three-hour event using the Big Map, participants involve themselves in simulations dealing with the structure of global problems, resource distribution, and political interconnections. Other programs deal with global food, energy, and economics; the "greenhouse effect"; and Africa's unique problems. All actively involve participants.

Fees vary according to location, length of program, and other factors.

Also available is *Global Recall*, an interactive atlas for Macintosh computers that permits users to see countries and their resources individually and in their global and regional contexts, and *Global Data Manager*, a spreadsheet program of global statistics that contains more than 100 different variables—including demographics, food, military, energy, environment, and health—for every country in the world. See "Map Software" for more information.

■ World Political Maps drawn with the Van der Grinten projection. Among them: 30" X 53"—available in Tyvek ($20) or laminated ($40); 34" X 53"—available in paper ($16.95) or laminated ($35); 27" X 40"—with country flags, available in paper ($14.95) or laminated ($30); 46" X 61"—available in paper ($21.95) or laminated ($60); and 17" X 27"—available in paper ($7.95), laminated ($20), or as a desk blotter ($14.95).
■ World Political Maps drawn with the Mercator projection. Among them: 22" X 39"—in Tyvek ($14.95) or laminated ($30); and 17" X 27"—

available in paper ($7.95) or laminated ($20).
■ World Environmental Maps drawn with the Van de Grinten projection. They are available in the following sizes: 27" X 40" ($11.95 paper, $30 laminated); 17" X 27" ($8.95 paper, $25 laminated); and a 9' X 12' eight-sheet wall map ($79.95 paper).
■ United States Political Maps drawn with the Albert's Equal Area projection. They are available in the following sizes: 33" X 53"—available in Tyvek ($20) or laminated ($40); 38" X 54"—available in paper ($16.95) or laminated ($35);

and 26" X 37"—available in paper ($12.95) or laminated ($25).

■ United States Environmental Map drawn in the Albert's Equal Area Projection. It is 26" X 37" ($12.95 paper, $25 laminated).

Interarts also distributes "Wearin' the World" sports jackets made from the Tyvek World Map (see "Map Stuff").

Kistler (4000 Dahlia St., Denver, CO 80216; 303-399-0900, 800-523-5485) produces a 34" X 22" raised-relief map of the world. It is available with or without a natural oak frame.

Modern School (1609 E. Kercher Rd., Goshen, IL 46526; 219-533-3111; 800-431-5929) produces a "New Earth Map," a world physical map with political overlay, 61" X 52". Printed on 200-pound Kimdura, the map includes all basic world landform information. A large key identifies land-feature information, and two insets include surface winds and ocean currents, as well as world agriculture. A political overlay includes national boundaries and place names. Both the basic map and overlay are markable/washable. The map is available on a spring roller, with nickel-plated steel map board and matching pull-down bar; it mounts on any map rail, or with hooks or button mounting. Price: $179.

Nystrom (3333 N. Elston Ave., Chicago, IL 60618; 312-463-1144; 800-621-8086) produces various world maps, including the educational "Readiness Map of the World" made with either the Van der Grinten or the Robinson projection ($105.50 each). A special Canadian edition shows adjacent provinces in contrasting colors. "Pacific Rim and the World" is a 76" X 52" map drawn with the Eckert IV Equal Area projection centered on the Pacific Rim area, with a shaded-relief inset map showing the Pacific region's "Ring of Fire" volcanoes and earthquake areas. Price: $167, with a teaching guide.

Rand McNally (P.O. Box 7600, Chicago, IL 60680; 312-673-9100) distributes Wenschow Maps: large, German-made, full-color relief maps drawn with the Molleweide Homographic projection for the U.S. and the world ($294 to $309).

■ **See also: "Antique Maps," "Foreign Country Maps," "Globes," "Ocean Maps," "Map Software," "Political Maps," "Selected Atlases," and "Space Imagery."**

BOUNDARY MAPS

Boundary Maps

When it comes to drawing the line, nobody does it better than Uncle Sam. The federal government has worked diligently to draw and maintain the intricate boundaries that separate it from Canada and Mexico, as well as those dividing the contiguous 48 states from one another. The United States isn't alone in this endeavor: The surveyors of most other countries have long strived to divide conquered kingdoms and define lands given as gifts in royal marriages or annexed after a war; so, too, have those who govern cities, counties, states, and provinces around the world. Throughout the world, boundary maps are helpful to police, border guards, and customs agents, as well as to geographers, landowners, developers, historians, and statesmen.

Though they are perhaps the simplest and most direct maps in the world—they merely show where one country, state, county, city, town, or land plat ends and another begins—there is a certain romance to a boundary map. To appreciate the mythical proportions some boundaries take, one need only recall Jean Renoir's classic film about World War I, *The Grand Illusion*. In the final scene, German soldiers cease their fire at escaping Frenchmen who have just made it over the Swiss border. Less dramatic scenes occur daily at borders, as it is necessary to determine where to build, whom to sue, how to tax, and other issues that are trivial to all but a few interested parties.

The men and women who survey boundaries follow a long tradition that includes such renowned American surveyors as Daniel Boone and George Washington. From drawing the lines of a cattle ranch or sheep farm to setting the borders of growing metropolises, the history of boundary mapping is one of expansion and intrigue. Surveyors like Charles Mason and Jeremiah Dixon (who tackled the 18th-century American wilderness to pinpoint the North-South dividing line that bears their names) did

so with a battery of men with axes in the lead to battle the vegetation, and often the Indians.

Boundary maps, however, are not the last word on borders. They merely illustrate the border lines set forth in treaties, annexations, or other agreements. If this sounds easy, consider the border specifications—uncomplicated by today's standards—of the first charter of Virginia as declared by England's King James in 1606:

> ...situate, lying, or being all along the Sea Coasts, between four and thirty degrees of Northerly Latitude from the Equinoctial Line and five and forty degrees of the same Latitude, and in the main Land between the same four and thirty and five and forty Degrees and the Islands therunto adjacent, or within a hundred miles of the coast thereof.

Sometimes, the process of correcting boundary lines that were carelessly mapped can require more words than the original boundary specification. In an 1875 document, the North Carolina Geological Survey described the incorrect mapping of the state's borders:

> ...it appears from the South Carolina geographical State survey of 1821-1825 that the course from the starting point is N. 47 degrees 30' W., and instead of pursuing the parallel of 35 degrees, it turns west about ten miles south of that line, and then, on approaching the Catawba River, turns northward, pursuing a zigzag line to the forks of the Catawba River...

The report estimated that such mapping errors had caused the state to lose between 500 and 1,000 square miles of territory. The course of boundary drawing may not run smoothly, but the importance of the process is boundless.

Boundary maps are available through a number of federal agencies, as well as through local and state land management offices and the cartographic offices of foreign countries.

GOVERNMENT SOURCES

The lines drawn on boundary maps produced by the federal government contain lines that are either solid (if their accuracy is absolutely established) or broken (if they are believed to be, but are not certainly, accurate). Monuments, such as engraved stones or monoliths, built as border markers are also shown along boundary lines, usually with a small square symbol. Lines within states are usually mapped by local or state agencies, and these bound-

aries are then incorporated into federal maps.

International Boundary Commission, United States and Canada (1250 23rd St. NW, Ste. 405, Washington, DC 20037; 202-736-9100) has boundary maps and corresponding books that show the detailed border locations separating the United States and Canada. The maps, drawn in 1922, are printed on heavy paper and show the vegetation, major waterways, and some topography in shades of blue, green, and brown. The commission's 226 maps that represent the entire U.S.–Canadian border are divided into seven subsections:

■ Source of the St. Croix River to the Atlantic Coast (18 maps).
■ Source of the St. Croix River to the St. Lawrence River (61 maps).

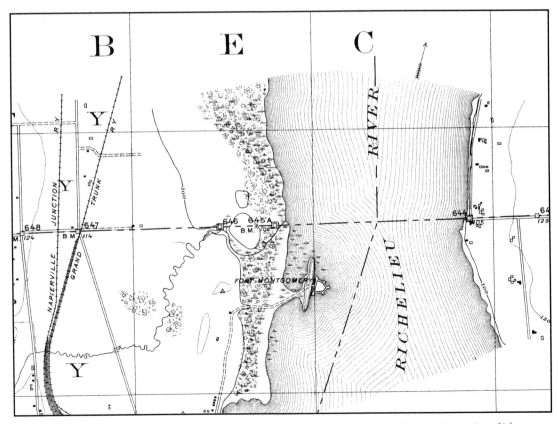

Portion of an International Boundary Commission map, sheet 3 in the St. Lawrence River–St. Croix River series, which illustrates the U.S.–Canadian boundary between New York and Quebec.

■ Northwesternmost Point of Lake of the Woods to Lake Superior (36 maps).
■ Gulf of Georgia to Northwesternmost Point of Lake of the Woods (59 maps).
■ 49th Parallel to the Pacific Ocean (one map).
■ Tongass Passage to Mount St. Elias (13 maps).
■ 141st Meridian from the Arctic Ocean to Mount St. Elias (38 maps).

Each map is $3. Write to the IBC for a free index of maps within each subsection.

International Boundary and Water Commission, United States and Mexico (The Commons, Bldg. C, Ste. 310, 4171 N. Mesa, El Paso, TX 79902; 915-534-6700). Has a U.S.–Mexico boundary map with projects of the International Boundary and Water Commission. Also available are maps of the U.S. and Mexico with the sister cities, the Lower Rio Grande Valley (Falcon Dam to the Gulf of Mexico), and the El Paso Project (Elephant Butte Dam to below El Paso). Maps vary in cost from $1 (photocopy) to $20. Prices are available upon request.

Bureau of the Census. The Census Bureau produces a number of outline map series, including:

■ Voting District Outline Maps. These county-based maps display all voting districts' boundaries and codes, the features and feature names (streets, railroads, rivers, and so on) underlying the boundaries, and the name of counties and county subdivisions (MCDs/CCDs), incorporated places, and American Indian/Alaska native areas. Map scales vary to minimize number of sheets. The maps may include one or more insets for densely settled areas.
■ Census Tracts/Block Numbering Areas Outline Map. These county-based maps depict the boundaries and codes of census tracts or block numbering areas, the features (streets, railroads, rivers, and so on), the feature names underlying the boundaries, and the boundaries and names of counties, county subdivisions,

places, and American Indian/Alaska native areas. Map scales vary to minimize number of sheets. The maps may include one or more insets for densely settled areas. This is the map most users will use when working with census data at higher geographic levels than blocks or block groups.
■ County Subdivision Outline Map. These maps are prepared for each state—usually on one sheet. They depict boundaries and names of all counties and statistically equivalent areas, county subdivisions, places, and American Indian/Alaska native areas. (The Census Bureau is publishing sectionalized versions of these maps in most 1990 census reports.)

Most maps produced by the **U.S. Geological Survey** include boundary lines for the area mapped. Topographical quadrangle maps include boundary lines drawn by local or state authorities. Only the maps of West Virginia contain boundaries established by the USGS at the request and compliance of the state (see "Topographic Maps" for more information on topographic quadrangles).

USGS also publishes an Alaska Boundary Map Series at 1:250,000 scale (1° X 2°), showing boundaries of federal lands ($2.50 each) and color photoimage quadrangle-size maps along the U.S.–Mexico border and along part of the U.S.–Canada border from Massena, NY, to East Richford, VT. These 20" X 22" maps center approximately on the border and sell for $2.50 each. See the USGS Catalog of Maps for ordering information.

The **Central Intelligence Agency** publishes hundreds of maps of foreign countries that include internationally accepted boundary lines. Some CIA maps are created specifically to illustrate border areas, such as "China-India Border Area" ($10; PB 86-928343) and "China-Vietnam Boundary Markers" ($10; PB 87-928335). The maps are available from the National Technical Information Service (see Appendix B).

Both the **Library of Congress** and the **National Archives** have boundary maps in their vast collections. The Library's collection consists of both American and international boundary maps, some dating to the 1300s. The Archives collection, which spans the two centuries between 1750 and 1950, contains American boundary maps commissioned by the federal government. While many of the best boundary maps are created privately by hired

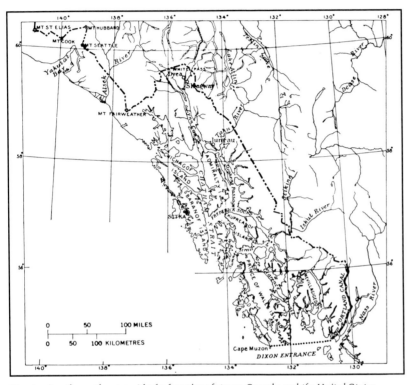

Map tracing the southeastern Alaska boundary between Canada and the United States.

surveyors and are rarely made public, the Library and the Archives have collected and made available many such maps of both domestic and foreign origin. Reproduction services are available for a modest fee from both collections (see "Uncle Sam's Treasure Chests").

State and Local Boundary Maps. These may often be obtained through local land-management or survey departments. Most cities have a records office where early land-ownership agreements and boundary maps may be available for study; local historical societies are

another good source for boundary maps of significance to an area. Some state cartographic offices provide maps or can direct you to good resources (see Appendix A).

Foreign Boundary Maps. These are often available through a country's cartographic agency. Another good source may be foreign tourism bureaus in the U.S.

COMMERCIAL SOURCES

Clarkson Map Co.
(1225 Delanglade St., P.O. Box 218, Kaukauna, WI 54130; 414-766-3000) distributes Canadian Boundary Waters maps ($13 each), including maps for Kabetogama Lake, Rainy Lake, and Lake of the Woods.

Ordnance Survey
(Export Sales Branch, Rm. C456, Romsey Rd., Southampton, England SO9 4DH) publishes a series of boundary maps for the United Kingdom, including "Great Britain—Local Government and European Constituency Boundaries" (North Sheet and Map Sheet); "England and Wales—Local Government Areas and Parliamentary Constituency Boundaries," a series of more than four dozen maps that show counties and districts overprinted with local government information; and "Wales—Local Government Boundaries."

■ **See also: "Foreign Country Maps," "Land-Ownership Maps," "Nautical Charts and Maps," "State and Provincial Maps," and "United States Maps."**

Congressional District Maps

Congressional district maps tell many tales. The history of congressional representation can be found in the shadings and boundaries that outline the voting realms—as well as the history of political deal-making and redistricting, also known as "gerrymandering."

The game of gerrymandering is one of the oldest in politics: redrawing the boundaries of a legislative district to create an imbalance of power, giving one political party an advantage at the voting booth. At times, congressional district boundaries meander around and through an area so sinuously as to include only the voters on the right side of one street, and only the voters on the left side of the street a block away. To look at maps of these districts, one might think the boundaries were astrological symbols—sea horses or snakes slithering across the land with no apparent method to their madness. Without maps to accurately define the district lines, few would believe the crazy-quilt patterns to be legal divisions of voting boundaries.

The term "gerrymander" was coined when Elbridge Gerry was elected governor of Massachusetts in 1812 with the aid of a bit of creative statewide redistricting. A clever cartoonist, noting the serpentine shape of the new boundaries, drew a caricature of the "gerrymander," a salamanderlike namesake of the governor.

Gerrymandering has helped more than a few politicians win elections in areas where they would normally have had little support. The Supreme Court sought to abolish the practice in a 1963 ruling, which established the "one man, one vote" precedent. Now, legislative districts must have relatively equal populations, effectively putting an end to the days when 500 bankers could elect three members of Congress, while 5,000 farmers elected just one. But even within these constraints, state legislatures still have the right to carve up voting districts as their political leaders see fit.

In most states, the party in power in the legislature has the right to draw up district boundaries. In the end, the district maps have the final say: once the maps are drawn, voters and politicians must follow their guidelines until a shift in power sparks the next bout of redistricting.

Some older, gerrymandered congressional district maps are works of art, colored and intricately drawn to include just the right citizenry. More recent maps are a bit less ornate—and less obvious about the purposes of redistricting—and though they may not be as pretty to look at, they paint an accurate portrait of the U.S. population's physical and political distribution.

Congressional district maps are useful to more than just members of Congress: business people use them to study population concentration; fund-raisers use them to pinpoint areas where certain political loyalties may create a donation base; teachers use them to educate students about American history and government. Anyone with an interest in U.S. political makeup and population distribution will find congressional district maps enlightening, even entertaining.

The federal government creates (and updates with each new Congress) a number of congressional district maps and atlases, as do several commercial map producers. Older congressional district maps are available from map dealers specializing in American history maps, or in reproduction form from map libraries, including the **Library of Congress** and the **National Archives**.

GOVERNMENT SOURCES

Government Printing Office. The following congressional district maps and atlases created by the Census Bureau are available from GPO:

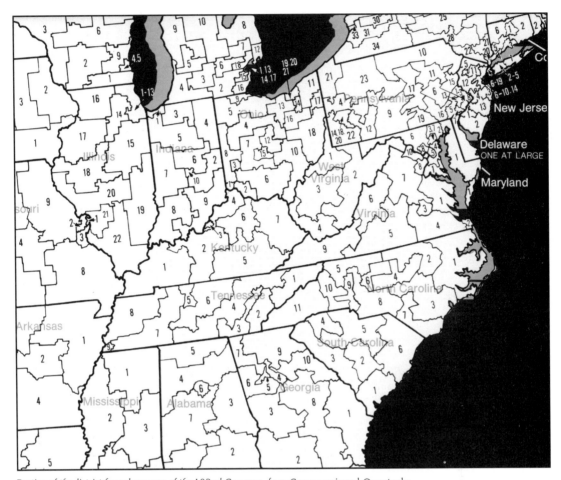

Portion of the district boundary map of the 102nd Congress, from Congressional Quarterly.

■ *Congressional District Atlas: 100th Congress of the United States* ($33; S/N 003-024-06234-8). This 696-page atlas contains maps depicting the boundaries of all congressional districts during the 100th Congress.

■ "Congressional Districts of the 100th Congress of the United States" ($4.75; S/N 003-024-06228-3), a 36" X 47" two-sided map. One side shows district boundaries for the 100th Congress; the other shows the districts for the first, 25th, 50th, 75th, and 100th Congresses.

U.S. Geological Survey. The National Atlas Program produced a colorful 1987 map, "Congressional Districts for the 100th Congress" ($3.10; US00446-38077-AT-NA-07M-00).

COMMERCIAL SOURCES

Congressional Quarterly (Book Distribution, 300 Raritan Center Pkwy., Edison, NJ 08818; 800-638-1710) sells a U.S. map of all the congressional districts, updated every two years. The 102nd Congress map is $14.95 prepaid, plus $1.95 postage and handling.

Western Economic Research Co., Inc. (8155 Van Nuys Blvd., Ste. 100, Panorama City, CA 91402; 818-787-6277) sells a 30" X 42" Congressional District Map of the Los Angeles five-county area ($30 paper, $40 laminated).

■ **See also: "Political Maps."**

Land-Ownership Maps

From land-grant maps to county plat maps, the portrayal of lands bought, granted, or inherited paints a picture of our perpetual need to own real estate. The detail with which some of these maps are drawn—every house, street corner, park, and fire hydrant in town diagrammed and labeled—preserves on paper one moment in the history of America's urbanization. By studying older ownership maps, one may locate the first house in which immigrant grandparents lived. By studying current ones, one may ascertain information about the land-holdings of neighbors and others.

The mapping of land ownership dates back to the Babylonian cadastral maps that delineated individual land-holdings. Somewhat later, according to legend, Ramses II established a cadastral survey in the 13th century B.C., but little of the papyrus on which the maps were made has survived. By the time of the Renaissance, the mapping of European estates was commonplace, and, by the 18th century, maps of counties were being published in England, with specific houses and residents named.

In the 19th century, the development of American county "land plats"—simple but detailed grid maps showing buildings, public lands, roads, and other features—became a necessity for the rapidly expanding nation. The importance of diagrams showing exactly who owned what and who lived where was immeasurable in a country where land-grant acts and squatters' rights were hotly debated. Today, county land plats, updated regularly by both commercial and government mappers, still serve as valuable land-planning tools; older plats serve as portraits of an area's past.

Everyone from genealogists to geographers uses land-ownership maps. Planners, builders, and investors can outline prospective developments by examining land-ownership blueprints. These maps sometimes reveal lands granted to, then taken from, native Indians, or the plantations of slave owners. And the exploding growth of cities, towns, and industrial centers is all recorded on these maps.

Boundary maps (see "Boundary Maps") are one form of land-ownership map, but most land-ownership maps do more than merely illustrate property lines. While boundary maps designate where one land plot ends and another begins, many land-ownership maps disclose to whom those lands belong.

Current land-ownership maps are available from several federal agencies, among them the **USGS**, the **Army Corps of Engineers**, and the **National Park Service**. Older boundary, land-grant, and plat maps may be found in the collections of the **Library of Congress** and the **National Archives**. State, county, and local mapping departments create their own land-ownership maps for taxation purposes, and some are available to the public. Land plat books and other ownership maps are also published by commercial map and blueprint companies around the country.

GOVERNMENT SOURCES

Uncle Sam owns a lot of land, and the surveying of this wealth of real estate is a job undertaken zealously by the federal government. Land-ownership maps are produced by several agencies or departments to diagram the continuing use of the land.

The **Bureau of Land Management** (BLM) is the largest federal source for plats of townships surrounding public land. In many cases, BLM's surveys were the first to establish boundary lines, and subsequent maps have detailed the growth of many American towns. The plats are simple black-and-white representations of an area, noting streets, houses, lakes, and parks. Other features, such as cultural centers and noteworthy topography, are included when possible. BLM no longer distributes its own land plats, but they can be obtained through two sources: BLM township plats of Illinois, Indiana, Iowa, Kansas, Missouri, and Ohio are available through the **National Archives and Record Administration**; township plats of other public-land states can be obtained from the Eastern States Office of the Bureau of Land Management (350 S. Pickett St., Alexandria, VA 22304; 703-461-1328).

The **National Park Service** keeps track of the purchase and development of federally protected parks. Maps showing the extent of each park's land-holdings are available at the parks themselves or from the Park Service (see "Recreation Maps").

The **Army Corps of Engineers** produces maps showing its public water-recreation areas. Land-ownership maps depict the boundaries of these lands and their potential for safe recre-

Land plat of Winnebago County, Illinois. Permission for reproduction granted by Rockford Map Publishers, Inc.

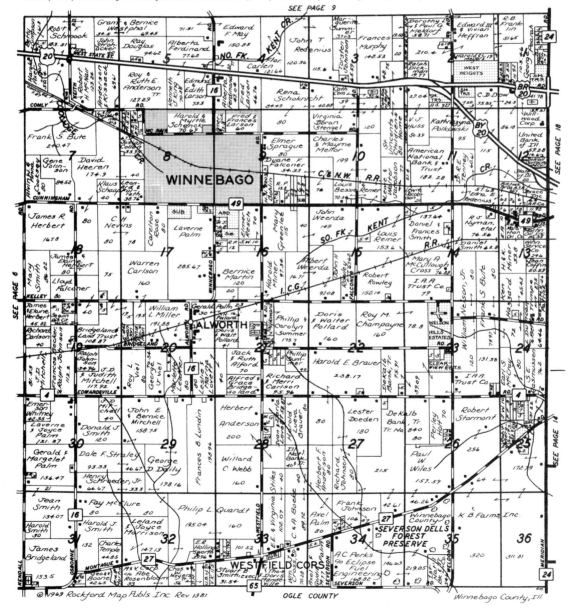

ational use. The maps are inexpensive (often free) and are available from the Army Corps of Engineers District Offices (see Appendix B).

The **Tennessee Valley Authority** has land maps and reservation property maps available for its 40,190-square-mile region, encompassing parts of Tennessee, Alabama, Georgia, Kentucky, Mississippi, North Carolina, and Virginia. TVA maps show property corner markers, boundaries, bearings, and distances for areas or reservations affected by TVA reservoirs. There are several sheets covering each reservoir area, and free indexes for these sheets are available.

Holdings in the **Library of Congress** of pre-20th-century land-ownership maps include 1,449 county maps, representing approximately one-third of all U.S. counties. The Library publishes *Land Ownership Maps: A Checklist of Nineteenth Century United States County Maps in the Library of Congress* ($6), available from the Library or the **Government Printing Office**, which lists these maps and gives a brief history of the collection. Copies of maps listed may be ordered from the Library's Photoduplication Service. The library also has 1,296 county land-ownership maps contained on 105-millimeter microfiche. Individual diazo microfiche copies may be purchased for $2 per fiche ($10 minimum), with the complete set available from the Photoduplication Service. Another microfiche collection is entitled "Ward Maps of United States Cities" and includes 232 pre-20th-century ward maps for 25 major cities. They are available from the Photoduplication Service on individual diazo microfiche ($2 each, with a $10 minimum) or as a complete set on either diazo microfiche ($645) or positive silver halide microfiche ($975).

The **National Archives** map collection includes the surveys of the Land Grant Office and later maps from the Bureau of Land Management. Indexes of these maps are available for study at the Archives' map research facilities in Alexandria, Virginia. Copies may be ordered through the Archives' reproduction service.

State, county, and local governments often produce land-ownership maps for such uses as settling zoning disputes or raising property taxes, and these may be available through local records or land offices. Other local sources include historical societies and long-established land sales companies, which may have ownership maps available for reproduction.

COMMERCIAL SOURCES

Publishing land-ownership maps is one of the oldest sources of income for commercial map companies. No sooner did a town spring up than the mappers arrived to plot boundaries and ownership agreements. Producers of land-ownership maps, especially land plats, may be found in most counties or population centers. Examples of maps being produced by such companies include:

M.A.P.S. Midwestern (32 N. Frederick, Oelwein, IA 50662; 319-283-3001) produces county/township maps depicting ownership and residency ($15 each). Maps are available for rural areas in Illinois, Minnesota, Missouri, South Dakota, Wisconsin, and eastern Iowa. Also available are books of residency ($15 each) for these areas.

Sanborn Map Company (629 5th Ave., Pelham, NY 10803; 914-738-1649) began producing detailed maps of U.S. urban areas in 1867, and by 1950 had mapped more than 12,000 cities and towns. The Sanborn archives contains about one million of these large-scale maps that show the size, shape, use, and other information about buildings and other structures. Each map sheet covers several city blocks. Currently, the maps are updated annually in 30 cities, and others at less frequent intervals. Reproductions of both current and historical editions of the maps are available from Sanborn as individual paper prints and microfilm sets.

■ **See also: "Boundary Maps."**

Political Maps

There are two types of political maps. In strict cartographic terms, a political map refers to maps that outline the political boundaries of the world. With their color-coded outlines of states and nations, these are the basic maps found in virtually every classroom, library, and home atlas—the ones that taught us early on that Italy looks like a boot "kicking" the island of Sicily, or that Mississippi was on the left and Alabama was on the right. This type of political map is created by practically every map-making company, as well as by most countries' governments. They can be found elsewhere in this book; see especially "Boundary Maps," "Foreign Country Maps," "Globes," "Selected Atlases," "State and Provincial Maps," "United States Maps," and "World Maps."

The other type of political map does more than simply divide nation from nation or state from state—it provides political characteristics, illustrating, for example, a ruling party's influence and role, or tracing a region's political development over time. These are "political" in the truest sense of the word, showing areas of human-rights abuse, for example, or countries under dictatorial rule. Many such maps are factual and unbiased; some are created by those intending to deliver a message.

One of the best collections of political maps may be found in a book, *The New State of the World Atlas*, by Michael Kidron and Ronald Segal (New York: Simon & Schuster, 1991; $30), a hardcover book chock-full of fascinating four-color maps, each of which compares the world's nations in some qualitative way. The choices and titles of the maps clearly reflect the authors' political leanings. Examples: "Shares in the Apocalypse" (which nations have what

"The United States as Seen from Canada." © *World Eagle, Inc., 64 Washburn Ave., Wellesley, MA 02181, U.S.A. Reprinted with permission.*

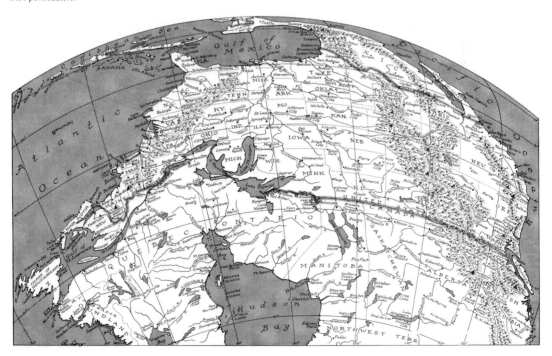

*Map of the military balance in the Caribbean, from the State
Department's* Atlas of Foreign Relations.

kinds of weapons and in what numbers); "The
First Slice of the Cake" (the percentage of
gross national product spent by each nation's
government); "Webs and Flows" (each
country's share of transnational parent
corporations); and "Exploitation" (ratios of the
price of manufactured products compared to
the wages of the workers who make them). In
the back of the book, the idea and rationale
behind each map is explained in simple terms.
For those anywhere along the political spectrum, this atlas provides a wealth of thought-
provoking maps.

While some commercial map publishers
and government agencies produce political
maps, most come from other sources, particularly public-interest groups, political organizations, and private foundations. There is no
single directory of such organizations or the
maps they produce. The gems must be uncov-
ered one by one. Many of the best political
maps are contained in atlases (see "Selected
Atlases").

GOVERNMENT SOURCES, UNITED STATES

Central Intelligence Agency. The CIA creates
several political maps, many of which are

available from the
National Technical
Information Service.
For information on
ordering CIA publica-
tions, see Appendix B.
CIA's political maps
and atlases include:

■ "Israeli Settlement
in the Gaza Strip"
($8.95; PB 88-928360).
■ "Lands and Waters
of the Panama Canal
Treaty" ($11.95; PB 88-
928328).
■ "Registered Afghan
Refugees in Pakistan"
($8.95; PB 88-928335).
■ "Major Insurgent
Groups of Afghanistan" ($10; PB 85-928040).
■ "Muslim Peoples in the Soviet Union" ($10;
PB 86-928358).
■ "China" ($12; PB88-928321).

Government Printing Office. The GPO
distributes "Eastern Europe, August 1990"
($16; S/N 041-015-00170-1), which shows
geographical, political, historical, and economic information about Eastern Europe prior
to the enormous changes in the region.

U.S. Geological Survey. As part of the
National Atlas Program, the USGS has published a two-sided map, "Presidential Elections, 1789-1968/1972-1984," that shows the
results of the 1789-1968 elections by state, and
the 1972-1984 elections by county, and
includes U.S. totals ($3.10; US05627-38077-
BH-NA-63M-00/38077-AY-NA-20M-00).

GOVERNMENT SOURCES, CANADA

Canada Map Office (615 Booth St., Ottawa,
Ontario, Canada K1A 0E9; 613-952-7000)
distributes maps of the *National Atlas of Canada*
series, including many in the "political geography" section, such as:

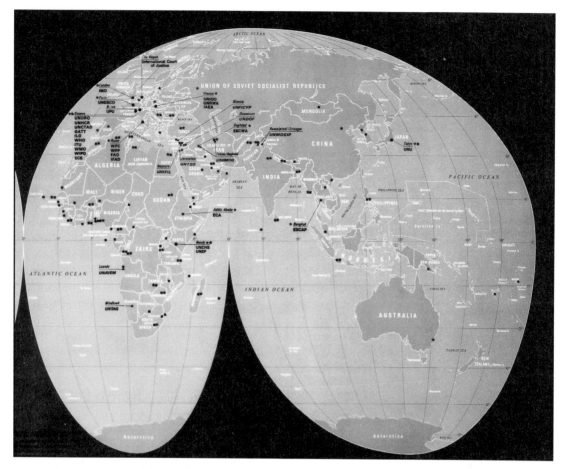

Portion of "Descriptive Map of the United Nations" (No. 3105, Rev. 10), courtesy United Nations.

■ "The 32nd Parliament" ($8.40 Canadian; MCR 4045).
■ "Confederation" ($8.40 Canadian; MCR 4051).
■ "Political Divisions" ($8.40 Canadian; MCR 4119).

Listings of *National Atlas* maps available from both the 4th and 5th editions, are available upon request.

COMMERCIAL SOURCES

Many map-making companies produce political maps. A sample is:

Delegation of the Commission of the European Communities (2100 M St. NW, Ste. 707, Washington, DC 20037; 202-862-9554) distributes free brochures about the European Community, including maps when available.

National Geographic Society (17th & M sts. NW, Washington, DC 20036; 301-921-1200) offers several foreign country maps, including:

■ "Africa Political" ($9.95; 20052; 46" X 60").
■ "British Isles" ($7.95; 02014; 23" X 31").
■ "Germany" ($7.95; 20814; 23" X 29").
■ "Japan and Korea" ($7.95; 20022; 23" X 30").
■ "Political United States" ($7.95; 02003; 30" X 43").

Unipub (4611-F Assembly Dr., Lanham, MD 20706; 301-459-7666; 800-274-4888; 800-233-

0504 in Canada) is the sole North American agent for the European Communities Office and the exclusive U.S. agent for United Nations Educational, Scientific, and Cultural Organization (UNESCO) publications and maps. Titles include "European Community Political Map," which shows EC regions and administrative units. In addition, the map contains a tabulation of the basic statistics on EC member states' area, population, gross domestic product at market prices, and per capita gross domestic product compared to the United States and Japan. Available in both a paper edition ($9) and laminated ($45).

United Nations Publications (Rm. DC2-0853, United Nations, New York, NY 10017; 212-963-8302) publishes "Descriptive Map of the United Nations" ($5; EF.87.90.I.22), a color poster map of the world showing U.N. member states, with population and area, as well as locations of U.N. offices and information centers. The U.N. publishes more than 6,000 other maps, not sold separately, which are parts of U.N. documents. As they are published, new U.N. maps are listed in UNDOC, a quarterly ($125 annually) that also gives ordering information.

UNDOC can be found in most public libraries.

World Eagle, Inc. (64 Washburn Ave., Wellesley, MA 02181; 800-634-3805) publishes Global Perspective Maps, black-and-white maps showing countries as they appear from certain neighboring countries. Ten titles are available: "U.S. as Seen from Canada," "Africa as Seen from India," "East Europe as Seen from West Europe," "Southeast Asia as Seen from People's Republic of China," "North Africa as Seen from Mideast," "People's Republic of China as Seen from Japan," "Central Africa as Seen from South Africa," "Soviet Union as Seen from Southeast Asia," "Latin America as Seen from Cuba," and "Mideast as Seen from Israel." The maps are available as a folded paper set for $31.95 (each sheet 24" X 38"), or $26.95 laminated (each map is $11^{1}/_{4}$" X $16^{1}/_{2}$"). Also available are six atlases of reproducible pages, including *Africa Today*, *Asia Today*, *The Middle East Today*, and *The United States Today*. Perfect-bound or three-hole-drilled; $26.50 each, plus $3.95 shipping.

■ **See also: "Census Maps," "Foreign Country Maps," "Military Maps," "Selected Atlases," and "World Maps."**

SCIENTIFIC MAPS

Agriculture Maps

Silicon Valley may be America's gold mine, but corn fields and cow pastures are still its heartland.

The history of American farmers is the history of America itself: the Indians who taught white settlers how to grow corn; the gentlemen planters who led the American Revolution and formed the federal government; the antebellum plantation owners, brought to their knees in the Civil War; the sharecroppers, cowboys, and immigrant farmers who helped tame the West. These are a few of the people who created America's agricultural legacy.

A century ago, farming in the United States was an enormous industry. New technology increased productivity, creating a need for greater knowledge of the land and its resources. In 1899, the **U.S. Department of Agriculture** began its soil-survey program. At the time, little was known about the quality or content of the nation's soil. But the methodological survey created a fund of knowledge that has grown over the years to encompass a complex system of soil testing, categorization, treatment, and usage.

The surveys contain soil maps as well as general information about soil quality and use. Since the turn of the century, USDA has published 3,653 surveys, 1,972 of which are still available. Surveys published since 1957 include a number of different interpretations for the various soils mapped in each area. Among these are interpretations of estimated yields of common crops, land capability, range land, soil-woodland, and soil suitability for community or recreational use. The maps in these later surveys are printed on a photomosaic base, usually at scales of 1:24,000, 1:20,000, or 1:15,840.

Older surveys are useful to agricultural or land-use historians, but the maps are more general and the interpretations out of date. More up-to-date soil surveys and other agricul-

ture maps are used by farmers, engineers, land planners, developers, geologists, and agricultural scientists.

Through its **Agricultural Stabilization and Conservation Service (ASCS)**, USDA also produces and maintains a large collection of aerial photographs of agricultural lands. The aerial photography program began in 1935, as a result of a law passed to alleviate the farm crisis brought on by the Depression. The law, designed to establish and maintain a balance between agricultural consumption and production, required the extensive and accurate measurement of the nation's farmlands. But the standard method of mapping since George Washington's time—the surveyor's chain—was too slow for USDA's purposes; so, in the mid-1930s, the agency began using "rectified-to-scale" aerial photomaps. With the use of aerial photomaps and a measuring device called a planimeter, it was possible to make land measurements that were 99 percent accurate. Today, the ASCS has aerial photomaps covering all major U.S. agricultural areas.

USDA's soil-survey and aerial-photomap programs are two parts of an extensive federal agriculture-mapping effort. The USDA's Forest Service creates maps that indicate the use of forest resources (see "Recreation Maps"). Other agriculture-map-producing agencies include the **Central Intelligence Agency**, which produces maps of foreign agriculture, and the **Army Corps of Engineers** and **National Oceanic and Atmospheric Administration**, both of which create agriculture-related maps about water sources (see "River, Lake, and Waterway Maps").

State, county, and local agriculture and conservation departments are good resources for agriculture maps of specific local areas. A few commercial cartographers create maps for classroom use.

GOVERNMENT SOURCES, UNITED STATES

Agricultural Stabilization and Conservation Service (Aerial Photography Field Office, P.O. Box 30010, Salt Lake City, UT 84130; 801-524-5856), part of the U.S. Department of Agriculture, produces aerial photographs of U.S. agricultural land. Products available include Landsat images; Skylab 2, 3, and 4 imagery; photographs taken as part of the National High Altitude Program; and photos taken by the Forest Service and Soil Conservation Service. Prices for copies of aerial photographs range from $6 for a 10" X 10" black-and-white paper contact print to $65 for a 38" X 38" paper print made from a color infrared positive. A price sheet (ASCS-441A) and order form (ASCS-441) are available upon request, as is an explanatory pamphlet, "ASCS Aerial Photography."

Central Intelligence Agency. The CIA produces hundreds of specialized maps, some depicting agriculture or vegetation in foreign countries, such as "Natural Vegetation in Africa" ($10; PB 86-928342), "China/Agricultural Regions" ($10; PB 86-928337), and "South Africa: Agricultural Activity" ($10; PB 86-928317). CIA maps and a map index are available from the National Technical Information Service (see Appendix B).

Forest Service. The U.S. Forest Service produces several forestry maps and atlases, many of them available from the Government Printing Office (see "Recreation Maps").

Government Printing Office. The following GPO publications contain agricultural maps or surveys and related text:

■ *Engineers and Irrigation: Report of the Board of Commissioners on the Irrigation of the San Joaquin, Tulare and Sacramento Valleys of the State of*

Soil types in the United States, from the U.S. Department of Agriculture's map "Soils of the World."

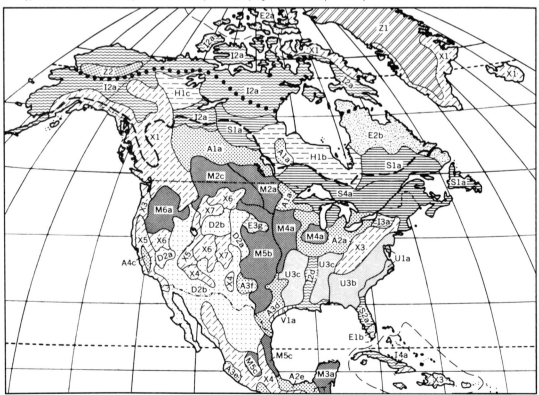

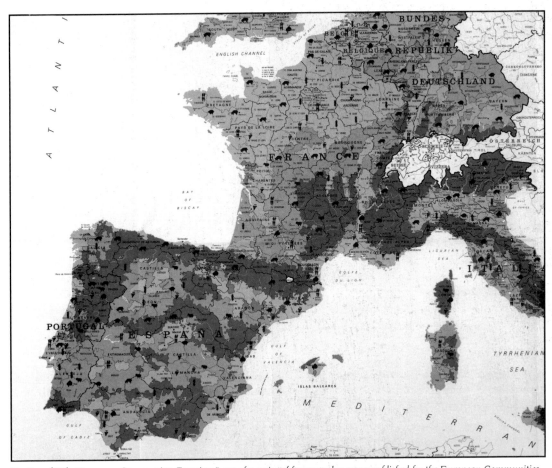

Portion of "The European Community: Farming," one of a series of four popular maps published by the European Communities Commission (distributed by Unipub).

California, 1873 ($14; S/N 008-022-00267-7), includes a large folded map.

■ *Environmental Trends* ($17; S/N 041-011-0084-0; 160 pages), contains maps, charts, and text that show key changes in the environment.

■ "USDA Plant Hardiness Zone Map" ($6.50; S/N 001-000-04550-4) is a waterproof chart showing 10 different zones, each of which represents an area of winter hardiness of plants for agriculture and natural landscape. The 1990 chart is 48" X 48", folded.

Soil Conservation Service (Info. Div., P.O. Box 2890, Washington, DC 20013; 202-720-6009) has soil surveys for almost all of America's farmland. There are 1,972 available surveys, although many are out of date; 1,681 are out of print. The surveys still in print can be obtained at no charge by land users and by representatives of state and local offices of the Soil Conservation Service. Many libraries have surveys on file for study and reproduction; these are good places to start the search for any of the out-of-print surveys. SCS publishes a free *List of Published Soil Surveys*, which includes a list of state offices. The most recent edition of this publication is available free upon request. Also available from the Publications Division of the Washington, D.C., office (see address above) and many state offices is a colorful and informative map that shows soils of the U.S.

(continued on page 133)

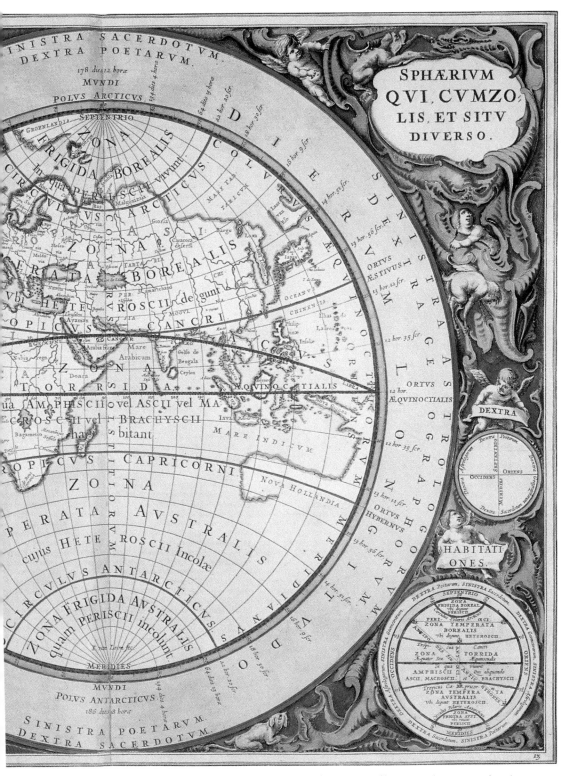

Portion of "The World in 1660," by Andreas Cellarius. Courtesy Hansen Planetarium Publications and University of Utah, Marriott Library Special Collections.

Aerial photograph of Wilmington, Delaware. Courtesy U.S. Geological Survey.

Space imagery of Grand Canary Island by the French satellite Spot. ©1988 CNES. *Provided courtesy* SPOT Image
Corporation, Reston, Virginia.

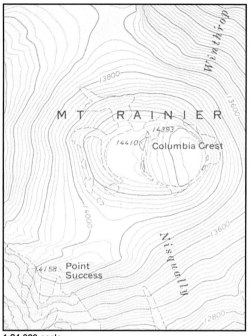

1:24,000-scale

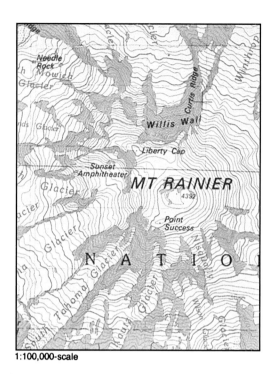

1:100,000-scale

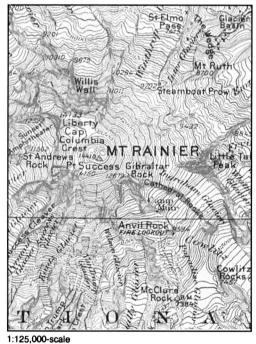

1:125,000-scale

Topographic maps of Mt. Rainier, Washington, illustrating three perspectives of the same region at different scales. Courtesy U.S. Geological Survey.

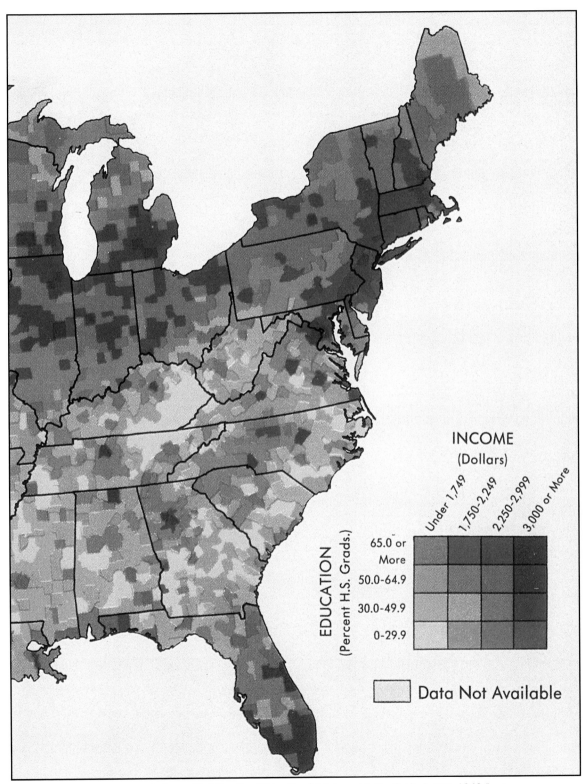

Portion of a Census Bureau statistical map, "Relationship of Educational Attainment to Per Capita Income, 1969."

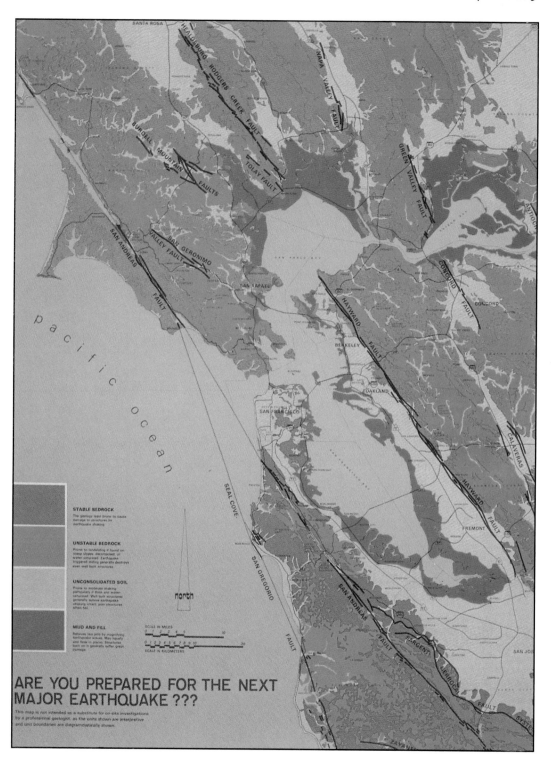

ARE YOU PREPARED FOR THE NEXT
MAJOR EARTHQUAKE ???

"Geology and Active Faults in the San Francisco Bay Area," from the Pt. Reyes National Seashore Association, showing the fault lines and adjacent geology, described in terms of relative stability during an earthquake.

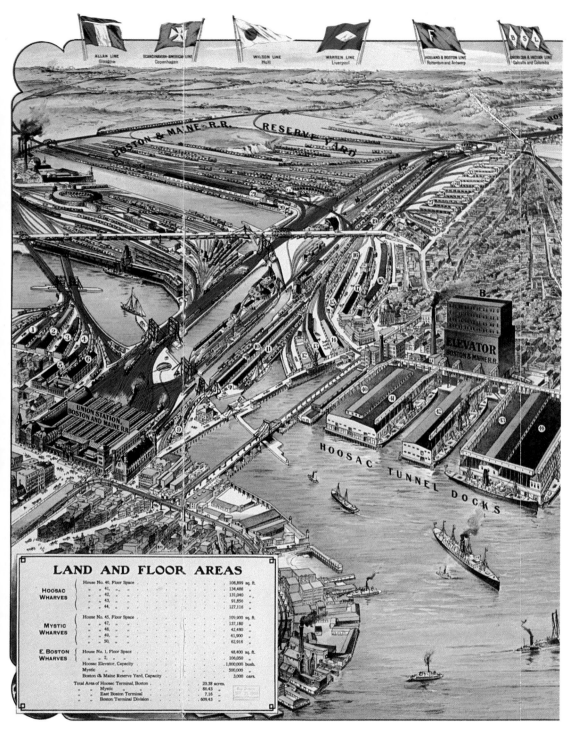

Portion of a 1905 bird's-eye-view map of Boston's railroad and shipyards, identifying individual buildings and facilities. Courtesy Library of Congress.

Computer-generated "European Reference Map," showing changes in Eastern Europe. © 1992 Computer Terrain Mapping, Inc./Zia Maps, Boulder, CO. Digital processing & film recording by GW Hannaway & Assoc., Boulder, CO.

(continued from page 124)

Tennessee Valley Authority. "Soils in the Tennessee Valley" ($2.50, plus $2 for mailing tube), compiled by TVA's Soils and Fertilizer Branch in cooperation with USDA's Soil and Conservation Service, is a colorful map describing in detail a variety of aspects of Tennessee Valley soils.

GOVERNMENT SOURCES, CANADA

Canada Map Office (615 Booth St., Ottawa, Ontario K1A 0E9; 613-952-7000) distributes maps from the *National Atlas of Canada*, 5th edition series, including: "Agricultural Lands" (MCR 4022), "Soil Capability for Agriculture" (MCR 4023), "Farm Operators" (MCR 4047), and "Farm Types" (MCR 4109). The maps, available with English or French text, are $8.40 Canadian each.

Maps Alberta (Land Information Services Div., Main fl., Brittania Bldg., 703 6th Ave. SW, Calgary, Alberta T2P 0T9; 403-297-7389) publishes numerous agricultural maps as part of the *Alberta Resource and Economic Atlas* (code 271). The Agriculture Production series consists of 16 maps, most produced in 1981, depicting the production of the following items: "Barley," "Canola," "Flaxseed," "Oats for Grain," "Tame Hay," "Rye," "Wheat," "Cattle and Calves," "Hogs, Milk Cows," "Poultry," "Poultry Hatcheries," "Sheep and Lambs," "Greenhouses," "Potato Growers," and "Vegetable Growers." The maps are 99 cents Canadian each. A "Soils" map from the Physical Features series of the atlas is also available (75 cents).

Maps Alberta also publishes Forage Inventory maps of Alberta's public land, which separate the natural vegetation into recognized plant associations ($3.47 Canadian each; code 232; 30" X 36"), and Canada Land Inventory Agriculture maps for Alberta, available in booklets ($6.80 each; code 481; series CLI/ALI). Write or call for latest catalog.

GOVERNMENT SOURCES, GREAT BRITAIN

Ordnance Survey (Export Sales Branch, Rm. C456, Romsey Rd., Southampton, England SO9 4DH) publishes European Community Maps, two of which are agriculture-related: "Farming" colorfully shows agricultural zones and products for each community region and includes an inset map with statistics for each member country and the entire European Community; "Forests" shows the forests of the EC in different shades of green, while statistical information is shown in an inset map.

COMMERCIAL SOURCES

Although most agriculture maps are created by government cartographers, there are a few commercial maps created as classroom tools that depict the development of agriculture in America. Among them:

American Geographical Society (156 Fifth Ave., Ste. 600, New York, NY 10010; 212-242-0214) distributes A. W. Kuchler's map, "Potential Natural Vegetation of the Conterminous U.S." ($26; 61" X 40"), which illustrates 116 types of vegetation, as well as states, major cities, water bodies, and topographic features.

George F. Cram Co. (P.O. Box 426, Indianapolis, IN 46206; 317-635-5564; 800-635-5564) produces a vibrant agricultural map—"Agricultural Regions of the United States"—as part of its United States History series. There are 19 52" X 40" maps in the series, which are mounted in a steel charthead on a metal tripod for classroom use ($320 for the set).

Librarie Pédagogique Mtl., Inc. (7957 Boul. St.-Michel, Montreal, Quebec, Canada H1Z 3C9; 514-729-3844) produces an agriculture map of the European Community ($104 Canadian; M-1036-MP) that shows the agriculture and formation of the European Community on one side, and participant countries' strongest economic characteristics on the other. A colorful "World Vegetation Map" ($99 Canadian; G-1777) is available, as well as thematic maps of Canada ($94 Canadian; MA-1244-MP), Japan ($104 Canadian; M-1196-MP), and China ($104 Canadian; M-1195-MP), with a physical/political country map on one side, and four themes on the other: agriculture, population, natural resources, and industry. All are available with French text; the European Community, World Vegetation, and Canada thematic map are also available in English.

Nystrom (3333 N. Elston Ave., Chicago, IL 60618; 312-463-1144; 800-621-8086) publishes a 50" X 80" brightly colored teaching map titled "Patterns of Agriculture in the United States" ($47 to $72), which depicts the products of America's major agricultural regions.

Omni Resources (1238 Anthony Rd., P.O. Box 2096, Burlington, NC 27216; 919-227-8300) distributes soil maps of many countries, acquired from various sources. Maps are available for countries such as Burkina Faso, Cameroon, Central African Republic, Great Britain, Italy, New Zealand, and the former Soviet Union. Also available is a "World Soils Map" created by the United Nations Educational, Scientific, and Cultural Organization (UNESCO) and a vegetation map of China.

Rand McNally (P.O. Box 7600, Chicago, IL 60680; 312-673-9100) publishes the American Studies series, which includes "Farm, Factory, and Forest (1900)" ($49; 112-12521-2), showing the impact agricultural and industrial development have had on the land. Measures 50" X 50".

Unipub (4611-F Assembly Dr., Lanham, MD 20706; 301-459-7666; 800-274-4888; 800-233-0504 in Canada) is the sole North American agent for the European Communities Office and the exclusive U.S. agent for United Nations Educational, Scientific, and Cultural Organization (UNESCO) publications and maps. Titles include "Soil Map of the European Community," a seven-sheet map with an explanatory booklet ($85 flat); "Map of Natural Vegetation of the Member States of the European Community and the Council of Europe," a four-sheet map with an illustrated explanatory booklet ($60); and "Vegetation Map of South America," a two-sheet map that was updated in 1991 ($45).

■ **See also: "Aerial Photographs," "Land-Use Maps," "Natural Resource Maps," "Recreation Maps," "Selected Atlases," and "Weather Maps."**

Geologic Maps

More than any other type of map, geologic maps are portraits of the Earth. Like any good portrait, a geologic map shows not only the face of its subject but also something of its inner nature.

Geologic maps show the Earth's face by delineating the characteristics and distribution of exposed rocks and surface materials. And they make it possible to infer the Earth's "inner nature"—the size, shape, and position of rock masses and mineral deposits they may contain—by means of symbols. These qualities are often interpreted with the help of slices, or cross-sections, made by combining surface observations with whatever subsurface information may be at hand from drill holes, mine workings, caves, or geophysical measurements.

Geologic maps are models of both space and time. The geologic history of an area can usually be reconstructed using a geologic map because the relative ages of rocks can often be determined (and even their ages in years estimated) if they contain fossils or certain naturally radioactive elements that decay at known rates. Geologic maps have been used to plot the pathways of meltwaters from glaciers that disappeared tens of thousands of years ago, leading, for example, to the discovery of groundwater reserves. Reserves of petroleum and natural gas are also found with the help of geologic maps.

Because they carry so much information, geologic maps are considerably more complex than topographic maps, which simply trace the surface contours of the earth (see "Topographic Maps"). Using a topo map requires mastering only two ideas beyond those needed to use a standard road map: the contour line and the interval between lines. Geologic maps, in contrast, convey a wealth of additional information. Some idea of their complexity may come from realizing that rocks, once formed—

on the ocean floor, on river floodplains, beneath glaciers, or around and below volcanoes—can be eroded; be lifted or lowered thousands of feet; be folded into troughs, basins, arches, domes, and far more intricate

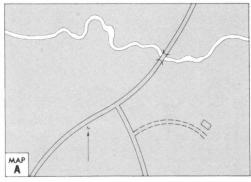

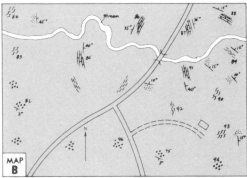

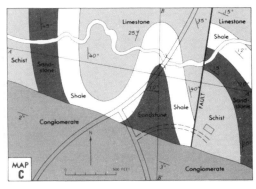

The development of a geologic map, from base map (top), to field map (center), to finished product (bottom).

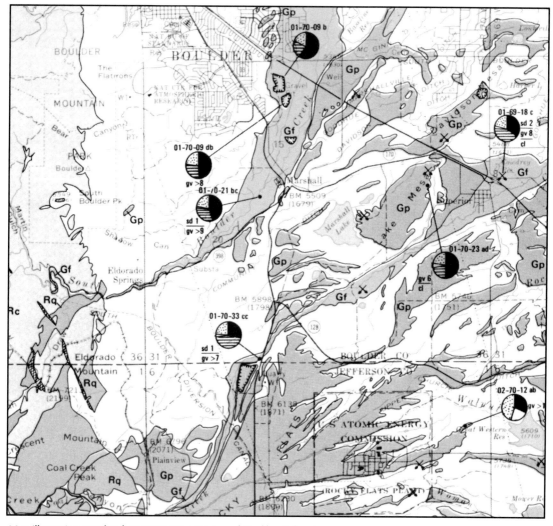

Map illustrating gravel and aggregate resources around Boulder, Colorado.

shapes; or be broken by great fractures and dragged or pushed hundreds of miles from their place of origin. The Earth has been actively making, deforming, eroding, and remaking rocks for more than four-and-a-half-billion years. This entire history can be shown through symbols, colors, and patterns on geologic maps.

A geologic map is important for two reasons:

■ It is the most effective means of recording observations about rocks in a way that shows their spatial relationships to one another.
■ Along with the cross sections that can be

drawn from it, it is a device for study and analysis of many kinds of geologic features and processes, such as sequence and thickness of rock formations, their geologic structure, and their history.

Scientists and engineers in many fields use geologic maps as basic tools. Because we know, for example, that certain kinds of rock or geologic structures are associated with certain kinds of mineral deposits, geologic maps can help an exploration geologist find oil, coal, copper, uranium, and many other minerals. Hydrologists use geologic maps to locate sources or movement paths of groundwater.

Geologic maps can be used for these and other purposes, whether or not the geologist who made them had such purposes in mind. A map prepared initially to solve a specific geologic problem may later help an engineering geologist choose between potential construction sites; a map made as part of a program of petroleum exploration may turn out, ultimately, to have far greater value in a search for uranium and potash.

GOVERNMENT SOURCES, UNITED STATES

The **U.S. Geological Survey** makes many kinds of geologic maps as part of the continuing program to ". . . examine the geologic structure . . . of the national domain," as its mission is described. These maps may be published singly or in one of several series:

■ **Geologic Quadrangle Maps** are multicolor geologic maps on topographic bases in 7 1/2- or 15-minute quadrangle units, showing bedrock, surficial, or engineering geology. They include text and some maps by structure and columnar sections.

■ **Geophysical Investigations Maps** are based on topographic or planimetric maps showing the results of surveys using geophysical techniques, such as gravity, magnetic, seismic, or radioactivity, which reflect subsurface structures that are of economic or geologic significance. Many are correlated with the geology.

■ **Miscellaneous Investigations Series Maps**, drawn on topographic or planimetric map bases, include a wide variety of format and subject matter, including 7 1/2-minute quadrangle photogeologic maps showing geology as interpreted from aerial photographs. The series includes maps of Mars and the moon.

■ **Coal Investigations Maps** show bedrock geology, stratigraphy, and structural relations in certain coal-resource areas; they are based on topographic or planimetric maps.

■ **Miscellaneous Field Studies Maps** are color or black-and-white maps of quadrangle or irregular areas. Pre-1971 maps show bedrock geology in relation to specific mining or mineral-deposit problems; post-1971 maps are preliminary black-and-white maps on various subjects such as environmental studies or wilderness mineral investigations.

■ **Mineral Investigations Resources Maps** show geographic distribution and grade of mineral-resource commodities.

■ **Hydrologic Investigations Atlases** are color or black-and-white maps based on topographic or planimetric maps, showing a wide range of geohydrologic data.

■ **State Geologic Maps** for 14 states: Alaska, Arizona, Arkansas, Colorado, Kentucky, Massachusetts, Montana, Minnesota, New Hampshire, New Mexico, North Dakota, Oklahoma, South Dakota, and Wyoming.

■ **Special Maps**, including "Geologic Map of the United States," "Coal Map of North America," "Subsurface Temperature Map of North America," and "Basement Rock Map of the United States, Exclusive of Alaska and Hawaii."

Geologic maps may also be published as folded sheets in envelopes bound with book-type series, such as "Bulletins," "Water-Supply Papers," and "Professional Papers," the texts of which contain descriptive and interpretive material that the maps alone cannot provide.

There are also several full-color 19" X 28" thematic maps from USGS's authoritative National Atlas Program, including "Geology" (1966), which shows the distribution of sedimentary, volcanic, and intrusive rock types; "Surficial Geology" (1979), showing the distribution of transported, untransported, and other deposits for the United States; "Classes of Land-Surface Form" (1964) and "Tectonic Features" (1968) covering the lower 48 states; "Land Surface Form" (1968) and "Tectonic Features" (1968) covering Alaska. Each is $3.10, available from USGS.

One of the best information resources at USGS is the **Geologic Inquiries Group** (GIG, USGS, 907 National Ctr., Reston, VA 22092; 703-648-4383). GIG provides specific responses to all geology-related questions from the public, other government agencies, and within the USGS. GIG specialists maintain up-to-date reference lists on popular geologic subjects, listing USGS publications (as well as those of other organizations) on frequently-asked-about subjects. These subjects include the geology and resources of each state; prospecting and mineral economics; oil and gas maps of the United States; earthquakes and volcanoes; state geologic maps; rocks, minerals, and gemstones; geology of the National Parks; plate tectonics; careers in the geosciences and environmental technology.

GIG also publishes Geologic Map Indexes (GMIs) for each state, and maintains the GEOINDEX data base. GMIs show outlines of published geologic maps more detailed than the state geologic maps. Publishers of geologic maps shown include the USGS, other federal agencies, state geoscience agencies, universities, professional societies, and private publishers. GIG helps inquirers find the geologic map for their area of interest, and directs them to the appropriate publisher. GEOINDEX is the bibliographic data base maintained by GIG that can be queried to answer most geologic map questions.

Two additional free publications available from GIG are *State Geologic Maps*, listing maps available for each state, and *Geologic Maps of the United States, North America, and Large Regions of the United States*, listing maps available from USGS and other sources.

Also available from GIG are two packets of earth-science teaching aids, which differ according to grade level and geographic location. The packets include lists of reference materials, various maps and map indexes, and a selection of general-interest publications. The packets are free to teachers who mail requests to GIG on school letterhead.

A complete description of USGS-produced maps can be found in the free publication *Guide to Obtaining USGS Information* (Circular 900), available from USGS Books and Open Files Reports Center, 25425 Federal Center, Denver, CO 80225, or any ESIC office.

USGS-published geologic maps range widely in scale depending on the type of information to be portrayed. A single mine or landslide may be drawn to a scale of 1:400, for instance, while the National Atlas series features geologic maps drawn to a scale of 1:7,500,000. However, most USGS maps come in one of five standard scales: 1:24,000, 1:48,000, 1:62,500, 1:100,000, or 1:250,000. The smaller-scale maps are used for general planning and resource evaluation over large regions. Larger-scale maps may be used for detailed planning, zoning, site selection, and resource evaluation. Geologic maps at 1:250,000 or larger scales are available for nearly 85 percent of the United States. The entire country has been mapped by USGS at 1:2,500,000 scale; only about 15 percent of the United States has been mapped at 1:24,000.

Geologic maps are available directly from USGS and its Earth Science Information Centers (see Appendix B). USGS maintains free geologic map indexes by state, which are available from USGS Books and Open Files Reports Centers in Denver, Colorado, and Fairbanks, Alaska, as well as from Earth Science Information Centers.

GOVERNMENT SOURCES, STATE

Regional USGS Earth Science Information Center offices also sell maps of local areas and books of local and general interest. In addition, most states have a Geological Survey, Bureau of Mines, or Department of Natural Resources that publishes and sells geologic maps. The **New Mexico Bureau of Mines & Mineral Resources** (Publications Rm., Socorro, NM 87801; 505-835-5410), for example, publishes dozens of geologic maps, including "Geology of Massacre Peak Quadrangle" (GM-51, $3.50) and "Geologic Map of Tres Hermanas Mountains" (GM-16, $1). **Oklahoma Geological Survey** (100 E. Boyd, Rm. N-131, Norman, OK 73019; 405-325-3031) sells a "Geologic Map of Oklahoma" for $7.30. There are countless others. See Appendix A for addresses of state geoscience agencies.

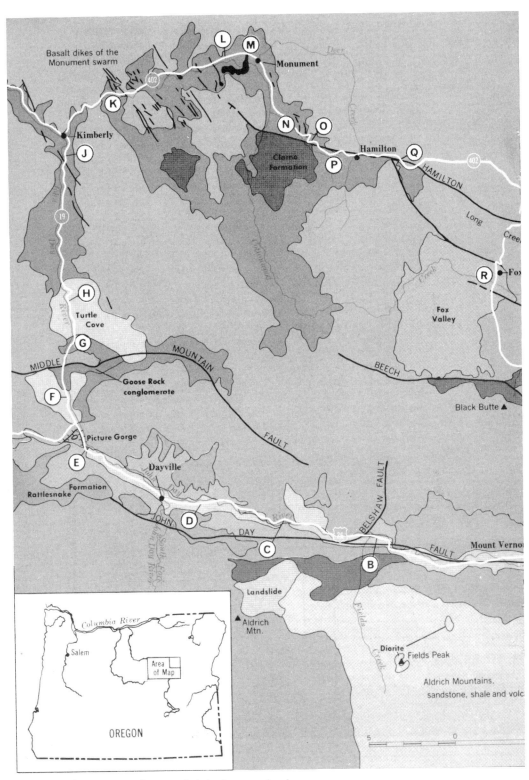

Map of the John Day region of Oregon, depicting its unusual geology.

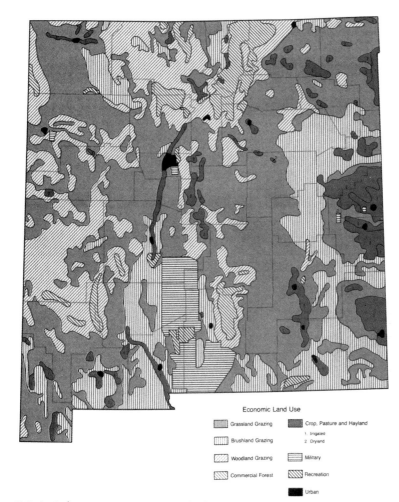

Economic Land Use

Grassland Grazing   Crop, Pasture and Hayland
1. Irrigated
Brushland Grazing   2. Dryland

Woodland Grazing   Military

Commercial Forest   Recreation

Urban

U.S. Agriculture Department's economic land-use map of New Mexico.

Maps Alberta (Land Information Services Div., Main fl., Brittania Bldg., 703 6th Ave. SW, Calgary, Alberta T2P 0T9; 403-297-7389) distributes geology maps produced by the Geological Survey of Canada. The color maps ($7.50 Canadian each; code 472) focus on various aspects of Canadian geology. Available maps are "Principal Mineral Areas of Canada" (900A), "Geological Map of Canada" (1250A), "Tectonic Map of Canada" (1251A), "Mineral Deposits of Canada" (1252A), "Glacial Map of Canada" (1253A), and "Physiographic Regions of Canada" (1254A). Some of these maps may not be availabe through Maps Alberta, but instead through the **Alberta Research Council** in Edmonton (403-438-1666).

GOVERNMENT SOURCES, CANADA

Canada Map Office (615 Booth St., Ottawa, Ontario K1A 0E9; 613-952-7000) distributes maps from *The National Atlas of Canada*, 5th edition, including "Glaciers" ($8.40 Canadian; MCR 4080).

Maps from the 4th edition of the *National Atlas* are also available ($3.45 Canadian each), including: "Geology" (MCR 1123), "Geological Provinces" (MCR 1124), "Tectonics" (MCR 1125), "Retreat of the Last Ice Sheet" (MCR 1126), "Glacial Geology" (MCR 1127), and "Post-Glacial Rebound" (MCR 1128). All *National Atlas* maps are available with either French or English text.

COMMERCIAL SOURCES

AAPG Bookstore (P.O. Box 979, Tulsa, OK 74101; 918-584-2555), affiliated with the American Association of Petroleum Geologists, distributes a series of "highway maps" that include state and regional geologic data with an overlay depicting major highways and landmarks. The lower 48 states are covered in 11 maps ($9 to $11 each) at a scale of one inch per 30 miles. AAPG's Map of the World Project consists of maps produced by the International Union of Geological Sciences. Titles include "Tectonic Map of South America" ($28) and "Tectonic Map of South and East Asia" ($88). AAPG stocks a wide variety of other geologic maps.

Circum-Pacific Map Project (U.S. Geological Survey, MS-952, 345 Middlefield Rd., Menlo Park, CA 94025; 415-329-4002) is an international cooperative effort between the Circum-Pacific Council for Energy and Mineral Resources and the USGS to assemble and publish new geological and geophysical maps of the Pacific Ocean Basin and surrounding land areas. The widely acclaimed maps are intended to show the relation of geology, tectonics, and crustal dynamics to known energy and mineral resources, and also to aid in exploration for new resources. The area has been divided into six regions (Northeast Quadrant, Northwest Quadrant, Southeast Quadrant, Southwest Quadrant, Antarctic Region, and Arctic Region) at a scale of 1:17,000,000. Map sheets are compiled for each of eight subjects—base, geographic, geologic, geodynamic, plate tectonic, energy resources, mineral resources, and tectonic; occasionally, data on such special subjects as natural hazards, tectonostratigraphic terrains and seafloor sediments are compiled on the Pacific Basin sheet, 1:17,000,000. As of mid 1992, 39 map sheets have been published, 35 by the American Association of Petroleum Geologists, and are available from the AAPG Bookstore (P.O. Box 979, Tulsa, OK 74101) for $7 each. Since 1990, publication of the series has been by the U.S. Geological Survey (USGS, Map Distribution, Box 25286, Federal Center, Denver, CO 80225). Costs range from $3.10 to $6.70 each, depending on number of sheets and pages of explanatory notes. Contact USGS Map Distribution for costs and new publications.

Crystal Productions (Box 2159, Glenview, IL 60025; 708-657-8144; 800-255-8629) sells four "Geologic Map Portfolios" ($39.95 for set): "Portfolio 1—Physical Geology" ($14.50), including eight full-color geologic maps with 23 color cross sections and a set of the same sections partially unfinished for student completion; "Portfolio 2—Historical Geology" ($14.50), containing 13 color maps showing major geologic provinces of the U.S.; "Portfolio 3—Physical Geology" ($15.50), including

bedrock and surficial geologic maps illustrating structures and stratigraphy across the U.S.; and "Geologic Quadrangles" ($8.50), with four full-color geologic maps and cross sections. Most portfolios come with a guide.

W. H. Freeman and Company (41 Madison Ave., New York, NY 10010; 800-877-5351) publishes "The Bedrock Geology of the World" ($41.95; 48" X 76"), a full-color map drawn to a scale of 1:23,230,300, showing the bedrock geology of continents as well as ocean basins.

Geological Map Service (P.O. Box 920, Sag Harbor, NY 11963; 516-725-0780) distributes a wide range of international geologic and tectonic maps, including many hard-to-find foreign-produced maps, some translated into English. Offerings include: "Arctic Atlas" ($125); "Deep Geological Sections of Northern Asia" ($94); "Geological Map of Eurasia" in 12 sheets ($64); and maps of Africa and Asia.

Geological Society of America (3300 Penrose Pl., P.O. Box 9140, Boulder, CO 80301; 303-447-2020; 800-472-1988) publishes several geologic maps in their Map and Chart series. Examples are "Geologic Map and Cross Section of the Eastern Ouachita Mountains, Arkansas" ($7.20 folded; $8.80 rolled), a color 46" X 28" map with an eight-page text; and "Map and Cross Section of the Sierra Nevada from Madera to the White Mountains, Central California" ($8 folded; $9.60 rolled), two full-color sheets with a four-page text. Also publishes Continent Ocean Transects and Continent Scale Maps as part of the Decade of North American Geology project. A catalog is available.

Gulf Publishing Co. (P.O. Box 2608, Houston, TX 77252; 713-529-4301) publishes two geologic maps: "The Breakup and Dispersion of Pangea" ($20; 30" X 40") and "Sinai Area Geological and Geomorphological Map" ($95; in two 38" X 20" sheets), created from Landsat imagery.

Mountain Press Publishing Co. (2016 Strand Ave., P.O. Box 2399, Missoula, MT 59806; 406-

728-1900) publishes Roadside Geology guides, giving a road-by-road study of geologic features as revealed from a car window; sketch maps appear throughout. The guides ($9.95 to $15.95 each) are available for Alaska, Arizona, Colorado, Idaho, Montana, New Mexico, New York, Northern California, Oregon, Pennsylvania, Texas, Utah, Vermont/New Hampshire, Virginia, Washington, Wyoming, and "Yellowstone Country."

National Geographic Society (17th & M sts. NW, Washington, DC 20036; 301-921-1200) sells "Earth's Dynamic Crust/Shaping of a Continent" ($7.95; 20005; 23" X 18"), a laminated map illustrating world geology and tectonics.

Omni Resources (1238 Anthony Rd., P.O. Box 2096, Burlington, NC 27216; 919-227-8300) is an excellent source for geologic maps of all types—bedrock geology maps, bouguer gravity maps, Quaternary geology maps, seismic maps, and tectonic maps of the U.S., states, and foreign countries. Selections include "Surficial Geology Map of Maine" ($8.95; 62-7105), "Magnetic Anomaly Map of South Australia" ($19.95; 64-1368), and "Seismotectonic Map of Iran/Afghanistan/Pakistan" ($15; 64-7820). Also available are geology maps of Bangladesh, Russia, and Slovenia, as well as detailed maps of much of Latin America. One noteworthy map is an "Archeological Map of Guatemala." A complete catalog is available.

Pt. Reyes National Seashore Association (Pt. Reyes National Seashore, Pt. Reyes, CA 94956; 415-663-1155) publishes a colorful 17" X 28" map, "Geology and Active Faults in the San Francisco Bay Area," showing the major fault lines as well as the four major rock types, color-coded by relative stability in an earthquake. The poster is $3 plus $2 postage; California residents add 22 cents sales tax.

Unipub (4611-F Assembly Dr., Lanham, MD 20706; 301-459-7666; 800-274-4888; 800-233-0504 in Canada) is the sole North American agent for the European Communities Office

and the exclusive U.S. agent for United Nations Educational, Scientific, and Cultural Organization (UNESCO) publications and maps. The selection varies from year to year; send for the latest catalog. Maps currently available include: "International Geological Map of Africa, 3rd ed.," published jointly by UNESCO and the Paris-based Commission for the Geographical Map of the World (six full-color sheets; $20 each); "International Geological Map of Europe" (49 sheets, each with a detailed legend, $25 or $30 each); and the "Geological World Map," a wall map consisting of three sheets drawn to a scale of 1:25,000,000. Polar, Atlantic, and Pacific regions each have their own sheet. Active volcanoes, faults, geological limits, overthrust, and subduction zones are represented, and colors identify the ages of major geological areas from the Jurassic to the Quaternary eras, as well as metamorphic and volcanic formations ($40).

Western GeoGraphics (Box 1984, Canon City, CO 81215; 719-275-8948) produces full-color state geologic highway maps for Colorado, Kansas, and Wyoming, and topographical maps of Colorado, Wyoming, Montana, Arizona, and New Mexico. The geologic highway maps ($6.95 each) are drawn to a scale of 1:1,000,000; sheet size is 24" X 37". The recreational maps ($3.95 each for Colorado and Wyoming, $2.95 each for western and eastern Montana) have a scale of 1 inch equals 12.5 miles on 24" X 37" or 24" X 33" sheets. Add $2 per order for folded maps or $3 for rolled maps.

Williams & Heintz Map Corp. (8119 Central Ave., Capitol Heights, MD 20743; 301-336-1144; 800-338-6228) sells "geologic portfolios" designed for teaching geology: Portfolio No. 1, "Physical Geology" ($8.50), consists of eight full-color geologic maps and sections, with accompanying text; Portfolio No. 2, "Historical Geology" ($8.50), consists of 13 full-color maps and text that cover the major geologic provinces of the United States; and Geologic Portfolio No. 3, "Physical Geology," consists of eight full-color bedrock and surficial geologic maps and text ($9.50). Another teaching package is Quadrangle Portfolio No. 1 ($5), containing four full-color geologic maps of four quadrangles with interesting geology, with accompanying text.

Williams & Heintz also produces and prints, but does not publish or sell, geologic maps. Examples include:

■ "New Mexico Highway Geologic Map" ($7 folded; $8.50 rolled), available from **New Mexico Geological Society, Inc.**, Campus Station, Socorro, NM 87801.
■ "Geologic Map of the Circum-Pacific Region, Antarctic Sheet, 1989," cat. 854 ($14), available from **AAPG Bookstore**, P.O. Box 979, Tulsa, OK 74101.
■ "Generalized Geologic Map of North Carolina, 1991" ($10.25), available from **North Carolina Geological Survey**, P.O. Box 27687, Raleigh, NC 27687.
■ "New York State Geological Highway Map 1990," educational leaflet 33 ($6.75), available from **New York State Geological Survey**, Publication Sales, 3140 CEC, New York State Geological Survey, Albany, NY 12230.
■ "Geology of the Coal-Bearing Portion of Tazewell North, Tip Top & Gary Quadrangles, Virginia, 1991," Pub. 110 ($6), available from **Virginia Div. of Mineral Resources**, P.O. Box 3667, Charlottesville, VA 22903.

M.P. Weiss (Dept. of Geology, Northern Illinois Univ., DeKalb, IL 60115; 815-753-1943) publishes "Map of Modern Reefs and Sediments of Antigua, West Indies" ($14 rolled; $11 folded), a full-color 27" X 40 1/2" map with descriptions and illustrations of bottom sediments and communities on the reverse side, and a record of changes over time. Also available is a 116-page guide, *Antigua* ($11), describing the bedrock geology, reefs, and island archaeology; a tourist map of the island is included. The guide and map are available together for $19.

■ **See also: "Emergency Information Maps," "Energy Maps," and "Natural Resource Maps."**

Natural Resource Maps

The modern world is paradoxically dependent on the natural world: The more technology we invent, the greater our need for resources to build or fuel this technology. From minerals to forests, natural gas to sunshine, all that the earth, sea, and air have to offer has been mapped, charted, and diagrammed.

The environmental movement of the past two decades, with its philosophy of conservation rather than depletion, led the way to a new consciousness about the Earth. "Use it or lose it" became "Save it or else." Today, forests that are harvested are simultaneously re-planted, "exotic" technologies such as solar and wind power are becoming commonplace, and the search for new sources of traditional energy has intensified. Maps often lead the way to finding and exploiting these resources wherever they lie—below the ground, beneath the ocean floor, or shining from above.

In 1871, when John Wesley Powell and his brother-in-law, Almon Harris Thompson, set out on a mapping survey of the American West, they were expected merely to fill in the details of an earlier, less-comprehensive map. But Powell had a new vision of the untamed land: He wanted to go beyond the precon-ceived notions of geologic and topographic mapping. Earlier maps had concentrated on geology for merely historical or industrial purposes. Topography was likewise treated with a narrow focus on the shape of the land and its suitability for agriculture and ranching. Powell believed that understanding the land and the way it was formed led to a deeper understanding of its usefulness for man. By surveying and mapping the land in relation to its ongoing development and specific uses, Powell predicted that future discovery and development of natural resources would be enhanced.

The Powell-Thompson maps are geologic landmarks, concentrating for the first time on mineral and soil development as well as studying the catalysts for the chosen path of a river or formation of a mountain. These studies shed new light on the search for and extraction of natural resources. One cartographic idea that Powell espoused but was never able to see carried out was the concept of "scientific classification" of the land. He believed that topographic maps were not descriptive enough in the nature of available resources; he wanted mappers to categorize the land in more specific terms of usefulness. Instead of "farm-land," for example, Powell believed maps should read "irrigation land" or "pasturage land," while mining lands should be labeled with the type of mineral or coal beneath the surface rather than just the generic term "mining." Although Powell's idea did not catch on at the time, his concept of mapping land classification now plays an important role in the exploration and use of natural resources.

The mapping of natural resources in America is an ongoing process for both government and commercial cartographers. As older resources are depleted, new ones found, and different methods of retrieval created, there are maps made to reflect the changes. And because even greater care is taken to protect the environment and nurture its riches, there will always be work for mappers of natural resources.

Energy and mining companies, farmers, builders, foresters, conservationists, and anyone else interested in land use find natural resource maps invaluable. The diagramming of natural resources includes solar-energy atlases and forest, oil-field, and mineral, coal, and gas investigations maps. There are maps of past, present, and potential energy sources, as well as maps detailing lands where energy explora-tion is prohibited. These and other maps are available from the government and from selected commercial organizations.

Northern portion of the "California Water Map," published by the Water Education Foundation. ©1987, revised 1989.

GOVERNMENT SOURCES, UNITED STATES

Fish and Wildlife Service. In 1977, the Fish and Wildlife Service began the National Wetlands Inventory in an effort to classify and map America's remaining wetlands. As part of the National Wetlands Inventory Program, the USGS has been mapping the marshes, swamps, ponds, and bogs of America, which currently represent about 5 percent of the total land surface of the lower 48 states. Of the 215 million acres of wetlands that originally existed in the conterminous U.S., the Fish and Wildlife Service estimates that there are only about 99 million acres left. More than 25,000 composite and overlay maps of the wetlands have been created

to date and are used for a variety of purposes, including zoning, flood-hazard planning, waste treatment, and water-quality planning. Information about NWI maps is available through Earth Science Information Center offices.

National Geophysical Data Center. NGDC produces maps depicting geothermal resources in the U.S., such as "Geothermal Energy in Alaska and Hawaii" ($10 folded), "Geothermal Resources of Kansas" ($10 folded), and "Geothermal Energy in the Western United States" ($10 folded; $15 rolled).

Tennessee Valley Authority. TVA has a mapping services branch that creates maps and charts for the Tennessee Valley region, including:

■ "Geologic Map of Georgia" ($3.50, plus $2 for mailing tube and $1 postage), 42" X 58".
■ "Mineral Resources of the Tennessee Valley Region" ($4, plus $2 for mailing tube and $1 postage). This 1970 map measures 35" X 49" and is printed in full color.
■ "Mineral Resources and Mineral Industries of Tennessee" ($2.50, plus $2 for mailing tube and $1 for postage). This 40" X 66" map illustrates the state's rich lode of mineral resources.

Other government sources of natural resource maps include state, county, and local departments of natural resources, ecology, forestry, and mining (see Appendix A for addresses).

U.S. Geological Survey. USGS's National Atlas Program includes the following maps on natural resources:

■ "Major Forest Types" ($3.10; US00420-38077-AM-NA-07M-00), a 1967 map showing the distribution of eastern, western, Hawaiian, and Alaskan forest and nonforest lands.
■ "Networks of Ecological Research Areas, 1983" ($3.10; US00725-38077-AO-NA-07M-00) shows the location of research areas designated by public and private agencies as secure sites for basic and applied studies of natural processes.
■ "Principal Lands Where Exploration and Development of Mineral Resources Are Restricted" ($3.10; US00421-38077-AP-NA-07M-00). This 1981

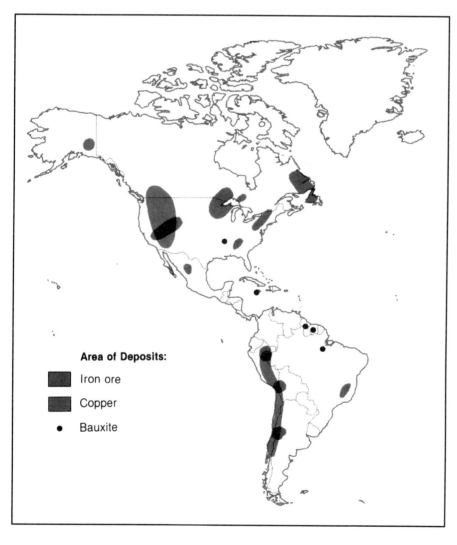

Area of Deposits:

■ Iron ore

■ Copper

● Bauxite

Portion of map showing mineral deposits of iron ore, copper, and bauxite, from the State Department's Atlas of United States Foreign Relations.

map shows areas of 5,000 acres or more where mineral development is prohibited or severely, moderately, or slightly restricted. Alaska and Hawaii are included on the reverse.

USGS also produces coal, oil, and gas investigations maps (see "Energy Maps"), as well as a series of Mineral Investigations maps and studies. Write to the nearest USGS Earth Science Information Center for listings of available maps and surveys (see Appendix B).

GOVERNMENT SOURCES, CANADA

Canada Map Office (615 Booth St., Ottawa, Ontario K1A 0E9; 613-952-7000) distributes two maps, both from *The National Atlas of Canada, 5th ed.*: "Distribution of Wetlands" (MCR 4107), showing the regional occurrence of wetlands, which cover 14 percent of the country; and "Wetland Regions" (MCR 4108), illustrating the types of wetlands found in Canada, and including descriptions of the ecology of major wetland types in each region. Other maps from the *Atlas* include maps of the entire country depicting "Coal" (MCR 4053) and "Mineral Commodity Flows" (MCR 4081). The maps, $8.40 Canadian each, are available in either English or French.

Maps Alberta (Land Information Services Div., Main fl., Brittania Bldg., 703 6th Ave. SW, Calgary, Alberta T2P 0T9; 403-297-7389) distributes a variety of natural resource maps of Alberta as part of the *Alberta Resource and Economic Atlas*, including: "Coal" (1984), "Movement of Coal Within Canada" (1983), "Forest Industry Development Area" (1984), "Potential Annual Forest Yield" (1984), "Metallic Minerals" (no date), "Minerals for Chemical and Metallurgical Industries" (1982), "Minerals for Construction Materials Industries" (1982), "Main Pipelines, Refineries and Gas Plants" (1984), "Movement of Oil and Gas" (1983), and "Oil, Gas and Oil Sands" (1984).

Maps Alberta also produces Aggregate Resource Maps, a series of 13 maps showing the distribution of major gravel deposits in the province, available in two scales: 1:250,000 (code 217), and 1:50,000 (code 216). Cost is $3.50 Canadian each; $22\frac{1}{2}$" X 29".

Also available is an "Oil Sands Agreements Map" ($7.50 Canadian; code 905; 40" X 28"), showing oil sands leases and dispositions.

COMMERCIAL SOURCES

Several commercial map publishers and geologic organizations produce maps of natural resources:

Circum-Pacific Map Project (U.S. Geological Survey, MS-952, 345 Middlefield Rd., Menlo Park, CA 94025; 415-329-4002) is an international cooperative effort between the Circum-Pacific Council for Energy and Mineral Resources and the USGS to assemble and publish new geological and geophysical maps of the Pacific Ocean Basin and surrounding land areas. The widely acclaimed maps are intended to show the relation of geology, tectonics, and crustal dynamics to known energy and mineral resources, and also to aid in exploration for new resources. As of mid 1992, 39 map sheets had been published, 35 by the American Association of Petroleum Geologists and available from the AAPG Bookstore (P.O. Box 979, Tulsa, OK 74101) at a close-out-sale price of $7 each. These include a Mineral Resources series that depicts mineral deposits by colored symbols showing location, geologic or geometric class, size of deposit, and age of mineralization, and an Energy Resources series that shows oil and gas fields, oil shale, tar sand, coal deposits according to rank, geothermal convection systems, and heat flow. Since 1990, publication of the series has been by the U.S. Geological Survey (USGS, Map Distribution, Box 25286, Federal Center, Denver, CO 80225). As of spring 1992, four maps had been completed, and 21 more were in various stages of compilation or production. Costs range from $3.10 to $6.70 each, depending on number of sheets and pages of explanatory notes. Titles include "Energy Resources Map, Southeast Quadrant, Sheet 1 and 2" (CP39) and

"Geodynamic Map, Arctic Sheet" (CP38). Contact USGS Map Distribution for costs and new publications.

Omni Resources (1238 Anthony Rd., P.O. Box 2096, Burlington, NC 27216; 919-227-8300) distributes natural resource maps for various countries, including the U.S. and Canada. Offerings include:

■ "China—Coal Map" ($29.95; 64-4040), a 34" X 23½," generalized map showing newly discovered deposits, mines, and processing plants.
■ "Mozambique—Mineral Map" ($14.95; 65-02940; 29½," X 40") illustrates the major ore deposits of metals, gemstones, gas, and uranium and comes with a 60-page booklet.
■ "Czechoslovakia—Mineral Deposits Map" ($18.95; 64-4640; 69" X 38"), two sheets depicting mineral deposits on a geologic base map with Slavic legend.
■ "Wyoming—Mineral Deposits Map" ($9.95; 63-0241; 49½," X 29½,"), a three-color map illustrating 176 deposits and including a list of 92 references.
■ "Nevada—Gold Districts Map" ($5.45; 62-8044; 29" X 33"), locating the major and minor gold districts of the state.
■ "Colorado—Geothermal Resources Map" ($3.95; 62-5785; 41½," X 53") illustrates known geothermal areas, thermal areas and springs, and heat-flow values.

Water Education Foundation (717 K St., Ste. 517, Sacramento, CA 95814; 916-444-6240) produces the "California Water Map," a 28" X

36" colorful map featuring natural and man-made water routes in the state ($7.50), and the "Colorado River Water Map," a 32" X 38" map depicting the seven Western states that share Colorado River water ($8.50).

Williams & Heintz Map Corp. (8119 Central Ave., Capitol Heights, MD 20743; 301-336-1144) produces but does not sell geologic and mineral maps (see also "Geologic Maps"). Examples of its resource maps include:

■ "Groundwater Vulnerability Regions of Iowa, 1991," Special Map, Series 11 ($6.05), from **Iowa Dept. of Natural Resources**, Geological Survey Bureau, 123 N. Capitol St., Iowa City, IA 52242.
■ "Recharge Potential of Louisiana Aquifers, 1989," free from **Louisiana Geological Survey**, P.O. Box G, University Station, Baton Rouge, LA 70893.
■ "Mineral Resources of West Virginia" ($9 folded; $10 rolled), from **West Virginia Geological Survey**, Publications Sales, P.O. Box 879, Morgantown, WV 26507.
■ "Availability of Federal Mineral Land Compared With Areas Favorable for Selected Locatable Minerals in New Mexico, 1989," Special Pub., Plate 1, available free from Office of Public Information, MS 1041, Columbia Plaza, 2401 E St. NW, Washington, DC 20241.

■ **See also: "Agriculture Maps," "Energy Maps," "Geologic Maps," and "Recreation Maps."**

Topographic Maps

A topographic map is a line-and-symbol representation of natural and selected artificial features plotted to a definite scale. "Topos," as they are often called, show the shape and elevation of the terrain in precise detail by using contour lines. Topos may show the location and shape of objects as big as mountains and as small as creeks and dirt roads.

The many uses of topographic maps make them the workhorses of cartography. They are of prime importance in planning airports, highways, dams, pipelines, and almost any type of building. They play an essential role in ecological studies and environmental control, geologic research, water-quality research, conservation, and reforestation. And, of course, they are widely used by hikers, hunters, bikers, and other outdoors enthusiasts. Topographic maps are also used as the basis for a wide range of other cartographic products, from aeronautical charts to road maps.

Topo maps come in a variety of scales, usually stated as a ratio or fraction showing the measurement of the map in relation to the land it covers (see "Map Scale" for more on this). In a 1:24,000 (or 1/24,000) topo map, for example, one unit (an inch, centimeter, or whatever) on the map equals 24,000 of the same unit on the ground.

Map scale is the basic classification of topographic maps, and each scale series fills a range of map needs:

■ Large-scale maps, such as 1:24,000, are useful for highly developed or rural areas where detailed information is needed for engineering planning or similar purposes. Large-scale topo maps are the ones used most often by hikers and campers and for use in other recreational activities.
■ Intermediate-scale maps, ranging from 1:50,000 to 1:100,000, cover larger areas and are

Portion of 1:24,000 topographic map of "Mt. Desert Island & Acadia National Park" in Maine, showing area around Northeast Harbor and Seal Harbor. Published by DeLorme Mapping Co.

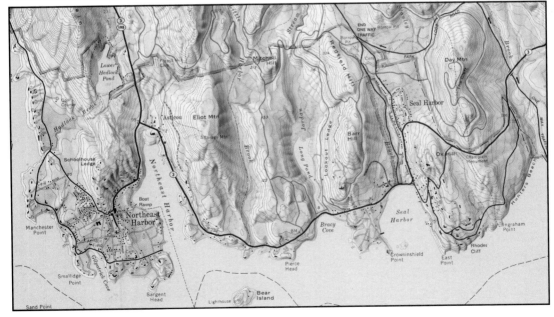

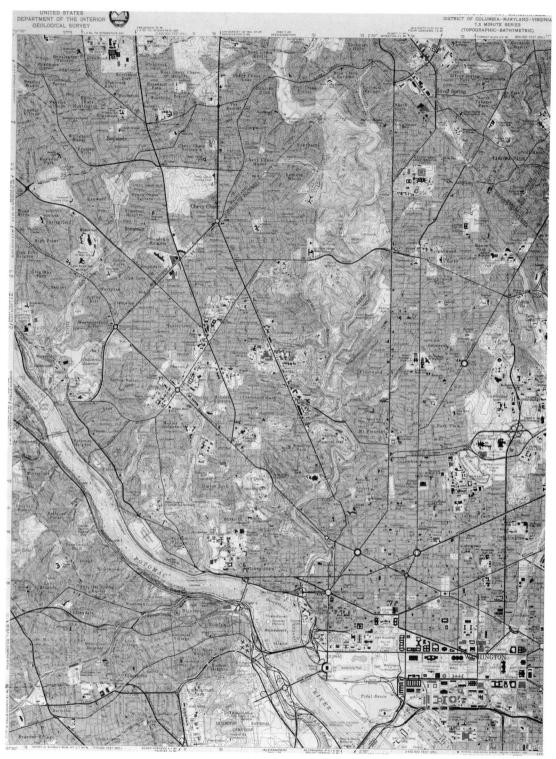

USGS 1:24,000-scale topographic map of "Washington West Quadrangle," showing portions of Washington, D.C., Maryland, and Virginia.

best suited for land management and planning. ■ Small-scale maps—1:250,000, 1:500,000, and 1:1,000,000—cover very large areas, on a single sheet, that are useful for comprehensive views of extensive projects or for regional planning.

(See page 128 for examples of topo maps covering the same area at different scales.)

For more than a century, the **U.S. Geological Survey** has been creating and revising topographic maps for the entire country at a variety of scales. There are about 60,000 USGS-produced topo maps, covering every square inch of U.S. territory. Each map covers a specific quadrangle (or "quad"), defined as a four-sided area bounded by parallels of latitude and meridians of longitude. Generally, adjacent maps of the same quadrangle can be combined to form a single large map.

USGS produces five series of topographic maps, each covering a different-size quad:

■ In the $7\frac{1}{2}$-minute series, each quad covers an area $7\frac{1}{2}$ minutes square (a minute is one-sixtieth of a degree in latitude and longitude). In this series, the scale is 1:24,000 (1:25,000 for Alaska and 1:20,000 for Puerto Rico); one inch represents about 2,000 feet, and each quad covers about 49 to 71 square miles.
■ In the 15-minute series, each quad covers an area 15 minutes square. In this series, the scale is 1:62,500 (1:63,360 for Alaska); one inch represents about one mile, and each quad covers about 197 to 282 square miles.
■ In the intermediate-scale quadrangle series, each quad covers an area 30 minutes by one degree. In this series, the scale is 1:100,000; one inch represents about $1\frac{1}{2}$ miles, and each quad covers about 1,145 to 2,167 square miles.
■ In the U.S. 1:250,000 series, each quad covers an area one degree by two degrees. In this series, as the name indicates, the scale is 1:250,000; one inch represents about four miles, and each quad covers about 4,580 to 8,669 square miles. Maps of Alaska and Hawaii vary from these standards.
■ In the International Map of the World series,

each quad covers an area four by six degrees. In this series, the scale is 1:1,000,000; one inch represents about 16 miles, and each quad covers about 73,734 to 102,759 square miles.

For comparison purposes, the area covered by one 1-by-2-degree map requires four 30-by-60-minute maps, 32 15-minute maps, 64 $7\frac{1}{2}$-by-15-minute maps, and 128 $7\frac{1}{2}$-minute maps.

When it comes to topos, the basic topographic map is just the tip of the cartographic iceberg. USGS also produces other special-purpose map data. These include:

■ **Orthophotomaps,** produced for selected topographic quadrangles, show land features primarily by color-enhanced photographic images that have been processed to show detail in true position. Orthophotomaps may or may not include contours. Because imagery naturally depicts an area in a more true-to-life manner than on a conventional topographic map, the orthophotomap provides an excellent portrayal of extensive areas of sand, marsh, or flat agricultural areas.
■ **Orthophotoquads** are a basic type of photoimage map prepared in a quadrangle map format. They can be produced quickly because they are printed in shades of gray without image enhancement or cartographic symbols. Orthophotoquads are valuable as map substitutes in unmapped areas and as complements to existing line maps.
■ A number of county maps at scales of 1:50,000 or 1:100,000 have been prepared cooperatively with some states. The maps are multicolored, show political boundaries, complete road networks, and a variety of topographical and cultural features. A series of 1:100,000-scale quad maps provides much of the detail shown on larger-scale maps yet covers enough geographic area to be useful as base maps for county-wide and regional study.
■ State maps at scales of 1:500,000 and 1:1,000,000 are available for all states except Alaska and Hawaii, which are covered by state maps at other scales. There are also shaded-relief editions for many states.

■ The National Park series, at various scales, covers many parks, monuments, and historic sites. Many of these maps are available with shaded-relief overprinting, in which the topography is made to appear three-dimensional by the use of shadow effects.

■ U.S. maps are available in sizes and scales ranging from letter size (1:16,500,000) to a two-sheet wall map (1:2,500,000). The complete series includes two maps, one at 1:6,000,000 and one at 1:10,000,000, that show all 50 states in their correct position and scale.

■ USGS is also engaged in a mapping program for Antarctica. The Antarctic maps are published at several scales, primarily 1:250,000, with shaded relief.

Although most topographic maps are produced by the USGS's National Mapping Program, other federal agencies—including the **Defense Mapping Agency**, **National Ocean Survey**, **Tennessee Valley Authority**, and the **National Park Service**—also prepare topographic maps as part of their regular activities, although such maps have been incorporated into the topographic map series published by USGS. They may also be obtained from the producing agencies (see Appendix B).

Colors, lines, and symbols. More than on most other map types, symbols are the graphic language of topographic maps. Color plays a key role, too:

■ symbols for water features are shown in blue;

■ man-made objects such as roads, railroads, buildings, transmission lines, and political boundaries are shown in black;

■ green distinguishes wooded areas from clearings;

■ red represents or emphasizes the more important roads, route numbers, fence lines, land grants, and the lines of townships, ranges, and sections of states subdivided by public-land surveys;

■ heavily built-up areas larger than three-fourths of a square mile are given a pink tint;

■ features added from aerial photographs during map revision are purple;

■ the contour lines that show the shape and elevation of the land surface are brown.

Color is just the beginning. The type of line on a topographic map also provides valuable information. For example, one type of black line designates national boundaries, another shows state boundaries, and still others indicate counties, parishes, civil townships, precincts, towns, barrios, incorporated cities, villages, hamlets, reservations, small parks, cemeteries, airports, and land grants. Additional black lines denote certain types of roads, trails, railroads, telephone lines, bridges, and tunnels. Similarly, there are a dozen or so different forms of blue lines that designate types of rivers, streams, aqueducts, and canals.

Symbols are another key feature. Some topo map symbols are "pictographs," resembling the objects they represent—a pick and ax designates a mine or quarry, for example; an exposed boat wreck appears as a partially submerged vessel.

All told, there are about 140 different topographic map lines and symbols. A complete directory of colors, lines, and symbols is contained in a free brochure, "Topographic Map Symbols," available by mail from USGS distribution centers. You may pick up the brochure in person from the distribution centers, the USGS's 14 sales counters, or the many commercial dealers that sell USGS topographic maps.

GOVERNMENT SOURCES, UNITED STATES

U.S. Geological Survey. The USGS distributes several indexes to its topographic maps, including "Index to Topographic and Other Map Coverage and Catalog of Topographic and Other Published Maps," available for each state; "Status and Progress of Topographic Mapping, U.S."; "Index to USGS/DMA 1:50,000-Scale, 15-Minute Mapping"; "Index to Intermediate-Scale Mapping/Index to County Mapping"; and "Index to USGS Topographic Map Coverage of National Park System." The USGS also distributes the informative pamphlet, "Topographic Map Symbols."

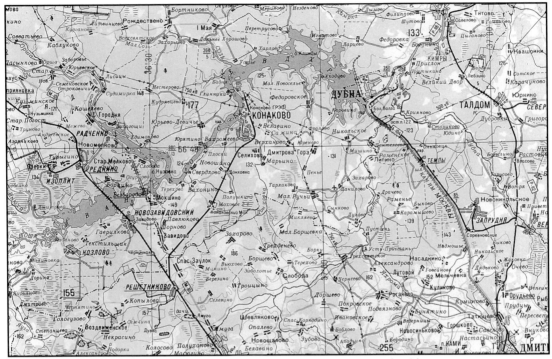

Portion of topographic of Russia, showing the Zagorsk quadrangle, north of Moscow. Distributed by Omni Resources.

GOVERNMENT SOURCES, CANADA

Canada Map Office (615 Booth St., Ottawa, Ontario K1A 0E9; 613-952-7000) distributes topographic maps covering Canada and its territories, as part of the National Topographic System series. Maps are available in various scales; indexes are available.

Manitoba Natural Resources (Surveys and Mapping Branch, 1007 Century St., Winnipeg, Manitoba R3H 0W4; 204-945-6666) distributes National Topographic System maps of Manitoba, in 1:50,000 and 1:250,000 scales. A pamphlet is available.

Maps Alberta (Land Information Services Div., Main fl., Brittania Bldg., 703 6th Ave. SW, Calgary, Alberta T2P 0T9; 403-297-7389) distributes various 1:250,000-scale topographic maps as part of the Provincial Access series ($4.43 Canadian each; code 201), as well as maps from the National Topographic series ($7.80 each). A catalog is available.

Québec Ministère de l'Energie et des Resources (Photocartothèque Québecoise, 1995 Blvd. Charest Ouest, Sainte-Foy, Quebec G1N 4H9; 418-643-7704) sells topographic maps for areas in Quebec drawn to 1:20,000 and 1:12,000 scales. An index, "Repertoire des Cartes, Plans, et Photographies Aeriennes," is available.

Saskatchewan Property Management Corp. (Central Survey and Mapping Agency, Distribution Center, 2045 Broad St., 1st fl., Regina, Saskatchewan S4P 3V7; 306-787-2799) distributes large-scale, detailed, color topographic maps of the major Saskatchewan cities and the immediate surrounding areas, available in the following scales: 1:25,000, 1:50,000, and 1:250,000 ($7.80 Canadian each, plus $4.50 handling per order).

COMMERCIAL SOURCES

CTM/Zia Maps (P.O. Box 4982, Boulder, CO 80306; 303-444-1670) produces a number of 3-D informational prints designed for framing and to cross-reference with topographic maps. These include:

■ "View to the West" (7" X 36"; $11), a horizon view of the Rocky Mountains as seen from above Limon, Colorado. Using digital data and photographs, it shows the Front Range to the Continental Divide, naming all the primary peaks and passes, many with elevations in feet and meters.
■ "Rocky Mountain National Park" (22" X 37$^1/_2$"; $10), a dramatic view of the park looking from the northwest to the southwest as seen from 50,000 feet above Fort Collins, Colorado. Elevations are shown in 1,000-foot color gradations.
■ "Colorado Front Range" (31" X 15"; $16) views the intersection of the Rocky Mountains and the Great Plains looking north from the Colorado/New Mexico state line to mid-Wyoming as seen from 90,000 feet above Maxwell, New Mexico. Primary highways and vital roads are shown linking the major incorporated population centers of the Front Range and the mountains. County lines show an interesting dissection of the landscape into geopolitical boundaries. In addition, the map shows all primary drainages and several major reservoirs.

DeLorme Mapping Co. (P.O. Box 298, Freeport, ME 04032; 207-865-4171) produces highly detailed topographic maps of recreation areas in New England, such as "Allagash & St. John Map and Guide" ($4.95), "Mount Desert Island/Acadia National Park" ($6.95), and "Trail Map & Guide to the White Mountain National Forest" ($6.95). DeLorme also publishes a 4' X 6' "Maine Wall Map," a laminated topographic and political map ($95).

Green Trails, Inc. (P.O. Box 1932, Bothell, WA 98041; 206-485-9144) publishes topographic maps for Washington State's Olympic Peninsula, the North Cascades, the Central Cascades, the South Cascades, and Northern Oregon. The color maps are numbered with a system compatible with the Uniform Map

System, which is used by search and rescue groups. Green Trails maps are available in a variety of retail outlets in the Pacific Northwest; a list of dealers and further information is available.

Omni Resources (1238 Anthony Rd., P.O. Box 2096, Burlington, NC 27216; 919-227-8300) distributes USGS 1:24,000/1:25,000 topographic maps for most states, as well as all 1:250,000 maps for the United States and Canada and all of Central America at 1:50,000; Canadian National Park topographic maps; and 1:50,000 and/or 1:200,000 maps of Eastern Europe, including Bulgaria, Czechoslovakia, Estonia, eastern Germany, Hungary, Latvia, Lithuania, and Poland. A sample of other titles available includes:

■ "Benin—Topographic Map" ($9.95; 64-2050).
■ "Cameroon—Topographic Quadrangle Maps" ($7.95 each; 64-2565). Seven of these bilingual maps are currently available.
■ "Norway—Topographic Quadrangle Map" ($7.95 each; set of 17 sheets, $99.95), a series offering complete coverage of Norway.
■ "Hungary—Topographic County Maps," by Cartographia ($6.95 each; set of 19 sheets, $76), 19 sheets that offer complete coverage of Hungary, county by county.

Raven Maps & Images (34 N. Central, Medford, OR 97501; 503-773-1436; 800-237-0798) produces 20 shaded-relief maps of states in the Western U.S. and the Northeast. The maps ($20 paper; $45 laminated) show towns, roads, and railroads, as well as geographical features. Maps are available for Alaska, Arizona, California, Colorado, Hawaii, Idaho, Maine, Massachusetts/Connecticut/Rhode Island, Montana, Nevada, New Mexico, New York, Ohio, Oregon, Pennsylvania/New Jersey, Utah, Vermont/New Hampshire, Washington, and Wyoming.

Trails Illustrated (P.O. Box 3610, Evergreen, CO 80439; 303-670-3457) publishes more than 100 topographic maps of recreational areas in

Colorado, Utah, as well as of more than 40 national parks. The waterproof, tearproof maps are updated annually and are available in retail stores or can be ordered directly. Trails Illustrated produces the following series:

■ Colorado Series ($7 each) includes maps for Indian Peaks, Tarryall Mountains, Poudre River, Steamboat Springs, Flat Tops, Maroon Bells, Kebler Pass West, and Weminuche/Chicago Basin.
■ National Park and Recreation Areas Series ($7 each), including Rocky Mountain National Park, Sequoia/Kings Canyon National Park, Grand Canyon National Park, Glacier/Waterton National Park, and Dinosaur National Monument.
■ Cross Country Series ($5 each) for Frisco-Breckenridge, Nederland-Georgetown, Vail-Leadville, and Aspen-Carbondale.
■ Utah Series ($7.95 each), including Timpanogos Peak, Dark Canyon, Fish Lake, and Grand Gulch.
■ Specialty Series ($5.95 each), including Triple David Peak, Old Faithful, Longs/McHenrys Peak, Mammoth Hot Springs, and Yellowstone Lake.

University of Hawaii Press (Univ. of Hawaii at Manoa, 2840 Kolowalu St., Honolulu, HI 96822; 808-956-8255) publishes the Reference Maps of the Islands of Hawai'i series by James A. Bier. The full-color, shaded-relief topographic maps available are: "Hawai'i" ($2.95; 25" X 31"); "Kaua'i" ($2.25; 22" X 15$\frac{1}{2}$"); "Maui" ($2.95; 24" X 18$\frac{1}{2}$"); "Moloka'i-Lana'i" ($2.95; 20" X 17"); and "O'ahu" ($2.95; 29" X 25"). Also available is James Bier's two-color, shaded-relief topographic "Islands of Samoa: Reference Maps of Tutuila, Manu'a, 'Upolu, and Savai'i" ($2.95; 35" X 18").

Warren Communications (P.O. Box 620635, San Diego, CA 92162; 619-236-0984) distributes topographic maps produced by the Mexican government. Warren sells the maps only on a wholesale basis; however, they can be pur-chased from **The Map Center**, 2611 University Ave., San Diego, CA 92104; 619-291-3830.

Wilderness Press (2440 Bancroft Way, Berke-ley, CA 94704; 510-843-8080) publishes a series of topographic maps to popular hiking areas in California. The maps contain updated changes in trails, roads, creeks, lakes, meadows, contour lines, and other features. Most maps are at a scale of 1:62,500 and measure 18" X 21"; all have a handy map-grid-and-index system. An added feature is the Polyart 2 plastic stock on which the maps are printed, which is tear-, water-, and grease-resistant, and easy to write on. Titles available include: "Devils Postpile," "Hetch Hetchy Reservoir," "Lassen Volcanic National Park and Vicinity," "Mt. Goddard," "Tuolomne Meadows," and "Yosemite National Park and Vicinity."

BOOKS ON READING TOPOGRAPHIC MAPS

Here are four titles on using maps and compasses that are especially geared to reading topographic maps; all include sample maps and explanations of map symbols:

■ *The Basic Essentials of Map and Compass*, by Cliff Jacobson (ICS Books, One Tower Plaza, 107 E. 89th Ave., Merrillville, IN 46410; 219-769-0585). 1988. $4.95 paper.
■ *Be Expert With Map & Compass: The Orienteering Handbook*, by Bjorn Kjellstrom (Charles Scribner's Sons, 866 Third Ave., New York, NY 10022; 212-702-2000). 1976. $14.95 paper.
■ *Land Navigation Handbook—The Sierra Club Guide to Map and Compass*, by W.S. Kals (Sierra Club Books, dist. by Random House, 201 E. 50th St., New York, NY 10022; 301-848-1900; 800-726-0600). 1983. $12.
■ *Outward Bound Map and Compass Handbook*, by Glenn Randall (Lyons & Burford, 31 W. 21st St., New York, NY 10010; 212-620-9580). 1989. $8.95.

■ **See also: "Tourism Maps and Guides."**

Wildlife Maps

Ah, wilderness! While we daily toil and play in our concrete-and-glass jungles, wildlife, by and large, has been relegated to a relative handful of sanctuaries, refuges, and other protective enclaves. Thanks largely to the federal government and an array of environmental groups, though, there is plenty of wildlife left, although the number of endangered species increases daily. Campers, bikers, hikers, botanists, entomologists, ornithologists, and zoologists are among those who use wildlife maps to keep track of Mother Nature.

The federal government, through the **Fish and Wildlife Service** (part of the Department of the Interior), is landlord to more than 90 million acres of wildlife habitat—home to more than 1,200 species of mammals, birds, reptiles, amphibians, and fish—the majority of which is in national wildlife refuges. These are lands where the only shooting permitted is done with a camera, where winged, finned, and furred creatures reign, and where humans are mere guests. The Fish and Wildlife Service administers these lands and provides maps, many of them free, to the public for each of its holdings. The **National Park Service** and the **U.S. Forest Service** also provide maps for the lands, rich with flora and fauna, that they administer.

State, county, and city governments are also good sources of wildlife maps, especially in regions where there is an abundance of locally protected forest and game land. Write to the appropriate conservation board or fish-and-game bureau to learn what maps are available (see Appendix A).

As for foreign wildlife, the travel and tourism bureaus in some countries known for their unusual wildlife (including Australia and many African nations) provide wilderness maps to visitors, as do privately run game parks both in the United States and abroad.

Other sources for wildlife maps include many of the organizations that promote conservation and protection of the environment, and scientific associations that study various species (although these are often technical and available only to members). Zoological parks and museums can also help locate wildlife maps; if there's nothing in their bookstores and gift shops, check with a curator or resident expert.

See "Recreation Maps" for sources of hunting and fishing maps.

Government Sources, United States

Fish and Wildlife Service. In 1977, the Fish and Wildlife Service began the National Wetlands Inventory in an effort to classify and map America's remaining wetlands. As part of the National Wetlands Inventory Program, the USGS has been mapping the marshes, swamps, ponds and bogs of America, which currently represent about 5 percent of the total land surface of the lower 48 states. In 1984, a report was published on the status and trends of our nation's wetlands from the mid-1950s to mid-1970s. Of the 215 million acres of wetlands that originally existed in the contermi- nous U.S., the Fish and Wildlife Service estimates that there were only about 105.9 million acres left in the mid-1970s. In 1991, the status and trends report was updated, and covered the mid-1970s to mid-1980s. In the mid-1980s, an estimated 103.3 million acres of wetlands remained. More than 25,000 compos- ite and overlay maps of the wetlands have been created to date, and are used for a variety of purposes, including town planning, waste treatment, zoning, flood-hazard planning, and water-quality planning. Information about NWI and the maps are available through Earth Science Information Center offices. The Fish and Wildlife Service also has free maps and brochures of wildlife refuges and fish hatcher-

Portion of "Wildlife Map of Acadia National Park" in Maine, showing area around Northeast Harbor and Seal Harbor. Published by American Nature Maps.

ies under federal protection. They are available at the locations themselves or by writing to the service's Division of Realty at the Washington, D.C., headquarters. The maps, which measure 8½" X 11", are black-and-white diagrams showing boundaries, wilderness areas, refuge headquarters, and driving directions from surrounding areas. Also available are three U.S. maps showing the land under the Fish and Wildlife Service's jurisdiction. The free maps, which are available on 8½" X 11" or 17" X 22" sheets, are titled "National Wildlife Refuge System," "National Fish and Wildlife Management Areas," and "National Fish Hatcheries and Fishery Assistance Stations." The U.S. maps, which are black-and-white with red lines denoting regional boundaries, are updated annually.

Government Printing Office. GPO offers wildlife maps and atlases, including:

■ "National Wildlife Refuges: A Visitor's Guide" ($1; S/N 024-010-00690-1), a 1991 map of the U.S. showing locations of all national wildlife refuges, including names, addresses, and descriptions of available activities.
■ *Gulf of Mexico Coastal and Ocean Zones Strategic Assessment: Data Atlas* ($138; S/N 003-017-00523-2), a 1985 atlas that includes 71 maps covering 73 species of living marine resources, as well as maps of physical environments, biotic environments, economic activities, environmental quality, and jurisdictions.

Tennessee Valley Authority. TVA has created a series of topographic maps of wildlife and game refuge areas in the Tennessee Valley region. The maps illustrate management boundaries, interior trails and roads, checking stations, and private lands within the TVA boundary. Available maps are:

■ "Catoosa Wildlife Management Area" ($2).
■ "Chuck Swan Wildlife Management Area" ($1.50).
■ "Prentiss Cooper Wildlife Management Area" ($1.50).
■ "Tellico Wildlife Management Area" ($2).
■ "Ocoee Wildlife Management Area" ($2).
■ "AEDC Wildlife Management Area" ($1.50).
■ "Fall Creek Wildlife Management Area" ($1.50).

There's a $1 handling charge for orders up to $10.

U.S. Geological Survey. USGS produces a series of topographic maps of the National Park System that includes maps of wildlife preserves and refuges under the care of the federal government. The "Index to USGS Topographic Map Coverage of the National Park System," a foldout map pinpointing park and wildlife areas covered in the topographic program, is available free from the USGS (see "Recreation Maps" and "Topographic Maps" for more information). The maps in the National Park series cost $4 each and are drawn at various scales; some parks require more than one sheet. Also available from USGS is a series of Coastal Ecological Inventory Maps ($4 each) that vividly illustrate the ecological setting, including flora and fauna, of the North American coastline. Maps are available for each major ecological coastal area.

GOVERNMENT SOURCES, CANADA
Canada Map Office (615 Booth St., Ottawa, Ontario K1A 0E9; 613-952-7000) distributes two maps from *The National Atlas of Canada,* 5th ed., "Distribution of Wetlands" (MCR 4107), showing the regional occurrence of wetlands, which cover 14 percent of the country; and "Wetland

U.S. *Fish and Wildlife Service's* "National Wildlife Refuges" *map.*

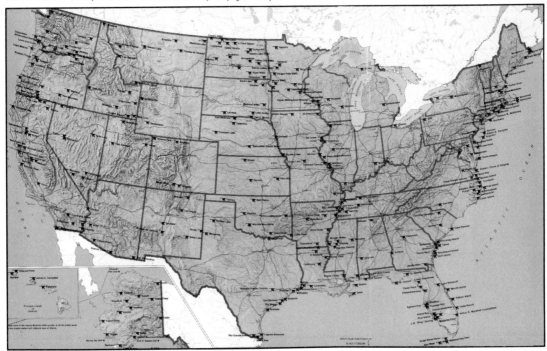

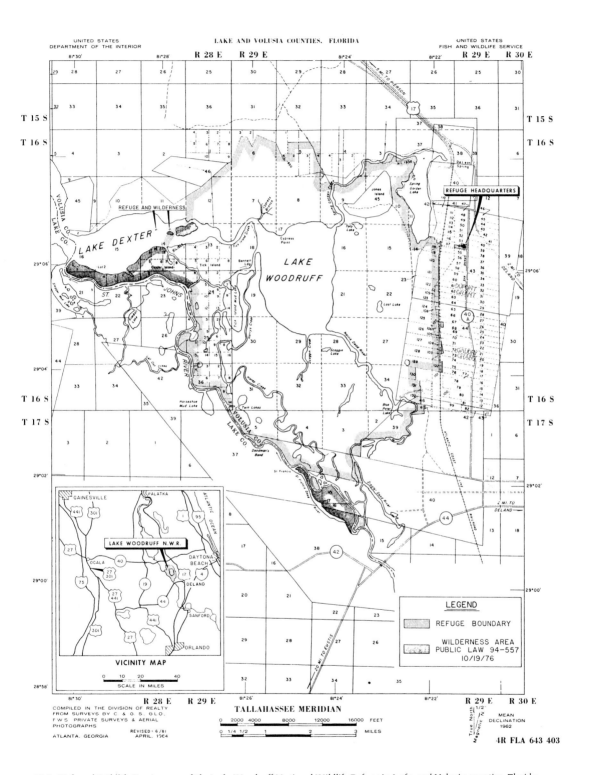

U.S. Fish and Wildlife Service map of the Lake Woodruff National Wildlife Refuge in Lake and Volusia counties, Florida.

Regions" (MCR 4108), illustrating the types of wetlands found in Canada, and including descriptions of the ecology of major wetland types in each region. The maps are $5.50 Canadian each.

Maps Alberta (Land Information Services Div., Main fl., Brittania Bldg., 703 6th Ave. SW, Calgary, Alberta T2P 0T9; 403-297-7389) distributes a "Canada Land Inventory" booklet ($6.80 Canadian; code 481), a survey of land capability designed for resource planning relating to agriculture, forestry, recreation, and wildlife. Maps depicting waterfowl wildlife as well as those showing wildlife ungulates (hoofed animals) are available in five-color paper or diazo for $2.91 Canadian each (code 482). An index of the maps is available upon request.

COMMERCIAL SOURCES
American Nature Maps (11620 Ivystone Ct., Ste. 201, Reston, VA 22091; 703-476-0378) produces wildlife maps for national parks. The maps provide complete listings of birds, mammals, reptiles, etc., and their locations within each park. Also depicted are prominent viewing sites, fall-color areas, ranger stations, campgrounds, and trails. Titles include "Wildlife Map of the Great Smoky Mountains National Park" ($4.95), "Wildlife Map of Acadia National Park" ($5.95), and "Wildlife Map of Yellowstone National Park" ($5.95).

Gabelli U.S. (1228 West Ave. #711, Miami Beach, FL 33139; 305-532-6956) distributes "The World of Wild Animals" map, which shows almost 200 animals—from the well-known to the lesser-known—in their natural environments. The 40" X 30" map is available in paper ($15) or flexible plastic ($29).

Hammond, Inc. (515 Valley St., Maplewood, NJ 07040; 201-763-6000) distributes "Loch Ness Monster" ($9.95; 6381-7), a map that depicts Scotland's Loch Ness and shows where the monster has been sighted.

National Geographic Society (17th & M sts. NW, Washington, DC 20036; 301-921-1200) sells "Whales of the World" ($7.95; 02819; 22" X 31"), with illustrations and notes.

World Conservation Union (Avenue du Mont-Blanc, CH-1196, Gland, Switzerland; 022-64-91-14) produces authoritative maps on the distribution of species and protected areas in all parts of the world, at the national system level and at the level of the particular site. It also has detailed maps of certain coastal and marine ecosystems, primarily in the Caribbean Sea, the Mediterranean Sea, and the enclosed seas of the Middle East. Write for more information.

■ **See also: "Bicycle Route Maps" and "Recreation Maps."**

HISTORY
THROUGH MAPS

Antique Maps and Reproductions

Old maps are beautiful and thought-provoking windows into our past, rich with the history of generations that have been outlived by the pictures they drew of their world. Short of stumbling across finds at auctions or on a store's dusty shelves, the best places to find antique maps are through the numerous collections of map libraries (see Appendix E), historical societies, or museums. There are also a number of publishers that create reproductions of historically significant—or simply artistically beautiful—maps and charts, as well as dealers with the resources to locate both originals and reproductions for a fee.

GOVERNMENT SOURCES

Two government agencies represent the lion's share of existing antique maps:

■ The Geography and Map Division of the **Library of Congress** holds one of the world's largest collections of antique maps and atlases, boasting more than four million maps and 52,000 atlases, plus hundreds of antique globes.
■ The **National Archives** has approximately two million maps and charts produced by the federal government between 1750 and 1950.

Both the Library of Congress and the Archives have reproduction services for their collections (see "Uncle Sam's Treasure Chests," page 174). These collections, as well as other government sources, are described in more detail in the *Scholar's Guide to Washington, D.C. for Cartography and Remote Sensing Imagery* ($15), available from the **Smithsonian Institution Press**, 470 L'Enfant

Right: Portion of 1755 map of Virginia and Maryland. Reprinted with permission of Historic Urban Plans, Ithaca, NY.

Plaza, Washington, DC 20560; 202-287-3738; 800-782-4612.

Federal government agencies that have older maps on file for study and reproduction include the USGS (dating to 1879) and the National Ocean Service (various marine and navigation charts from the 18th century on; Civil War maps detailing certain marches and campaigns).

The Library of Congress also sells reproductions of several antique maps in its collection. These may be ordered from the Library of Congress, Information Office, Box A, Washington, DC 20540. Include $2 postage for orders under $50; $3.50 for orders over $50. Titles include:

■ "Map of Manhattan" ($17^3/_4$" X $26^1/_2$"; $15), drawn in 1639, the earliest-known map of the island and its environs.
■ "Map of the World" ($34^1/_4$" X $22^1/_2$"; $20), drawn in 1565 by Paolo Forlani of Verona, an excellent example of the maps printed from copperplates in Italy in the mid-16th century.
■ "Map of the World" ($19^3/_4$" X $13^5/_8$"; $10), drawn in 1544 by Battista Agnese, showing Magellan's route around the world.
■ "Map of the North Pacific" ($31^1/_2$" X $20^3/_4$"; $20), drawn around 1630 by Joao Teixeira Albernaz I, the most notable Portuguese cartographer of his day.
■ "A Chart of the Gulf Stream" ($17^1/_4$" X 11"; $10), commissioned by Benjamin Franklin in 1786, the first map to show the Gulf Stream as a continuous feature flowing from Florida to Newfoundland.
■ "Chart of the Mediterranean Sea and Western Europe" (27" X 39"; $20), a 1559 drawing by Mateus Prunes, a leading member of one of the well-known families of 16th-century Majorcan cartographers.

COMMERCIAL SOURCES, REPRODUCTIONS

Several map publishers carry one or more antique map reproductions. Examples include:

American Geographical Society (156 Fifth Ave., Ste. 600, New York, NY 10010; 212-242-0214) distributes "World Map" ($4; 14" X 14"), reproduced from the small *Under Heaven Map Book*, published in Korea in the late 17th or early 18th century.

Historic Urban Plans (P.O. Box 276, Ithaca, NY 14850; 607-272-MAPS) sells reproductions of old city plans and urban panoramic maps, both U.S. and foreign. Prices range from $5.50 for the 145 maps in the Historic America Maps and Urban Views series to $5 to $17.50 for the worldwide selection of 400 maps in the Historic City Plans and Views series.

International Map Services, Ltd. (P.O. Box 2187, Grand Cayman, Cayman Islands, British West Indies; 809-949-4700) reproduces a map showing North America and the Caribbean in 1776. The map, originally printed in London in 1777 in two sheets, has been reproduced in a single sheet. The hand coloring is based upon that used in a similar map in the collection of the British Museum.

COMMERCIAL SOURCES, ANTIQUE MAPS

There are two excellent sources for information about antique maps and map dealers: One is *The Map Collector*, a British quarterly published in March, June, September, and December. The journal features articles on types of maps ("Understanding Engraved Maps" is one example), events in cartographic history ("The Geographic and Cartographic Work of the American Military Mission to Egypt, 1870-1878"), and specific maps, such as Johann Gabriel Doppelmayr's 1720 map of the world, as well as news of events in the antique map world, and, of course, advertisements from antique map dealers. Subscription is £29 annually for UK residents; £32 for all other countries. Write to Map Collector Publications, 48 High St., Tring, Hertsfordshire HP23 5BH, England; 442-891004. The other is *Imago Mundi* (c/o King's College London, The Strand, London WC2R 2LS), an international journal with articles on early maps and cartographic history. For subscription details, write to the address above.

Researching Old Maps

Because there are many different kinds of old maps, stored in many different collections, they are difficult to research. However, with a little imagination and a lot of perseverance, you can probably find just the map you want. There are many sources for you to investigate, ranging from historical societies to the cartographic offices of your state or local government to the **National Archives** and the **Library of Congress**.

The best place to begin a search for an old map is your local library. Two reference books—*The Directory of Historical Societies in the United States and Canada* (**American Association for State and Local History**, 172 Second Ave. N, Ste. 202, Nashville, TN 37201; 615-255-2971) and *Map Collections in the United States and Canada: A Directory* (**Geography and Map Division of the Special Libraries Association**, 1700 18th St. NW, Washington, DC 20009; 202-234-4700)—are excellent sources for finding local antique map collections; they may be found on many libraries' reference shelves. These books may lead you to organizations that have their own collections, or who can suggest other places to look.

One event of note to antique map buffs is the **Antiquarian Map & Print Fair** (26 Kings Rd., Cheltenham GL52 6BG, England; 0242-514287;), called "the only monthly antique map and print fair in the world." It is held at the Bonnington Hotel, Southampton Row, London WC1 4BH; admission is free.

ANTIQUE MAP DEALERS

Following is a select list of antique dealers and their specialties:

Alaska
Alaskana Book Shop
4617 Arctic Blvd.
Anchorage, AK 99503
907-561-1340
(*Alaska, mountain climbing, hunting*)

California
Argonaut Book Shop
792 Sutter St.
San Francisco, CA 94109
415-474-9067
(*rare books, maps, prints*)

Holy Land Treasures
1200 Edgehill Dr.
Burlingame, CA 94010
415-343-9578
(*rare and antique maps of the Holy Land*)

The Holmes Book Co.
274 14th St.
Oakland, CA 94612
510-893-6860

Houle Rare Books & Autographs
7260 Beverly Blvd.
Los Angeles, CA 90036
213-937-5858

Jill Scopazzi
278 Post St., Ste. 305
San Francisco, CA 94108
415-362-5708
(*antique maps*)

Colorado
Art Source International
1237 Pearl
Boulder, CO 80302
303-444-4080

Connecticut

Cedric L. Robinson, Bookseller
597 Palisado Ave.
Windsor, CT 06095
203-688-2582
(*American atlases, maps, and travelers' guides prior to* 1900)

Florida

Capt. Kit S. Kapp
P.O. Box 64
Osprey, FL 34229
813-966-4181
(*antiquarian maps, the Americas and rest of world; catalog, $3*)

Mickler's Floridiana
P.O. Box 38
Chulota, FL 32766
305-365-3636
(*books, atlases, maps on Florida; search service for out-of-print maps*)

Illinois

J.T. Monckton, Ltd.
730 N. Franklin St.
Chicago, IL 60610
(*early maps, prints, and books; cartographic facsimiles; scholarly monographs; catalogs upon request*)

Kenneth Nebenzahl, Inc.
P.O. Box 370
Glencoe, IL 60022
708-835-0515
(*15th- to 19th-century atlases, maps, and globes*)

George Ritzlin, Books & Maps
P.O. Box 6060
Evanston, IL 60204
708-328-1966
(*antiquarian maps and atlases; cartographic history*)

Harry L. Stern, Ltd.
1 N. Wacker #206
Chicago, IL 60611
312-372-0388
(*all types of rare and out-of-print maps and atlases*)

Maryland

Old World Mail Auctions
5614 Northfield Rd.
Bethesda, MD 20817
301-657-9074
(*16th- to 19th-century maps; free catalog*)

Massachusetts

David Jolly Antique Maps
P.O. Box 1003
Brookline, MA 02146
617-232-6222
(*mailing lists of antique maps dealers; publishes* Price Record and Handbook *and* Maps of America in Periodicals Before 1800)

Michigan

Clifton F. Ferguson
4999 Meandering Creek Dr.
Belmont, MI 49306
616-874-9297
(*antique maps, atlases, and sea charts*)

Missouri

Phyllis Y. Brown
736 De-Mun
St. Louis, MO 63105
314-725-1023
(*17th-, 18th-, and 19th-century engravings, woodcuts and lithographs; antique prints, maps, books*)

Elizabeth F. Dunlap, Books & Maps
6063 Westminster Pl.
St. Louis, MO 63112
314-863-5068
(*maps of North America prior to* 1885)

New Hampshire

G.B. Manasek, Inc.
35 S. Main St.
Hanover, NH 03755
603-643-2227
(*Japan, Mideast, and medieval maps*)

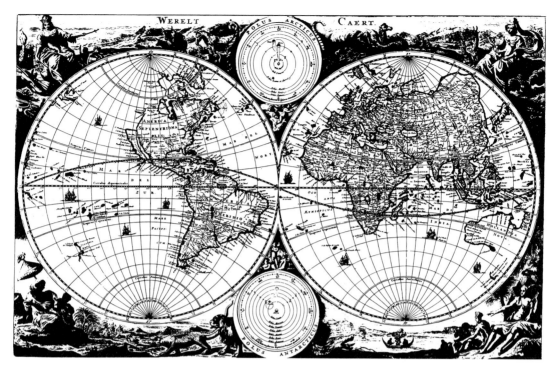

A Dutch "Bible-map" from 1690, probably created by Daniel Stoopendaal, a preeminent Dutch map-maker.

New Jersey
Grace Galleries, Inc.
75 Grand Ave.
Englewood, NJ 07631
201-567-6169
(*antiquarian maps and sea charts from 17th century to early 20th century*)

Maps of Antiquity
P.O. Box 569
Montclair, NJ 07042
201-744-4364
(*specializes in items of New Jersey as well as 19th-century maps of other locations*)

New Mexico
Richard Fitch
2324 Calle Halcon
Santa Fe, NM 87505
505-982-2939
(*North American antique maps and prints*)

New York
Antiquarian Booksellers' Center
50 Rockefeller Plaza
New York, NY 10020
212-246-2564

W. Graham Arader III
29 E. 72nd St.
New York, NY 10021
212-628-3668
(*antique maps and books; offices throughout U.S.*)

Richard B. Arkway, Inc.
538 Madison Ave.
New York, NY 10022
212-751-8135
(*antique maps*)

Jo-Ann and Richard Casten, Ltd.
4 Dodge Ln.
Old Field, NY 11733
516-689-3018
(*antique maps, atlases, and books*)

High Ridge Books, Inc.
Box 286
Rye, NY 10580
914-967-3332
(*19th-century maps of America*)

Martayan Lan, Inc.
10 W. 66 St.
New York, NY 10023
212-595-1776
(*maps of the world and the Americas*)

Rare Collectibles, Ltd.
94 Kaydeross Ave.
Saratoga Springs, NY 12866
518-584-2810

Thomas Suarez
RD 2, Box 297
Yorktown Heights, NY 10598
914-248-6650
(*maps, atlases, and prints relating to exploration*)

Pennsylvania
Antiquarian Map & Book Den
217 E. New St.
Lititz, PA 17543
717-626-5002

The Cartophile
934 Bridle Ln.
West Chester, PA 19382
215-692-7697
(*U.S. explorations, battle maps, land surveys, gazetteers, pocket maps, geographies*)

Heritage Antique Maps
551 Christopher Ln.
Doylestown, PA 18901
215-340-9662

The Philadelphia Print Shop, Ltd.
8441 Germantown Ave.
Philadelphia, PA 19118
215-242-4750
(*prints, maps and rare books; send $4 for most recent catalog, or $18 for next six*)

Tennessee
Murray Hudson Books & Maps
109 S. Church St., P.O. Box 163
Halls, TN 38040
901-836-9057
(*antiquarian maps, and books with maps; specialty: U.S. South and West prior to 1900*)

Vermont
Tuttle Antiquarian Books, Inc.
P.O. Box 541
Rutland, VT 05701
(*maps and atlases of America*)

Virginia
Cartographic Arts
P.O. Box 2202
Petersburg, VA 23803
804-861-6770
(*antique and rare maps and atlases*)

Chartifacts
P.O. Box 8954
Richmond, VA 23225
804-272-7120
(*U.S. Coast Survey charts and reprints, 1840s to 1900s*)

Paul Roberts Stoney
P.O. Box F
Williamsburg, VA 23187
804-220-3346
(*colonial America; catalogs periodically*)

Washington
The Shorey Bookstore
110 Union St.
Seattle, WA 98101
206-624-0221
(*Western Americana, Alaska, and the Arctic*)

Wisconsin
Sadlon's, Ltd.
1207 Fox River Dr.
De Pere, WI 54115
(*antique maps*)

Reproduction or Original?
by David C. Jolly

How can you tell an original antique map from a reproduction?

An **original** generally refers to a copy printed more or less at the time the map or view first appeared. In some cases, maps were printed for a century or more from the same copperplate or woodblock, occasionally with updating to include newer information. In such cases, as long as the plate or block was being employed commercially, impressions from it were considered to be "originals." Sometimes the block or plate survived to a later time, and was used to print restrikes. These are often identified by special watermarks or stamps. In any event, restrikes of old maps are almost unheard-of on the commercial market.

Reproductions are a different matter. They can be defined as impressions made by some process, nowadays usually photographic, based on an original impression. Reproductions are not necessarily printed recently. Some 19th-century reproductions exist, many of excellent quality, but most reproductions encountered will have been done in the past few decades. A small number of reproductions can be distinguished only by experts. Most, however, require only a little knowledge. Some of the factors to be considered in detecting reproductions include:

■ **Size.** Reproductions not intended to deceive are often produced slightly larger or smaller than the original. Of course, one must know the size of the original. My book, *Antique Maps, Sea Charts, City Views, Celestial Charts, and Battle Plans, Price Record and Handbook*, gives dimensions that can be helpful in this regard, but remember that some dimensions are rounded off by dealers and that paper can expand somewhat as the humidity rises.

■ **Coloring.** Colored reproductions often employ halftone colors. These consist of patterns of small dots, geometrically arranged, which can be seen quite readily with a magnifying glass. A few reproductions, however, are colored by hand, just like the originals.

■ **Printing quality.** Sometimes reproductions have a slightly blurred appearance. The black lines do not have the fine, dense quality of a true engraving. This can show up especially in cross-hatched areas, where the lines may fuse together.

■ **Plate mark.** When an engraved map is printed, the impression of the metal plate crushes the paper, resulting in a depressed area. The depressed area   *(continued)*

FOREIGN COUNTRIES

Australia
Antique Print Room
130 King William Rd.
Goodwood 5034, SA
08-272-3506
(*Australian and world maps*)

Bibliophile
24 Glenmore Rd.
Paddington N.S.W. 2021
Sydney
02-331-3411

Read's Rare Book Shop
62 Charlotte St.
Brisbane 4000
07-229-3278
(*maps of Australia to 1850*)

is usually rectangular and extends slightly beyond the printed area. This can often be seen, or felt, as a slight step or ridge. In a few cases, where the paper is thin, or where the map has been trimmed to the border, the plate mark may not be visible. On a very few reproductions, plate marks have been added to enhance realism. While visible on steel and copper engravings, a plate mark is normally not found on woodcuts, because much less pressure is used in printing them.

■ **Legends.** On most reproductions, there is a legend, usually in fine print, saying something like "Copyright 1968" or "From an original in the Library of Congress." It may seem unnecessary to even mention this, but people sometimes overlook the obvious. The legend can be hard to find. I have seen tiny legends embedded in the borders of wood-cut maps. If outside the border, the legend may have been trimmed. Someone may also have tried to erase it, though this should leave a thin spot or scuff marks.

■ **Paper.** Probably the best method of distinguishing is to study the paper. Chain marks, rectangular grids of lines on hand-made rag paper that can be seen when paper is held up to the light, are visible on paper made before about 1800. Some reproductions are printed on modern paper with chain marks, but the markings tend to be more regular on the modern paper. Water-marks can also be an important clue, but some expertise may be needed in interpreting them. Many of the folio-size maps have watermarks, but smaller maps often do not. The paper on originals tends to have an aged appearance—perhaps browned or even brittle, and sometimes with spotting or "foxing" (small, usually brown, spots on the paper caused by mold that are the result of storage under damp conditions). Some originals show signs of use, such as stains, soiling, wear, and tears. Originals often show slight offsetting, either of color or printer's ink, depending on how they were originally bound or folded. If colored, the pigments sometimes oxidize the paper, which can be seen by looking for browning on the verso (reverse side) corresponding to the colors on the map.

The above advice can help, but there is no substitute for long-term experience. Before investing money in an antique map, it is best to consult an experienced dealer. Some may charge a small amount for authenticating an item. Local libraries, art galleries, or museums may also be able to help.

Excerpted from *Antique Maps, Sea Charts, City Views, Celestial Charts and Battle Plans, Price Record and Handbook*, David C. Jolly, ed., revised annually. Available for $36.50 from David C. Jolly, Publishers, P.O. Box 931, Brookline, MA 02146; 617-232-6222.

Spencer Scott Sandilands
546 High St.
East Prahran 3181
Victoria
03-51-5709

Belgium
Librarie van Loock
51 rue St. Jean
1000 Brussels
02-512-7465

Canada
Beach Antique Maps & Prints
3 Firstbrooke Rd.
Toronto, Ontario M4E 2L2
416-694-8119

D&E Lake, Ltd.
239 King St. E.
Toronto, Ontario M5A 1J9
416-863-9930
(*Americana/Canadiana; catalog available*)

North By West
1016 Fort St.
Victoria, BC V8V 3K4
604-383-3442
(*antique maps*)

Ptolémée Plus
C.P. 344, succ. Cartierville
Montreal, Quebec H4K 2J6
(*North America*)

England
Avril Noble
2 Southampton St., Covent Garden
London WC2E 7HA
01-240-1970
(*16th- to 19th-century antique maps and engravings*)

Channel Bookshop
5 Russell St.
Dover, Kent CT16 1PX
0304-213016

Ivan R. Deverall
Duval House
The Glen, Cambridge Way
Uckfield, Sussex TN22 2AB
0825-2474
(*professional coloring of maps and prints*)

Susanna Fisher
Spencer, Upham
Southampton S03 1JD
048-96-291
(*16th- to 19th-century sea charts*)

Garwood & Voigt
15 Devonshire Bldg.
Bath BA2 4SP
0225-24074

Mrs. D. M. Green
7 Tower Grove
Weybridge, Surrey KT13 9LX
0932-241105
(*antique county maps, town plans, and road maps*)

Intercol
1A Camden Walk
Islington Green
London N1 8DY
01-354-2599
(*16th- to 19th-century atlases, maps, prints; world maps*)

J.A.L. Franks, Ltd.
7 New Oxford St.
London WC1A 1BA
01-405-0274
(*early maps of most types and areas*)

Jonathan Potter, Ltd.
21 Grosvenor St.
Mayfair, London W1X 9FE
01-491-3520
(*rare, interesting, and decorative old maps*)

Leicester Map Galleries, Ltd.
Well House
Arnesby, Leicester LE8 3WJ
053-758-462
(*16th- to 19th-century antique maps*)

Maggs Brothers
50 Berkeley Sq.
London W1X 6EL
01-493-7160

The Map House
54 Beauchamp Pl.
Knightsbridge, London SW3 1NY
01-589-4325
(*antique maps*)

Northwood Maps, Ltd.
71 Nightingale Rd.
Rickmansworth, Herts WD3 2BU
0923-772258

Paul Orssich
117 Munster Rd.
London SW6 6DH
01-736-3869
(*rare books and maps; lists on request*)

Pierpoint Gallery
10 Church St.
Hereford HR1 2LR
0432-267002

Warwick Leadlay Gallery
5 Nelson Rd.
Greenwich, London SE10 9JB
01-858-0317
(*antique maps worldwide; specializes in maps of southeast London and northwest Kent*)

Finland
Atikki-Kirja
Kelevankatu 25
Helsingfors SF-100
90-611775
(*northern regions, Russia, Scandinavia*)

France
Librairie Ancienne—Curiosités
3 rue de l'Université
75007 Paris
42607594
(*rare and antique maps*)

Librairie Dudragne
86 rue de Maubeurge
Paris 75010
878-50-95
(*France, Africa, Middle East, America*)

Germany
Antiquariat Wolfgang Staschen
Potsdammerstr. 138
D-1000 Berlin 12
030-262-2075

Werner Weick Galerie
Sterstrasse 2 am Markt
D-5300 Bonn 1
0228-657822

Greece
K.E.B.E.
Odos Sina 44
10672 Athens
21-361-5548
(*Cyprus, Greece, Malta, and the Near East*)

Ireland
Neptune Gallery
41 S. William St.
Dublin 2
01-715021

Italy
Libreria Antiquaria Soave
Via Po 48
10123 Torino
011-878957
(*Italian topographic, rare, and antique maps*)

The Netherlands
Antiquariaat C. Broekema
Postbus 5880
1007 AW Amsterdam
020-629510
(*old maps, atlases, travel books*)

Jan J. Van Waning Galerie
Westersingel 35
3014 GS Rotterdam
010-4360198

Scotland
Billson of St. Andrews
15 Greyfriars Garden
Fife KY 16 9DE
St. Andrews
0334-75063
(*antiquarian Scottish atlases, maps, county maps, town plans, road maps, and sea charts*)

The Carson Clark Gallery
Scotia Maps-Mapsellers
173 Canongate
The Royal Mile
Edinburgh EH8 8BN
031-556-4710
(*antique maps and charts of all parts of the world*)

Switzerland
Antik-Pfister Antiquariat
Postfach 784
8025 Zurich
01-476232
(*antique Swiss maps and prints of all parts of the world*)

History Maps

Maps of history are modern diagrams that illustrate a region's trends or events over decades or centuries. Instructors use history maps to teach everything from archaeology and anthropology to military history and literature. Scholars use them to track trends in a society or culture. As study tools, they provide valuable overviews of the evolution of a society's traditions, explorations, and advances.

There is a wide range of history maps available. There are maps that trace the routes of famous explorers (see page 176 for maps commemorating the voyage of Christopher Columbus), and maps of the history of medicine, religion, theater, poetry, art, and technology. There are maps of the most significant developments in the history of civilization. Many history maps are poster-size and intended for both decoration and study. Others are accompanied by texts that provide both background and analysis of the events illustrated on the maps.

The best overall sources for history maps are the larger commercial map publishers, especially those with an educational market. Historical maps, as well as atlases of American and world history, military history, and social history, are produced in great numbers by these publishers. Many smaller companies often publish history maps related to the other products in which they specialize. The federal government produces little in the way of history maps, but some state and local governments produce maps related to local and regional development.

GOVERNMENT SOURCES, UNITED STATES

U.S. Geological Survey. USGS has published a National Atlas map, "Territorial Growth," that shows the territory of the United States at various times between 1775 and 1920, including a final map of the U.S. and territories as of March 1986 ($3.10; US00664-38077-AV-NA-

34M-00). USGS Base Map 8-A shows the routes used by principal explorers between 1501 and 1844 ($2.40; 05365). USGS also produced a special-edition map sheet to commemorate the bicentennial of the signing of the U.S. Constitution: "Maps of an Emerging Nation—The United States of America, 1775-1987." One side of the map sheet shows the first map of the U.S. produced by an American in 1774; the reverse side has a series of 14 maps showing the expansion of the U.S. between 1775 and 1987, along with depictions of flags appropriate to the years of the maps ($4; 38077-HI-UG-05M-18).

Some local or state agencies produce or distribute maps describing local history. Write to the local historical societies for further information, or contact state mapping agencies where applicable (see Appendix A).

GOVERNMENT SOURCES, CANADA

Canada Map Office (615 Booth St., Ottawa, Ontario K1A 0E9; 613-952-7000) distributes various historical maps, including:

■ Historic Maps of Canada, a special series produced by the Department of Energy, Mines and Resources of Canada. The maps trace the expanding knowledge of the New World as well as changing cartographic techniques. The series includes: "America Septentionalis, 1639" (MCR 2300), "Amerique Septentrionale, 1695" (MCR 2302), "An Accurate Map of Canada, 1761" (MCR 2303), "British North America, 1834" (MCR 2304), and "Le Canada, ou Nouvelle France, 1656" (MCR 2305). The five maps can be purchased separately ($5.15 Canadian each) or as a set ($18.75 Canadian; MCR 2301).

Also available as part of the *National Atlas of Canada* series is "Canada Then and Now," a set

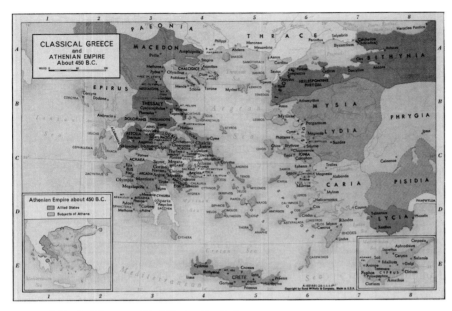

"Map of Classical Greece and the Athenian Empire."
Reprinted with permission from Rand McNally & Company's
Historical Atlas of the World. ©1965.

containing three maps that portrays the early geography of Canada and the evolution of provincial and territorial boundaries. Maps in the series include "Canada—Confederation," "Canada—Territorial Evolution," and "Canada," a 1982 map of the country. The set is $10 Canadian.

Maps Alberta (Land Information Services Div., Main fl., Brittania Bldg., 703 6th Ave. SW, Calgary, Alberta T2P 0T9; 403-297-7389) also distributes maps from the *National Atlas* series.

COMMERCIAL SOURCES

George F. Cram Co. (P.O. Box 426, Indianapolis, IN 46206; 317-635-5564; 800-227-4199) publishes three series of 52" X 40" maps— United States History (set no. 50), Modern European and World History (set no. 60), and Early European History (set no. 70). Each set contains 19 maps that cover important historical highlights. Latitude and longitude markings are clearly identified to make it easy for teachers and students to locate historical happenings on a current map. The maps are set in a steel

charthead on a metal tripod ($320 for each set).

Hammond, Inc. (515 Valley St., Maplewood, NJ 07040; 201-763-6000) publishes several atlases of world history in cooperation with Times Books of London, as well as a small series of its own, including Bible atlases and atlases of American and world history. Hammond also distributes Bartholomew Maps, which produces several pictorial maps on historical subjects, including "Cathedrals and Abbeys." Atlases are $85 for hardcover editions; Bartholomew pictorial maps, $9.95.

Modern School (1609 E. Kercher Rd., Goshen, IL 46526; 219-533-3111; 800-431-5929) produces 13 history maps for classroom use, including "Indian Tribes & Cultures," "Early Exploration," "Territorial Expansion to 1848—The Mexican War," and "World War II: Europe." The series is available in two different mountings, ranging from $303 to $395.

National Geographic Society (17th & M sts. NW, Washington, DC 20036; 202-921-1200) produces a number of history maps. Titles include "France/Historical France" ($7.95; 20041; 22" X 33"), "Making of Quebec" ($7.95; 20055; 27" X 20 1/2"), and "United States/Territorial Growth" ($7.95; 20025; 43" X 30"). National Geographic maps are full-color with illustrations and are usually suitable for framing. A list of publications is available.

Nystrom (3333 N. Elston Ave., Chicago, IL 60618; 312-463-1144; 800-621-8086) specializes

Uncle Sam's Treasure Chests

The world of maps is so vast that you practically need a map to find one. Two of the best resources for historical map research are the map collections of the Library of Congress and the National Archives, both in or around Washington, D.C. Funded and operated by the federal government, both collections contain millions of maps, charts, atlases, and globes, as well as a myriad of valuable research tools for the study of cartographic information.

Library of Congress, Geography and Map Division (Washington, DC 20541; 202-707-6277). When the Library of Congress was established in 1800, some of its earliest acquisitions were maps and atlases. In 1897, the Geography and Map Division was given its own room; it has since moved to specially designed quarters on Capitol Hill. The collection, the largest in the world, consists of more than four million maps, 53,000 atlases, 2,000 plastic-relief models, 350 globes, and 8,000 reference works. Among its most prized possessions are three sailing atlases and 19 sailing charts dating back to

the 14th through 17th centuries. There are also numerous early American maps and charts, some predating the Revolutionary War, and the Sanborn Map Company's 19th-century fire insurance maps, which detail the growth of 12,000 American cities and towns. The rest of the world is well represented, too, including rare Asian maps in the Hummel and Warner collections.

Although there is no single catalog of all the division's holdings, there are specialized card and book catalogs, as well as computerized magnetic tapes listing newer maps. The library publishes selected lists on specialized topics, including annotated lists of Civil War maps, railroad maps, land-ownership maps, and Indian land maps. The Geography and Map Division's "List of Publications" is free upon request. The Geography and Map Division's collections are meant for research purposes only, and lending privileges are restricted to members of Congress, federal agencies, and authorized libraries. A reference service is available to the public, and staff can handle phone and mail requests. The Library's Photoduplication Service can make reproductions of maps and atlases for

in learning materials for schools. Its series of American and world history maps are 50" X 38". Among the 33 maps in the American history series are "Indian Tribes and Settlements in the New World, 1500-1750" and "Transportation Unites the Nation." Titles in the series of 32 world history maps include "Christian Europe and the Crusades." Prices of single maps range from $47 to $72, depending on type of mounting. Set prices range from $373 to $823.

Ordnance Survey (Export Sales Branch, Rm. C456, Romsey Rd., Southampton, England SO9 4DH) publishes two full-color 224-page books, *Smugglers' Britain* and *Great British Ruins*. The former is compiled primarily from unofficial

accounts of 18th- and early 19th-century smuggling; in addition to photos and engravings, outline Ordnance Survey maps and grid references lead the reader on the trail of the smugglers. The latter book is a county-by-county guide to unusual and romantic ruins; each site is shown on one of the Ordnance Survey maps that accompany the text. In addition, the Ordnance Survey's Record Map Library holds more than a half-million superseded maps, some of which date to the early 19th century.

Rand McNally (P.O. Box 7600, Chicago, IL 60680; 312-673-9100) produces three sets of American history and one set of world history

a fee, except where copyright or other restrictions apply.

The Library's Photoduplication Service handles all reproduction orders. Prices range from $10 for a 2" X 2" color slide (minimum order, $25) and $12 for a black-and-white photodirect paper print to hundreds of dollars for exhibition-quality prints, depending on size and reproduction quality desired. Minimum reproduction time is six weeks.

National Archives, Cartographic and Architectural Branch (841 S. Pickett St., Alexandria, VA 22304; 703-756-6700). The Archives' Cartographic and Architectural Branch holds one of the largest collections of American maps in the world. Established as the repository for maps commissioned or created by the government, its holdings date from 1750 to 1950. The branch has more than two million maps and charts, 800,000 in manuscript form, as well as 500,000 architectural drawings and engineering plans and eight million aerial photos.

The maps of the Lewis and Clark and other explorations of North America are among the treasures in the collection. Virtually every aspect of American society and expansion can be found in the files of the branch, located in a suburb of Washington, D.C. A number of special catalogs and reference information papers are available through the Archives, their subjects running the gamut from 18th-century Indian lands to 20th-century transportation growth. The free pamphlet "Cartographic and Architectural Branch, National Archives and Records Administration," available directly from NARA, lists many of the categories and reference materials in the collection. Reproduction services of varying degrees of quality and price are available; orders usually require four to six weeks for completion.

The Archives staff can produce black-and-white photocopies of some maps while you wait for $1.80 per linear foot of copy. If you need a better-quality reproduction, the Archives Reproduction Service can make many types of copies, but not while you wait. Prices range from $3.50 for a 2" X 2" color slide, to $18 for a 4" X 5" color negative, to $33.25 for a 16" X 20" color print. Reproduction time can take up to eight weeks. For information and the free pamphlet, write Cartographic Branch (NNSC), National Archives, Washington, DC 20408. Hours for in-person research are 8 a.m. to 4:30 p.m., Monday through Friday.

maps intended for school use. It also distributes the Breasted-Huth-Harding series of world history maps. The three U.S. series are American History Maps (for intermediate grades), American Studies (all levels), and Our America, which includes time lines and text on each map. The world history series covers the development of civilization in most areas of the globe. The 62 maps in the Breasted-Huth-Harding series include "Barbarian Migration" and "Air Age."

OTHER SOURCES

Following is a sample of the history maps produced by smaller map companies or organizations involved in studying or promoting specific subjects:

Celestial Arts (P.O. Box 7327, Berkeley, CA 94707; 510-845-8414; 800-841-2665) publishes a "wall visual" poster ($9.95) called "The Aztec Cosmos," a stylized ancient history map demonstrating the Aztec culture's artistic, mathematical, and stone-carving accomplishments. The map includes an educational 32-page booklet describing Aztec symbols and religion.

Facts On File, Inc. (460 Park Ave. S., New York, NY 10016; 800-322-8755; 800-443-8323 in Canada) produces Historical Maps on File

Tracking Columbus

The 500th anniversary of the voyage of Christopher Columbus to the "New World" inspired several publishers, map-makers, and others to create products that help us understand his route and his voyage. A sampling:

Aristoplay (P.O. Box 7028, Ann Arbor, MI 48107; 313-995-4353; 800-634-7738) sells "Land Ho!" ($22), a board game designed to depict the perils of 15th-century ocean travel, and to permit players to sail with Columbus to the New World. Designed for three players, ages 8 to adult, "Land Ho!" can be played by English- or Spanish-speaking players, or in both languages simultaneously in two levels of play. A ship's log cites the most current historical data relevant to the voyage in both languages.

GeoLearning Corp. (Box 2042, Sheridan, WY 82801; 307-674-6436) sells "Voyages of Columbus" ($12.95), a 100-piece inlaid tray jigsaw puzzle with educational information about Columbus and his trip to the New World. The colorful puzzle provides information about the explorer's four voyages, including a chronology of key events and the routes taken by the Niña, Pinta, and Santa Maria. Two other puzzles in the company's Columbus Collection include "Departure from Palos in 1492" ($9.95), a 500-piece jigsaw box puzzle of the painting by Emanuel Leutze, and "Caravels of Columbus" ($12.95), a 550-piece double-sided 24" X 18" jigsaw puzzle depicting the ships of Columbus on one side and the bust of Columbus on the reverse.

Rand McNally (P.O. Box 7600, Chicago, IL 60680; 708-673-9100) publishes the *Atlas of Columbus & the Great Discoveries*, a 176-page compendium of the maps and charts created and followed by the world's early explorers. In compiling this book, map historian Kenneth Nebenzahl combed the world's museums, libraries, and private collections. His search turned up more than 50 antique maps, most of which are printed as double-page spreads with section enlargements. The text, which follows the development of the Age of Discovery and the contributions of Columbus and his successors, concisely conveys each map's significance and detail. Price is $75. Editions have also been published in England, France, Germany, Italy, and Spain.

Tab Books (Blue Ridge Summit, PA 17294; 717-794-5461) publishes *The Log of Christopher Columbus*, a 272-page account of Columbus' first voyage written in his own words. Translated and annotated by Columbus scholar Robert H. Fuson, Professor Emeritus of Geography at the University of South Florida, the book recreates a day-to-day account of Columbus' original travel log. In addition to the log, there are drawings, woodcuts, and authentic charts from Columbus' time. Price: $29.95 hardover and, appropriately, $14.92 softcover.

($145). The more than 300 copyright-free maps in this loose-leaf collection are simple black-and-white diagrams of major historical trends or events. Titles include "Greece During the Persian Wars," "Expedition of Coronado, 1540-1542," and "Adams-Onis Treaty, 1819." These are useful for students or researchers who need to copy maps for reports and presentations.

Travel Genie (3714 Lincolnway, Ames, IA 50010; 515-232-1070) offers a reproduction of a map of Iowa in 1855 originally published by J.H. Colton ($4.95, plus $1.50 shipping).

Williams & Heintz Map Corp. (8119 Central Ave., Capitol Heights, MD 20743; 301-336-1144), primarily a producer of technical maps for various customers, also publishes a series of geologic maps. Its Historical Geology portfolio ($8.50) has 13 maps that trace the history of major U.S. geologic provinces.

Historic Site Maps

Civil War battlefields, presidents' homes, and monuments to long-gone explorers dot the American landscape, as do countless other historic sites of major and minor importance to our national heritage. Some sites are operated under the auspices of the federal government or a state or local historic society. Others are privately run. For virtually all, there is a map available to guide one to and through the places where history was made.

Government Sources

National Park Service. The National Park Service is the guardian of national historic sites. "The House Where Lincoln Died," Bunker Hill, and Mesa Verde are three of the hundreds of historic sites operated and preserved under the Park Service's care. Maps are usually available at these sites or through the agency's Office of Public Inquiries.

U.S. Geological Survey. USGS publishes National Park maps, which include some maps of national historic landmarks, such as "Custer Battlefield National Monument" in Montana, "Home of Franklin D. Roosevelt" in New York, and "Colonial National Historical Park" covering Williamsburg and Yorktown in Virginia ($4). USGS also pinpoints certain historic landmarks on its maps of America. There must be a substantial object (a house, a battlefield, or a grave, for example) for the site to be included on a USGS map; small monuments or signs do not merit note. Maps depicting national historic sites and areas are listed by state, in an "Index to USGS Topographic Map Coverage of National Park System," available from Earth Science Information Centers and the USGS Distribution Centers in Denver, Colorado, and Fairbanks, Alaska.

Government Printing Office. GPO has maps and guidebooks to several popular historic sites. Prices range from $2.25 for a simple guidebook to $10 or more for comprehensive texts, complete with maps, of various sites. Examples of maps and guides available from GPO include: "Fort Sumter: Anvil of War" ($3; S/N 024-005-00919-1), "Fort Vancouver National Historic Site, Washington" ($7; S/N 024-005-00816-1), and "Guide to United States Army Museums and Historic Sites" ($5.50; S/N 008-020-00561-4).

State historic societies (see Appendix A) and building preservation societies sometimes publish maps or guides to historic sites preserved by states or local jurisdictions. State tourist agencies (Appendix A) and local chambers of commerce often publish walking-tour maps or guidebooks to area attractions.

■ **See also: "Antique Maps," "Selected Atlases," "Military Maps," "Recreation Maps," and "Railroad Maps."**

Military Maps

Among the precious few consolations of war are the resulting technological advances that often have applications in nonmilitary life. Over the years, the need for accurate military maps has led, time after time, to the creation of newer and more sophisticated mapping techniques.

In 1777, the Military Cartographic Headquarters was established at Ringwood, New Jersey, to create maps for General George Washington's campaign against the British. The attacks and marches planned with these maps led the Americans to an unprecedented victory against Mother England, and the legacy of American military mapping began.

In the decades that followed, the young nation found itself embroiled in a series of conflicts with other nations, and finally, with itself. Cartographic agencies were created to keep pace with the changing needs of the military, and these agencies in turn gave birth to numerous advances in surveying and mapping techniques.

The War of 1812 pointed out the need for nautical military maps to accommodate an expanding Navy, which resulted in the establishment of the Navy Depot of Charts and Instruments in 1830. The Civil War led to the development of aerial-reconnaissance mapping, with surveyors rising above the fray in hot-air balloons to diagram enemy territory. In 1907, aerial reconnaissance reached new heights with the establishment of the Aeronautical Division of the Army Signal Corps.

The Spanish-American War gave U.S. military cartographers their first real chance at mapping foreign soil, an exercise that paid off during the trench and field battles of the First World War. The use of aerial photography for military purposes was also perfected during World War I. The fine art of cartographic cooperation was honed during World War II, as the federal government's civilian map agencies joined with the Army Map Service and the Navy

Hydrographic Office to help battle the Nazi menace.

GOVERNMENT SOURCES, UNITED STATES

The mapping agencies of the Defense Department were combined in 1972 to form the Defense Mapping Agency. Today, DMA's Topographic, Hydrographic, and Aerospace Centers produce many of the maps used by the American military. Aside from updating and producing a steady stream of military maps for everyday use, the DMA is currently creating a digitized map of the world to help guide missiles and other military systems. Many of DMA's regular maps are available to the public, although they are among the most expensive in the federal government's map collection, and some require special software to run them.

Besides DMA, there are several other government sources of military maps:

■ The **National Oceanic and Atmospheric Administration** distributes military aeronautical and nautical charts and maps.
■ The **Central Intelligence Agency** creates maps of foreign countries (see "Foreign Country Maps"), which are distributed by the National Technical Information Service.
■ The **Defense Department**, **State Department**, and other agencies produce maps sometimes used for military purposes; they are distributed by the GPO.
■ The collections of the **Library of Congress** and the **National Archives** are filled with military maps available for study. The Archives contains maps created by government mapping agencies, while the Library of Congress's collection includes both domestic and foreign military maps. For a fee, the reproduction services of both collections make copies of their maps (see "Uncle Sam's Treasure Chests").
■ Maps of historic battlegrounds that are preserved by the federal government can be

MAP NO. 2

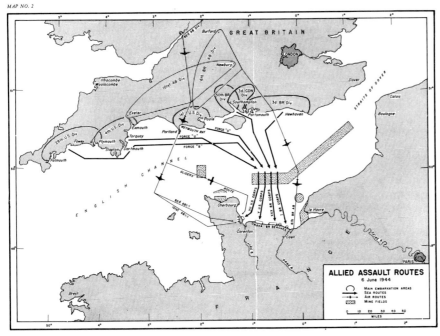

The routes of the Allied assault on D-Day, from a set of maps contained in the GPO book Utah Beach to Cherbourg.

- *Ardennes, Battle of the Bulge* ($21; S/N 008-029-00069-5).
- *Omaha Beachhead* ($8.50; S/N 008-029-00128-4).
- *Saint Lo, July 7-19, 1944* ($8.50; S/N 008-029-00127-6).
- *Cassino to the Alps* ($19; S/N 008-029-00095-4).
- *Global Logistics and Strategy, 1940-1943* ($19; S/N 008-029-00056-3).
- *War in the Pacific: Campaign in the Marianas* ($19; S/N 008-029-00040-7).
- *Guadalcanal: The First Offensive* ($20; S/N 008-029-00067-9).
- *Okinawa: The Last Battle* ($22; S/N 008-029-00066-1).

obtained from the **National Park Service,** while state and local bureaus of tourism or historical preservation usually hand out free maps of the memorials or battlegrounds under their auspices.

If you're searching for a military map, here are some strategic places to look:

Government Printing Office. GPO has several publications with military maps, including:

- *South to the Naktong, North to the Yalu (June-November 1950)* ($25.50; S/N 008-029-00079-2).
- *Military Advisors in Korea: KMAG in Peace and War* ($6; S/N 008-029-00002-4).
- *Civil War Maps: An Annotated List of Maps and Atlases in the Library of Congress* ($46; S/N 030-000-00209-1).
- *Russian Combat Methods in World War II* ($4.50; S/N 008-029-00182-9).
- *Siegfried Line Campaigns* ($22; S/N 008-029-00068-7).

Tennessee Valley Authority. TVA produces several inexpensive blueline lithoprint repro-ductions of original Civil War maps depicting campaigns fought in the Tennessee Valley region. Available maps include:

- "Map of the approaches and defense of Knoxville during the Civil War" ($1.50; 455 K 90), a 25" X 31" blueline print, surveyed in 1863.
- "Map of the Army movements around Chatta-nooga made to accompany the report of Major General Grant in January, 1864" ($1; G MD 453 G 754), a litho measuring 18" X 24".
- "Battlefield of Chickamauga, Georgia, April, 1864" ($1; G MD 453 G 754-1), a blueline print measuring 18" X 22".
- "Map showing the operations of the National Forces under the command of General W.T. Sherman during the campaign of Atlanta, September 1864" ($1; G MD 453 G 754-2), a blueline print measuring 16" X 21".

■ "Chattanooga and its approaches" ($1.50; G MS 453 K 754-3), a blueline print measuring 22" X 28" that shows the Union and Rebel advances during the battles of November 1863.

■ "Maneuver ground, Chickamauga Park and Vicinity" ($1; G CF 8141 G), a blueline print measuring 18" X 24" of a topographic map made in April 1910.

■ "Map of the Battlefields of Chattanooga" ($1; 5-438), a blueline print measuring 18" X 24", dated 1901, showing movement against Orchard Knob.

■ "Military Map Showing the Marches of U.S. Forces Under General Sherman, 1863-1865" ($1.50; 453 M 754-8), measuring 23" X 38".

U.S. Geological Survey. USGS's topographic mapping program, which covers the National Park System, has mapped many historic forts, battlegrounds, and military memorials and parks. A free map pinpointing topographic maps, "Index to USGS Map Coverage of the National Park System," is available from USGS. The maps in the National Park series cost $4 each and are drawn to various scales; some parks require more than one sheet (see "Recreation Maps" and "Topographic Maps" for more information).

National Archives and **Library of Congress.** Both agencies contain thousands of military maps providing worldwide coverage.

National Oceanic and Atmospheric Administration. For reasons no one can explain, the NOAA maintains an extraordinary collection of Civil War charts and diagrams drawn by the cartographers of the Confederate Army. A catalog of NOAA's Civil War collection is available from GPO.

The collections of the Library of Congress, National Archives, and NOAA are available to the public for study only. Reproduction facilities are available at each collection, although reproductions can take up to eight weeks. See "Uncle Sam's Treasure Chests" for more information on the collections of the Library of Congress and National Archives.

GOVERNMENT SOURCES, CANADA

Canada Map Office (615 Booth St., Ottawa, Ontario K1A 0E9; 613-952-7000) distributes, as part of *The National Atlas of Canada*, 5th ed., the map "The Northwest Campaign, 1885" ($8.40 Canadian; MCR 4106).

COMMERCIAL SOURCES

Older maps of military campaigns or battles can be found through antique map and military paraphernalia dealers; many print and art dealers carry antique military map reproductions. Reproductions can also be obtained from bookstores at many museums and libraries.

Other sources for military maps include those commercial map companies that produce classroom maps tracing military campaigns or battles. Some companies also publish decorative reproductions of military maps, as well as up-to-date, utilitarian maps pinpointing current military bases.

Another good source for historical military maps are local or regional military clubs for devotees of a certain era or war. Pennsylvania and West Virginia have several Civil War organizations, for example, while the New England area is rife with Revolutionary War buffs. The museums and gift shops of military battlefields and parks are also good hunting grounds for commercial military maps.

Several educational map publishers produce maps depicting military history. Here's a sampling:

George F. Cram Co. (P.O. Box 426, Indianapolis, IN 46206; 317-635-5564; 800-227-4199) publishes a series of 52" X 40" United States History maps (set no. 50) that includes such titles as "The Civil War 1861-1865" and "The Mexican War and Compromise of 1850." The Modern European and World History series (set no. 60) includes "World War I—1914-1918," "The Nations at War in 1918," "World War II—

European and African Theaters," and "World War II—Pacific Ocean Theater." The Early European History series (set no. 70) includes "Ancient Enemies," "Campaigns and Empire of Alexander," and "Crusading Europe, 1095-1291." Each series includes 19 maps, which are mounted in a steel charthead on a metal tripod for classroom use ($320 for the set).

Europe Map Service/OTD, Ltd. (1 Pinewood Rd., Hopewell Junction, NY 12533; 914-221-0208) distributes reproductions of the official German Reich administrative World War II maps showing borders of the Third Reich from 1937 to May 1945. The series of 1:25,000-scale maps consists of 2,557 sectional maps showing topographic features, buildings, railways, and roads in exceptional detail. The maps, some in color, some black-and-white, measure approximately 23" X 24" and cost from $9 to $12 each.

Hubbard Scientific, Inc. (P.O. Box 760, Chippewa Falls, WI 54729; 800-323-8368)

introduced the "Desert Storm Raised Relief Commemorative Map" in 1992, a 25" X 26" topographic map that shows the entire area of involvement in the Desert Storm conflict. The map shows elevations, land formations, water sources, and political boundaries, as well as key missile sites, ship locations, air bases, and major battlegrounds, which are depicted in full-color vinyl. The custom matte displays the Desert Storm logo and includes four die-cut openings with pictures of the troops. A hardwood frame is included in the $62.95 price.

National Geographic Society (17th & M sts. NW, Washington, DC 20036; 301-921-1200) has "Battlefields of the Civil War" ($7.95; 20019), a full-color map that measures 30" X 23".

Nystrom (3333 N. Elston Ave., Chicago, IL 60618; 312-463-1144; 800-621-8086) sells two richly colored series of history teaching maps. The maps ($47 to $72, depending on mounting) measure 50" X 38". Titles relating to military

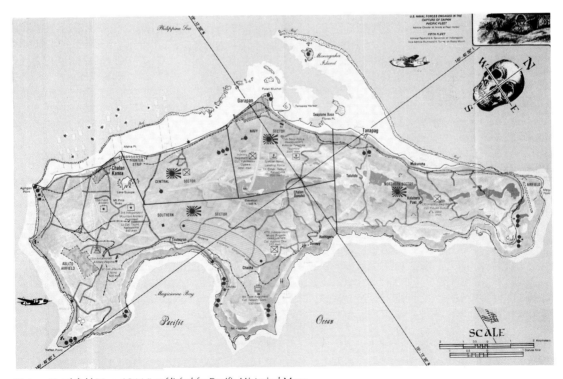

"*Saipan Battlefield Map—1944*," *published by* Pacific Historical Maps.

1937 topographic map of Chemnitz, Germany, from Europe Map Service/OTD, Ltd. The area, now known as Karl Marx Stadt in eastern Germany, was devastated during World War II.

Japanese sectors, and railways on the island. With copious text in the margins, it provides a historical summary of events, along with information on everything from "Coastal Defenses" to "Japanese Strategy." The reverse side features a 1944 aerial photograph of the island, with various war photos in the margins. The map is available from **Marianas Visitors Bureau**, Box 861, Saipan MP 96950.

■ "Dive Map of Ghost Fleet of Truk Lagoon" ($3.50), a combination map and pictorial depicting the 1944 U.S. aircraft carrier attack on Japanese fleets. Shipwrecks from this battle are located and described. The map is available from the **Truk Visitors Bureau**, P.O. Box FQ, Moen, Truk, F.S.M. 96942.

■ "Battlefield Map of Peleliu" ($4.50), describing the American attack of 1944 and the Japanese defense. The map is available from **Western Caroline Trading Co.**, Box 280, Koror, Palau 96940.

■ "Ghost Fleet of Truk Lagoon" ($11.50), a book describing the U.S. naval attack on the Japanese fleet, illustrated with maps and photos, available from **Pictorial Histories Publishing**, 713 S. Third W., Missoula, MT 59801.

■ **See also: "Aerial Photographs," "Aeronautical Charts," "Antique Maps," "History Maps," "Native American Land Maps," and "Selected Atlases."**

history in the American series include "The Revolutionary War," "The War of 1812," "The War Between the States, 1861-1865," and "Korean War; Vietnam War." Maps in Nystrom's World History series include "Mongol-Turkish Conquests—Eastern Trade Routes," "Napoleonic Empire, 1812," "World War II in Europe and Northern Africa," and "Russian and Japanese Expansion in the Far East."

Pacific Historical Maps (P.O. Box 201 [CHRB], Saipan, Mariana Islands 96950) publishes historical maps and books of World War II Pacific battlefields, which are distributed by other companies and agencies. Offerings include:

■ "Saipan Battlefield Map—1944" ($3.50), a four-color map illustrating the U.S. route of advance and Japanese defensive positions,

UTILITY AND SERVICE MAPS

Business Maps

For the traveling salesperson, the road map is as vital a tool as the telephone and the motel, but it isn't the only kind of map available to people in sales and other aspects of business. Maps are increasingly being used in businesses large and small, as computer and other data are combined with territorial maps to create visual representations for a variety of business applications, primarily in the areas of sales and marketing.

Business maps come in many shapes and forms. Among them are:

■ demographic maps ranking areas by population, income, age, race, and other factors;
■ thematic maps showing manufacturing and trade areas;
■ simple, uncluttered black-and-white or color maps of countries, states, counties, cities, and major transportation routes;
■ zip code maps with population data;
■ maps showing the major television and radio markets;
■ travelers' maps and atlases showing efficient routes, convention centers, hotels, and other amenities; and
■ various marketing and sales atlases combining many of the above elements.

Most of these are manufactured by a few large companies that either specialize in, or have departments devoted to, business maps. The federal government's contribution to the business map field comes in the form of census maps (see "Census Maps"), many of which are also available, often with enhancements, from commercial publishers. The cartographic offices of foreign countries (see Appendix C) can often locate the necessary business maps for their regions.

One of the fastest-growing areas of business maps is "desktop mapping"—the creation of maps on desktop and other computers. A

growing number of businesses, as well as government agencies and educational institutions, are finding myriad uses for these technologies, particularly in the areas of marketing and sales. For more on desktop mapping, see "Map Software."

GOVERNMENT SOURCES

Several Census Bureau maps are available through the Government Printing Office, including:

■ "Metropolitan Areas (MSAs, CMSAs and PMSAs)" ($5.50; S/N 003-024-07228-9). This 1990 map shows the locations of three standardized census regions—consolidated metropolitan statistical areas (CMSAs), primary metropolitan areas (PMAs), and metropolitan statistical areas (MSAs)—for the United States and Puerto Rico. The map (35" X 44") is printed on both sides; the continental U.S., Alaska, Hawaii, Puerto Rico, Guam, and American Samoa are on the front and a large map of New England is on the back. The map is updated annually. (See "Census Maps" for additional titles.)

COMMERCIAL SOURCES

Many commercial business maps are made with utility in mind: some atlases can slide into glove compartments; larger maps are designed to be mounted and displayed for presentation. Graphics tend to be minimal, as are details about tourist attractions or other extraneous features found on most general-use maps.

American Map Corp. (46-35 54th Rd., Maspeth, NY 11378; 718-784-0055; 800-432-6277) produces a variety of business-related maps. Its Cleartype series is a collection of black-and-white outline maps in varying sizes showing place-names and borders for U.S. cities, counties, and states, as well as maps of Canada and the world. Cleartype maps can be drawn or written on and are available with a variety of mounting styles. Below is a sample of available titles.

■ "U.S. State Outline" shows the continental United States, Alaska, and Hawaii with each state outlined and identified. There are six sizes available, from 11" X 8$\frac{1}{2}$" (60 cents) to 38" X 50" ($14).

■ "Individual States/County Outline" shows all counties within a single state. Maps are available for all 50 states, in 8$\frac{1}{2}$" X 11" (55 cents).

■ "Individual States/County and Town Outline" are the same as above, but show both towns and counties.

■ "World Outline" shows outlines and names of continents and countries on a map drawn on a Mercator projection. The three sizes and prices available range from 11" X 8$\frac{1}{2}$" (55 cents) to 50" X 38" ($22).

■ "Continents and Oceania Outline Maps" show outlines of countries, individual continents, and Oceania (17" X 22"; $2.75).

Other Cleartype maps include sets of principal U.S., Canadian, and world cities, and major U.S. metropolitan areas.

Colorprint maps are similar to Cleartype maps in detail but are produced in full-color. Available sales maps include:

■ "World Map Murals" ($25 to $150; 64" X 42" to 110" X 68").

■ "Laminated Sales Maps," county maps showing towns of 2,500+ population ($40),

New York City and surrounding areas are illustrated in this portion of a "Principal City Map." Reprinted with permission of the American Map Corp.

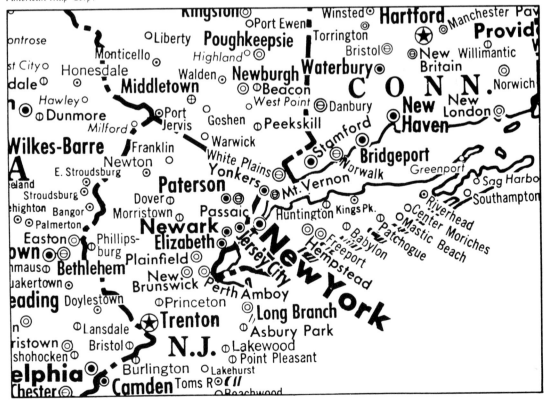

This simple, concise U.S. map is intended for use in sales planning, marketing, and other business applications. ©1982 by Rand McNally & Company. Reprinted with permission.

towns of 5,000+ population ($28), and towns of 10,000+ population ($18); and U.S. maps showing principal cities of 20,000+ population ($5), 10,000+ population ($6), and 5,000+ population ($6).

Cismap, Inc. (P.O. Box 770369, Houston, TX 77215; 713-783-5728) distributes *Gulf Coast Industrial Handbook* ($150), a directory/atlas showing more than 200 processing facilities and featuring full-color maps. Information on the facilities is cross-referenced to maps, making it easy to locate key businesses.

M.A.P.S. Midwestern (32 N. Frederick, Oelwein, IA 50662; 319-283-3001) produces county/township maps and books depicting ownership and residency, targeted toward commercial use. Books and maps are available for rural areas in Illinois, eastern Iowa, Minnesota, Missouri, South Dakota, and Wisconsin. Also available for these areas are books of

residency that show who lives where (books, $20; county wall maps, $25; area maps, $35 and up).

The National Survey (Chester, VT 05143; 802-875-2121) produces "Township Outline Maps" as well as "School Outline Maps" for the New England states. Map sizes vary from 8½" X 11" to 22" X 34"; prices range from 50 cents to $4 each. Also available are wall maps for New England states and New York.

Northwest Map and Travel Center (W. 525 Sprague Ave., Spokane, WA 99204; 509-455-6981) publishes "Inland Northwest" ($40 paper; $60 laminated), a 42" X 60" map that covers an area east of the Cascades to the Rockies and from Baker City, Oregon, to Calgary, Alberta.

Pierson Graphics Corp. (899 Broadway, Denver, CO 80203; 303-623-4299) produces maps for Colorado metropolitan areas. Titles range from "Denver/Boulder Wall Map" (48" X 72"; $90)—including block numbers, zip codes, municipal and county boundaries, and township ranges—to the Close Up series, atlases of the Denver regional and metropolitan areas, as well as Boulder/Longmont, and a *Colorado State Atlas*. Prices range from $7.95 to $29.95.

Pittmon Map Co. (732 SE Hawthorne Blvd., Portland, OR 97214; 503-232-1161; 800-547-3576 in Western states) sells Outline Maps used to mark sales areas. Maps are available for most Western states; sizes range from 8$\frac{1}{2}$" X 11" to 22" X 34" ($1.25 to $3.00). Pittmon also distributes zip code and freeway maps for the Portland metropolitan area.

Rand McNally (P.O. Box 7600, Chicago, IL 60680; 312-673-9100) has a line of business atlases, including:

■ *Zip Code Atlas + Market Planner*, which has full-color, 11" X 15" state, city, and metro area maps. Five-digit zip code boundary maps are printed on acetate overlays for the maps. The atlas comes in a portfolio with a 10-ring binder and Velcro closure ($475).
■ *Commercial Atlas + Marketing Guide* ($295), the oldest continuously published atlas in the country, revised annually.
■ *The Business Travelers Road Atlas* ($16.95), a 160-page wire-bound atlas that contains the standard *Rand McNally Road Atlas* maps, plus maps of major airports and reference data on area codes, state gas taxes, and driving time. Also included is a state-by-state list of convention facilities, toll-free hotel and car-rental telephone numbers, and expense-account information.

Thomas Bros. Maps (17731 Cowan Dr., Irvine, CA 92714; 714-863-1984; 800-899-6277) offers business maps for California. Products include:

■ Arterial Wall Maps of the Bay Area and Los Angeles, showing freeways, major highways, and major streets. Prices range from $24.95 for the "Bay Area and Vicinity Arterial" map (28" X

40") to $119.95 for the "Southern California Sales & Marketing" map (69" X 52").
■ Thomas Zip Code Editions ($18.95 to $37.95) for Los Angeles and Orange counties, San Bernardino/Riverside counties, San Diego County, Santa Barbara and San Luis Obispo/Ventura counties; and, in Northern California, Sacramento County, San Francisco/Alameda/Contra Costa counties, and Santa Clara/San Mateo counties.
■ Census Tract Editions ($39.95 to $59.95) for the following counties: Los Angeles/Orange, San Bernardino/Riverside, San Diego, Santa Barbara and San Luis Obispo/Ventura, Alameda/Contra Costa, San Francisco/Marin, Santa Clara/San Mateo, and Sacramento; also available for King/Pierce/Snohomish counties in Washington ($69.95).

T. R. Map Co. (16403 W. 126th Terr., Olathe, KS 66062; 913-782-6168) publishes full-color Metro Area Office Wall Maps (38" X 50"; $74.50), which include house numbering systems, railroads, water features, city limits, subdivision names, public buildings, shopping centers, and various other landmarks. Maps are available for metro areas in Arkansas, Iowa, Kansas, Missouri, Nebraska, and Oklahoma. Also available is a one-color map of suburban Johnson County, Kansas (52" X 63"; $49).

Visual Planning Division, MagnaPlan Corp. (6805 Blvd. Decarie, Montreal, Canada H3W 3E4; 514-739-3116) distributes business maps from various sources. The company claims to be able to fulfill virtually any request for business maps and map accessories, including magnets, pins, and adhesive dots.

Western Economic Research Co. Inc. (8155 Van Nuys Blvd., Ste. 100, Panorama City, CA 91402; 818-787-6277) produces a full line of business maps for most metropolitan areas. Map categories include 5-Digit Zip Code Outline Maps, Census Tract Outline Maps, Updated 5-Digit Zip Code Annual Demographic Estimates, Major Street and Highway—Freeway Community Maps, and 1990 Census Demo-

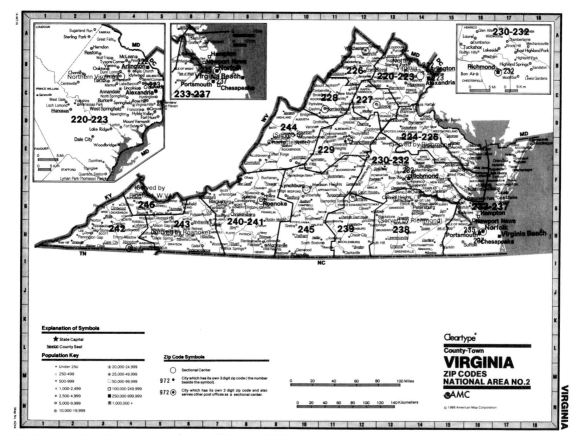

An American Map Corporation zip code map of Virginia. ©1986 American Map Corporation. Reprinted with permission.

graphic Maps. It also offers Annual Demographic Estimates for all zip codes in the U.S., either printed or on diskette. Western Economic Research offers extensive specialty business maps for the Los Angeles County area, including a "Hispanic Growth Map" (1991-92; 11" X 17"), a "Hi-Rise Office Building Map," and "Distribution of Manufacturing Employment Map."

Wide World of Maps, Inc. (2626 W. Indian School Rd., Phoenix, AZ 85017; 602-279-2323) publishes various maps of the Phoenix and Tucson metropolitan areas. Titles include

black-and-white, color, and zip code wall maps of both metropolitan areas (60" X 42"; black-and-white, $41.95). It also produces arterial street maps for both areas, as well as a "Proposed Freeway and Expressway Routes" map detailing existing, planned, or under-construction freeways and expressway routes (85 cents each; 8$\frac{1}{2}$" X 11").

■ **See also: "Census Maps," "Energy Maps," "Land-Ownership Maps," "Map Software," "Natural Resource Maps," "Selected Atlases," "Urban Maps and City Plans," and "Utilities Maps."**

Census Maps

Every 10 years, the Bureau of the Census compiles and tabulates millions of statistics about Americans. Between these decennial censuses, it gathers and disseminates monthly, quarterly, and annual information on other demographic and economic areas, including its economic, agriculture, and government censuses every five years. Summary reports that present the data collected usually display appropriate maps. A variety of other maps can be purchased separately from the publications and computer tape files, either from the **Government Printing Office** or directly from the **Census Bureau**. The census data and maps are useful to businesses looking for prospective markets; to developers in search of sites for new homes, offices, or factories; to analysts concerned with demographic data and population trends; and to anyone else with an interest in the numbers, distribution, incomes, life-styles, and so on, of Americans.

For the 1990 census, the Census Bureau has prepared an automated geographic data base for the United States and its territories. This data base is called TIGER (for Topologically Integrated Geographic Encoding and Referencing). The 1990 census maps will be available as publication-size or full-size (approximately 36" X 42") map sheets. For the 1990 census, as it did for the 1980 census, the bureau is producing three categories of map types: 1990 census maps, summary reference outline maps, and thematic or statistical maps. Many maps will be of publication quality. Most maps will be black-and-white, but the bureau will present a few thematic maps in color.

Selected maps will be included in various printed 1990 report series: the 1990 Census of Population and Housing (1990 CPH series), the 1990 Census of Population (1990 CP series), and the 1990 Census of Housing (1990

CH series). Similar to the 1980 census reports, plans call for the national summary report in each series to include a few thematic maps.

The 1990 map products, with the notable exception of the 1990 census map series, are similar to the 1980 census products. The 1990 county block series replaces five map series that comprise the 1980 census maps. The 1980 census maps include the Metropolitan Map Series, the Vicinity Map Series, the County Map Series, the Place Map Series, and the Place-and-Vicinity Map Series; these maps are still available for purchase, primarily from the Census Bureau. Two map products are new for 1990: the Voting District Outline Map Series and the Urbanized Area/Highway Map Series.

The 1990 census block maps are detailed summary-reference outline maps. The map series is county-based, consisting of one or more—usually more—full-size map sheets for each county or statistically equivalent area, supplemented by an index map. They are available for American Indian/Alaska Native Lands, Incorporated Places, and Census Designated Places also. The map sheets for each county are at one of several standard scales. Like the 1980 census maps, the 1990 maps portray most of the elements of census geography, from census block to international boundary. Most of the various geographic entities recognized for the census are identified by boundary, name, and, in most cases, Federal Information Processing Standards (FIPS) code. The maps also show a wide range of linear base features—primarily roads, streams, and railroads—along with landmark features such as schools, military installations, and major parks.

Whereas the 1990 census block map series portrays most geographic entities for which the Census Bureau tabulates decennial census data, the other summary-reference outline map series focus on specific levels of informa-

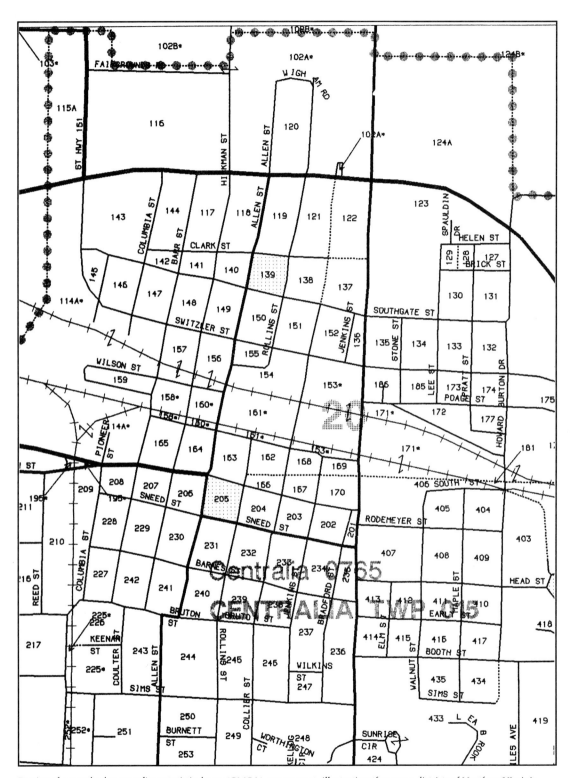

Portion of a standard metropolitan statistical area (SMSA) census tract, illustrating the census districts of Northern Virginia.

tion and depict only selected geographic entities. Geographic entities are identified by boundary symbology, type style, name, and, usually, code. Most of the summary-reference outline map series identify linear base features that coincide with the displayed geographic entity boundaries. Summary-reference outline maps include the following:

■ "County Subdivision Outline Maps." This is a state-based map series. The maps for each state or statistically equivalent entity will be produced at one of several standard scales as full-size map sheets. A page-size version of the county subdivision maps, in sections, will be included in the 1990 CPH, 1990 CP, and 1990 CH series of printed reports for each state. A full-size, plotted wall map is available for each state. The subdivision map series portrays all appropriate international, state, American Indian/Alaska Native area (AI/ANA), county, county subdivision, and place-boundaries names.

■ "State/County Outline Maps and State Metropolitan Area Outline Maps." The State/County map series is issued at various scales in a page-size format. For each state or equivalent area, the maps portray the included counties. The State/Metropolitan Area map shows the three types of metropolitan areas defined by the Office of Management and Budget: metropolitan statistical areas (MSAs), consolidated MSAs (CMSAs), and primary MSAs (PMSAs); it also shows the capital and selected large cities in each state.

■ "Voting District (VTD) Outline Maps." This is a county-based map series, produced at one of several standard scales as one or more full-size map sheets. The maps show international, state, county, AI/ANA, county-subdivision, place, and VTD boundaries and names. The maps also identify selected linear base features that coincide with or approximate VTD boundaries available or those counties for which states delineated the VTDs for the bureau only. VTDs are shown separately on the PL94-171 County Block Maps as well.

■ "Census Tract/Block Numbering Area (CT/

BNA) Outline Maps." This is a county-based map series, produced at one of several standard scales as one or more full-size map sheets. The maps show international, state, AI/ANA, county, county-subdivision, place, and CT/BNA boundaries and names. The maps also identify selected linear base features that coincide with CT/BNA boundaries.

■ "Urbanized Area (UA) Outline Maps." The UA Outline Maps are a UA-based map series. Scale varies within a page-size format. A large UA may be shown as a multipage map, whereas several small UAs will be grouped on a single page. This map displays international, state, AI/ANA, county, county-subdivision, and place boundaries and names. Additionally, the UA Outline Maps depict the boundary and the shade coverage of each UA.

■ "UA/Boundary Maps." This map series shows the extent of each urbanized area in relation to major roads and water bodies, as well as international, state, AI/ANA, county, county-subdivision, and place boundaries; it also displays and identifies other linear features that coincide with the UA boundaries.

■ "Census Regions and Divisions of the United States." This is a single-page map of the conterminous U.S., with Alaska and Hawaii shown as insets. The map shows the names and boundaries of the four census regions and nine divisions, as well as the states.

■ "Metropolitan Areas of the United States, Urbanized Areas of the United States, and American Indian/Alaska Native Areas of the United States." These are individual, two-page maps of the conterminous U.S., with Alaska and Hawaii shown as insets. Each map displays state and county boundaries, as well as the outlines or locations and names of the geographic areas specified in the map title.

Thematic, or statistical, maps depict a wide variety of topics. A thematic map presents the distribution or structure of a specific set of data. The GE-90 series is a wall-size (approximately 35" X 46") map series, generally at a scale of 1:5,000,000, that depicts data by county or displays names and boundaries of specific

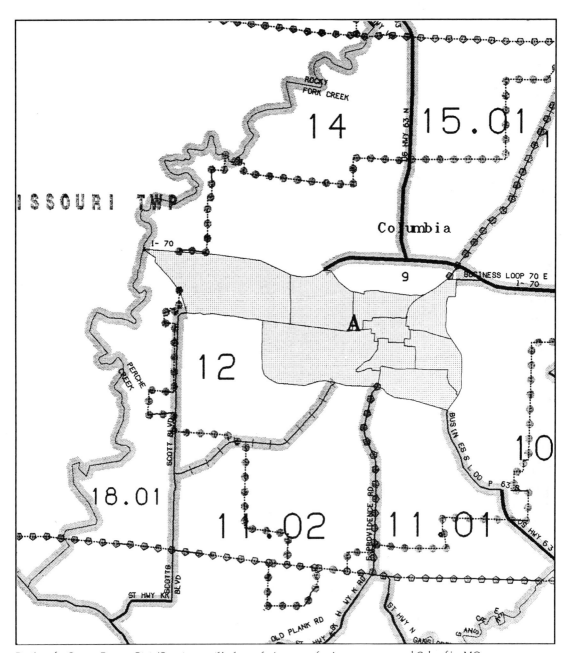

Portion of a Census Bureau State/County tract/block numbering map showing an area around Columbia, MO.

geographic entities for the entire United States. Subject titles in this series include "United States Base Map," "Metropolitan Areas" (for the most recent year for which changes were announced), "1980 Population Distribution" (both "daytime" and "nighttime" versions), and "Race as a Percentage of Total Population."

Most of the GE-90 series are four-color maps.

The Census Bureau also prepares page-size thematic maps for inclusion in the national summary reports for the several censuses. The maps in the Census Bureau's 1980 *Number of Inhabitants, U.S. Summary* report are either state- or county-based maps. The 1990 census map

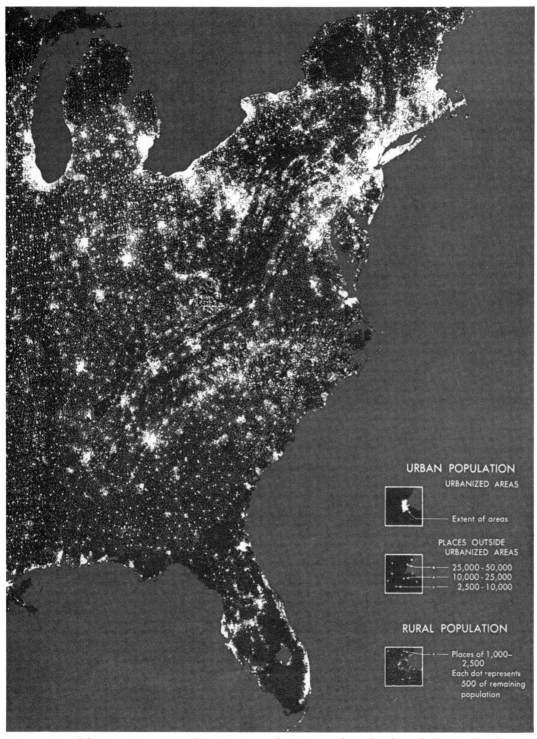

URBAN POPULATION
URBANIZED AREAS

Extent of areas

PLACES OUTSIDE
URBANIZED AREAS

25,000 - 50,000
10,000 - 25,000
2,500 - 10,000

RURAL POPULATION

Places of 1,000–
2,500
Each dot represents
500 of remaining
population

Eastern portion of the Census Bureau's "Nighttime View" map, illustrating population distribution by depicting how the country might appear from above at night.

titles include "Major Acquisitions of Territory by the United States and Dates of Admission of States," "Metropolitan Areas of the United States," "Urbanized Areas of the United States," "Regions and Census Divisions of the United States," and "Center of Population for the United States: 1790 to 1990" (both mean and median versions).

The Census Bureau has published graphic summaries portraying data for the 1977 Economic Censuses and for each Census of Agriculture from 1967 through 1982; a similar atlas for the 1987 Census of Agriculture is also now available (approximately 54 reports; single copies vary in price). The maps are for the United States, showing state outlines, with the data displayed by dots or in color shading.

The Census Bureau published a *Congressional District Atlas* for the 100th Congress and plans to produce one for the 103rd Congress to show the new congressional districts resulting from

the use of the 1990 census data; replacement pages will be made available as required to reflect any revisions for the 104th and subsequent Congresses. These maps are included in CPH-4, "Characteristics for Congressional Districts of the 103rd Congress." The atlas contains one page-size map for each state, and page-size insets for counties located in two or more CDs. The state maps include international, state, CD, and county boundaries and names. The inset maps display and identify appropriate geographic entities and CD boundaries of members as well as features that coincide with CD boundaries.

■ **See also: "Business Maps," "Energy Maps," "Map Software," "Native American Land Maps," "Political Maps," "United States Maps," and "Urban Maps and City Plans."**

Emergency Information Maps

The adage "Forewarned is forearmed" is especially true when it applies to rising flood-waters or tremors signaling a major quake. Maps of potential or past disasters can often avert serious injury and property loss. But mapping for emergencies can be a tricky thing. Not knowing what emergency will occur, or when and where it might strike, makes it virtually impossible to plan for every event. Still, areas that are flood- or earthquake-prone, seaside towns frequently hit by hurricanes or tidal waves, and any place with a history of disaster will probably have maps for evacuation and insurance purposes.

Emergency maps have been around for as long as there have been emergencies. Over the centuries, there have been "plague maps" showing the spread of disease; flood and fire maps showing damage to life and property; and countless other diagrams, charts, and maps attempting to illustrate and evaluate the havoc nature, man, or both can have on the environ-

ment. There have been preventive maps as well: countless lives and valuable property have been saved by use of maps of floodplains, faults, unstable areas prone to mud slides and avalanches, and tornado "alleys" that seem to attract nearby twisters.

Among the most common emergency information maps are flood maps. While flooding damage takes its toll in billions of dollars and hundreds of lives annually, flood maps have been highly successful in helping potential victims prepare for the onslaught of mud and water. In some regions, simply having a map of floodplain locations—and avoiding building on them—can make the difference between financial ruin and survival.

Seismicity maps of earthquake regions are also frequently compiled. Their usefulness for pinpointing regions where earthquakes have occurred or may strike make them valuable tools for planning and constructing new roads, industries, or communities. Seismicity maps

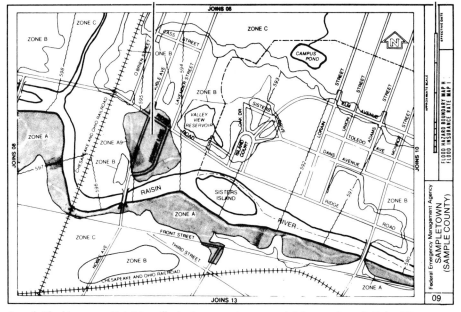

Sample Flood Insurance Rate Map, illustrating property areas and risk zones, from the Federal Emergency Management Agency's Flood Insurance Program.

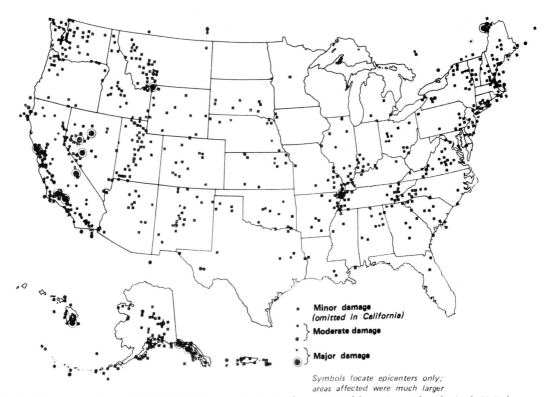

National Oceanic and Atmospheric Administration map pinpointing the epicenters of damaging earthquakes in the United States.

are also helpful in the study of faults, shifts, and movement in the Earth's crust.

Other emergency maps available include civil evacuation maps, maps of dangerous tides or currents, maps of active volcano regions, and maps predicting or tracing the paths of such natural disasters as avalanches and hurricanes. But emergency information maps are useful in another way: they have historical value.

The fire-insurance maps the **Sanborn Map Company** began creating in 1867 were certainly utilitarian at the time. Now, however, they are among the **Library of Congress**'s most prized collections. Because of the regularity with which Sanborn updated its maps, historians use the works to study the growth of hundreds of American towns and cities. The maps are so detailed that over a single decade one can trace the advances made in building materials or the changing demographics of a neighborhood.

Even the earliest Sanborn map in the Library's collection, an 1867 fire atlas of Boston, categorizes buildings, materials, construction, and contents by level of fire hazard.

Certain emergency maps, especially those for civil evacuation, are created by local, county, or state officials rather than by the federal government. Uncle Sam does, however, produce numerous seismicity, floodplain, storm-tracking, and tidal-warning maps through its agencies, including the **U.S. Geologic Survey**, the **National Geophysical Data Center**, and the **Federal Emergency Management Administration**.

GOVERNMENT SOURCES, UNITED STATES

Federal Emergency Management Agency. FEMA runs the National Flood Insurance Program, which creates and distributes Flood Hazard Boundary Maps, designed to show

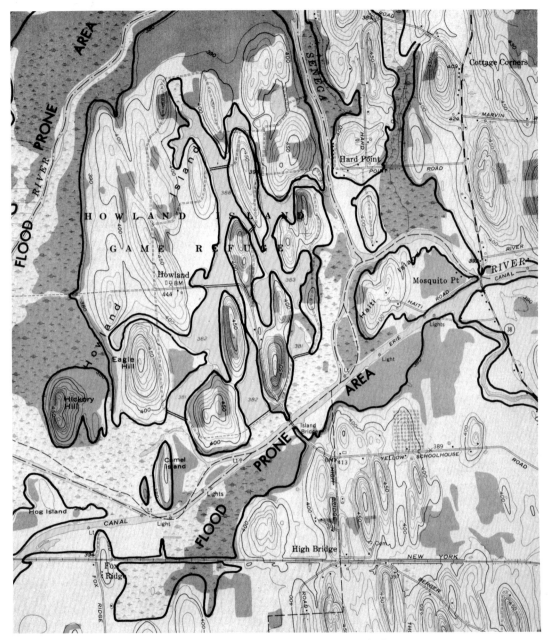

Portion of a Montezuma, N.Y., quadrangle map of flood-prone areas, drawn to a scale of 1:24,000.

where flooding may occur within communities, and Flood Insurance Rate Maps (FIRMs), which illustrate the varying severity of flood-hazard zones and aid in establishing flood-insurance rates for specific properties within a community. The maps in both series are created in two forms: the "flat-map format" contains a map index, a legend on the cover sheet, and 11" X 17" map pages covering the community; the "multiple-fold format" (also known as the "z-fold" format) resembles a standard folded road map and includes a map index only if more than one map page is required for the community.

A free pamphlet, "Guide to Flood Insurance Rate Maps" (FIA-14), is available free from FEMA (see Appendix B). Boundary maps for your area may be obtained by calling FEMA toll-free (800-333-1363).

National Geophysical Data Center. The NGDC, part of the **National Oceanic and Atmospheric Administration**, produces numerous seismicity and tsunami maps, useful for seeing where earthquakes and tsunamis have occurred historically. Examples of maps available include:

■ "Significant Earthquakes Map, 1900-79" ($10 folded; 41" X 54"), a world map produced in 1980.
■ "Seismicity Map of the Middle East, 1900-83" ($10 folded; 41" X 54"), produced in 1985.
■ "Seismicity Map of Middle America, 1900-79" ($10 folded; 35" X 41"), created in 1982.

■ "Tsunamis in Pacific Basin, 1900-83" ($10 folded; 43" X 60"), produced in 1984.

COMMERCIAL SOURCES

Williams & Heintz Map Corp. (8119 Central Ave., Capitol Heights, MD 20743; 301-336-1144) produces, but does not sell, many kinds of geologic maps. The maps are custom-made for a number of companies, state geologic offices, and other groups needing specialized work. Recently, they have produced "Earthquake Planning Scenario on the Newport-Inglewood Fault Zone in Southern California" and "Planning Scenario for a Major Earthquake, San Diego–Tijuana Metropolitan Area, 1990" ($22 each), available from the **California Division of Mines & Geology**, P.O. Box 2980, Sacramento, CA 95812.

■ **See also: "Geologic Maps" and "Weather Maps."**

Energy and Utilities Maps

From light bulbs to limousines, we are as dependent on electricity, gas, and oil as our primitive ancestors were on clubs, stones, and knives. The search for new energy sources has become a serious endeavor for scientists and engineers—and mappers. Without the means to pinpoint these resources, the wealth of the Earth's natural energy would remain hidden.

There are energy and utilities maps for every type of energy source. Sunshine maps show the locations on Earth where sunlight is most plentiful; coal- and oil-investigation maps point out where these resources can be found. There are maps of hydroelectric and nuclear power plant sites, gas pipelines, and oil refineries, as well as maps of the sediment on the ocean floor where retrievable hydrocarbons can be found. And there are maps showing modern communications systems.

The federal government produces many of these maps, reports, and charts used by those in both the public and private sectors. Other sources of energy maps are public utilities, mining or oil companies, and geologic map companies or organizations.

GOVERNMENT SOURCES, UNITED STATES

The U.S. government is a primary source for energy maps because of its subsidized utilities projects (such as the Tennessee Valley Authority) and its awareness of the strategic importance of energy independence. Some of the agencies producing energy-related maps include:

Federal Energy Regulatory Commission (FERC). FERC produces a map illustrating interstate natural gas pipelines in the U.S. "Major Natural Gas Pipelines" ($3.75; 13" X 18") shows major existing pipelines, as well as those proposed or under construction; locations of natural gas fields; and imports and exports of gas from Canada and Mexico. It is available from the Government Printing Office and the FERC Public Reference Branch.

Central Intelligence Agency. The CIA has several international energy maps available through the National Technical Information Service, including:

■ "China: Fuels, Power, Minerals and Metals" ($7.50; PB 83-928207).
■ "Eastern Europe: Major Power Facilities" ($11.50; PB 82-927905).
■ "Middle East Area Oilfields and Facilities" ($11.95; PB 88-928368).
■ "Soviet Union Electric Power," including its petroleum-refining and chemical industry ($10; PB-88-928311).

National Climatic Data Center. A good source for historical maps of solar energy is the NCDC (Federal Bldg., Asheville, NC 22801; 704-259-0682), which produces "A History of Sunshine Data in the United States, 1891-1980" ($1; available in fiche only) as part of its Historical Climatology series. The study gives digitized, summarized monthly and annual totals, when available, of "duration of sunshine" from 239 observation sites between 1891 and 1980. An accompanying map shows the sunshine station network as it existed in 1891, 1900, 1920, 1940, 1960, and 1980.

U.S. Geological Survey. USGS's National Atlas Program has two sunshine map sets:

■ "Monthly Sunshine." This 1965-edition sheet map contains theoretical maximum and mean actual hours of yearly sunshine for selected locations, as well as 12 monthly maps of mean actual sunshine ($3.10; US00478 38077-AI-NA-17M-00).
■ "Annual Sunshine, Evaporation, and Solar

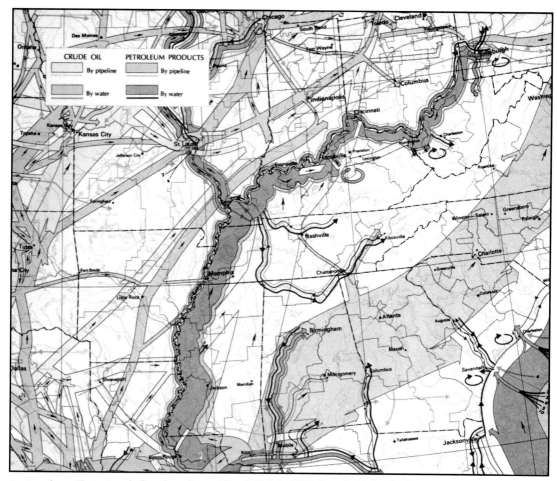

Portion of map illustrating the flow of petroleum within the U.S. in 1974, from the National Atlas.

Radiation." This 1969 sheet contains three maps of mean actual sunshine, annual pan evaporation, and May-October evaporation, and five maps of annual solar radiation and mean solar radiation for January, April, July, and October ($3.10; US00565 38077-AJ-NA-17M-00).

Also available from the U.S. Geological Survey are a number of gas-, oil-, and coal-investigation maps, many of which are produced by the Bureau of Mines. (See also "Geologic Maps.") For listings of these maps, write or call the nearest USGS Earth Science Information Center (see Appendix B).

Tennessee Valley Authority. TVA produces two maps illustrating the transmission lines and

private utilities of TVA's roughly 40,910-square-mile territory, covering parts of Tennessee, Alabama, Georgia, Kentucky, Mississippi, North Carolina, and Virginia. The map, revised in 1992 ($5, plus $1 postage), is 31" X 40" and shows TVA and private-utilities transmission lines, dams, generating plants, highways, railroads, county and state boundaries, cities and towns, and rivers and lakes.

GOVERNMENT SOURCES, CANADA

Canada Map Office (615 Booth St., Ottawa, Ontario K1A 0E9; 613-952-7000) distributes maps from *The National Atlas of Canada*, 5th ed. series ($8.40 Canadian each), including "Oil Pipelines" (MCR 4048), "Natural Gas Pipelines"

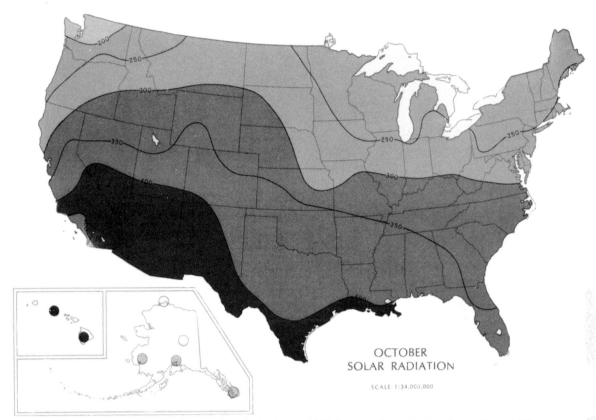

OCTOBER
SOLAR RADIATION

SCALE 1:34,000,000

Inset map depicting nationwide levels of mean solar radiation in the mid-20th century during October, from a National Atlas sheet of solar radiation maps.

(MCR 4049), and "Electricity, 1987" (MCR 4144). Maps from the 4th ed. (1973) are also available, and include: "Fossil Fuels and Pipelines, Eastern Canada" (MCR 1199), "Fossil Fuels and Pipelines, Western Canada" (MCR 1200), "Electricity, Eastern Canada" (MCR 1227), and "Electricity, Western Canada" (MCR 1228). The maps cost $3.45 Canadian each, plus shipping. All maps are available with either English or French text.

Maps Alberta (Land Information Services Div., Main fl., Brittania Bldg., 703 6th Ave. SW, Calgary, Alberta T2P 0T9; 403-297-7389) produces various energy maps as part of its *Alberta Resource and Economic Atlas*, including:
■ "Main Pipelines, Refineries and Gas Plants, 1984" (99 cents Canadian).
■ "Movement of Oil and Gas, 1983" (99 cents Canadian).

Maps Alberta also distributes maps from *The National Atlas of Canada, 5th ed.*, including:
■ "Electricity Generation and Transmission" ($9.30 Canadian; code 418 MCR 4069).
■ "Energy" ($9.30 Canadian; code 418 MCR 4002).
■ "Mineral Commodity Flows" ($9.30 Canadian; code 418 MCR 4081).

COMMERCIAL SOURCES

Some of the best sources for energy maps are geologic map companies or associations. Here are several that produce high-quality maps:

American Association of Petroleum Geologists (P.O. Box 979, Tulsa, OK 74101; 918-584-2555) is a membership organization for petroleum geologists. Although members receive a discount on AAPG products, the publications are also available to nonmembers. Products include:

■ "The Arabian Plate Producing Fields and Undeveloped Hydrocarbon Discoveries" ($10). This 23 1/2" X 31 1/2" color oil-field map of the Middle East denotes 560 producing fields and undeveloped hydrocarbon discoveries. The map was compiled in 1990 by Ziad Beydoun for enclosure with his AAPG Studies in Geology #33 volume, *Arabian Plate Hydrocarbon Geology and Potential—A Plate Tectonics Approach*, and is available as a stand-alone map.
■ "Sedimentary Provinces of the World" ($27, plus $1.90 shipping). This 40" X 54" map uses the latest data to classify, inventory, and rate those sedimentary deposits that may contain recoverable hydrocarbons. A 36-page booklet included with the map lists each province and shows potential hydrocarbon productivity.
■ "Geological Provinces: Contiguous 48" ($12, plus $1.90 shipping). This code map by the AAPG Committee of Statistics of Drilling was prepared for reporting well information from a standardized index map. The map lists codes for the 48 contiguous states.
■ "Geologic Provinces: Alaska" ($12, plus $1.90 shipping). Same as above, for Alaska.
■ AAPG also sells maps made by the Circum-Pacific Map Project, a series of which shows mineral resources in the Pacific Ocean region (see "Geologic Maps" for more information on this project).

Canadian Society of Petroleum Geologists (206 7th Ave. SW, #505, Calgary, Alberta T2P 0W7; 403-264-5610) produces a variety of specialized maps of sedimentary basins in Canada. A listing of maps is available.

Gulf Publishing Co. (P.O. Box 2608, Houston, TX 77252; 713-529-4301) publishes an 80-page *USSR Energy Atlas* ($35), with full-color maps and photos along with a 22" X 36" foldout color reference map.

MAPSearch Services (9800 Richmond Ave., Ste. 375, Houston, TX 77042; 713-781-7211)

publishes pipeline and facilities maps emphasizing interconnected data for natural gas, crude oil, refined-product, liquid petroleum gas, and petrochemical systems. Products include wall maps, atlases, textual data, and digital data-base information, as well as custom mapping. Recent titles include 1992 *Natural Gas Atlas of the* U.S. & Canada ($750) and 1992 *Crude Oil Atlas of the* U.S. & Canada ($750).

Omni Resources (1238 Anthony Rd., P.O. Box 2096, Burlington, NC 27216; 919-227-8300) distributes a vast array of energy maps of U.S. states and foreign countries, including:

■ "Illinois—Oil & Gas Industry Map" ($5.95; 62-6580), a four-color map illustrating oil and gas fields, pipelines, refineries, pumping stations, and underground storage fields.
■ "Oklahoma—Oil & Gas Fields Map" ($8.95; 62-8880) outlines 3,083 active and 35 abandoned fields.
■ "Finland—Energy Production and Supply" ($24.95; 64-5583). This Finnish/English map depicts energy data for nuclear, steam, gas-turbine, and hydroelectric plants, and by-products of heat from industry.
■ "Venezuela—Petroleum Resources Map" ($14.95; 65-5180). This black-and-white, Spanish-text map shows petroleum-producing regions, producing and nonproducing wells, oil and gas pipelines, and refineries.

PennWell Books (P.O. Box 21288, Tulsa, OK 74121; 918-831-9421; 800-752-9764) produces maps depicting U.S. energy resources and distribution systems. Among them:

■ "Products Pipelines of the United States & Canada" ($115; 40" X 57") uses seven colors to show liquid petroleum gas and natural gas liquid pipelines, carbon dioxide pipelines, and refined-product pipelines, along with insets of several major metropolitan areas.
■ "Natural Gas Pipelines of the United States & Canada, 3rd Ed." ($115; 40" X 57") uses nine colors to identify 220 major gas pipeline systems, including features such as pipe

diameter, compressor-station locations, and LNG terminals.

■ "Crude Oil Pipelines of the United States & Canada, 3rd ed." ($115; 40" X 57") uses seven colors to identify 116 pipeline operators, diameters, pumping stations, refinery locations and terminals, and detailed insets of major metropolitan areas.

■ "EL&P Electric Power Generation and Transmission Systems Map of the U.S." ($65; 42" X 58") is a detailed, eight-color map that identifies major transmission lines, power generation plants, operators, megawatt capacities, type of fuel, and North American Electric Reliability Council zones. A handy index lists investor-owned utility service areas with information on holding companies, subsidiaries, and headquarters locations.

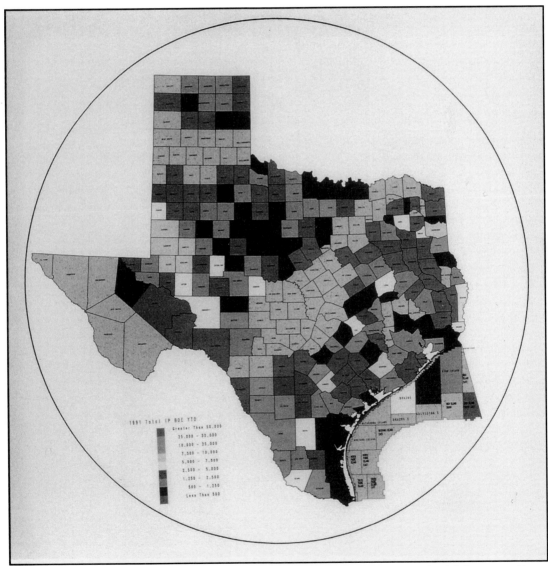

Example of map produced by Petroleum Information Corporation's Voyager GIS system, depicting the oil-drilling potential in Texas. Courtesy Petroleum Information Corporation.

Petroleum Information Corp. (4100 E. Dry Creek Rd., Littleton, CO 80122; 303-740-7100; 800-645-6277) offers a variety of map products useful to natural resource exploration and production industries. It publishes production maps, which display land survey net and oil and/or gas production values; lease maps, which depict current lease status, oil and gas wells, surface ownership, land survey net and culture; base maps, which display township range, section, latitude and longitude, culture and well spots; display maps, which are color maps showing oil and gas fields, major geologic features, states, counties, and townships; photogeologic-geomorphic maps, which illustrate geological outcrop patterns, strike and dip of beds, synclinal and anticlinal axes, fractures, faults, alignments, and geomorphic features; and structure countour maps, which show township, range and section, operating units, culture, well spots, and formation depth contours. Many of the maps are digitally produced, and options for variations in coverage are offered. Digitally produced maps are also available in digital form. Digital cartographic data containing mineral ownership status, lots, tracts, and special surveys gathered from public-land records, and digitized culture data derived from USGS topographic quads at 1:24,000 is available. PI also offers custom mapping services utilizing PI, public, and/or customer proprietary data, as well as Voyager, which is the oil and gas industry's interface to ARC/INFO Geographic Information System. A free catalog is available.

Williams & Heintz Map Corp. (8119 Central Ave., Capitol Heights, MD 20743; 301-336-1144) produces, but does not sell, many kinds of geologic maps custom-made for companies, state geologic offices, and other groups needing specialized work. Williams & Heintz energy maps available from these sources include:

■ "Map of Indiana Showing Oil, Gas & Products Pipelines, 1991," Miscellaneous Map No. 53 ($5, plus $1.50 postage), from **Indiana Geo-**

logical Survey, Publications Section, 611 N. Walnut Grove, Bloomington, IN 47405.
■ "Coal Map of Wyoming, 1991," Map Series 34 ($10 folded; $4.50 rolled), from **The Geological Survey of Wyoming**, Box 3008, University Station, Laramie, WY 82071.

UTILITIES MAPS

Like energy maps, most utilities maps generally aren't suitable for framing or gift-giving (unless the recipient is a lineman for the county); they are typically black-and-white, with perhaps a color or two to delineate utilities lines. Still, they are necessary tools for developers and construction workers, as well as for utilities companies themselves. Even the weekend gardener may have need of these maps to avoid that awful moment when hoe meets underground cable. As important as it is to know where utility lines are, it sometimes helps to know where they aren't.

The typical utility map is a straightforward representation of the lines, pipes, cables, and wires carrying one or more commodities, and pinpoints the stations or sources generating them. Utilities maps run the gamut from simple diagrams of phone lines, gas pipes, and water mains to complex depictions of sewer systems, television cables, hydroelectric plants, and any other utility that serves a given area.

The best sources for local utility maps are the utilities companies themselves. Sewer- and water-system maps are created and distributed by local and county departments of public works. Several branches of the federal government produce or distribute national and regional maps of power plants and telephone systems. Federal producers of utilities maps include the **Tennessee Valley Authority**, which has a number of power maps for its region, the **Bureau of the Census**, with a statistical map on home-heating fuel use, and the **Central Intelligence Agency**, which produces several maps detailing energy sources in the former Soviet Union and the Middle East. The **Government Printing Office** also distributes a number of utilities maps from various federal agencies.

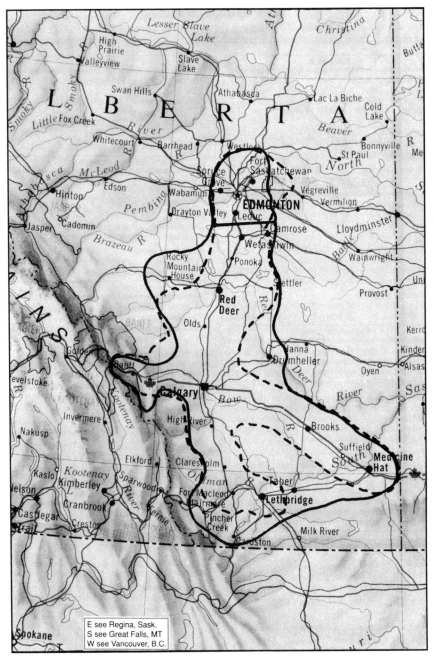

Boundaries of cellular-telephone service in portion of Alberta, Canada. The solid and dotted lines each denote one of the two competing cellular companies offering service in the area. From The Cellular Telephone Directory.

GOVERNMENT SOURCES, UNITED STATES

U.S. Geological Survey. USGS publishes the following energy resource maps, all produced in 1974: "Natural Gas Movements by Pipelines" ($3.10; US 00422), "Electric Power Transmission" ($3.10; US 00430), and "Total Interstate Energy Movement" ($3.10; US 00437), as part of the National Atlas series of maps.

GOVERNMENT SOURCES, CANADA

Canada Map Office (615 Booth St., Ottawa, Ontario K1A 0E9; 613-952-7000) distributes maps from *The National Atlas of Canada*, 5th ed., which include ($8.40 Canadian each): "Air Transportation Network" (MCR 4102), "Electricity Generation and Transmission" (MCR 4069), and "Telecommunications Systems" (MCR 4105).

Cartographic departments of foreign countries can assist in finding utilities maps for those lands, while the local tourism, sanitation, or utilities commissions of specific provinces may also be of help in locating maps for their regions.

Maps Alberta (Land Information Services Div., Main fl., Brittania Bldg., 703 6th Ave. SW, Calgary, Alberta T2P 0T9; 403-297-7389) also distributes the above maps from *The National Atlas of Canada*, 5th ed.

COMMERCIAL SOURCES

Communications Publishing Service (Box 500, Mercer Island, WA 98040; 800-366-6731, 206-232-3464) publishes *The Cellular Telephone Directory*, 4th ed., ($19.95), a 1,000-page guide including maps of the coverage areas of all U.S. and Canadian cellular-telephone companies. The guide tells how to place and receive calls as a visitor in each city, lists rates charged, and includes a listing of cellular-telephone companies, with addresses and telephone numbers.

■ **See also: "Energy Maps," "Geology Maps," "Land-Use Maps," and "Natural Resource Maps."**

WATER MAPS

Nautical Charts and Maps

Rivers, lakes, oceans, and other bodies of water are portrayed on both maps and charts, the distinction between which even some veteran old salts don't really understand. Charts differ from maps primarily in the amount of navigation information shown. Charts are much more detailed, showing a main channel sailing line, for example, as well as safety harbors, the general shape and elevation of river or lake bottoms, hazard areas, and other key symbols that enable a boat pilot to wend safely through a potentially treacherous body of water. Maps, in contrast, are much more superficial, primarily showing landmarks. They are limited more to the requirements for small-craft navigation and for general recreation guidance.

The **National Ocean Service** (NOS), part of the National Oceanic and Atmospheric Administration (itself an agency of the U.S. Depart-

ment of Commerce), produces several types of maps and charts:

■ **Coast charts** (scales from 1:50,000 to 1:150,000), the most widely used nautical charts, are intended for coast-wide navigation inside offshore reefs and shoals, entering bays and harbors of considerable size, and navigating certain inland waterways.
■ **General charts** (scales from 1:150,000 to 1:600,000) are designed for use when a vessel's course is well offshore, and when its position can be fixed by landmarks, lights, buoys, and characteristic soundings.
■ **Sailing charts** (scales smaller than 1:600,000) are plotting charts used for offshore sailing between distant coastal ports and for approaching the coast from the open water.
■ **Harbor charts** (scales larger than 1:50,000)

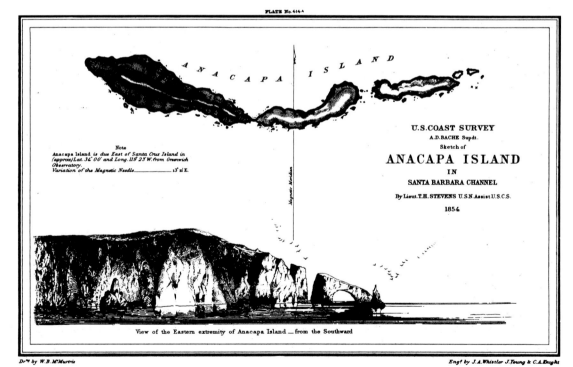

An 1854 U.S. Coast Survey sketch of Anacapa Island, off the southern California coast, engraved by a young James Whistler during his short career as an illustrator with the Survey.

are for navigation and anchorage in harbors and smaller waterways.

■ **Small-craft charts** (scales from 1:10,000 to 1:80,000) include specific information pertinent to small-craft operators. They show a great variety of information, such as tide and current data, marina and anchorage facilities, and courses. These charts are published both as folded sheet maps and in book form, for handling convenience on small boats.

■ **Canoe charts**, a series of charts of the Minnesota-Ontario border lakes, are designed to suit the needs of small, shallow-draft vessels.

■ **Coast pilots** and **Great Lakes pilots**, published in nine volumes, provide detailed navigation information that cannot be shown conveniently on charts, such as radio service, weather service, port data, sailing directions, and natural features.

■ **Special maps and data**, byproducts of the nautical charting program, are generally for non-navigational use. They include topographic surveys and planimetric shoreline maps, aerial photographs, hydrographic smooth sheets, graphic depth records, descriptive reports of surveys, and sedimentology sample data (see "Ocean Maps" for details of such map products).

GOVERNMENT SOURCES, UNITED STATES

Defense Mapping Agency. DMA, through its Hydrographic Center, publishes a variety of maps covering foreign regions, most priced around $13.25. A complete list of nautical charts available from DMA is contained in DMA's *Catalog of Maps, Charts, and Related Products—Hydrographic Products* (Part II, Vol. 1; $10.50), available from DMA's Combat Support Center. The catalog includes DMA's series of "world charts," showing major oceans and shipping regions, and its several hundred "coastal, harbor, and approach charts," covering smaller regions throughout North America. The DMA catalog is color-coded, indicating which charts are available from DMA, NOS, and the Government Printing Office, and which must be

obtained from other nations' hydrographic offices or sales agents. The catalog contains a complete name-and-address listing of DMA nautical chart agents throughout the U.S. and in 40 countries, as well as order forms for ordering charts available directly from DMA.

National Ocean Service. NOS publishes free chart catalogs—actually large, folded maps—that list nearly a thousand available charts. There are five catalogs: number one covers the Atlantic and Gulf Coasts, including Puerto Rico and the Virgin Islands; number two covers the Pacific Coast, including Hawaii, Mariana and Samoa Islands; number three covers Alaska, including the Aleutian Islands; number four covers the Great Lakes and adjacent waterways, and number five covers bathymetric and fishing maps, including topographic/bathymetric maps. Catalogs one through four are useful for another reason: Each contains a listing of the hundreds of authorized NOS nautical chart dealers throughout the U.S. and Canada.

NOS also provides information and indexes on the following lake and river charts: "Lakes" (Cayuga, Champlain, Great Lakes, Mead, Minnesota-Ontario border lakes, Okeechobee, Oneida, Pend Oreille, Franklin D. Roosevelt, Seneca, Tahoe); and "Rivers" (Columbia, Connecticut, Delaware, Hudson, James, Kennebec, Neuse, New, New York State Barge Canal, Pamlico Sound, Penobscot, Potomac, Rappahannock, Savannah, St. Johns, St. Lawrence to Cornwall, York, and others).

A separate free publication, Dates of Latest Editions of Nautical Charts, is issued quarterly by NOS to aid mariners in obtaining up-to-date charts. Notice to Mariners, also available from NOS, is a pamphlet issued weekly by the Defense Mapping Agency in cooperation with NOS, the U.S. Coast Guard, and the U.S. Army Corps of Engineers to keep mariners advised of new publications and information on marine safety.

Tennessee Valley Authority. Since its inception in 1933, TVA has operated a Maps and

Surveys Branch that produces a great variety of nautical maps and charts. Among them are navigation charts and maps, published for the TVA main-river reservoirs, and recreation maps for each of the TVA lakes (see also "Recreation Maps"). TVA publishes a price catalog that may be obtained free from the TVA Mapping Services Branch.

U.S. Army Corps of Engineers. The Corps of Engineers publishes nautical charts of selected rivers showing water depths and other navigation data, and indexes showing water areas and the number of charts required to cover them. Covered rivers include the Allegheny, Atchafalaya, Big Sandy, Big Sunflower, Calcasieu, Cumberland, Illinois, Kanawha, Mississippi, Missouri, Monongahela, Ohio, Tennessee, and the Gulf Intracoastal Waterway. Maps and indexes may be obtained from any of the Corps of Engineers district offices.

GOVERNMENT SOURCES, CANADA

Canadian Hydrographic Service (Dept. of Fisheries and Oceans, 1675 Russell Rd., P.O. Box 8080, Ottawa, Ontario K1G 3H6; 613-998-4931) produces a wide range of publications, including standard nautical charts, small-craft charts and guides, and sailing directories for the Great Lakes and other Canadian waterways. A complete publications list is available.

Maps Alberta (Land Information Services Div., Main fl., Brittania Bldg., 703 6th Ave. SW, Calgary, Alberta T2P 0T9; 403-297-7389) produces nautical charts for many areas in Alberta and neighboring provinces. The charts show bearings, soundings, heights, lake and river resolutions, monthly water levels, buoy markers, radar reflectors, mileage, beacon range, port and starboard targets, rocks, rapids, and shoals. Prices vary; a catalog containing chart information is available upon request. Also available is "Symbols and Abbreviations Used on Canadian Nautical Charts" ($3 Canadian). Maps Alberta also sells hydrographic maps depicting water depths of lakes through-

out the province ($2.85 Canadian each, ordered by lake name; code 240).

Saskatchewan Property Management Corp. (Central Survey and Mapping Agency, Distribution Center, 2045 Broad St., 1st fl., Regina, Saskatchewan S4P 3V7; 306-787-2799) produces hydrographic charts for Lake Athabasca, Lac La Ronge, Poplar Point to Stony Rapid, and Slave River to Mackenzie River ($12 Canadian each). Bathymetric maps are also available for more than 525 lakes in the province. Costs are $1 to $3 each, and map sizes vary; a list is available upon request.

COMMERCIAL SOURCES

While the federal government is the primary producer of up-to-date nautical maps and charts, there are some commercial sources as well. At least one source distributes renderings of sailing days long past.

Better Boating Association, Inc. (295 Reservoir St., Needham, MA 02194; 617-449-3314) produces "Chart Kits," books containing full-color reproductions of government charts. Titles available include: The Bahamas; Canadian Border to Block Island, Rhode Island; Cape Cod Canal to Cape Elizabeth; Cape Elizabeth to Eastport, Maine; Cape Sable—Clearwater; Chesapeake and Delaware Bays; Florida East Coast; Florida Keys; Florida West Coast; The Intracoastal Waterway—Norfolk, Virginia to Jacksonville, Florida; Jacksonville to Miami; Lake Michigan; Long Island Sound; Narragansett Bay to Nantucket; New Orleans to Panama City, Florida; New Orleans to Texas Border; Southern California; and Texas. Prices range from $49.95 to $94.95; sizes range from 12" X 17" to 17" X 22."

Bluewater Books & Charts (1481 SE 17th St., Ft. Lauderdale, FL 33316; 305-763-6533; 800-942-2583) is one of the largest volume nautical charts agents in North America, with worldwide chart coverage and more than 25,000 nautical books and charts in stock. Bluewater is an

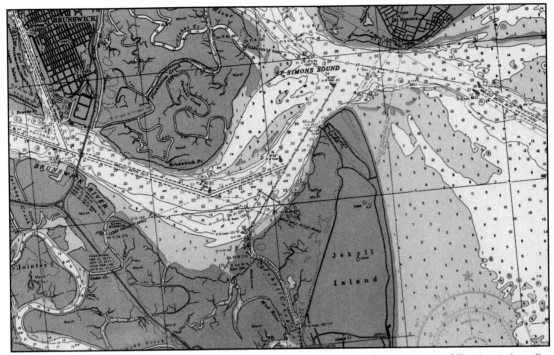

Portion of the southern Georgia coast, from the Better Boating Association's Chart Kit for Region 6: "Norfolk, VA to Jacksonville, FL—The Intercoastal Waterway."

agent for Defense Mapping Agency, National Ocean Service (NOAA), British Admiralty, Canadian Hydrographic Service, Imray-Iolaire, Chart Kit, and other chart publishers. They also have a worldwide selection of hard-to-find cruising guides and courtesy flags for yachts.

Chartifacts (P.O. Box 8954, Richmond, VA 23225; 804-272-7120) offers both originals and reprints of antique U.S. Coast Surveys, 1851-71, the most active period of this first federal mapping of our ocean shores, harbors, and tributary rivers. Reprints are $7.50 for a small 1854 sketch of Duwamish Bay & Seattle Harbor; $20 for a large, 1865 map of New York Bay & Harbor. Old-style charts often show fascinating detail: docks, town streets, buildings, outlying roads, farm plots, railroads, shoreline views, and other details as they were more than 100 years ago. Originals are $10 to $200, based on location, detail, and condition. Ask for the 24-page catalog 3A, covering Maine through Georgia, or catalog 3B, listing items for Florida,

Gulf and Pacific coasts. Price for the catalogs is $1 each or three first-class stamps.

Clarkson Map Co. (1225 Delanglade St., P.O. Box 218, Kaukauna, WI 54130; 414-766-3000) distributes nautical charts ($13 each) of Lake Michigan, Lake Superior, and "Canadian Boundary Waters." Also available is a handy 36-page booklet, *Chart Symbols and Abbreviations* ($2.50).

Gulf Publishing Co. (P.O. Box 2608, Houston, TX 77252; 713-529-4301) publishes ChartCrafter's Mariner's Atlas series of books packed with full-color government nautical charts and "chartlets," supplements of nautical data for harbors, inlets, rivers, and other tricky waters. The 10" X 14" paperbacks are available for the following areas: *Florida Gulf Coast/The Florida Keys; Lake Michigan; Long Island Sound/ South Shore; New England; Southeast Florida/The Florida Keys; Southern California;* and *Texas Gulf Coast.*

Richardson's Marine Publishing (600 Hartrey Ave., Evanston, IL 60202; 708-491-0991; 800-873-4057) distributes nautical charts and cruising guides, including: *Richardson's Chartbook and Cruising Guides*, 12" X 18" spiral-bound chart books combining reproduced NOAA and Canadian Hydrographic Service charts with information on facility and marina services, towns, navigation and cruising, harbor photos, emergency and radio communication notes, and U.S. and Canadian customs requirements. Each book contains charts of the entire lake, including the Canadian side. Overlap lines and page references make transition from page to page as well as from small-scale to large-scale charts easy. Available for Lake Michigan, Lake Huron, Lake Superior, Lake Ontario, and Lake Erie ($63.95 each). Richardson's also sells chart book accessories, including a watertight carrier for protection of the chart book in wet weather. A catalog of products is available upon request.

Waterway Guides (6255 Barfield Rd., Atlanta, GA 30328; 404-256-9800; 800-233-3359) sells a variety of nautical charts for pleasure boaters, including Waterway Guide "ChartBooks" ($49.50 to $84.95 each) for seven areas such as "Newport to Canada," "Norfolk to Jacksonville," and "Lower Florida and Keys." Also available are Waterway Guides ($31.95 each) containing useful information on locations of bridges, docks, and the like. Guides are available for the following regions: Northern U.S., Southern U.S., Mid-Atlantic, and Great Lakes.

■ **See also: "Ocean Maps," "Recreation Maps," "River, Lake, and Waterway Maps," and "Tide and Current Maps."**

Ocean Maps

When it comes to mapping, there are essentially three "oceans." One is the geographic ocean: the ocean as it appears from space. Another is the geologic ocean: the nature of the coasts, continental margins, and the deep-sea floor. Still another is the biologic ocean: the fish, plants, and assorted other life forms that populate the deep blue sea. (There is also the nautical ocean, of course, the sailing routes used by pilots of boats and ships. See "Nautical Charts and Maps" for information on those maps.)

The earliest world maps were, in effect, maps of the oceans, which served as boundaries for earlier civilizations' perspectives of their planet. Indeed, some of the earliest surviving maps are European nautical charts that date back to the second half of the 13th century. Today's maps of the seas are somewhat more accurate, based on the digital recordings made by satellites instead of visual recordings made by seamen.

Scientists have been fascinated with the bottom of the ocean almost as long as they have studied the lands ashore. Geologists in the early 19th century speculated that the ocean floors were dull expanses of mud—featureless and flat. For centuries, naturalists thought that the oldest rocks on Earth were on the ocean floors. They believed that the present-day ocean basins formed at the very beginning of the Earth's history and that throughout time they had slowly been filled by a constant rain of sediment from the lands. Data gathered since the 1930s have enabled scientists to view the seafloor as relatively youthful and geologically dynamic, with mountains, canyons, and other topographic forms similar to those found on land. The seafloor, they found, is no more than 200 million years old—a "young" part of the globe's crust compared to the continents that contain rocks nearly twenty times that age.

Research conducted since World War II has produced an ocean of data on the seafloor, much of it based on the studies of the federal **National Ocean Service** conducted by the National Oceanic and Atmospheric Administration, an agency of the U.S. Department of Commerce. Actually, it was the war itself that produced the technology for this research. In testing different sound frequencies to help locate submarines, scientists found that certain frequencies were capable of sending sound waves through the seafloor and getting reflections from deeply buried layers of rock. This revolutionized the study of marine geology and the quality of maps of the ocean floor.

Among the most spectacular cartographic products of this technology is the glow-in-the-dark "Map of the Ocean Floor" published by **Celestial Arts** (P.O. Box 7327, Berkeley, CA 94707; 510-845-8414; 800-841-2665). The 36-inch-square map provides accurate and highly illustrated details of the mysterious terrain that underlies our oceans—in effect, what the Earth would look like without water—showing all four hemispheres from several different viewpoints. With the lights out, areas of volcanic activity glow in the dark. The map ($9.95, plus $2 postage) comes with a helpful 28-page "guide and tourbook."

NOS produces a variety of ocean maps (see "Nautical Charts and Maps" for other NOS products). Among them are:

■ **Bathymetric maps**, which are topographic maps of the seafloor. Through the use of detailed depth contours and other data, the size, shape, and distribution of underwater features are vividly portrayed. These serve as the basic tool for performing the scientific, engineering, geophysical, and environmental studies that are often required for development of energy and marine resources.

■ **Topographic/bathymetric maps** are multipurpose maps showing the topography of the ocean floor and the land nearby. These are cooperatively produced by NOS and the U.S. Geological Survey to support the coastal-zone-management and environmental-impact programs. They may also be used by land-use planners, conservationists, oceanographers, marine geologists, and others interested in the coastal zone and the physical environment of the continental shelf.

■ **Bathymetric fishing maps** are topographic maps of the seafloor designed primarily for use by commercial and sport fishermen. This series of maps, produced at a 1:100,000 scale, includes information about the type and distribution of bottom sediment and known obstructions on the seafloor, in addition to the basic information found on a standard bathymetric map. It is intended to aid fishermen in identifying where the "big ones" are biting.

■ **Geophysical maps** consist of a base bathymetric map, a magnetic map, a gravity map, and, where possible, a sediment overprint. The bathymetric map, when combined with the others, serves as a base for making geological-geophysical studies of the ocean bottom's crustal structure and composition. There are two series of geophysical maps. The 1:250,000-scale series contains the geophysical data for the continental shelf and slope. The 1:1,000,000-scale series covers geophysical data gathered in the deep-sea areas, sometimes including the adjacent continental shelf.

GOVERNMENT SOURCES, UNITED STATES

National Geophysical Data Center. The NGDC, part of NOAA, distributes a full-color "Gravity Field of the World's Oceans," a 35" X 46" map that portrays the gravitational effect of seafloor topography such as sea mounts, ridges, and fracture zones ($15).

U.S. Geological Survey. The USGS is mapping the ocean floor in the Exclusive Economic Zone (EEZ), using imaging sonar along with seismic, magnetic, and bathymetric data. (The EEZ, established by presidential proclamation in 1983, gives the U.S. jurisdiction over the living

and natural resources in the ocean area extending 200 nautical miles seaward from the offshore three-mile limit off the coast of the U.S. and its territories.) To date, a number of atlases have been published that show 2-degree-by-2-degree computer-enhanced sonar mosaics of the ocean floor, at a scale of 1:500,000. Facing each sonar mosaic is a matching image map containing preliminary geologic interpretation, names of major features, and bathymetric contours. *Atlas of the Exclusive Economic Zone Western Conterminous United States* (I-1792; 152 pages) is available for $45. Atlases of the East Coast, Alaska, and Hawaii are in preparation.

GOVERNMENT SOURCES, CANADA

Canadian Hydrographic Service (Dept. of Fisheries and Oceans, 1675 Russell Rd., P.O. Box 8080, Ottawa, Ontario K1G 3H6; 613-998-4931) produces a Natural Resource Maps series of the ocean floor adjacent to Canada. The maps, available in 1:250,000 scale, are used to identify areas of geological and geophysical significance in the search for new resources. CHS also publishes 1:10,000,000-scale bathymetric charts of Canadian areas as part of a "General Bathymetric Chart of the Oceans," sponsored by the International Hydrographic Organization and the United Nations Educational, Scientific and Cultural Organization (UNESCO). The 19 maps in the series, which includes two polar sheets at 1:6,000,000 on a Polar Stereographic projection and a world map at a scale of 1:35,000,000 on a Mercator projection, can be purchased individually or as a boxed set, which includes a supporting volume of documentation. Special-purpose maps are also produced along with descriptive text in the Marine Science Paper series.

COMMERCIAL SOURCES

AAPG Bookstore (P.O. Box 979, Tulsa, OK 74101; 918-584-2555), affiliated with the American Association of Petroleum Geolo-

Portion of the "World Ocean Map (Spilhaus Projection)," from GeoLearning Corp., showing "the whole world ocean and all the continents uncut by the edge of the map."

gists, distributes geologic maps of ocean floors, such as: "Magnetic Lineations of the World's Ocean Basins" ($33), depicting seafloor-spreading magnetic anomalies in the world's ocean basins; and "Sediment Thickness Map of the Indian Ocean" ($27), showing total sediment thickness between the seafloor and oceanic basement.

Circum-Pacific Map Project (U.S. Geological Survey, MS-952, 345 Middlefield Rd., Menlo Park, CA 94025; 415-329-4002) produces various maps of the Pacific Ocean area. See "Geologic Maps."

GeoLearning Corp. (555 Absaraka St., Sheridan, WY 82801; 307-674-6436; 800-843-

6436) distributes the "World Ocean Map," drawn with the Spilhaus projection, showing continents and oceans uncut by map edges; text provides facts about the oceans of planet Earth. The map measures 24" X 36" and costs $6.

Marie Tharp, Oceanographic Cartographer (1 Washington Ave., South Nyack, NY 10960; 914-358-5132) produces beautiful color maps of the world ocean floor, including "Floor of the Oceans" ($23.50), a 27" X 41" map created in 1975; "World Ocean Floor Panorama" ($23.50), measuring 24" X 38", available laminated or in Kimdura plastic; "Seismicity of the Earth" ($28.50), showing areas with frequent seismic activity; and "Ocean Floor Sediment and Polymetallic Nodules Map" ($18.50), measuring 44" X 76". Also available are physiographic diagrams of the South Atlantic, the Indian Ocean, and the Western Pacific ($11 each).

National Geographic Society (17th & M sts. NW, Washington, DC 20036; 301-921-1200) sells five ocean-floor maps:

■ "Arctic Ocean Floor Physical" ($7.95; 20049; 20 1/2" X 21 1/2").
■ "Atlantic Ocean Floor Physical" ($7.95; 20048; 21" X 32").
■ "Pacific Ocean Floor/Political Pacific Ocean" ($7.95; 02024; 18" X 24").
■ "World Physical/Ocean Floor" ($7.95; 02359; 43" X 30").
■ "World Physical/Ocean Floor" ($9.95; 02683; 68" X 48"), a 1992 map.

■ **See also: "Antique Maps," "Map Software," "Nautical Charts and Maps," "Selected Atlases," "Space Imagery," "Tide and Current Maps," and "World Maps."**

River, Lake, and Waterway Maps

For mapping purposes, rivers, lakes, and waterways fall primarily into the jurisdictions of three federal agencies: the Army Corps of Engineers, the U.S. Geological Survey, and the Tennessee Valley Authority, all of which are prolific cartographers. Some of their products are covered in two other sections of this book: "Nautical Charts and Maps" and "Recreation Maps."

GOVERNMENT SOURCES, UNITED STATES

U.S. Geological Survey. General information about individual major U.S. rivers may be found in a series of free brochures, "River Basins of the United States," produced by USGS. The series, which covers the Colorado, Delaware, Hudson, Potomac, Suwannee, and Wabash rivers, includes general rather than highly detailed maps of the river basins, each of which spans two or more states. Also included is information about each river's early exploration; its headwaters and mouth; its major tributaries; a description of its course, length, width, depth, and rate of flow; the river's dams, reservoirs, and canals; its geologic setting and drainage area; its water quality and use; and the major cities it passes along its route. These brochures are available from USGS publication-distribution centers (see Appendix B) and are listed in a free catalog, "General Interest Publications of the U.S. Geological Survey."

Another USGS series is its State Hydrologic Unit Maps, highly detailed maps showing the hydrographic boundaries of major U.S. river basins that have drainage areas greater than 700 square miles. (Hydrology is the study of the water cycle, from precipitation as rain and snow through evaporation back into the atmosphere.) The four-color maps provide informa-

tion on drainage, culture, hydrography, and hydrologic boundaries for each of 21 regions and 222 subregions. The maps, which cost from $2.50 to $8 each, are used primarily by water-resource planners for managing water resources and flood potential, and by land-resource planners for managing natural resources and recreation areas. The maps are available from USGS Distribution Centers (see Appendix B). A free brochure, "State Hydrologic Unit Maps," is also available from USGS.

Army Corps of Engineers. The big picture of U.S. waterways is contained in a 15" X 22" black-and-white Corps of Engineers map, "Major Waterways and Ports of the United States." On the map, navigable waterways are shown as heavy black lines, with other rivers shown with less emphasis. For the shipping rivers and waterways, there are symbols indicating locks, ports, and principal cities.

The Corps also produces maps of major rivers—considerably more colorful than the USGS versions—containing much the same types of information, with one major exception: a detailed chart of recreational facilities along each river, such as boat ramps, sanitary facilities, camping facilities, and picnic tables. The sites on the charts are keyed to the map.

The Corps of Engineers' series of maps of U.S. lakes provides considerably more detail, right down to the lakes' boat ramps, campgrounds, and concession stands. Most helpful is a series of nine regional maps: "Lakeside Recreation in New England," "Lakeside Recreation in the Mid-Atlantic States," "Lakeside Recreation in the Southeast," "Lakeside Recreation in the Great Lakes States," "Lakeside Recreation in the Upper Mississippi Basin," "Lakeside Recreation in the South Central States," "Lakeside Recreation in the

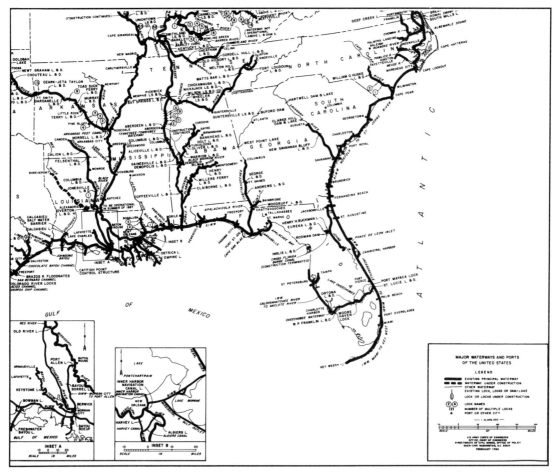

Section from the U.S. Army Corps of Engineers' map "Major Waterways and Ports of the United States," showing existing and planned waterways and ports.

Great Plains," "Lakeside Recreation in the Northwest," and "Lakeside Recreation in the Southwest." Each contains a map of the states covered along with a detailed chart that shows the facilities available at each lake—everything from the type of campsites (developed or primitive) to boat-launching ramps, showers, hunting, ice fishing, and nearby hotels and restaurants. In addition to the regional maps, there are detailed maps covering dozens of individual lakes. These show recreation areas in considerable detail, including information about all facilities. Both river and lake maps are available at all Corps offices and from the U.S. Army Corps of Engineers' Washington, D.C. office.

Unfortunately, each of the Corps' divisions and districts publishes its own maps and publications, and there is neither a central distribution center nor a single listing of all the agency's maps. The Missouri River Division, for example, distributes a "Descriptive List of Maps and Charts for Sale to the Public," available from its two offices, in Omaha and Kansas City, Missouri. Similarly, the Ohio River Division distributes maps and charts of that river, and the Chicago District distributes maps of the middle and upper Mississippi River and the Illinois Waterway to Lake Michigan; lower Mississippi maps come from the Corps' Vicksburg (Mississippi) District. And then there are the Black Warrior, Alabama, Tombigbee,

Apalachicola, and Pearl rivers, all of whose maps come from the Corps' Mobile (Alabama) District. When seeking maps of a particular area, your best bet is to contact the Corps of Engineers office closest to the area (see Appendix B).

Tennessee Valley Authority. TVA's Mapping Services Branch produces a wide range of maps and publications, all listed in a free TVA Maps price catalog. In addition to its recreation maps of TVA lakes (see "Recreation Maps"), there is also a series of full-color Tributary Watershed Maps, showing drainage basins, topography, highways, railroads, and nearby cities, and a series of full-color Reservoir Area Maps, showing reservoirs and surrounding regions. TVA also publishes navigation maps of its many rivers and tributaries.

GOVERNMENT SOURCES, CANADA

Canada Map Office (615 Booth St., Ottawa, Ontario K1A 0E9; 613-952-7000) distributes Inland Water Directorate (IWD) Maps for Canadian areas. IWD-series maps available are "Peyto Glacier Map" (IWD 1010; $5.35), and "Columbia Icefield" (IWD 1011; $5.85). A map index/price list will be sent upon request.

Saskatchewan Property Management Corp. (Central Survey and Mapping Agency, Distribution Center, 2045 Broad St., 1st fl., Regina, Saskatchewan S4P 3V7; 306-787-2799) produces two special 1:50,000-scale waterway maps: "Churchill River from Otter Lake to Nistowiak Lake," and "Churchill River—MacKay Lake" ($6 Canadian each). The agency also produces hydrographic charts for Lake Athabasca, Lac La Ronge, Poplar Point to Stony Rapid, and Slave River to Mackenzie River ($12 Canadian each).

Bathymetric maps are also available for more than 525 lakes in the province. Map sizes and prices vary; a list is available upon request.

COMMERCIAL SOURCES

Clarkson Map Co. (1225 Delanglade St., P.O. Box 218, Kaukauna, WI 54130; 414-766-3000) sells maps for lakes in Minnesota, upper Michigan, and Wisconsin (90 cents each). A free map index is available.

Map Works, Inc. (2125 Buffalo Rd., Ste. 112, Rochester, NY 14624; 716-426-3880; 800-822-6277 in New York) publishes large, full-color travel guide maps to four New York State regions—Central Leatherstocking, Finger Lakes, North County, and Western Region— that include boat launches, canal locks and parks, and marinas. The Finger Lakes map, which measures 38" X 45" and covers a 14-county region, has a special emphasis on fishing in the lakes ($3.95).

Northwest Map and Travel Center (W. 525 Sprague Ave., Spokane, WA 99204; 509-455-6981) publishes nautical and facilities maps of Roosevelt Lake in Washington ($5.50 each; 24" X 35"). Also available: "Banks Lake Bathymetric/ Topographic and Facilities Map" ($5.50; 24" X 30") and "Nautical & Facility Information for Coeur d'Alene" ($4.95; 23" X 32").

Ozark Map Co. (Hwy. 135, Rte. 2, Box 324-B, Gravois Mills, MO 65037; 314-374-6553) produces a map of the Truman Reservoir in South Central Missouri ($1.95).

■ **See also: "Nautical Charts and Maps," "Recreation Maps," and "Tide and Current Maps."**

Tide and Current Maps

Among the many remarkable qualities of Mother Earth is her ability to perform certain rituals with uncanny regularity. Tides, for example, can be predicted with astounding accuracy and plotted on tidal-current charts. These are available from the **National Ocean Service**, part of the Commerce Department's National Oceanic and Atmospheric Administration. The NOS tidal-current charts each consist of a set of 12 charts that depict, by means of arrows and figures, the direction and velocity of the tidal current for each hour of the tidal cycle. The charts, which may be used for any year, present a comprehensive view of the tidal-current movement in the respective waterways as a whole and also supply a means for rapidly determining, at any given moment, the direction and velocity of the current at various points throughout the water areas covered.

There are 11 available charts ($8 each), covering Boston Harbor, Charleston Harbor, Narragansett Bay (two charts), Long Island and Block Island Sounds, New York Harbor, Upper Chesapeake Bay, Tampa Bay, San Francisco Bay, and Puget Sound (two charts). All but the Narragansett Bay chart require that you also purchase one of the NOS Tidal Current Tables ($10). There are two: one covering the Atlantic Coast, the other covering the Pacific Coast and Asia. All NOS charts, tables, and publications are available directly from NOS (see Appendix B) or one of its authorized dealers.

Maps Alberta (Land Information Services Div., Main fl., Brittania Bldg., 703 6th Ave. SW, Calgary, Alberta T2P 0T9; 403-297-7389) distributes "Tides in Canadian Waters" ($2 Canadian). The publication is available through the Calgary Information Centre at the above address (403-297-6324).

■ **See also: "Nautical Charts and Maps," "Ocean Maps," and "River, Lake, and Waterway Maps."**

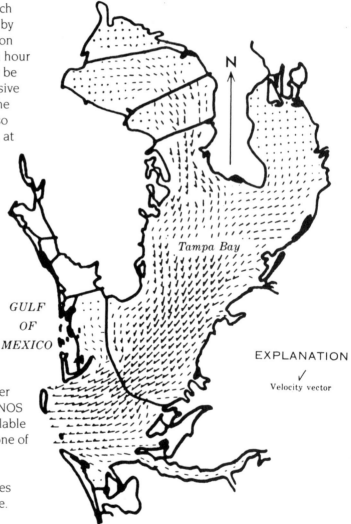

Map showing current flow and velocity in Tampa Bay, Florida, from information compiled from Landsat satellite imagery.

SKY MAPS

Aeronautical Charts

Aeronautical charts provide a wealth of fascinating information, regardless of whether you intend to take over a Beechcraft or a Boeing. Granted, these are not simple maps to read. At first glance, they seem filled with colorful circles, arrows, and other strange markings, and the little text that exists consists primarily of cryptic letters and numbers—"Picket 3 MOA 4000' to and incl. 10,000'" is one example.

But with a bit of patience, you can spot areas that are prohibited or restricted to fly over—usually military bases and other high-security locations. And you are likely to find dozens of heretofore unknown landing strips in your region—possibly belonging to a tycoon down the road who may have quietly constructed a runway capable of handling a jumbo jet. You'll find out exactly where low-flying aircraft are permitted and where they're banned, perhaps giving you the informational ammunition to inform the authorities about a commercial airliner that has been repeatedly flying over your home at an altitude a bit too close for comfort. It's all there, if you know how and where to look.

Aeronautical charts are published by both government and private publishers. Both create charts covering the skies over the United States as well as the rest of the world.

GOVERNMENT SOURCES, UNITED STATES

The **National Ocean Service** (NOS), part of the Commerce Department's National Oceanic and Atmospheric Administration, publishes and distributes U.S. aeronautical charts. Charts of foreign airways are published by the Defense Mapping Agency. In addition to the NOS's two distribution centers, domestic aeronautical charts and related publications are available through a network of several hundred sales agents, usually located at or near airports. A free publication, *Aeronautical Charts and Related Products*, includes a list of such dealers, as well

as detailed descriptions of the various charts and publications distributed by the NOS.

According to the NOS, the date of an aeronautical chart is important if you are using it for aviation purposes. The agency notes that when charted information becomes obsolete, **using the chart or publication for navigation may be dangerous**. Critical changes occur constantly, and it is important for pilots to purchase up-to-date charts. To ensure that only the latest charts are used, NOS publishes *Dates of Latest Edition*, available free from NOS distribution centers.

Available NOS charts include:

Aeronautical planning charts, used for preflight planning of long flights. Portions of the flight route can then be transferred to more detailed charts for actual use in flight. NOS publishes two types of flight-planning charts. "VFR/IFR Wall Planning Charts," at a scale of 1:2,333,232, are large (82" X 56") charts in two pieces that can be assembled to form a composite visual-flight-rules (VFR) planning chart on one side and an instrument-flight-rules (IFR) chart on the other. The chart is revised every 56 days. A one-year subscription is $45.50; single copies are $6.50. Another planning chart, the "Flight Case Planning Chart," is a somewhat smaller (30" X 50"), folded chart (scale 1:4,374,803) designed for pre- and in-flight use. It contains the same information as the VFR/IFR chart, with the addition of selected flight-services stations and National Weather Service airport offices, parachute-jumping areas, a tabulation of special-use airspace areas, a mileage table listing distances between 174 major airports, and a city-airport location index. This chart is revised every 24 weeks. A two-year subscription is $20; single copies are $4.

Visual aeronautical charts, multicolor charts designed for visual navigation of slow- to medium-speed planes. The information featured

Portion of a NOAA *sectional chart for the New York City area, showing airports, controlled airspace, restricted flying areas, and other vital information for pilots.*

includes selected visual checkpoints, including populated places, roads, railroads, and other distinctive landmarks. There are three types: Sectional Aeronautical Charts (1:500,000; 20" X 60") show the airspace for a large region of several hundred square miles; Terminal Area Charts (1:250,000; 20" X 25") show the airspace designated as Terminal Control Areas around airports; and World Aeronautical Charts (1:1,000,000; 20" X 60") cover much larger areas with much less detail. Two-year subscriptions

are $6 to $22; single-copy prices are $3 and $5.25. One helpful publication is NOAA's *Aeronautical Chart User's Guide* ($4), a colorful 36-page booklet intended as a learning tool for all three types of charts. It includes detailed definitions of the dozens of symbols used on these charts and can help any aeronautical chart reader to understand them.

Instrument navigation charts, providing information for navigation under instrument-flight rules. There are different series for low-altitude flights (below 18,000 feet), high-altitude flights, and instrument-approach-procedure (IAP) charts.

The **Defense Department** also publishes aeronautical charts, which primarily provide information about flying over airspace outside the U.S. These can be ordered through Defense Mapping Agency Distribution Services (Washington, DC 20315; 301-227-2495; 800-826-0342).

■ **FLIP (Flight Information Publications) charts** are available for most parts of the world, including Africa, Asia, and Antarctica. Each set of maps provides the information needed for flying in foreign airspace.
■ **Operational navigation charts** provide information on high-speed navigation requirements at medium altitudes.
■ **Tactical pilotage charts** provide information on high-speed, low-altitude, radar, and visual navigation of high-performance tactical and reconnaissance aircraft at very low through medium altitudes.
■ **Jet navigation charts** are used for long-range, high-altitude, high-speed navigation.
■ **Global navigation and planning charts** are suitable for flight planning, operations over long distances, and en route navigation in long-range, high-altitude, high-speed aircraft.

GOVERNMENT SOURCES, CANADA

Canada Map Office (615 Booth St., Ottawa, Ontario K1A 0E9; 613-952-7000) distributes aeronautical charts for Canada, including VFR Navigation Chart ($12.70 Canadian), drawn to a 1:500,000 scale; World Aeronautical Chart (WAC) ($12.70 Canadian); and VFR Terminal Area Chart ($10.45).

Manitoba Natural Resources (Surveys and Mapping Branch, 1007 Century St., Winnipeg, Manitoba R3H 0W4; 204-945-6666) distributes World Aeronautical Charts, Canadian Pilotage Charts, and VFR Navigational Charts for Canada. A pamphlet is available.

Maps Alberta (Land Information Services Div., Main fl., Brittania Bldg., 703 6th Ave. SW, Calgary, Alberta T2P 0T9; 403-297-7389) distributes World Aeronautical Charts, Canadian Pilotage Charts, Aeronautical Planning and Plotting Charts, and VFR Terminal Area Charts for Canada. A catalog is available.

Saskatchewan Property Management Corp. (Central Survey and Mapping Agency, Distribution Center, 2045 Broad St., 1st fl., Regina, Saskatchewan S4P 3V7; 306-787-2799) distributes World Aeronautical Charts ($12.70 Canadian each) for all areas in Canada.

COMMERCIAL SOURCES

One of the oldest and largest producers of aeronautical charts is **Jeppesen Sanderson** (55 Inverness Dr. E., Englewood, CO 80112; 303-799-9090), which creates a wide range of charts and other publications for pilots. "Jeppesens," as they are known among pilots, are available only by subscription, which includes the initial charts for a particular area plus updates (biweekly for the U.S. and Canada, weekly for other areas). In addition to the Airway Manual Service, the company offers navigational information in a wide variety of paper-based and electronic formats. It also provides a number of other aviation information services, including airport information, flight planning services, computerized weather, and pilot-training materials. A free catalog is available by writing or calling the company.

WHERE TO BUY CHARTS

The best place to purchase government and nongovernment aeronautical charts is at almost any general-aviation airport—that is, an airport, or portion of an airport, that serves private, noncommercial flights. The "fixed-base operators" (or FBOs) that run these private airport facilities typically sell charts covering the immediate region surrounding the airport; some also sell other domestic or international charts. In addition, there are many other

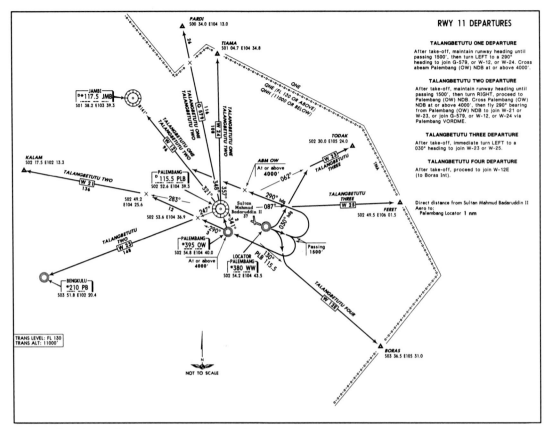

Jeppesen chart showing departure routes at Sultan Mahmud Badaruddin II Airport, Palembang, Indonesia. Copyright 1989 Jeppesen Sanderson, Inc.

retailers of the charts, including many map stores; a list of select retailers is below.

Government-produced charts, besides being available at many airports, may also be purchased through three NOS offices:

■ 439 W. York St., Norfolk, VA 23510; 804-441-6616.
■ 1801 Fairview Ave. E., Seattle, WA 98102; 206-442-7657.
■ Federal Bldg. and U.S. Courthouse, 222 W. 7th Ave., #38, Anchorage, AK 99513; 907-271-5040.

These three NOS offices also can send you NOS's free catalog mentioned earlier.

Some of the many authorized NOAA aeronautical chart sales agents are:

Aero-Supply, Inc.
Daytona Beach Regional Airport
1624 Aviation Center Pkwy.
Daytona Beach, FL 32014

Air-Delphia, Inc.
1834 E. High Ave.
New Philadelphia, OH 44663

American Aviation
Dexter Municipal Airport
Dexter, ME 04930

Aviation Management Corp.
195th St. & Bernham Ave., Bldg. 3
P.O. Box 553
Lansing, IL 60438

Bodas Aero Mart
3930 Campus Dr.
Newport Beach, CA 92660

Cableair, Inc.
1749 W. 13th St.
Upland, CA 91786

Cape Cod Aero Marine
Chatham Municipal Airport
George Ryder Rd.
Chatham, MA 02633

Denison Aviation, Inc.
Municipal Airport
Denison, IA 51442

El Cajon Flying Service, Inc.
1825 N. Marshall Ave.
El Cajon, CA 92020

Elliott Flying Service, Inc.
Quad City Airport
Moline, IL 61265

Gydan Import & Export
4137 Donald Douglas Dr.
Long Beach, CA 90808

JEM Aero, Inc.
2003 Quail St.
Newport Beach, CA 92660

Jameco Air Service
Grand Galize Airport
Osage Beach, MO 65065

Kingman Aero Services, Inc.
5070 Flightline Dr.
Kingman, AZ 86401

Leavenworth Aviation Services
2619 S. 4th St.
Leavenworth, KS 66048

Marv Golden Discount Sales, Inc.
8690 Aero Dr., Ste. 102
San Diego, CA 92123

Midway Aviation, Inc.
Rte. 1
Kearney, NE 68847

The Pilot Shop
106 Access Rd.
Norwood, MA 02062

Plane Things
1875 W. Commercial Blvd., Ste. 180
Ft. Lauderdale, FL 33304

Prescott Pilot Shoppe, Inc.
Ernest A. Love Field
Prescott, AZ 86301

San-Val Discount, Inc.
7444 Valjean Ave.
Van Nuys, CA 91406

Skyridge Aviation, Inc.
201 Airport Rd.
Franklin, NC 28734

Sportsmans Market, Inc.
Clermont County Airport
Batavia, OH 45103

Wings, Inc.
501 N. Daleville Ave.
Daleville, AL 36322

Wings and Things
1954 Airport Rd., Ste. 66
Atlanta, GA 30341

Astronomical Charts and Maps

For thousands of years observers have tried to unlock the secrets of the heavens. And with that effort has come a never-ending stream of celestial charts and maps. Today there are maps showing the landscapes of the planets and satellites that our spacecraft have visited or flown by and charts that show the bright stars of the Milky Way galaxy; some catalog the positions of other galaxies. The charts are redrawn every 50 years (a period known as an epoch), with additional updating done in the intervening years.

There are several kinds of star charts. Some are decorative, made to be put on a wall for classroom use or to pique the interest of curious passersby. The most stunning chart of this variety is "The Map of the Universe," published by **Celestial Arts** (P.O. Box 7327, Berkeley, CA 94707; 510-845-8414; 800-841-2665). Printed on black paper, this brightly colored map glows in the dark. Major constellations and zodiacal signs are vividly illustrated, as are comet paths, meteor showers, and other celestial wonders. A 16-page booklet accompanies the map.

For beginners, a novel and effective way to get to know the sky is an audio star chart. Called *Tapes of the Night Sky* ($23.95 postpaid from **Astronomical Society of the Pacific** (390 Ashton Ave., San Francisco, CA 94112; 415-337-1100), the two cassette tapes feature four "guided tours" of the bright stars and constellations of each season and come with a 60-page book of instructions, transcripts, maps, and readings. The nonprofit society publishes a 48-page, illustrated catalog that includes a wide variety of interesting products, including posters, charts, software, and a video from the Magellan spacecraft in orbit around Venus. The catalog is available for three first-class stamps

by writing to the Catalog Requests Dept. at the above address.

Young astronomers may find it easier to work with a planisphere, a wheel that is dialed to the time and date of the visible stars and constellations in the sky. Planispheres may be the most basic and helpful astronomical tool for the novice.

Many amateur astronomers interested in using star charts for outdoor gazing turn to star-atlas field guides. Often these are printed on vinyl or on a durable paper that can withstand inclement weather and other hazards that may be encountered outdoors. As you peruse what's available, think about how much information you need. A weekend observer may need charts that show only stars visible to the naked eye. Such charts are less cluttered and a lot easier to use. If you plan to take your chart outside to use while viewing, make sure that it is visible at night (stars printed in white on a black field) and that it is compact enough to accompany you, your telescope, and other necessities. If you plan to use the chart to make observations, make sure you bring along a flashlight with a red filter so you can use the atlas without being blinded by white light.

Sky Publishing Corp., **Kalmbach Publishing Co.**, and **Willmann-Bell Inc.** are the three major companies publishing reputable star charts used by amateur astronomers. Government agencies also publish star charts, as well as maps of planets and the solar system. The **National Geographic Society** offers individual maps and two beautiful star charts in its comprehensive *Atlas of the World*. Finally, a few additional companies sell planispheres and other unique types of star charts. Following is some of what's out there to make your journey through the stars easier and more enjoyable.

Night-sky planisphere from David Chandler Co. allows you to dial in on the constellation of your choice according to the current date and time.

GOVERNMENT SOURCES

The **Government Printing Office** has the following selection of astronomical charts and maps:

■ *Astronomical Almanac* ($21; 1992 edition: S/N 0-16-002117-0) is an annual publication that contains data for astronomy, space science, geodesy, surveying, navigation, and other applications.

■ *Astronomical Phenomena for the Year*, 1993 contains information on the sun, the moon, planets, eclipses, Gregorian calendar and Julian date, time zones, and related phenomena ($3.50; 0-16-035922-8).

■ *Air Almanac* ($39; 1992 edition: S/N 0-16-

034909-5) is a technical, 900-page almanac of charts that provide the astronomical data and ephemerides for navigation.

■ *Stars in Your Eyes: A Guide to the Northern Skies* explains how to locate several summer constellations of the northern sky and includes famous mythological lore ($1.50; S/N 008-022-00155-7).

U.S. Geological Survey. The USGS maintains an extensive stock of moon and planetary maps. Titles range from a topographic map of the Syrtis Major region of Mars to a geological map of the first Apollo landing site, made in 1970. Prices vary; a catalog is available.

(continued on page 237)

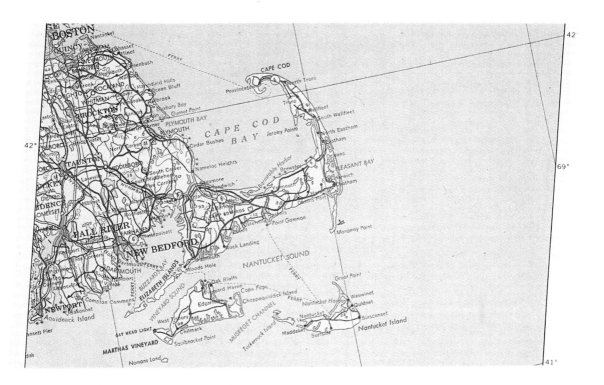

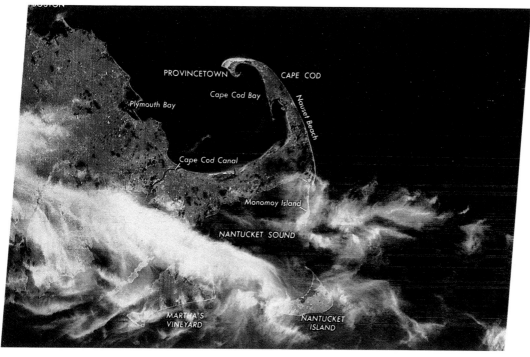

Two views of Cape Cod, Massachusetts. Top: Part of the Boston sheet of the Defense Mapping Agency's "International Map of the World." Bottom: A Landsat image covering the same region. Courtesy U.S. Geological Survey.

A polar projection of the North Pole from the Nimbus-5 weather satellite. Colors indicate variations in microwave radiometric temperature. See also "Space Imagery," page 255, and "Weather Maps," page 242.

"Map of the Universe," compiled and designed by Tomas J. Filsinger, showing astronomical and astrological phenomena. The Milky Way and other highlights glow in the dark on this poster-sized map. ©1981. Used with permission of Celestial Arts, P.O. Box 7327, Berkeley, CA 94707.

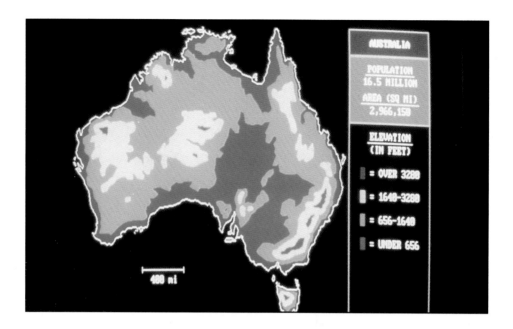

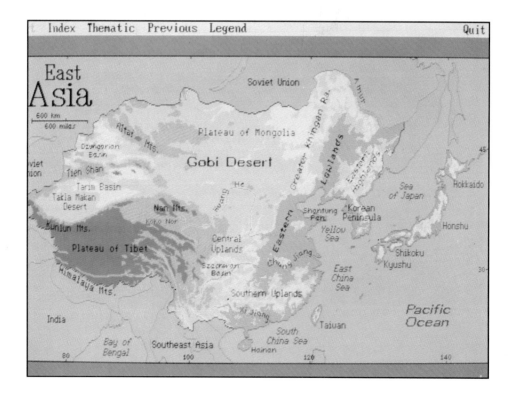

Two samples of geography education software. Top: Screen from PC Globe, courtesy Comwell Systems, Inc. Bottom: Electromap World Atlas, courtesy Electromap, Inc. See also "Geography Education Materials," page 276, and "Map Software," page 291.

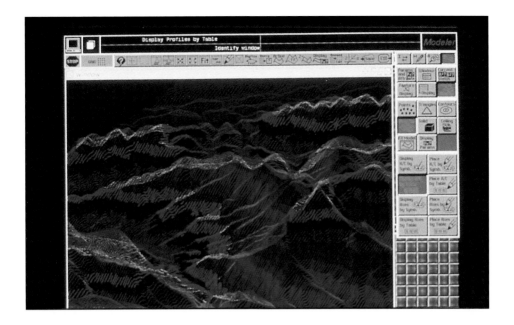

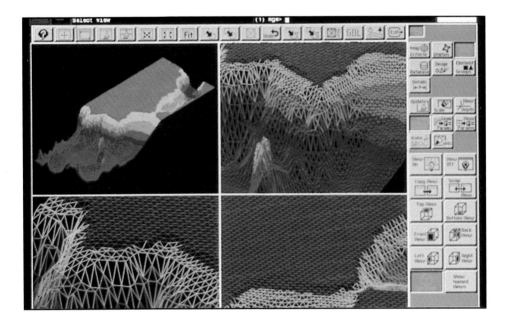

Two maps created with Intergraph Corporation's MicroStation computerized map-making system. Top: Color-coded surface mesh showing the Blue Ridge Mountains, created with TIGRIS Modeler, using a dataset from the U.S. Geological Survey. Bottom: A bathymetric model of the Straits of Gibraltar.

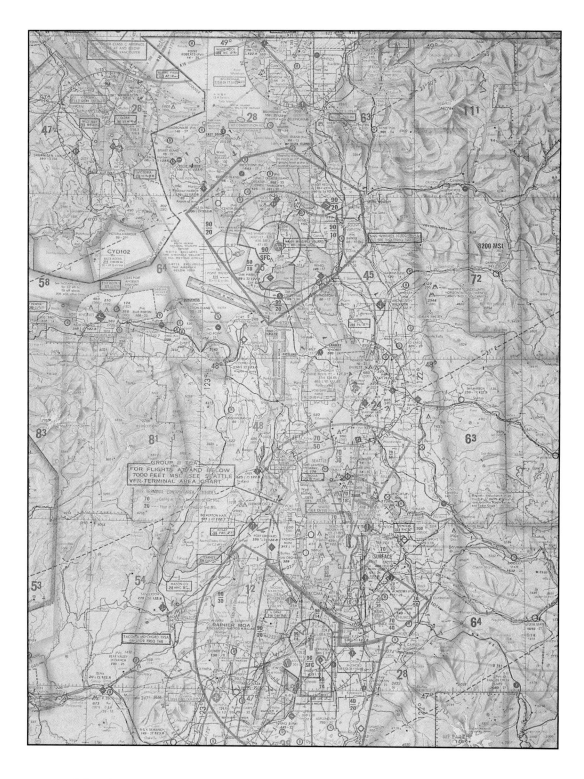

Aeronautical chart of western Washington, including Seattle, the San Juan Islands, and part of Vancouver, B.C. See also
"Aeronautical Charts," page 222.

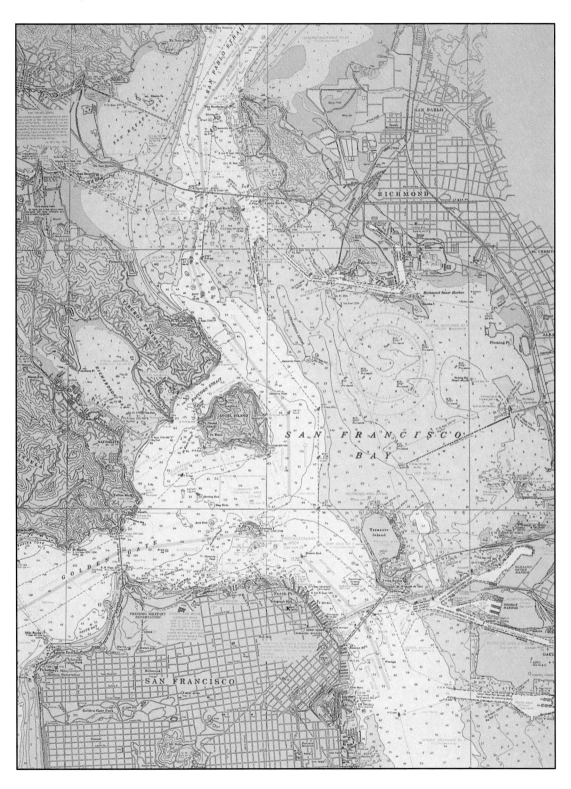

Nautical chart of San Francisco Bay, showing depth markings and other navigation information for sailors. See also "Nautical Charts and Maps," page 208.

Computer-processed wetland map of the Chincoteague Bay salt-marsh complex in the Virginia Eastern Shore.

(continued from page 228)

COMMERCIAL SOURCES

Abbeville Press (488 Madison Ave., New York, NY 10022; 212-888-1969; 800-227-7210) publishes *Maps of the Heavens*, a 148-page book featuring full-color maps of the zodiac and the constellations ($29.98).

Celestial Arts (P.O. Box 7327, Berkeley, CA 94707; 510-845-8414; 800-841-2665) offers four 36" X 36" posters showing: a map of the universe, a map of the solar system, the phases and faces of the moon, and the cosmos as perceived by the Aztecs. They have the added benefit of glowing in the dark. The maps are $9.95 each.

David Chandler Co. (P.O. Box 309, La Verne, CA 91750; 714-988-5678) has created a night-sky planisphere that allows you to dial in on the constellations of your choice according to the current date and time. Chandler's 10-inch chart is double-sided to accommodate both the northern and southern sky views, and four different versions are available for the following latitudes: Northern United States/Canada/Europe; Southern United States; Mexico/Far Southern United States; and South America/Australia/New Zealand. Chandler's book *Exploring the Night Sky With Binoculars* provides additional information about stargazing. Price for the planisphere is $3.25; the book is $3.95. These are also available through **Sky Publishing Corp.** and the **Astronomical Society of the Pacific.**

Exploration USA (P.O. Box 456, College Park, MD 20740; 301-490-2236) produces a 35" X 37" "Mars Map," based on USGS and NASA information, which includes the latest official names approved by the International Astronomical Union (IAU). The 1:25,000,000-scale map comes with a glossary and is available directly from Exploration USA for $5, plus $2 shipping.

Hubbard Scientific, Inc. (P.O. Box 760, Chippewa Falls, WI 54729; 800-323-8368)

produces several teaching charts and tools. Among the products are:

■ "Globe Kit" ($19.45), a working model of the Earth that enables students to solve various problems in such broad areas as earth measurements, astronomy, and seismology.
■ "Astronomy Study Prints" ($19.45), a set of twelve 9" X 15" charts for teaching the basics of astronomy. The set includes prints of star charts of the Northern and Southern Hemispheres, as well as prints of the planets, the sun, the moon, and the galaxies.
■ "Star Charts" ($33.50), reversible 44" X 44" sky maps of the Northern and Southern Hemispheres. The stars, nebulae, planets, constellations, and phenomena are depicted with light colors against a dark background for easy reference.
■ "Star Finder/Zodiac Dial" ($4.75), a reversible wheel for finding stars and identifying zodiac constellations.
■ "Celestial Star Globe" ($128.50), a clear model of the celestial sphere that provides a physical demonstration of star and planetary movement. It shows constellations, stars to the 5th magnitude, major nebulae, bright star clusters, and the Milky Way. Included are an Earth globe, a movable sun, a chrome meridian ring and horizontal mounting, and a study guide.

Kalmbach Publishing Co. (P.O. Box 1612, Waukesha, WI 53187; 414-796-8776) produces a wide range of astronomy materials, including magazines, books, and posters. Here are a few samples from Kalmbach's list:

■ *The Star Book*, by Robert Burnham ($9.95), is a good basic field guide to the constellations of the Northern Hemisphere. Half of the 18 pages illustrate the changes in the night sky for both the early and late portions of the four seasons. The other half describe the constellations and their history. Illustrations are white on blue for easier nighttime reference. The accompanying text and illustrations clearly explain how to identify stars and constellations.
■ *Leslie Peltier's Guide to the Stars: Exploring the Sky*

With Binoculars ($11.95) is a detailed guide on how to use binoculars to see constellations, stars, variable stars, the sun, the planets, the moon, and comets and meteors. Easy-to-read seasonal star charts and diagrams are included.
■ "Our Galaxy: The Milky Way Poster" ($16.95) shows the entire sky visible from Earth. What sets this star chart apart is that everything in the sky is shown in relation to the Milky Way. The poster shows more than 9,000 stars, all 88 constellations, and more than 250 of the brightest and most significant deep-sky objects.
■ *Philips Color Star Atlas*, by John Cox and Richard Monkhouse ($19.95), is an easy-to-use atlas showing the colors of all naked-eye stars. Ideal for amateur astronomers—naked-eye, binocular, small telescope, and armchair. Twenty wide-angle charts locate all stars down to a magnitude of +6.55, plus deep-sky objects such as galaxies, nebulae, and clusters.
■ *Observing the Moon With a Backyard Telescope*, by Michael T. Kitt ($11.95), lets every amateur astronomer begin a voyage of understanding and exploration to our closest celestial neighbor, the moon. Equipped with this handy guidebook and a telescope, readers will have all they need to embark on unforgettable lunar adventures. From the publishers of *Astronomy* magazine.
■ *Beyond the Solar System: 100 Best Deep-Sky Objects for Amateur Astronomers*, by David J. Eicher ($12.95), is an organized tour of the 100 best deep-sky objects viewed through binoculars or a backyard telescope. Readers will head out under the stars to observe spiral galaxies, glowing gas clouds, binary stars locked by gravity, and clusters of newborn blue-white suns. The description of each object includes a photograph and information about its discovery, evolution, location, and characteristics. From the publishers of *Astronomy* magazine.

Millennium Enterprises (2740 W. Olive Ave., #30, Fresno, CA 93728; 209-266-2239) publishes a "World Star Atlas" ($12.50 postpaid), an attractive 23" X 35" two-color star chart. Although not drawn to scale, it provides a clear perspective of the key celestial objects.

Using the NightStar star globe.

National Geographic Society (17th and M sts. NW, Washington, DC 20036; 301-921-1200) offers the *Atlas of the World*, 6th ed. ($59.95 softcover, $74.95 hardcover), which includes two magnificent star charts of both the northern and southern skies. Magnitudes up to 6 are included, as well as quasars, pulsars, stars, nebulae, and even a possible black hole. Also included is a map of the solar system and maps of both the near side and far side of the moon. Another astronomical map is "The Heavens" (1989; $7.95; 20037; 23" X 35").

The NightStar Co. (1334 Brommer St., Santa Cruz, CA 95062; 408-462-1049; 800-782-7122) manufactures three models of star globes that are made of soft plastic, then deflated and sealed in the shape of a bowl. The models have a movable surface that can be adjusted for any time and place on Earth and include the whereabouts of all 88 constellations. There are several versions available: NightStar Traveler ($25) is compact enough to fit in your pocket or backpack; the package includes a full-feature, foldable two-color (white on dark blue) map with simplified instructions. NightStar Classic ($45) is the top-of-the-line model; it includes glow-in-the-dark stars, a comprehensive activities handbook, two planet-finder overlays showing one full year of planetary movements, and two snap-on dials that offer the option of presetting the sky for any time, date, or latitude. The NightStar Classic Stowaway ($43) combines features of both models; it comes with the same handbook as the Classic and is as compact as the Traveler.

Two additional NightStar products are *Learning Astronomy With NightStar* ($10) and *Teaching Astronomy With NightStar* ($10)—student and teacher editions of an easy-to-follow activities book for beginning students of the stars.

Replogle Globes, Inc. (2801 S. 25th Ave., Broadview, IL 60153; 708-343-0900), the world's largest manufacturer of globes, offers a 12-inch moon globe and a 12-inch celestial globe. Developed under the auspices of NASA, the moon globe ($35.95; 38245) has a three-dimensional look that reveals craters, seas, and mountains. The celestial globe ($39.95; 38848) locates 1,200 stars from 1st to 4th magnitude and shows constellations, star clusters, new stars, and double stars. The company's newest product is called "Planet Earth" ($75; 80200), the first globe as seen from space. The 12-inch globe was drawn by an artist using hundreds of satellite photos and images.

Sky Publishing Corp. (P.O. Box 9111, Belmont, MA 02178; 617-864-7360) offers a wide variety of books and products related to astronomy and space science, for all levels and experience. Its monthly magazine, *Sky & Telescope*, provides information on viewing the stars, planets, and other celestial objects; timely astronomy news and features; articles on telescope making, astrophotography, computing; equipment reviews; and more. Sky's product line includes

Replogle Globes's moon globe.

numerous star charts and atlases, astronomical globes and photographs, planet and moon maps, software, videos, laserdiscs, CD-ROMs, and a large selection of books. A free "Sky Publications Catalogue" is available upon request. Sky Publishing's products include:

■ *The Sky & Telescope Guide to the Heavens* ($1; #S2000), published annually. It features a full-color chart showing which planets are visible on any given night, the phases of the moon and its rising and setting times, meteor shower activity, and more. The eight-page guide also contains four-seasonal star charts for easy identification of constellations and a map of the moon.

■ "Sky's Mars Map" ($7.95; #S1961), a 39" X 40" color Mercator projection of the red planet's surface that shows thousands of craters, mountains, valleys, and other topographical features.

■ "Mercury Map" ($6.95; #S1171), a fully documented multicolor airbrush map (41" X 25") showing topography and albedo features (bright and dark areas) of the crater-pocked planet nearest the sun.

■ "Lunar Quadrant Maps" ($12.95 per set; #46239), a set of four highly detailed maps of the moon's near side produced by the University of Arizona's Lunar and Planetary Laboratory. The 23" X 27" maps show all craters and other features measuring at least two miles in diameter labeled with their official names.

■ *Sky Atlas* 2000.0, by Wil Tirion (deluxe color version, bound, $44.95, #46336; black-on-white version, unbound, $19.95, #46328). *Atlas* 2000.0 is a detailed, large-format collection of star charts of the entire sky. Its 27 13" X 18" charts accurately depict the positions and magnitudes of more than 43,000 stars down to 8th magnitude and 2,500 deep-sky objects.

■ "Chart of the Heavens," by Wil Tirion ($4.95; #S0032), a wall chart of all the stars visible to the naked eye from Earth's Northern and Southern Hemispheres. Measuring 27" X 10", the chart depicts white stars on a blue background, with lettering and constellation lines in black.

■ "Sky & Telescope's Star Finder" ($9.95; #50058), a handy star wheel that displays a miniature map of the night sky as seen from anywhere between latitudes 25 and 55 degrees (all of U.S.). Just dial in the current date and time and it shows you which stars and constellations are visible right then. The Star Finder is 10 inches in diameter, made of weatherproof plastic, and includes instructions for use on the back.

■ "The Sky & Telescope Mars Globe" ($84.95; #39214), a 12-inch-diameter scale model of Mars that depicts more than 100 identified topographic features, including volcanoes, impact basins, craters, canyons, and river valleys, as well as major albedo features visible from Earth. Produced in cooperation with NASA and the U.S. Geological Survey, the globe was illustrated using data from Viking and Mariner spacecraft. It rests on a clear pedestal and includes an information booklet.

■ "The NASA Moon Globe" ($38; #S0059), which allows anyone to explore the Moon's myriad craters, "seas," and mountains, many of which are labeled with their official names. Endorsed by NASA, the globe is 12 inches in diameter and sits on a plastic base. A booklet entitled *The Story of the Moon* is included.

■ "The Great Celestial Sphere" ($29; #S0060), a 16-inch, clear acrylic globe with more than 1,100

stars, deep-sky objects, and all 88 constellations precision-painted on its inner surface. Stars are labeled with their names, Greek letters, and distances in light years. A rotatable six-inch Earth globe, a sun ball, and an adjustable horizon ring inside the star sphere allow the user to simulate the view of the heavens from anywhere on Earth at any time.

■ "The Planet Earth Globe" ($74; #S0064), the first 12-inch-scale model of our planet as seen from space. It shows the Earth's geography without political boundaries or country labels. Rich colors distinguish vegetation, mountains, deserts, rivers, islands, and clouds. Included with each globe is a full-color *Planet Earth Discovery Guide*.

Spherical Concepts, Inc. (2 Davis Ave., P.O. Box 1215, Frazer, PA 19355; 215-296-4119) produces silk-screened clear-acrylic celestial globes, including:

■ "Astro Disk" ($29 to $39), nine-inch or 13-inch star finders, hand-crafted of the finest-quality acrylic. Simply match the date and time on the two disks to see what stars and constellations appear at any time of night, any day of the year. Comes with display stand and instructions.

■ "Star Ball" ($32), a five-inch celestial globe featuring all 88 constellations with names and patterns, and including a booklet of interesting "sky facts."

■ "The Stars Above" ($75 to $95), designed to show the actual sky at any time on any given night of the year by matching the date and time on the rims of the two 14-inch hemispheres. Constellations and stars of first and second magnitude are shown, along with the Milky Way and the path of the planets. It comes mounted on a clear base with an eight-page booklet and wax marking pencil; available illuminated or not.

■ "Starship Earth," a fascinating clear celestial globe with a small, inner globe of the Earth and a "sun ball." With the Starship, it is possible to see planetary movements and deep-sky objects, and to trace the movements of the sun. The globe comes with a "certificate of authenticity," a wax marking pencil, and a 36-page booklet

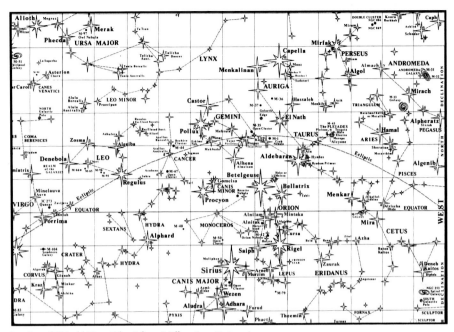

Portion of "World Star Atlas," from Millennium Enterprises.

written by astronomical columnist George Lovi. The globe is available in a 16-inch diameter ($299 to $425, depending on base) or 30-inch diameter ($1,295).

■ "S.C.I. Celestial Globe," a six-color globe showing most naked-eye stars in their true colors (temperatures) and magnitudes (brightness), and constellations, star clusters, nebulae, and the like. The globe comes with an instruction booklet written by George Lovi ($289 to $325, depending on base).

Star Finders Inc. (2406 Lawrence St., Eugene, OR 97405; 503-686-6754) produces a glow-in-the-dark star chart ($9; 24" X 28") of the northern sky for learning the stars indoors. It shows all the constellations of the Northern Hemisphere. Star Finders also produces a brass-and-vinyl planisphere ($12) for learning the same stars and constellations outdoors. The planisphere comes with a red plastic filter for use with a flashlight and a primer to stargazing.

Sunstone Publications (RD 4, Box 700A, Cooperstown, NY 13326; 607-547-8207) offers

"Astro-Dome" ($9.95), a three-dimensional map of the night sky developed by Klaus Hunig. With easy-to-follow directions, the precut pages transform into an attractive miniature planetarium depicting the stars and constellations of the Northern Hemisphere. Astro-Dome measures 20" in diameter when assembled, and includes a 24-page *Constellation Handbook* explaining the history and details of the major constellations. The map glows in the dark and is intended for children ages 12 and up.

Willmann-Bell, Inc. (P.O. Box 35025, Richmond, VA 23235; 804-320-7016) is one of the largest retail book dealers in astronomy-related materials. It carries 1,500 titles, many of which are also carried by Sky Publishing and Kalmbach Publishing. The catalog costs $1. The company's own star chart, *Uranometria 2000.0*, by Wil Tirion, Barry Rappaport, and George Lovi ($39.95), charts the heavens in two volumes. Volume 1 shows the Northern Hemisphere to − 6 degrees. Volume 2 shows the Southern Hemisphere to +6 degrees. Each volume contains 259 charts.

Weather Maps

Weather has always been a provocative and mystical element of the natural world. From the songs and poems it has inspired to the conversations it has started (or saved), our romance with blue skies and blustery winds is as old as weather itself. Because weather is often unpredictable and erratic, the maps, charts, and tables that trace its patterns and behavior can be lifesaving tools for pilots, sailors, and others.

Weather maps, by their very nature, are usually out of date within a few days or even hours of their creation. There are exceptions—including historical climatology maps, general tracking guides, do-it-yourself prediction kits, and National Weather Service charts—but most specific weather maps are useful only for an extremely limited period of time.

The federal government produces a number of weather maps, charts, atlases, and guides aimed at educating and informing the public. The **National Weather Service** (part of the Commerce Department's National Oceanic and Atmospheric Administration), which provides the information for the telephone recordings and radio and TV station forecasts upon which many people rely, also issues daily weather charts and maps.

The Weather Service's daily maps (available by subscription from NOAA and the **Government Printing Office**) show the surface weather of the United States as it is observed at 7 a.m. Eastern time each morning. A weekly series, also available by subscription, includes each day's maps for the seven-day period, plus smaller maps showing high and low temperatures, precipitation, and wind patterns. These maps are widely used by airplane pilots and boat captains.

Another set of useful weather maps produced by the Weather Service are the 15 Marine Weather Services Charts, covering the waters of the United States and Puerto Rico, which illustrate the locations of visual storm-warning

display sites and of weather radio stations broadcasting Weather Service information.

Other weather maps and charts produced by the federal government include the Historical Climatology series of maps and atlases published by the **National Climatic Data Center**, the sunshine temperature maps that are included in the **U.S. Geological Survey**'s National Atlas Program, and a variety of climatic, storm, and weather-pattern data and maps available from the Government Printing Office.

In addition to these printed materials, there are several new technologically advanced methods of getting up-to-date weather maps. For example, through on-line weather services, you may tap into data bases via a modem.

GOVERNMENT SOURCES

Government Printing Office. The GPO sells a variety of weather-related publications. A sampling is:

■ *Aviation Weather for Pilots and Flight Operations Personnel* ($8.50; S/N 050-007-00283-1) explains weather facts every pilot should know and discusses high-altitude, Arctic, tropical, and soaring weather.
■ *Aviation Weather Services* ($8.50; S/N 050-007-00705-1), a supplement to the above, explains weather service in general and how to use and interpret both observed and prognostic weather charts, forecasts, and coded weather reports.
■ *Climatological Atlas of the World Ocean* ($11; S/N 003-017-00509-7). This 189-page atlas has maps, charts, graphs, and tables that synthesize National Ocean Survey data about the temperature and other climatological information.
■ *United States Navy Hindcast Spectral Ocean Wave Model Climatic Atlas: North Atlantic Ocean* ($39; S/N 008-042-00074-8). This 393-page atlas, created

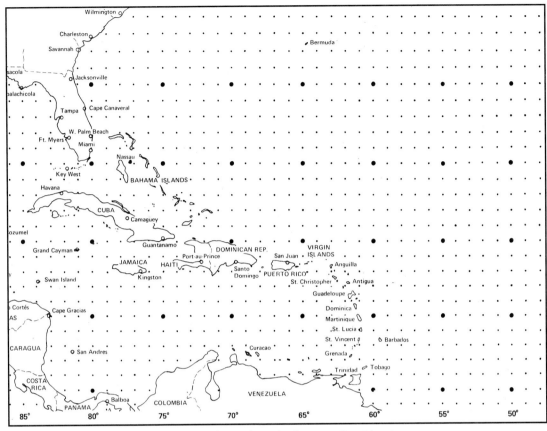

From NOAA's "Storm Search and Hurricane Safety With North Atlantic Tracking Chart."

in 1983, is filled with maps, charts, and other historical data about the wind and wave climatology of the North Atlantic Ocean.

National Climatic Data Center. The National Climatic Data Center (Federal Bldg., Asheville, NC 28801; 704-259-0682), part of the **National Oceanic and Atmospheric Administration**, has a Historical Climatology series that includes 11 weather-related atlases. The maps in the atlases depict local, regional, and continental climatological parameters, showing climate changes over a relatively long time. A service charge of $5 per order must be included when purchasing the atlases by mail (a $13 minimum order, in addition to the $5 service charge, is required). Available atlases include:

■ *Atlas of Mean Winter Temperature Departures From*

the Long-Term Mean over the Contiguous U.S., 1895-1983 ($3; series title 3-1), with seasonal maps of departures from mean winter temperatures in the U.S. from the late 19th to late 20th centuries.

■ *Atlas of Monthly and Seasonal Temperature Departures, 1895-1983* (four volumes; $10.50 each, or $36 for all four; series titles: 3-2 [winter]; 3-3 [spring]; 3-4 [summer]; and 3-5 [fall]). This series includes maps of departures from long-term, statewide average monthly and seasonal temperatures.

■ *Atlas of Monthly Palmer Hydrological Drought* ($12; series title 3-6), with maps showing drought conditions in the U.S. according to the Palmer Hydrological Drought Index, an objective measure of moisture conditions. A companion volume, for years 1931-1983 ($17; series title 3-7), is also available.

How to Read a Weather Map

All weather maps use common symbols. Here is a description of the symbols used to represent different weather phenomena:

■ **Sky conditions** are indicated by small circles (representing key cities) that are completely filled in (overcast skies), partially filled in (partly cloudy conditions), or empty (clear conditions). If it is raining or snowing, the circle may contain an R or an S. On some maps, symbols are used—for example, jagged lines for lightning or snowflakes for snow.

■ **Wind** is represented by a line drawn from a sky-condition circle. To determine wind direction, assume that the top of the circle is north; the bottom, south; the right, east; and the left, west. The line is drawn in the direction from which the wind is originating. Barbs representing 10 miles per hour each are drawn horizontally from the wind direction line to indicate wind speed. So a 30-mph wind would have three barbs. Some maps use arrows rather than barbs that point in the direction the wind is blowing.

■ **Temperature** is usually written directly on the map in degrees Fahrenheit, although Celsius may also be used.

■ **Barometric pressure** is represented by isobars — solid, curved black lines. *High-pressure* weather systems (clear weather) are drawn as ascending isobars. *Low-pressure* weather systems (cloudy weather) are drawn as descending isobars.

■ **Fronts** can be shown in three ways. A *cold front*, a leading edge of a moving mass of cold air, is drawn as a solid black line with small triangles. The points of the triangles face the direction in which the front is moving. A *warm front*, the leading edge of an advancing mass of warm air, is drawn as a solid black line with solid black semicircles. A *stationary front*, separating two air masses, neither of which is moving, is indicated by a solid black line that has alternate triangles and semicircles.

For a complete list of atlases and other products in the Historical Climatology series, write to the NCDC and ask for the *Environmental Information Summary* (C-24).

The NCDC also produces an Annual Average Climatic Maps of the United States series, including "Temperature, 1941-70," "Total Precipitation, 1941-70," "Relative Humidity, Generally 1948-77," "Dew Point Temperature, Generally 1946-65," "Annual Average Daily Global Solar Radiation on a South Facing Surface, Generally 1953-75," "Mean Annual Number of Thunderstorms, Generally 1948-77," and "Normal Annual Heating Degree Days (Contiguous U.S. and Alaska), Generally 1951-80." The climatic maps are free from NCDC.

National Oceanic and Atmospheric Administration. NOAA publishes "Storm Search and Hurricane Safety With North Atlantic Tracking Chart" (NOAA/PA 78019), a brochure with a chart included. It is free from the NOAA Logistics Supply Center (1500 E. Bannister Rd., Bldg. 1, Kansas City, MO 64131; 816-926-7993; 800-669-1099).

U.S. Geological Survey. USGS's National Atlas Program includes several weather-related maps. The maps are colorful and suitable for framing, albeit a bit out of date. Prices shown include surface mailing within the U.S. The following maps are available:

■ "Monthly Sunshine" ($3.10; 00478, ref. code 38077-AI-NA-17M-00), created in 1965.
■ "Annual Sunshine, Evaporation, and Solar Radiation" ($3.10; 00565, ref. code 38077-AJ-NA-17M-00), created in 1969.
■ "Monthly Average Temperature" ($3.10; 00661, ref. code AK-NA-17M-00), created in 1965.
■ "Monthly Minimum Temperatures" ($3.10; 00662, ref. code 38077-AL-NA-17M-00), created in 1965.

GOVERNMENT SOURCES, CANADA
Canada Map Office (615 Booth St., Ottawa,

Ontario K1A 0E9; 613-952-7000) distributes 11 weather-related maps as part of the *National Atlas of Canada*, 5th ed. series: "Annual Solar Radiation" (MCR 4076), "Length of Day" (MCR 4068), "Last Frost in Spring" (MCR 4035), "Growing-Degree Days" (MCR 4034), and "Temperature—January and July" (MCR 4058). The maps are $5.50 Canadian each.

Maps from the *National Atlas of Canada*, 4th ed. (1973) are available for $2 Canadian each. Titles include: "Soil Climate" (MCR 1132), "Weather Stations and Average Annual Precipitation" (MCR 1134), "Frost" (MCR 1137), "Precipitation—Regions" (MCR 1139), "Precipitation—Monthly Average, April-Sept." (MCR 1140), "Precipitation—Seasonal Average" (MCR 1141), "Temperature—Winter" (MCR 1142), "Temperature—Spring" (MCR 1143), "Temperature—Summer" (MCR 1144), "Temperature—Autumn" (MCR 1145).

Maps Alberta (Land Information Services Div., Main fl., Brittania Bldg., 703 6th Ave. SW, Calgary, Alberta T2P 0T9; 403-297-7389) distributes various weather maps of the province, which are part of the *Alberta Resource and Economic Atlas*. Part of the Physical Features series of the atlas, the weather maps (75 cents Canadian each) are drawn to a scale of 1:5,000,000 and include: "Sunshine" (D10), "Precipitation" (D11), "Snowfall" (D12), "Mean Temperature" (D13), and "Average Frost-Free Days" (D14).

COMMERCIAL SOURCES
American Association of Weather Observers (401 Whitney Blvd., Belvidere, IL 61008; 815-544-9811), founded in 1984, acts as a clearinghouse for people interested in pooling weather data. Information submitted by members is published monthly in the organization's newsletter, *American Weather Observer*; it also becomes part of the organization's permanent data base, which is available to members. The newsletter includes other information close to weather watchers' hearts: new tools of the trade, reports from other organizations, and a

weather map based on members' data, among other things. The group has about 1,500 members, who pay $12 a year ($18 for those who are not members of AAWO-affiliated groups), which includes 12 issues of the *Observer*.

American Weather Enterprises (P.O. Box 1383, Media, PA 19063; 215-565-1232) sells books, software, and educational materials, in addition to weather instruments. Some items from the catalog include a sturdy wall chart (55" X 33") that details global atmospheric influences, meteorological motion, severe weather, clouds and precipitation, aviation meteorology, and more in an easy-to-understand flow-chart design ($16.50), and Geochron, an attractive chalkboard-size electronic map that continually shows the exact time of day and amount of sunlight anywhere in the world (basic unit is $1,200; deluxe models up to $2,000).

Blue Hill Observatory (P.O. Box 101, East Milton, MA 02186; 617-698-5397) sells a hurricane-tracking chart that includes two 11" X 24" maps and data on hurricanes covering the Atlantic, Gulf, and Pacific coasts. Included are instructions on how to plot a hurricane's course using longitude and latitude, a hurricane-survival checklist, and a list of current hurricane names. The observatory offers weather-related publications, including a quarterly bulletin, available to all members; membership is $10 a year. Write for a free brochure.

Hammond, Inc. (515 Valley St., Maplewood, NJ 07040; 201-763-6000; 800-526-4953). Of special interest to weather watchers is the Hammond Weather Kit, complete with chart and wheel. The 25" X 28" weather chart offers graphic explanations of popular weather terms, including cloud types, weather fronts, tornado formation, and more. The weather wheel helps amateurs create their own forecasts.

Hubbard Scientific, Inc. (P.O. Box 104, Northbrook, IL 60065; 708-272-7810; 800-323-8368) distributes a 44" X 50" fluorescent-green weather map and plotting chart of the U.S. The

map and chart are laminated, so weather conditions can be written on and wiped off ($30).

New Orleans Map Co. (3130 Paris Ave., New Orleans, LA 70119; 504-943-0878) distributes a 29" X 35" "Hurricane Tracking Chart" that covers the Gulf of Mexico, the Yucatán Peninsula, the northern coast of South America, the West Indies, and the Atlantic coast of the U.S. north to Baltimore ($10, plus tax and shipping). The map is laminated, so hurricanes can be tracked with a grease pen; when the hurricane is over, the markings can be wiped off and the map rolled up and stored until the next one.

Omni Resources (1238 Anthony Rd., P.O. Box 2096, Burlington, NC 27216; 919-227-8300) distributes various weather-related maps of foreign countries, such as the "China—Annual Rainfall Map" ($10.95).

COMPUTER SOFTWARE AND ON-LINE SERVICES

The **National Weather Service** offers various data lines that can be subscribed to for up-to-the-minute weather information. The problem is that most of this data is in coded form. You can't really read it without computer software and hardware to help you decipher what is being sent. A number of companies offer software packages to help translate the data. Other companies offer menu-driven systems that are not dependent on NWS data. Each of these systems has its own strengths and limitations.

Accu-Data (Accu-Weather, Inc., 619 W. College Ave., State College, PA 16801; 814-237-0309) is a complete, real-time weather data base that interfaces with most terminals, personal computers, and business computers. Available data from Accu-Data include hourly surface observations; digitized radar signals; upper-air data; worldwide observations; DIFAX, LFM/NGM, MOS, and other modal output; plain-language and coded forecasts; severe-weather bulletins; watches and warnings; climatological summaries; and marine data. Data are transmitted as both charts and maps. The data base is compat-

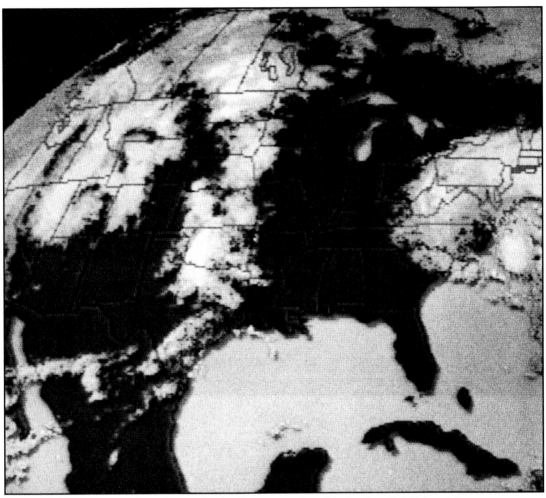

Screen image from Accu-Data, an on-line weather data base, courtesy Accu-Weather, Inc., State College, PA.

ible with both IBM and Apple computers. There are three different prices for Accu-Data. Commercial users pay $69 an hour and secondary schools $42 an hour; both have access to a toll-free "800" number. Hobbyists pay $16.95 an hour, but must also pay long-distance charges; prices are for 1200 baud.

National Geographic Society (17th & M sts. NW, Washington, DC 20036; 202-857-7000; 800-368-2728) distributes the "Weather Machine," which allows students to select a packet of weather data culled from the National Weather Service's Domestic Data Service (held in a National Geographic com-

puter) that is then translated into color computer maps superimposed over a map of North America. Readings include temperature, air pressure, wind speed and direction, dew point, cloud cover, and more. The Weather Machine can be used on the Apple IIc, IIe, or IIgs; a modem is needed if users plan to tap into the daily updates offered. A detailed curriculum is part of the package.

Weathervane Software (P.O. Box 277, Grafton, MA 01519; 508-839-6777) is the publisher of "Atlantic Hurricane Watcher" ($30), a menu-driven program that allows you to plot and compare the tracks of hurricanes on a color or black-and-white map of the U.S., western Atlantic Ocean, Caribbean, and Gulf of Mexico. New storms can be included easily in the 1985 data base. IBM-PC compatible.

WEATHER BY SHORTWAVE RADIO AND FAX

It's not generally known, but you can pick up current weather information via a variety of media. For example, some weather stations transmit in a facsimile, or fax, mode, which means that they send photos and maps over shortwave radio bands. These are picked up by news and weather services around the country, but anyone with a little know-how can tap into the system.

For some shortwave radios, you won't need a special antenna. Two sources are:

Stephens Engineering Associates, Inc. (7030 220th St. SW, Mountlake Terrace, WA 98043;

206-771-2182) offers the SEAFAX weather facsimile digital signal processor, with high-resolution printouts. The system must be attached to a single-side-band radio receiver and a printer. Price is $995, or $1,145 with IBM-compatible serial output.

Universal Amateur Radio, Inc. (1280 Aida Dr., Reynoldsburg, OH 43068; 614-866-4267). If you'd like to tap into the weather map scene, take a look at the Information-Tech M-800 ($349), which can be hooked up to a shortwave radio and an Epson printer for a crisp, clear map. A variety of other electronic gear is also offered in the Universal catalog.

■ **See also: "Aeronautical Charts," "Emergency Information Maps," "Energy Maps," "Nautical Charts and Maps," and "Tide and Current Maps."**

IMAGES AS MAPS

Aerial Photographs

Ever since humans have been able to fly and hold a camera at the same time, aerial photographs have been an important part of the mapping process, as well as a means of preserving images of the Earth and its development. Images of the land taken from above are valuable tools that are suitable for use as finished products, but they are also starting points for creating most types of land maps. Cartographers often use stereoscopic aerial photos—two aerial photos of the same site taken from two different aerial camera positions—to create the three-dimensional perspective needed for some map-making. Aerial photos are also used in such fields as aeronautics, agriculture, engineering, and land planning.

Cameras in airplanes photograph land section by section. The resulting photographs must first be corrected to eliminate distortion, camera tilt, and optical effects created by the land itself. Through a series of enhancements or overlays, the photos are then transformed into a variety of map types:

■ Cartographers often use aerial photographs to create or update **planimetric** or **topographic** maps, for example.
■ The addition of mapping symbols (such as major roads, borders, and selected place names) to photographs results in **photoimage** maps, also known as **pictomaps**.
■ **Orthophotoquads** and **orthophotomaps** result from further enhancements, such as eliminating most distortion and adding color and enhanced definition of coastlines, rivers, mountains, and other land forms.

GOVERNMENT SOURCES, UNITED STATES

Nearly every federal agency involved with land preservation, planning, or management maintains collections of aerial photographs that span the nation from picture-perfect coast to picture-perfect coast (see Appendix B for addresses).

The **U.S. Geological Survey**'s Aerial Photography Summary Record System, established in 1976 as the first Earth Science Information Center data base, catalogs the in-progress and completed aerial photographs for the U.S. to assist in locating a desired photograph. The USGS, through its ESIC offices, can sell prints of photographs taken by a number of federal agencies, such as the Bureau of Reclamation, the U.S. Navy, and the Environmental Protection Agency. A pamphlet, "How to Obtain Aerial Photographs," available from USGS, may be helpful in obtaining aerial photos.

The **National Archives** has a large stockpile of older aerial photographs of the U.S. The Archives also maintains a large collection of World War II-vintage Allied-generated aerial photographs of foreign areas, as well as World War II-era Luftwaffe-produced aerial prints covering much of Europe and North Africa. These may be located through queries to Archives staff (see "Uncle Sam's Treasure Chests").

The **Earth Resources Observation Systems (EROS) Data Center**, near Sioux Falls, South Dakota, is the depository of the Department of the Interior's aerial photography, radar imagery, and other federal-government-produced aerial photographs, all of which are available for sale (see "Space Imagery").

The **U.S. Department of Agriculture** Aerial Photography Field Office in Salt Lake City, part of the Agricultural Stabilization and Conservation Service, has thousands of aerial photographs covering most of the nation's major

Aerial photograph of the rapidly growing Tysons Corner, Virginia, area. Courtesy Air Photographics, Inc., Wheaton, Maryland.

croplands. USDA's National Forest Service has aerial photographs of the nation's forests.

The **Department of the Interior**'s Bureau of Land Management has aerial photographs of most federally maintained land, available through its offices or through the EROS Data Center.

The **Defense Mapping Agency** has aerial photographs of military installations and other defense-related areas around the world.

The **Department of Commerce**'s National Ocean Service has aerial photographs of the nation's coastline.

The **Tennessee Valley Authority** has aerial photos covering the entire Tennessee River Drainage Basin with varying dates and scales.

GOVERNMENT SOURCES, CANADA

Manitoba Natural Resources (Surveys and Mapping Branch, 1007 Century St., Winnipeg, Manitoba R3H 0W4; 204-945-6666) maintains the Manitoba Air Photo Library, a collection of more than one million aerial photographs, some dating to 1923. Copies and enlargements of any photo in the collection can be ordered. There are photos for every area of Manitoba, although coverage is more extensive for some areas; it's best to visit, phone, or write the Air Photo Library before placing an order.

Maps Alberta (Land Information Services Div., Main fl., Brittania Bldg., 703 6th Ave. SW, Calgary, Alberta T2P 0T9; 403-297-7389) maintains all the aerial photographs taken for the provincial government dating to 1949. Most of the photos are black-and-white, although some are in color. Contact prints, laser prints, color-contact prints, and enlargements of the aerial photos can be requested. Flight Index Maps and an Aerial Photography Project Index, available from Maps Alberta, are handy resources when searching for aerial photographs of a specific area. Prices range from $3.36 for a contact print ($9\frac{1}{2}$ inches square, printed on matte photographic paper) to more than $30 for a 40" X 40" enlargement. Laser prints are $4 Canadian per print, while laser enlargements—a section of a print may be enlarged up to four times—are $8 each. Laser prints are generally processed within three days, contact prints within one week; other services usually require about two weeks. A catalog explaining Maps Alberta's aerial photograph distribution is available upon request.

Quebec Ministère de l'Énergie et des Resources (Photocartothèque Québecoise, 1995 Blvd. Charest Ouest, Sainte-Foy, Quebec G1N 4H9; 418-643-7704) produces aerial photographs for areas in Quebec in scales of 1:40,000, 1:36,000, 1:31,680, 1:30,000, 1:25,000, 1:15,840, 1:15,000, and 1:10,000. An index of available photographs, "Repertoire des Cartes, Plans et Photographies Aeriennes," is free.

Saskatchewan Property Management Corp. (Central Survey and Mapping Agency, Distribution Center, 2045 Broad St., 1st fl., Regina, Saskatchewan S4P 3V7; 306-787-2799) produces Township Photomaps, at a scale of about 1:20,000, from aerial photography rectified to theoretical township corners. Photomaps ($10 Canadian per township) are available for all areas of Saskatchewan.

COMMERCIAL SOURCES

Aerial maps are also available from the following sources and reference libraries:

Alabama
Atlantic Aerial Surveys, Inc.
803 Franklin St.
Huntsville, AL 35804
205-722-0555

Arizona
Kenny Aerial Mapping, Inc.
1130 W. Fillmore St.
Phoenix, AZ 85007
602-258-6471

Arkansas
AMI Engineers
1615 Louisiana St.
Little Rock, AR 72206
501-376-6838

California
Ace Aerial Photo
P.O. Box 2040
Laguna Hills, CA 92654
714-830-2960

Aerial Map Industries
2012 S. Main St.
Santa Ana, CA 92707
714-546-7201

Aeroeco, Inc.
16996 Sky Valley Dr.
Ramona, CA 92065
619-788-6802

Foster Air Photo
9312 Florence Ln.
Garden Grove, CA 92641
714-539-3890

Aerial photograph of Boston, courtesy USGS/EROS Data Center.

Western Economic Research Co., Inc.
8155 Van Nuys Blvd., Ste. 100
Panorama City, CA 91402
818-787-6277

Colorado
Intra Search, Inc.
5351 S. Roslyn St.
Englewood, CO 80111
303-741-2020

Florida
Aerial Cartographics of America
1722 W. Oak Ridge Rd.
Orlando, FL 32809
407-851-7880; 800-426-0407

Georgia
Georgia Aerial Surveys
4451 N. Log Cabin Dr., Ste. 124
Smyrna, GA 30080
404-434-2516

Hawaii
Air Survey Hawaii
544 Ohohia St., Ste. 1
Honolulu, HI 96819
808-833-4881

Idaho
Moore's Photography
7128 Snohomish St.
Boise, ID 83709
208-362-3820

Valley Air Photos
5001 Aviation Way
Caldwell, ID 83605
208-454-1344

Kentucky
GRW Aerial Survey, Inc.
801 Corporate Dr.
Lexington, KY 40503
606-223-3999

Park Aerial Surveys
40209 Harding Ave.
Louisville, KY 40217
502-366-4571

Maryland
Air Photographics, Inc.
11510 Georgia Ave., Ste. 130
Wheaton, MD 20902
301-933-5282

Massachusetts
Airmap America
Airmap Park
Washington St.
Braintree, MA 02184
617-848-8000

Michigan
Abrams Aerial Survey Corp.
124 N. Larch St.
Lansing, MI 48901
517-372-8100

Nevada
Cooper Aerial of Nevada, Inc.
3750 S. Valley View Dr., Ste. 6
Las Vegas, NV 89103
702-362-4776

New Jersey
Aerial Data Reduction Associates, Inc.
P.O. Box 557
Pennsauken, NJ 08110
609-663-7200

New York
Aerographics, Inc.
P.O. Box 248
Bohemia, NY 11716
516-589-6045

Ohio
Cleveland Blueprint
1478 St. Clair Ave.
Cleveland, OH 44114
216-241-1815

Oregon
Insight Reconnaissance
525 SE Goodnight Ln.
Corvallis, OR 97333
503-754-6488

Pennsylvania
Eastern Mapping Co.
280 Kappa Dr.
Pittsburgh, PA 15238
412-967-9577

Texas
International Aerial Mapping Co.
8927 International Dr.
San Antonio, TX 78216
512-826-8681

Adams Aerial Surveys
P.O. Box 476
South Houston, TX 77587
713-946-0830

Space Imagery

Modern science has created new tools that have not only revolutionized techniques for making maps, but have also given rise to new types of map products. Among the most important of these tools is "remote sensing," the process of detecting and monitoring chemical or physical properties of an area by measuring its reflected and emitted radiation.

The earliest remote-sensing experiments took place using photographs taken aboard the first manned missions: Mercury, Gemini, and Apollo. Astronauts used hand-held cameras to produce historic pictures that were examined by scientists worldwide, although no actual maps were made from the pictures.

In 1969, the first scientific space photographic experiment was performed on Apollo 9. Four 70-mm cameras were mounted on a metal frame that fit the spacecraft's command module hatch window. Taking a variety of pictures of the Phoenix, Arizona, region, scientists later interconnected them—a process called "mosaicking"—and printed them as a single image to produce a standard line map. Although crude by today's standards, the experiment led the way for what would become highly sophisticated photomapping techniques using manned and unmanned spacecraft.

Landsat I (originally called the Earth Resources Technology Satellite, or ERTS), launched in 1972, was the first American spacecraft designed specifically to record images of the Earth. Since then, subsequent Landsat satellites have recorded thousands of images of the planet. At an altitude of 567 miles, each satellite circles the globe 14 times daily, scanning a particular scene every 18 days, or more than 40 times per year. Each image covers an area approximately 115 miles square, and Landsat can detect an area as small as 100 feet square. Since 1972, images from the five Landsat satellites have become valuable tools for farmers, oil companies, geologists, foresters, foreign governments, and others interested in land resource management. In 1985, ownership of Landsat was transferred by the federal government to the Earth Observation Satellite Co. (EOSAT), a partnership of Hughes Aircraft Co. and RCA Corp.

Although Landsat produces pictures of Earth, its principal viewing instruments are not cameras but two digital-sensor systems known as multispectral scanner systems. Digital cameras have several advantages over other cameras in terms of signal-to-noise ratio, weight, reliability, and simplicity of operation—and thus have been flown on almost all planetary probes. Another advantage is that their digital information can be manipulated in a computer, allowing enhancement or suppression of images.

In multispectral scanner systems, satellites record information in two visible (red and green) wavelengths and two infrared wavelengths not visible to the human eye. The procedure results in four separate black-and-white digital images, combined by computer into a "false-color" portrait. In thematic mapper systems, satellites record information in three visible (blue, green, red) wavelengths, three infrared wavelengths, and one thermal (heat-measuring) wavelength. Two of the visible and two of the infrared wavelengths are combined to make standard "false-color" images. Different colors describe the land below:

■ Healthy vegetation appears in shades of red and contrasts with unhealthy vegetation, which appears blue-green.
■ Water appears dark blue or black unless it is sediment-laden, in which case it takes on a light-blue tone.
■ Most buildings, streets, and other "cultural features" appear a steely blue-gray.

Another, newer space-imagery vehicle is *Spot*, a French-owned satellite launched in 1986, the first commercially owned satellite-sensing system. *Spot*'s sensing abilities enable it to record images as small as 10 meters (about 33 feet) square—about half the size of a tennis court—and at a higher resolution than Landsat. Airplanes, bridges, ships, roads, even some houses, can be detected by *Spot* with impressive clarity. One reason is that *Spot* uses a system of mirrors that can "look" to the side as well as straight down, enabling the satellite to "view" an object from two or more directions. Among other things, this allows for production of stereoscopic images that create a three-dimensional perspective of land images. Still, Landsat can produce bigger pictures than *Spot*, and in more wavelengths of light.

The uses of space imagery are widespread and growing. There is the sheer beauty of space maps, of course—some have been likened to French Impressionist paintings—but there are myriad practical uses. Space imagery, for example, has been used to:

■ Analyze geologic structures, from earthquake faults to mountain ranges, and to detect oil and mineral deposits.
■ Manage water resources and improve stream-flow characteristics and water quality in lakes, rivers, and bays.
■ Map, measure, and analyze glaciers and ice caps to predict reservoir inflow and potential flooding.
■ Create thematic maps of forested and cultivated land and coastal waterways.
■ Produce computer-aided mapping and land-use analysis.
■ Monitor forest fires, air pollution, oil-well fires, and changes in vegetation.
■ Analyze archaeological sites, detect road alignment, and monitor wildlife migration.

Ordering space imagery. The EROS Data Center (EDC), near Sioux Falls, South Dakota, operated by the U.S. Geological Survey, reproduces and sells copies of manned-spacecraft photographs as well as aerial photographs (see "Aerial Photographs"), NASA aircraft data, and other remote-sensing products. EDC reproduces and sells copies of

imagery products of the USGS as well as photographs, geophysical data, and computer products collected by 16 different federal agencies.

Landsat images. Landsat images are available for the 50 states and for most of the Earth's land surface outside the U.S. There are several products available for any given location, including:

■ Single black-and-white images, available as film negatives, film positives, or paper prints.
■ Complete sets of four black-and-white images and a false-color composite. All false-color composites are available as film positives or paper prints.
■ Computer tapes containing digital data.

Each Landsat image covers about eight million acres. Images do not reveal outlines of small areas, like houses or small towns and villages, but provide views of broad areas and large features, such as mountain ranges and the outlines of major cities.

Landsat images are available through EOSAT's offices located at the EROS Data Center, where orders are processed. When ordering, it is important to describe the exact area in which you are interested, including, if possible, the geographic coordinates or a map marked with the specific area. You should also indicate:

■ the type of product (black-and-white, false-color, or digital tapes);
■ the minimum image quality acceptable;
■ the maximum percentage of acceptable cloud cover (10 percent to 90 percent); and
■ the preferred time of year.

To order specific images of the 48 contiguous United States, you can use the form "Landsat 4 Coverage Index" (NOAA Form 34-1205, available free from EROS and USGS Earth Science Information Centers), which includes a map of the U.S. showing the locations of individual Landsat images selected for their clarity and

Portion of Landsat image showing parts of western Bolivia, southern Peru, and northern Chile. Courtesy USGS/EROS Data Center.

lack of cloud cover. USGS has also prepared a number of photomaps, mosaics, and other images produced from Landsat, Spot, and other imagery, including an impressive view of the entire U.S. Prices for most of these range from $3 to $8, not including postage and handling charges for mail orders.

Ordering Spot images. Spot images may be obtained directly from Spot Image Corp. (1897 Preston White Dr., Reston, VA 22091; 703-620-2200), the wholly owned subsidiary of the French company created to market *Spot's* services. This satellite imagery is the most detailed commercially available and can be acquired in either black-and-white or color infrared. Imagery is available of any location in the world. The SPOTView product line provides up-to-date (less than one year old) image maps corresponding to any 1:24,000 or other standard U.S. Geological Survey map. Several other types of images are also available in digital form on magnetic computer tape, CD-ROM, Exabyte tape or QIC tape, or in hard copy as photographic prints or transparencies. Specialty products produced from Spot imagery include posters ($25), watches ($65), and museum-quality photographic prints ($150 to $300). Commercial products for computerized mapping, GIS, AM/FM, AutoCad, image processing, or manual interpretation range in price from $750 to $3,000, depending on product type and processing level.

Satellite-image maps. USGS has published satellite-image maps for selected areas in the

U.S. and such areas as Antarctica, the Bahamas, and Iceland from multispectral-scanner, thematic-mapper, and Spot imagery. Most of these image maps are printed in false-color infrared; prices range from $2.50 to $8. Notable examples are "Denali National Park, Alaska," at a scale of 1:250,000, with a standard topographic map on the reverse side ($7); "Washington, DC," at a 1:50,000 scale ($5.50); and "Point Loma, California," at a scale of 1:24,000, with a standard quadrangle map on the reverse side ($4). An order form listing these maps is available from USGS ESIC offices, or from the Distribution Center in Denver, Colorado.

Other space imagery. Also available are older space-based images that predate Landsat and *Spot*, including those made from traditional photographic processes using both fixed on-board and handheld cameras. A limited number of photographs from space are available from the Gemini and Apollo programs, for example, made between 1965 and 1970, and from the Skylab program in 1973 and 1974. The Gemini and Apollo images are limited by those spacecrafts' flight paths and cover primarily the Southwest, the Gulf Coast, and Florida. Skylab, however, includes extensive photographic coverage of most of the U.S., much of South America, and parts of Africa, Europe, and the Middle East. These photos are available from ESIC and EROS.

COMMERCIAL SOURCES

National Air Survey Center Corp. (4321 Baltimore Ave., Bladensburg, MD 20710; 301-927-7177) sells a variety of satellite mosaics in false-color infrared. Prints and transparencies are available in sizes ranging from 8" X 10" to 40" X 60", and prices range from $25 to $350. Prints/transparencies are available for the contiguous United States, individual states, and a few countries. A brochure, "Satellite Photography—Space Portrait U.S.A.," is available.

Omni Resources (1238 Anthony Rd., P.O. Box 2096, Burlington, NC 27216; 919-227-8300)

distributes many USGS satellite-image maps, many with topographic maps on the reverse side. Most titles it distributes portray areas of geologic interest. Titles available include "Anchorage, Alaska: Glacial Terrain"; "Kansas City, Missouri: Meandering Rivers"; "Pahute Mesa, Nevada: Eroded Mesas"; and "Downtown Washington, D.C." All are $6 per sheet. Also available are Spaceshot satellite-image poster/maps (see below), as well as Spot images, including Hong Kong, New York, and Paris. One of the prettiest is the "Satellite Image Map of Israel" ($19.95).

Spaceshots, Inc. (526 S. Francisca Ave., Redondo Beach, CA 9026; 310-792-5692; 800-272-2779) produces prints of satellite images of the Earth. More than 45 images are available for areas in North America, including "Cape Cod," "Idaho," "New Orleans," "Montreal," "Spokane," and "Toronto." In addition, nine foreign locations are available, including "Bahamas," "Hong Kong," "Jerusalem," and "Lake Geneva," and a dozen Earth shots from space are also available. Print size and area covered vary; prints are available on paper or laminated, and in some cases slides, T-shirts, and wall murals are also available. Prices for prints range from $13 to $30.

Worldsat Productions, Inc. (1495 Bonhill Rd., Unit 10, Mississauga, Ontario, Canada L5T 1M2; 800-387-8177, 416-670-5670) sells the striking 40" X 72" "Earth From Space" wall mural ($43.45, paper; $69.95, laminate; $99.95, polyvinyl) and other posters that use raw data from *Landsat*-5. Posters include "North America From Space," "Canada From Space," "Europe From Space," "Earth From Space—Atlantic," "Earth From Space—Pacific," "Six Global Views—Europe," "Six Global Views—Americas," and "London/Home Counties." Posters range in size from 19" X 24" to 24" X 36". Prices are $14.95 for paper and $21.95 for laminate.

■ **See also: "Aerial Photographs" and "Weather Maps."**

ATLASES AND GLOBES

How to Choose an Atlas

by June Crowe and James O. Minton

The atlas is a unique cartographic format valuable to students, teachers, travelers, and families who wish to have the world at their fingertips. The term "atlas" was first applied to a cartographic work by Gerhard Mercator, a Flemish geographer and map-maker, who in 1595 placed the Greek mythological figure of Atlas on the title page of a collection of maps in a book format.

Technically speaking, an atlas is a collection of maps that treat a specific subject in a systematic manner. Some atlases are broad in scope, such as the *Times Atlas of the World*, a general world atlas, while others are more specific, such as the *Atlas of Georgia*, which is a thematic atlas of that state. As with geographic area, subject matter can also vary, covering political, physical, economic, or social themes. Some examples of thematic atlases are *We The People: An Atlas of America's Ethnic Diversity*, *Cultural Atlas of Japan*, *Historical Atlas of Washington*, *Mariner's Atlas*, *Southwest Florida and the Florida Keys*, *Atlas of Oregon Lakes*, and *USSR Energy Atlas*. Most comprehensive world atlases focus on political and physical features with a limited selection of thematic maps.

Because there is a variety of possibilities to choose from, you must first decide which type of atlas will best satisfy your needs. Since many world atlases today cost more than $100, it is important that your selection process be deliberate and address the essential elements of quality atlas production. These criteria should cover the basic technical elements of maps (projection, scale, grids, etc.) and the physical properties of book design, layout, and printing and take into consideration your own individual preferences.

Here are some basic guidelines for selecting a world atlas for purchase:

Reputation and background of cartographer and publisher. The American Library Association's Reference and Subscription Books Reviews Committee (50 E. Huron St., Chicago, IL 60611; 312-944-6780) maintains information on a variety of atlas publishers and may answer your questions about a publisher's experience and reputation. A variety of library journals also contain reviews of atlases. Unfortunately, most atlas reviews appear many months after publication and are often difficult to locate. A selected list of journals that publish reviews on a regular basis is included at the end of this section. Ask the reference librarian at a local library for assistance in locating these reviews.

The cartographer is the person responsible for drafting the maps contained in an atlas. The cartographer (or cartographers) of individual atlas sheets is usually difficult to determine. The book's introduction may provide this information; if not, you may want to contact the publisher directly. General world atlases are not usually produced by a single cartographer, although thematic atlases often are. The cartographer's experience may be reflected in the accuracy, legibility, and clarity of the maps included in the atlas. Whether the cartographer or publisher is well known or relatively obscure, check the atlas for information on areas with which you are most familiar. Though omissions and errors are rare, they can be overlooked by even the best map-makers.

Your individual needs. Why are you buying an atlas? To plan your travels? To keep on your coffee table? Do you want the atlas to provide demographic and related information? Are you interested in the entire world or only a specific area? All these questions should be answered before selecting an atlas. In some situations, a

geographical dictionary, almanac, gazetteer, or encyclopedia may be better suited to your needs. Personal preference for size, binding, and other considerations should also be taken into account.

Technical aspects of cartographic materials.
The type of map projection (the method of getting the spherical Earth on flat paper) used in map-making will affect the size, shape, distance, and directional characteristics of the world (see page 18 for more on this). The intended use of a map determines the preferred projection. A clear explanation about the projections used in the atlas should be provided in the introduction. Moreover, the projection used should appear on each map. A variety of projections are normally used in a world atlas, including polar projections, equal-area azimuthal projections, Bonne projections, Albers conical projections, Winkel triple projections, and the Robinson projection.

The single most important technical element on a map is its scale. Scale determines the size

of paper necessary to cover a particular geographical area and the amount of detail you can expect from a map. There are three widely used methods of indicating scale on a map: geographic or bar scale, a verbal scale, and the R.F. (representative fraction) or natural scale. Maps contained in atlases may indicate scale with any one, or all, of these methods. (Better-quality atlases usually indicate scale in all three manners.) It is recommended that serious map users learn the R.F. method, because it allows you to work with any system of measurement—centimeters, inches, meters, feet, kilometers, or miles. Maps are referred to as either large-scale or small-scale. Small-scale (such as 1:35,000,000) maps show little detail and emphasize only major elements of world geography. Large-scale (such as 1:15,000) maps show greater detail and may even depict individual streets and buildings. If you are interested in such "big picture" things as global-transportation patterns or bird-migration routes, a small-scale map showing the entire world on one page may satisfy your needs. However, if you are interested in finding the name of a specific street, a much larger-scale map will be necessary. World atlases generally contain small-scale maps of continents and nations with a few larger-scale maps of selected cities. Don't expect a world atlas to contain a street index to your hometown, for example.

Legends and symbols are also important. Maps use lines, points, and polygons (enclosed areas) to depict various physical, economic, social, and worldwide cultural features. These elements form the symbols used on maps that allow you to visually interpret information at a glance. Well-produced maps contain a legend or list of symbols. Most atlases contain a legend or symbol sheet in the front of the publication. Some publishers print a separate legend sheet that can be moved easily from page to page while using the maps without having to leaf to the specific legend page every time you need to consult it. All symbols used on the maps should be included and be clearly distinct from one another, especially if a range of colors is used to depict graduated changes.

Atlases are most often used in locating cultural and physical features—cities, lakes, mountains, and so forth. A variety of methods of grids is used to index these features. Some atlases contain lists of features (generally at the end of the publication) with a grid indicating its location on a page and specific spot within the map—"B-21," for example. Most good atlases, however, also list the latitude and longitude of the place along with the plate (or page) number. It is recommended that you become familiar with the systems of degrees, minutes, and seconds used to determine latitude and longitude. (Each degree of latitude or longitude is made up of 60 minutes; each minute consists of 60 seconds. Thus, 28° 40' 35"N refers to a latitude that is 28 degrees, 40 minutes, and 35 seconds north of the equator.) You shouldn't even consider an atlas whose index does not indicate latitude and longitude.

Publishing information. There are a number of considerations:

■ *Date of publication*. You should scan the title page and other introductory pages for the date of publication, place of publication, copyright, and revision information. Be aware that most atlases are revised or reprinted. However, some less-than-reputable publishers issue a "new" atlas containing older maps without updating them. Select a particular section of the world that has undergone change and review the atlas to see if the changes have been incorporated. (For example: Do maps of China show the capital as "Beijing" or "Peking"?) Check for changes in names, roads, boundaries, and other pertinent information.

■ *Adequacy of coverage*. An important aspect in selecting an atlas is whether it contains detailed maps of an area important to you. If you are interested in detailed maps of Papua New Guinea, for example, it is unlikely that a world atlas will suffice. The place of publication is an important hint as to the depth of coverage you can expect. If the atlas were printed in Papua New Guinea or Australia, there would be a greater likelihood that it would contain more maps at larger scales of that region than those published elsewhere.

■ *Arrangement and organization of material*. Atlases have evolved into a somewhat standard format: title page, table of contents, general thematic maps, larger-scale maps, supplementary materials, and indexes. Atlas organization determines how efficiently it can be used. For example, you may want to quickly locate a place whose name you heard on the evening news. Is your atlas arranged to find it easily? Is there a recognizable geographic arrangement to the maps within the atlas?

■ *Indexes*. These are the most important parts of an atlas. Two types of indexes are common: a textual index to place names and a graphic index indicating map coverage and plate numbers. Textual indexes are generally included in an alphabetical arrangement at the end of the atlas along with the plate number (or page) and grid location (preferably latitude and longitude). Pay particular attention to the textual index. Do all names listed in the index appear on the maps? Are all names on the maps listed in the index? Are the spellings of names in both English and the native language of the country on the map? If not, you may have difficulty locating specific places. (Is it listed as Köln or Cologne?) Are physical features included in the index? Better-quality atlases have large indexes that include the map and the geographic location of each entry. The *Times Atlas of the World* and *Rand McNally's New International Atlas* each contain more than 200,000 entries. Select several place names from the index to determine whether these names appear on the map plates. According to *Kister's Atlas Buying Guide* (Oryx Press, 2214 N. Central Ave., Phoenix, AZ 85004; 602-254-1483; 1984), a general world atlas should contain between 30,000 and 50,000 entries to adequately cover the world's places and features.

Graphic indexes consist of outline maps indicating map coverage with plate or page number. These indexes provide quick access to most of the maps in an atlas. If you wish to locate a map of the island of New Guinea, for example, a quick glance at the graphic index should yield the plate number immediately, whereas the textual index will require locating the name in alphabetical order, noting the plate number, then locating the map. However, if you wanted to locate the city of Lae in Papua New Guinea, the textual index would provide a more efficient way to do so.

■ *Supplementary materials.* Most atlases contain material that is non-cartographic in nature. This may include bibliographies, charts, text, tables, population figures, and photographs. Many atlas publishers include such extraneous material to enhance marketing. But much of this type of information can be found in other publications providing better coverage and reliability than an atlas. Atlases should contain a limited number of pages devoted to supplementary material.

SELECTED JOURNALS THAT REVIEW ATLASES

■ *American Cartographer* (American Congress on Surveying and Mapping, 5410 Grosvenor Ln., Ste. 100, Bethesda, MD 20814; 301-493-0200).
■ *The Booklist* (American Library Association, 50 E. Huron St., Chicago, IL 60611; 312-944-6780).
■ *Bulletin* (Special Libraries Association, Geography and Map Division, 1700 18th St. NW, Washington, DC 20009; 202-234-4700).
■ *The Cartographic Journal* (British Cartographic Society, c/o T.A. Adams, Laser-Scan, Ltd., Cambridge Science Park, Milton Rd., Cambridge, England CB4 4FY).
■ *Choice* (Association of College and Research Libraries, 50 E. Huron St., Chicago, IL 60611; 312-944-6780).
■ *Geographical Journal* (Royal Geographical Society, 1 Kensington Gore, London SW7 2AR, England; 071-589-5466).
■ *Geographical Review* (American Geographical Society, 156 Fifth Ave., Ste. 600, New York, NY 10010; 212-242-0214).
■ *GeoTimes* (American Geological Institute, 4220 King St., Alexandria, VA 22302; 703-379-2480).
■ *Information Bulletin* (Western Association of Map Libraries, c/o Stanley D. Stevens, University Library-University of California, Santa Cruz, CA 95064; 408-429-2364).
■ *Library Journal* (R.R. Bowker, Bowker Magazine Group, Cahners Magazine Div., 245 W. 17th St., New York, NY 10011; 212-916-1600).
■ *Professional Geographer* (Association of American Geographers, 1710 16th St. NW, Washington, DC 20009; 202-234-1450).
■ *Surveying and Mapping* (American Congress on Surveying and Mapping, 5410 Grosvenor Ln., Ste. 100, Bethesda, MD 20814; 301-493-0200).

June Crowe is head of the Information Resource Center at International Technology Corp. in Knoxville, TN. James O. Minton heads the Cartographic Information Center at the University of Tennessee, Knoxville.

Selected Atlases

Mention the word "atlas" and it usually brings to mind the word "world," although "world atlases" represent a mere fraction of atlases published. There are atlases of nearly every place and thing: agriculture atlases, Bible atlases, state atlases, country atlases, history atlases, plant and animal atlases, road atlases, celestial atlases, war atlases, and on and on. The Library of Congress, in Washington, D.C., has more than 11,000 books containing the word "atlas" in their titles—representing only books the library has cataloged since 1968!

WORLD ATLASES

Here are some of the world atlases currently available:

■ *Goode's World Atlas*, 18th ed. (Chicago: Rand McNally, 1990; 368 pages; $26.95). This is one of the most popular world atlases used in schools (its 1922 through 1949 editions were titled *Goode's School Atlas*) because it provides more than 100 special-purpose maps typically used by students on subjects such as population, economics, and agriculture. Goode's maps are particularly clear and readable, and the book's bindings were designed for rugged school-library use.

■ *Great World Atlas* (Maspeth, N.Y.: American Map Corp., 1989; 384 pages; $49.95). A revised and expanded edition, it includes chapters covering astronomy and earth science, a large section of satellite photos, along with well-executed maps, several thematic and statistical maps, and an index.

■ *Hammond Gold Medallion World Atlas* (Maplewood, N.J.: Hammond, Inc., 1991; 692 pages; $85). Hammond publishes several world atlases, but this is the most comprehensive,

with more than 600 maps providing a wide range of data.

Hammond also publishes an *Ambassador World Atlas* (1991; 548 pages; $54.95); *Citation World Atlas* (1991; 420 pages; $22.95 soft, $32.95 hard); *Discovery World Atlas* (1991; 248 pages; $19.95 hard, $13.95 soft); *Nova World Atlas* (1988; 184 pages; $10.95); *Headline World Atlas* (1991; 48 pages; $3.95); *Hammond Physical World Atlas* (1991; 40 pages; $6.95); and *Passport Travelmate and World Atlas* (1991; 128 pages; $4.95).

■ *National Geographic Atlas of the World* (Washington, D.C.: National Geographic Society, 1990; 411 pages; $59.95 soft, $74.95 for deluxe hardcover edition with magnifier). Published by this venerable institution, the atlas is a comprehensive and attractive work, featuring clear, easily readable maps. Of particular note is the coverage of the oceans of Africa, which are presented in detail not generally found in other world atlases. National Geographic also publishes *Atlas of North America: Space Age Portrait of a Continent* (1985; 264 pages; $51.95).

■ *Rand McNally New International Atlas* (Chicago: Rand McNally, 1989; 560 pages; $125). Compiled by more than 100 cartographers worldwide, it is known for its generally balanced coverage and attractive maps. It includes detailed maps of major world metropolitan areas at 1:1,000,000 and 1:3,000,000 scales, a helpful glossary giving translations of geographic terms in 52 languages, and a thorough 160,000-name index. It does not feature thematic or special-purpose maps.

Rand McNally also publishes the *Rand McNally Cosmopolitan World Atlas* (1987; 392 pages; $60); *Rand McNally Images of the World* (1984; 160 pages; $24.95); *Rand McNally Desk Reference World Atlas* (1987; 528 pages; $17.95); *Quick Reference World Atlas* (1991; 64 pages; $4.95); *New Century*

World Atlas (1991; 256 pages; $11.95); and
International Geographic Atlas (1991; 256 pages;
$19.95).

■ *Times Atlas of the World* (New York: Times
Books, 1990; 520 pages; $159.95). *The Times of
London* has produced world atlases since 1895,
and they are consistently lauded for their
comprehensive, balanced coverage and top-
quality indexes. In addition to the "comprehensive" edition, there is also a "concise
edition": *The New York Times Atlas of the World*
(New York: Random House; 1987; 288 pages;
$49.95).

Other world atlases include:

■ *The Bantam Illustrated World Atlas* (New York:
Bantam, 1989; $39.95).
■ *Britannica Atlas* (Chicago: Encyclopedia
Britannica, 1989; $99.50).
■ *Illustrated World Atlas* (New York: Franklin
Watts, Inc., 1988; $14.90).
■ NBC *News Rand McNally World News Atlas and
Almanac* (Chicago: Rand McNally, 1992; $9.95).
■ *Rand McNally World Atlas of Nations* (Chicago:
Rand McNally, 1988; $34.95).
■ *Reader's Digest Atlas of the World* (Chicago:
Rand McNally, 1990; $39.95).

UNITED STATES ATLASES

Other atlases that primarily cover the U.S.
include:

■ *The City to City Atlas* (Maspeth, N.Y.: Ameri-
can Map Corp., 1992; $17.95).
■ *Contemporary Atlas of the United States* (New
York: Macmillan, 1990; $90).
■ *Rand McNally Road Atlas & Vacation Guide*
(Chicago: Rand McNally, 1990; $14.95), an
annual.
■ *Rand McNally Road Atlas* (Chicago: Rand
McNally, 1992; $7.95).
■ *The United States Road Atlas* (Maspeth, N.Y.:
American Map Corp., 1992; $6.95).

SPECIALIZED ATLASES

These vary widely—in form, content, and
availability. While there are thousands of
specialized atlases, we've listed below some of
the more interesting, comprehensive, or useful
ones. Many, but not all, are still in print; a few
are difficult to find outside of major metropolitan and university libraries.

STATE ATLASES

■ *Atlas of Georgia* (Athens, Ga.: Institute of
Community & Area, University of Georgia, 1985;
$47.50).
■ *Atlas of Hawaii*, 2nd ed., (Honolulu: Univ. of
Hawaii Press, 1983; $29.95).
■ *Atlas of the State of South Carolina: Prefaced with a
Geographical, Statistical & Historical Map* (Easley,
S.C.: Southern Historical Press, 1980 reproduc-
tion of 1825 edition; $50).
■ *Historical Atlas of Kansas* (Norman, Okla.:
University of Oklahoma Press, 1989; $26.95).
■ *Maine Atlas & Gazetteer* (Freeport, Me.: DeLorme

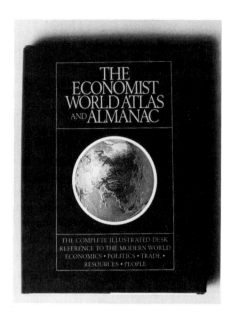

Mapping Co., 1989; $11.95).

■ *New Jersey Road Maps of the Eighteenth Century* (Princeton, N.J.: Princeton University Library, 1981; $10).

■ *New Mexico in Maps* (Albuquerque, N.M.: University of New Mexico Press, 1986; $14.95).

■ *Trakker Maps Florida State Road Atlas* (Miami, Fla.: Trakker Maps, Inc., 1989; $7.95), an annual.

■ *Vermont Atlas & Gazetteer* (Freeport, Me.: DeLorme Mapping Co., 1988; $11.95).

■ *Vermont Road Atlas* (Burlington, Vt.: Northern Cartographics, 1989; $12.95).

FOREIGN COUNTRY & REGIONAL ATLASES

■ *Atlas of Central America and the Caribbean* (New York: Macmillan, 1985; $60).

■ *Atlas of Ireland* (New York: St. Martin's Press,1980; $99.50).

■ *Atlas of Israel* (New York: Macmillan, 1985; $185).

■ *Atlas of the Middle East* (New York: Macmillan, 1988; $60).

■ *Atlas of South Asia, Annotated* (Boulder, Colo.: Westview Press, 1985; $19.95).

■ *Atlas of Southeast Asia* (New York: Macmillan, 1988; $95).

■ *Atlas of the Third World* (New York: Facts On File, 1989; $95).

■ *The Contemporary Atlas of China* (Boston: Houghton Mifflin Co., 1988; $39.95).

■ *Cultural Atlas of Africa* (New York: Facts On File, 1981; $45).

■ *Cultural Atlas of China* (New York: Facts On File, 1983; $45).

■ *The Cultural Atlas of Islam* (New York: Macmillan, 1986; $115).

■ *Cultural Atlas of Japan* (New York: Facts On File, 1988; $45).

■ *Cultural Atlas of Russia and the Soviet Union* (New York: Facts On File, 1989; $45).

■ *Hammond Atlas of the Middle East* (Maplewood, N.J.: Hammond, Inc., 1991; $7.95).

■ *Rand McNally Road Atlas & City Guide of Europe* (Chicago: Rand McNally, 1992; $18.95).

■ *Rand McNally Road Atlas of Britain* (Chicago: Rand McNally, 1992; $18.95), an annual.

■ *Rand McNally Road Atlas of Europe* (Chicago: Rand McNally, 1992; $9.95), an annual.

■ *Third World Atlas* (Philadelphia: Taylor & Francis, Inc., 1984; $69 hardcover, $28 softcover).

HISTORICAL ATLASES

■ *Atlas of African History* (New York: Holmes & Meier Publishers, Inc., 1978; $45 hardcover, $29.50 softcover).

■ *Atlas of African History* (New York: Penguin Books, 1980; $8.95).

■ *Atlas of American History* (New York: Macmillan, 1985; $60).

■ *Atlas of American History* (New York: Facts On File, 1991; $19.95).

■ *Atlas of Ancient America* (New York: Facts On File, 1986; $45).

■ *Atlas of Ancient Egypt* (New York: Facts On File, 1980; $45).

■ *Atlas of Ancient History* (New York: Penguin Books, 1967; $9.95).

■ *Atlas of the British Empire* (New York: Facts On File, 1991; $40).

■ *Atlas of British Social and Economic History Since 1700* (New York: Macmillan, 1989; $80).

■ *Atlas of Classical History* (New York: Macmillan, 1985; $50).

■ *Atlas of Early American History: The Revolutionary*

Era (Princeton, N.J.: Princeton University Press, 1976; $250).

■ *Atlas of the Greek World* (New York: Facts On File, 1981; $45).

■ *Atlas of Medieval Europe* (New York: Facts On File, 1983; $45).

■ *Atlas of Medieval History* (New York: Penguin Books, 1968; $9.95).

■ *Atlas of Modern History* (New York: Penguin Books, 1973; $9.95).

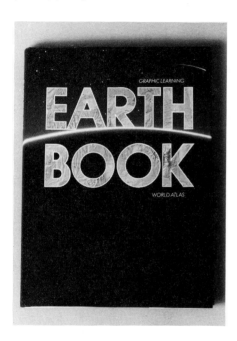

■ *Atlas of Nazi Germany* (New York: Macmillan, 1987; $60).

■ *Atlas of North American History* (New York: Penguin Books, 1988; $9.95).

■ *Atlas of Recent History* (New York: Penguin Books, 1986; $9.95).

■ *Atlas of the Roman World* (New York: Facts On File, 1982; $45).

■ *Atlas of United States History* (Maplewood, N.J.: Hammond, Inc., 1989; $11.95).

■ *Atlas of World History* (Chicago: Rand McNally, 1987; $18.95).

■ *Hammond Atlas of World History* (Maplewood, N.J.: Hammond, Inc., 1987; $11.95).

■ *Historical Atlas of Canada*, Volume I (Toronto: University of Toronto Press, 1987; $95).

■ *Historical Atlas of the Outlaw West* (Boulder, Colo.: Johnson Books, 1984; $15.95).

■ *Historical Atlas of Political Parties in the United States Congress: 1789-1989* (New York: Macmillan, 1989; $190).

■ *Historical Atlas of the United States* (Washington, D.C.: National Geographic Society, 1989; $76.95).

■ *Historical Atlas of the World* (Chicago: Rand McNally, 1965; $6.95).

■ *Peoples and Places of the Past: The National Geographic Illustrated Cultural Atlas of the Ancient World* (Washington, D.C.: National Geographic Society, 1983; $69.95).

■ *Poland: A Historical Atlas* (New York: Hippocrene Books, 1989; $27.50).

■ *The Times Atlas of World History* (Maplewood, N.J.: Hammond, Inc., 1989; $85).

■ *The Times Concise Atlas of World History* (Maplewood, N.J.: Hammond, Inc., 1988; $24.95).

■ *Past Worlds: The Times Atlas of Archaeology* (Maplewood, N.J.: Hammond, Inc., 1988; $21.25).

POLITICAL, CULTURAL, AND SOCIOLOGICAL ATLASES

■ *Atlas of African Affairs* (New York: Methuen, Inc., 1984; $14.95).

■ *Atlas of American Women* (New York: Macmillan, 1986; $90).

■ *Atlas of Disease Distribution* (New York: Basil Blackwell, Inc., 1988; $150).

■ *Atlas of Environmental Issues* (New York: Facts On File, 1989; $16.95).

■ *Atlas of Global Strategy* (New York: Facts On File, 1985; $29.95).

■ *Atlas of the North American Indian* (New York: Facts on File, 1989; $16.95).

■ *Atlas of Nuclear Energy* (Atlanta: Georgia State University, Dept. of Geography, 1984; $6).

■ *Atlas of the Arab World* (New York: Facts On File, 1991; $50).

■ *Atlas of World Affairs* (New York: Methuen, Inc., 1987; $45.95 hardcover, $13.95 softcover).

■ *Atlas of World Cultures* (Pittsburgh, Pa.: University of Pittsburgh Press, 1981; $18.95).

■ *Atlas of World Issues* (New York: Facts On File, 1989; $16.95).

■ *The Cambridge Encyclopedia of the Middle East & North Africa* (New York: Cambridge University Press, 1987; $55).

■ *The Coin Atlas* (New York: Facts On File, 1990; $40).

■ *National Population Atlas of the People's Republic of China* (New York: Oxford University Press, 1987; $275).

■ *New State of the World Atlas* (New York: Simon & Schuster, Inc., 1991; $30).

■ *The Nuclear War Atlas* (New York: Basil Blackwell, Inc., 1988; $14.95).

■ *Oxford Economic Atlas of the World* (New York: Oxford University Press, Inc., 1972; $24.95).

■ *Oxford Regional Economic Atlases: The United States & Canada* (New York: Oxford University Press, Inc., 1975; $19.95).

■ *Strategic Atlas: A Comparative Geopolitics of the World's Powers* (New York: HarperCollins, 1990; $29.95).

■ *The Stamp Atlas* (New York: Facts On File, 1987; $29.95).

■ *We the People: An Atlas of America's Ethnic Diversity* (New York: Macmillan, 1987; $85).

■ *Wine Atlas of Italy and Traveler's Guide to the Vineyards* (New York: Simon & Schuster, 1991; $60).

■ *The Women's Atlas of the United States* (New York: Facts On File, 1987; $60).

■ *Women in the World: An International Atlas* (New York: Simon & Schuster/Touchstone, 1986; $12.95).

■ *The World Bank Atlas* (Washington, D.C.: IBRD/The World Bank, 1989; $5.95), an annual.

MILITARY AND WAR ATLASES

■ *State of War Atlas: Armed Conflict—Armed Peace* (New York: Simon & Schuster, 1983; $9.95).

■ *World Atlas of Military History, 1945-84* (New York: Hippocrene Books, 1985; $24.95).

ATLASES OF RELIGION

■ *Atlas of the Bible Lands* (Nashville, Tenn.: Broadman Press, 1979; $6.95).

■ *Atlas of the Bible Lands* (Maplewood, N.J.: Hammond, Inc., 1989; $11.95).

■ *Atlas of the Bible* (New York: Facts On File, 1984; $45).

■ *Atlas of the Christian Church* (New York: Facts On File, 1987; $45).

■ *Atlas of the Islamic World Since 1500* (New York: Facts On File, 1982; $45).

■ *Atlas of the Jewish World* (New York: Facts On File, 1984; $45).

■ *Maps of the Holy Land* (New York: Abbeville Press, 1985; $29.98).

■ *Oxford Bible Atlas* (New York: Oxford University Press, 1985; $27.95 hardcover, $14.95 softcover).

■ *Reader's Digest Atlas of the Bible* (New York: Random House, 1982; $28).

CELESTIAL ATLASES

■ *Atlas Australis* (Belmont, Mass.: Sky Publishing Corp., 1964; $49.95).

■ *Atlas Borealis* (Belmont, Mass.: Sky Publishing Corp., 1964; $49.95).

■ *Atlas of Deep Sky Splendors* (New York: Cambridge University Press, 1984; $59.50).

■ *Atlas of Selected Areas* (Belmont, Mass.: Sky Publishing Corp.; $33).

■ *Maps of the Heavens* (New York: Abbeville Press, 1989; $29.98).

■ *Norton's Star Atlas and Reference Handbook* (Belmont, Mass.: Sky Publishing Corp., 1986; $29.95).

■ *Sky Atlas* (Belmont, Mass.: Sky Publishing Corp., not dated; $15.95).

NATURE ATLASES

■ *An Atlas of Massachusetts River Systems: Environmental Designs for the Future* (Amherst, Mass.: Univ. of Massachusetts Press, 1990; $17.95).

■ *Atlas of Living Resources of the Seas* (New York: Food and Agricultural Organization/Unipub, 1981; $115).

■ *Atlas of Natural Wonders* (New York: Facts On File, 1988; $35).

■ *Atlas of the Environment* (New York: Prentice Hall Press, 1990; $29.95).

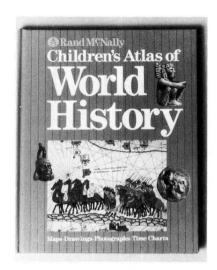

■ *Atlas of Wintering North American Birds* (Chicago: University of Chicago Press, 1989; $60).
■ *Climatic Atlas of the United States* (Asheville, N.C.: National Climatic Data Center, 1969; $17).

OCEAN ATLASES

■ *Climatological Atlas of the World Ocean* (Washington, D.C.: Government Printing Office, 1982; $11).
■ *Oceanographic Atlas of the Bering Sea Basin* (Seattle, Wash.: University of Washington Press, 1980; $35).
■ *Oceanographic Atlas of the Pacific Ocean* (Honolulu, Haw.: University of Hawaii Press, 1969; $25).
■ *Random House Atlas of the Oceans* (New York: Random House, 1991; $40).
■ *Sea Ice Climatic Atlas* (Asheville, N.C.: National Climatic Data Center, 1989; free), an annual in three volumes.

RAILWAY AND SHIPPING ATLASES

■ *Trucker's Atlas* (Wood Dale, Ill.: Creative Sales Corp., 1989; $9.95), an annual.
■ *Rand McNally Handy Railroad Atlas* (Chicago: Rand McNally, 1988; $14.95).

ATLASES FOR YOUNG PEOPLE

■ *Atlas of Ancient Egypt* (New York: Facts On File, 1990; $17.95).
■ *Atlas of Ancient Greece* (New York: Facts On File, 1989; $17.95).
■ *Atlas of Ancient Rome* (New York: Facts On File, 1989; $17.95).
■ *Atlas of the Middle Ages* (New York: Facts On File, 1990; $17.95).
■ *Children's Illustrated World Atlas* (Philadelphia, Pa.: Running Press, 1989; $9.98).
■ *Discovering Maps: A Young Person's World Atlas* (Maplewood, N.J.: Hammond, Inc., 1991; $10.95).
■ *Facts On File Children's Atlas* (New York: Facts On File, 1987; $14.95).
■ *Rand McNally Children's Atlas of World Wildlife* (Chicago: Rand McNally, 1991; $14.95).
■ *Rand McNally Children's Atlas of World History* (Chicago: Rand McNally, 1989; $14.95).
■ *Rand McNally Children's World Atlas* (Chicago: Rand McNally, 1989; $14.95).
■ *Rand McNally Children's Atlas of the Environment* (Chicago: Rand McNally, 1991; $14.95).
■ *Rand McNally Children's Atlas of the United States* (Chicago: Rand McNally, 1989; $14.95).
■ *Rand McNally Picture Atlas of the World* (Chicago: Rand McNally, 1991; $19.95).
■ *World Atlas* (Chicago: Nystrom, 1991; $4.25).

■ **See also: "Geography Education Materials."**

Globes

The globe—the most accurate distortion-free representation of the Earth's surface—has the greatest utility of any visual aid in geography. It is the only map of the world that shows the true size and shape of all land and water areas, as well as the true distances and geographical relationships between them. As a model of the rotating Earth, the globe can be used to illustrate illumination from the sun, the relationship of time and longitude, and related concepts.

Although mounting a world map onto a sphere does have special advantages, it also creates some unique problems that usually make flat maps more practical. Only part of the world can be seen at one time, for example. And whatever its size, a globe takes up more space than a flat map of equal scale, is not easily portable, and usually contains insufficient detail.

Perhaps the greatest disadvantage of globes is their greater cost compared to maps of similar scale. Like any material printed on a flat surface, maps can be produced cheaply in large quantities. Unfortunately, a satisfactory spherical printing press has yet to be invented, so globe maps are also printed on a flat surface and then transformed into a hemisphere by one of several manufacturing processes.

How globes are made. For centuries, globes were made by printing the world map onto 30-degree-wide gores, which were cut and pasted onto a wooden sphere by hand. In the Replogle and Cram globe factories, paper gores are still applied by hand on some models, but the wooden sphere has been replaced by pressboard or plastic.

This handmade process proved too slow to satisfy the public's growing demand for globes. By the middle of the 20th century, machine-made globes were being mass-produced by a method in which northern and southern polar projections were printed directly onto sheet aluminum and stamped into hemispheres with a hydraulic press. Susceptibility to dents and map stretching during the hemisphere-stamping process increases with globe size, however, and these globes could not be larger than 12 inches in diameter.

In the early 1960s, a new type of globe made from chipboard was introduced and has since become the most common type in current use. The maps are printed as interrupted polar projections resembling a propeller with 12 blades, referred to in the business as "rosettes." Each map is glued to chipboard, die-cut into the rosette shape, then glued to another rosette-shaped piece of chipboard, with seams overlapping, before the hydraulic press forms it all into a hemisphere.

One recent development in globe manufacture was the introduction of plastic, raised-relief globes. Using a procedure similar to that of making metal globes, the polar projections are printed onto sheet plastic, then formed using a vacuum process into their hemispheric shape. This process creates more accurate relief than is possible on chipboard globes. As with metal globes, the maps printed on plastic are drawn with some deliberate distortion, which occurs when the hemispheres are formed. Place names near the equator still appear vertically stretched, however. The Northern and Southern Hemispheres of plastic, chipboard, and metal globes are matched at the International Date Line or the South Pacific island of Celebes when they are joined. A narrow strip of tape is applied over the equator to cover any gaps and to give a better appearance before the mounting and base are attached.

Types of globes. Terrestrial globes can be classified into three basic groups by type of coloring and information contained: political globes, physical globes, and political-physical combination globes.

The political globe is characterized by multicolor political units and solid-blue oceans. There is quite a variety in the amount of political information different manufacturers include on their globes. Some political globes show national units only. Other globe-makers add multicolor U.S. state units; and on some models Canada's provinces are also shown in different colors. Still other models show only provincial boundaries of non-North American countries. Names stretched across the length of bodies of water, deserts, and mountain ranges are typically the only evidence of the physical Earth on political globes, although some models also show ocean currents, steamship routes, and one type of relief portrayal.

The physical globe is primarily a representation of the world's relief features. The traditional method showing relief is by tints, with

"Planet Earth," a 12"-diameter model of Earth as seen from space, from Replogle Globes, Inc.

The third type of globe is the political-physical combination. It is similar to the political globe in that political units or boundaries are multicolor, but it also contains features found on a physical globe, such as raised and shaded relief, bathymetry of the ocean floor, and spot heights.
"Two-way illuminated" political-physical globes, available from some manufacturers, feature political cartography when not illuminated. When the light is turned on, the ocean floor is revealed in shaded relief, for example, or eco-region cartography. These globes can be considered two globes in one, unlike older illuminated globes, in which light is used for merely decorative purposes.

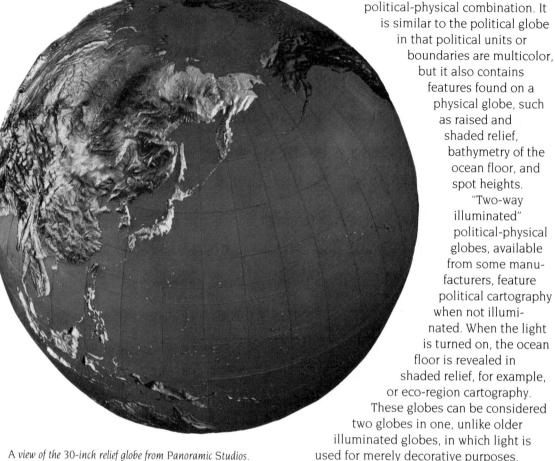

A view of the 30-inch relief globe from Panoramic Studios.

green for lowlands and lighter green, yellow, and brown for higher elevations. The use of hysometric tints has recently been subject to the criticism that it does not give a realistic image of the planet's surface. Perhaps as a response to this, some manufacturers have produced "eco-region" globes that use various shades of green, yellow, and brown to portray forests, grasslands, deserts, and other natural regions on land, and shades of blue to portray the ocean floor. Raised and shaped relief are used extensively on physical globes. Some even feature the ocean floor in indented relief. Almost all physical globes show place names of physical features and selected cities, and some also include spot heights, ocean currents, and political unit boundaries and names.

Special and extraterrestrial globes. Other types of globes include:

■ Outline or project globes, showing only the shapes or outlines of continents on a smooth plastic or slated surface. These are designed to be marked with pens or chalk to show various global concepts.
■ Political globes with either French or Spanish text. Globes with text in other foreign languages can be obtained from European globe companies.
■ Globes of celestial bodies other than the Earth, including the moon, Mars, and the solar system. Most are produced from NASA photographs. Celestial globes are available in two versions. One type has yellow stars and planets

printed on an opaque blue sphere with lines connecting stars in constellations or the outlines of the characters these constellations represent. The other is a clear plastic sphere with the stars and planets printed on the inside surface and a small Earth model mounted in the center.

COMMERCIAL SOURCES

While thousands of globes exist, only a handful are readily available from globe manufacturers. Most map libraries have several terrestrial— and sometimes extraterrestrial—globes for study; the Library of Congress's map division has 400 globes on hand.

Globe prices range from less than $10 to well over $1,000, depending on size, quality of artwork, and such extras as floor stands, illumination, and raised relief.

George F. Cram Co. (P.O. Box 426, Indianapolis, IN 46206; 317-635-5564; 800-227-4199) manufactures 38 different globes, from a series of nine-inch "gift" globes ($16 to $140) to 16-inch deluxe illuminated models ($230 to $410).

GeoLearning Corp. (P.O. Box 2042, Sheridan, WY 82801; 307-674-6436; 800-843-6436) distributes the "Magnetic Globe Puzzle" ($149.95), a 15-inch-diameter metal sphere with 470 magnetized puzzle pieces that, when assembled, gives an accurate, to-scale representation of the world. Individual replacement pieces ($3 each) may be ordered as political boundaries change, meaning the globe will never be obsolete.

Modern School (1609 E. Kercher Rd., Goshen, IN 46526; 219-533-3111; 800-431-5929) produces six globes for classroom use, ranging from a 12-inch model to three 16-inch models on floor stands and casters ($58 to $195).

National Geographic Society (17th & M sts. NW, Washington, DC 20036; 301-921-1200) sells two 12-inch and three 16-inch globes, one illuminated, two on wooden floor stands,

ranging from $59.95 to $160.

Nystrom (3333 N. Elston Ave., Chicago, IL 60618; 312-463-1144; 800-621-8086) produces 12-inch and 16-inch raised-relief globes with a variety of mountings. Made of vinyl, they are designed to be touched and are advertised as guaranteed against peeling or breaking. Models range from $79.50 to $243. Another Nystrom product is "Form-a-Globe," designed for classroom use, a build-it-yourself paper globe demonstrating how maps and globes differ from and are related to each other. A set of 30 "Form-a-Globes" is $21.

Omni Resources (1238 Anthony Rd., P.O. Box 2096, Burlington, NC 27216; 919-227-8300) produces the "Drift Globe" ($175), a 12-inch globe created to aid in understanding continental drift. The globe features 9 continents that may be positioned anywhere on the globe with Velcro. Orientation marks on each continent match crosses on the globe, which represent 50-million-year intervals. The globe comes with a cartoon-illustrated guide that discusses climate and fauna during each era.

Panoramic Studios (1104 Churchill Rd., Wyndmoor, PA 19118; 215-233-4235) has manufactured large, intricate globes used by many news organizations, as well as in classrooms and boardrooms. It produces a 30-inch relief globe ($2,500), which is a popular geographic tool for teachers of the blind; other relief globes and maps are custom made.

Rand McNally (P.O. Box 7600, Chicago, IL 60680; 312-673-9100) produces about 15 globes for educational use, ranging in price from $40 to $695. The terrestrial globes are divided into three series: Political, featuring country boundaries in contrasting colors; International, showing political boundaries in ribbons of blue; and World Portrait, showing the Earth as seen from space, with natural vegetation and underwater topography. Rand McNally also makes the "Geography-Physical Globe," the largest model of the Earth manufactured today, in six-foot and three-foot diameters. In addition, the company produces Geography-Physical plaques, each depicting a single continent, with diameters ranging from two feet to 60 inches.

Replogle Globes, Inc. (2801 S. 25th Ave., Broadview, IL 60153; 708-343-0900) produces a variety of 12-, 16-, 20-, and 32-inch globes in both blue-ocean and antique styles, including several illuminated models. The "President" ($2,425; 65015) is a 20-inch illuminated globe with "touch-on" light control; three levels of brightness can be obtained by touching the meridian. The nine-inch "Weather Watch" ($139.95; 51403), a raised-relief globe, has a specially designed base that can aid in tracking global weather. Other popular models include the 16-inch nonilluminated "Commander" (22803), an antique-style floor model that retails for $85, and the 16-inch "Lafayette" (64105), an illuminated globe that comes with a hardwood base and is priced at $605.

Replogle also offers a 12-inch moon globe and a 12-inch celestial globe. Developed under the auspices of NASA, the moon globe ($35.95; 38245) has a three-dimensional look that reveals craters, seas, and mountains. The celestial globe ($39.95; 38848) locates 1,200 stars from 1st to 4th magnitude and shows constellations, star clusters, new stars, and double stars. The company's newest product is called "Planet Earth" ($75; 80200), the first globe as seen from space. The 12-inch globe was drawn by an artist using hundreds of satellite photos and images.

Spherical Concepts, Inc. (2 Davis Ave., P.O. Box 1215, Frazer, PA 19355; 215-296-4119) produces silk-screened clear-acrylic globes, available in various colors. Models include "The Continental," in 8-, 12-, 16-, or 30-inch diameters, and "The International," a 12-inch political globe. Most models come with a wax marking pencil to use on the globe and instruction booklet. All globes can be customized to show specific locations, route lines, and so on, for corporate advertising specialty work. Prices range from $29 for the five-inch "Earthball," to $995 for the 30-inch "Continental" globe. Several celestial globes are also available (see "Astronomical Charts and Maps").

Trippensee Planetarium Co. (301 Cass St., Saginaw, MI 48602; 517-799-8102) produces handcrafted clear-acrylic globes that are fashioned of individually blown hemispheres. The graphics are silk-screened on the interior surface, permitting the globe to be marked with a china marker, which is easily wiped off. Globes available include the "Explorer & Starlite Celestial Globes," in 12- and 16-inch sizes ($175 to $385); the "Flair Globe" ($32 to $60; 5 3/4 inches), in three color schemes and a variety of bases; and the "Spectrum Globe" ($145 to $330; 12 and 16 inches), a nine-color globe depicting countries, oceans, major cities, and states and provinces.

■ **See also: "Astronomical Charts and Maps," "Map Software," and "World Maps."**

ET CETERA

Geography Education Materials

If you read the news, you've heard the stories: Today's young people—and Americans in particular—are geography illiterates. The tales would be funny if they weren't so serious. For example:

■ In one survey of the University of Miami, 30 percent of the students could not locate the Pacific Ocean on a world map.
■ Nearly half of the college students in a California poll could not identify the location of Japan.
■ In Baltimore, 45 percent of those tested could not respond correctly to the instruction: "On the attached map, shade in the area where the United States is located."
■ Twenty-five percent of the students tested in Dallas could not identify the country that borders the United States on the south.
■ In Boston, 39 percent of the students could not name the six New England states.
■ When a television station in Washington, D.C., asked 500 high school students to name the large country north of the United States, 14 percent guessed incorrectly. One said Delaware.

The statistics go on and on. According to a 1988 Gallup poll, Americans ranked among the bottom third in an international test of geographic knowledge, and those aged 18 to 24 came in last. Even less encouraging is that in this day of global communications, test scores are getting worse. Compared to surveys taken in the 1950s, American students know even less about the world than ever.

In response to this crying need, the 1980s saw the rebirth of geography education, in the form of "Geography Awareness Weeks," "Geography Bees," and dozens of new products designed specifically to help fill the void. A few

states, including South Dakota and California, have implemented geography requirements for graduation. From members of Congress to local schoolteachers to map dealers to the National Geographic Society—which budgeted some $4 million to improve geography education—everyone seems to have gotten into the act. Geography is at last finding its way back onto the map.

While most of the hundreds of maps, globes, atlases, software, and related products are worthy of being enlisted in this campaign, here are some of the products specifically aimed at the education market:

GAMES AND PUZZLES

Aristoplay (P.O. Box 7028, Ann Arbor, MI 48107; 313-995-4353; 800-634-7738) sells "Where in the World?" ($35), a colorful multi-use game designed to enhance world awareness for children six years old to adult. Included are "Crazy Countries" card games acquainting players with the countries of each continent, and "Statesman, Diplomat and Ambassador" board games introducing players to geographical locations and cultural and economic aspects of countries of the world. Also available is "Land Ho!" ($22), a board game designed to depict the perils of 15th century ocean travel, and to permit players to sail with Columbus to the New World. Designed for three players, ages 8 to adult, "Land Ho!" can be played by English- or Spanish-speaking players, or in both languages simultaneously in two levels of play. A ship's log cites the most current historical data relevant to the voyage in both languages.

Educational Insights (19560 S. Rancho Way, Dominguez Hills, CA 90220; 213-637-2131; 800-933-3277) produces various fun games focusing

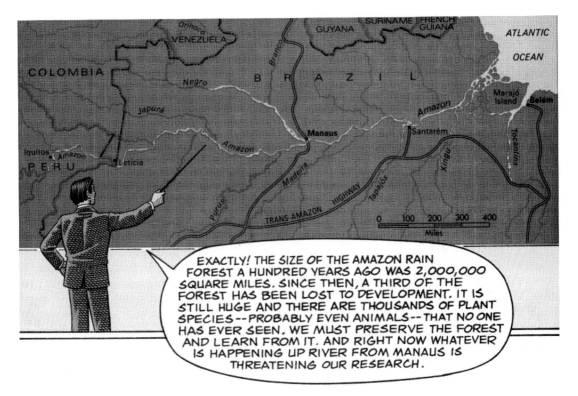

Panel from Captain Atlas and the Globe Riders®, Mystery of the Amazon, part of a series of educational comic books from Hammond designed to teach geography and other skills. © Hammond, Inc., Maplewood, New Jersey.

on geography education. One example is "Geo-Safari" ($99.95), an electronic map game suitable for classroom or individual use that can both teach and quiz users. The game comes with 18 maps; two sets of additional maps, "U.S. Geography" and "World Geography," are $14.95 each. "3-D Landforms" ($14.95) is a tactile teaching tool to help students visualize such geographic features as mesas, straits, reservoirs, and isthmuses. The kit includes reproducible maps and a teacher's guide. "Project: Earth" ($29.95) is a make-your-own-globe kit, consisting of a 14-inch Styrofoam sphere that you cover with papier-mâché, on which you then trace the outlines of the continents, add physical features, paint the countries, then plant flags. The company's catalog features additional games and map-skill products.

GeoLearning Corp. (555 Absaraka St., Sheridan, WY 82801; 307-674-6436; 800-843-6436) produces many fun and interesting games, available in stores or directly from GeoLearning:

■ "The Spilhaus GeoGlyph" ($24.95), a puzzle showing the continuous surface of the world. More than 100 correct maps can be created from the pieces.
■ "GeOdyssey—The World Game" ($14.95), a game in which players compete to build a world map, tile-by-tile, testing their geography knowledge by identifying continents, coastlines, and other geographical features.
■ "GeOdyssey Deluxe" ($29.95), a version of GeOdyssey that features larger nine-color playing tiles and labeled oceans.
■ "GeoCards" ($7.95), a colorful game featuring a deck of 48 cards, with each card representing a different geographical location.
■ "TectoniCube" ($4.50), a fascinating seven-sided geometric form showing how the Earth's tectonic plates fit together. The cube illustrates

The National Geography Bee

In which two hemispheres is North America located? Which continent contains no countries? The geographic center of North America is located in which state? Name the four oceans.

These are among the kinds of questions asked each year of thousands of fourth-through eighth-graders around the United States. Those who give the most correct answers qualify to participate in the National Geography Bee and vie for college scholarship and other prizes ($25,000 goes to the winner, $15,000 to the runner-up, and $10,000 to the third-place contestant).

The annual event was established in 1989 by the National Geographic Society, part of the organization's multimillion-dollar campaign to improve geography education in the United States. Much like the age-old spelling bees, the geography bee is con-ducted in an oral format, with questions addressing a broad range of geography topics, from the Earth itself to its inhabitants and cultures. Competitions begin in January at the school level, then proceed to the state level, and culminate with the National Championships, held in the spring in Washington, D.C.

To date, more than 43,000 public, private, and parochial schools across the nation have registered to participate. Only school principals may register their schools; for more information on the National Geography Bee, contact the **National Geographic Society**, 17th & M sts. NW, Washington, DC 20036.

(By the way, the answers to the above questions are: northern and western; Antarctica; North Dakota; and Atlantic, Arctic, Indian, and Pacific.)

---

the plates' various ridges, boundaries, zones, and faults.

■ "Flight Lines" ($5.95), a game featuring "Geography-Triangles," such as Los Angeles to Sydney, Paris to Rio, Tokyo to Chicago, and many more.

The Map Store (142 E. 5th St., Ste 70, St. Paul, MN 55101; 800-654-1599, 612-227-2280) offers colorful map puzzles ($16.95) showing counties, watersheds, freeways, and other highlights. Available puzzles include California, Florida, Illinois, Michigan, Minnesota, New York, and Texas, as well as a world map, a U.S. map, and a puzzle of U.S. flags.

National Geographic Society (17th & M sts. NW, Washington, DC 20036; 301-921-1200) sells "Global Pursuit" ($21.95), with nearly 1,000 geography trivia questions to test the global knowledge of students and adults alike. Includes a world map.

The Nature Co. (P.O. Box 2310, Berkeley, CA 94702; 510-524-9052, 800-227-1114, plus more than 75 retail stores in the U.S., as well as outlets in Japan and France) sells "GeoSafari" ($100), a geography game with 20 map lessons and a guide that lets you explore countries, capitals, cities, states, oceans, and so on.

Nystrom (3333 N. Elston Ave., Chicago, IL 60618; 312-463-1144; 800-621-8086) produces 12- and 16-inch raised-relief globes with a variety of mountings. Made of durable vinyl, they are designed to be touched and are claimed to be unbreakable. Models range from $73 to $227. Another Nystrom product is "Form-a-Globe," designed for classroom use, a build-it-yourself paper globe demonstrating how maps and globes differ from and are related to each other. A set of 30 "Form-a-Globes" is $21.

Omni Resources (1238 Anthony Rd., P.O. Box 2096, Burlington, NC 27216; 919-227-8300) produces the "Drift Globe" ($175), a 12-inch globe created to aid in understanding continental drift. The globe features nine continents, which may be positioned anywhere on the globe with Velcro. Orientation marks on each continent match crosses on the globe, which represent 50-million-year intervals. The globe comes with an illustrated guide that discusses climate and fauna during each era.

Pacific Puzzle Co. (378 Guemes Island Rd., Anacortes, WA 98221; 206-293-7034) offers colorful, hand-cut hardwood puzzles, including three maps of the U.S. ($24 to $70), a political world map ($16), a Dymaxion world map ($22), and five continent puzzles ($16 to $19 each). Shipping is extra; write for catalog.

Parkwest Publications (238 W. 72nd St., Ste. 2F, New York, NY 10023; 212-877-1040) distributes the British-made "Tarquin Globe" ($7.95), a paper build-it-yourself globe in full color, featuring all countries and some 1,200 major

cities, seas, rivers, and other features. The kit is accompanied by a 24-page booklet full of facts and ideas. A similar product, "The Tarquin Star-Globe" ($7.95), is for constructing a three-dimensional globe of the night sky.

Pendergrass Publishing Co. (P.O. Box 66, Phoenix, NY 13135; 315-695-7261) publishes *Our United States* ($7.95; teacher's key free), a 256-page book at a fourth- to fifth-grade reading level that introduces students to American history and geography with full-page graphically illustrated maps, as well as text.

Puzzles 'N Such, Inc. (19 Prairie Dunes, Hutchinson, KS 67502; 316-663-4192) produces the colorful, information-packed Puzzlin' World series of jigsaw puzzles. The puzzles of each state feature county boundaries, county seats, rivers, lakes, points of interest, and historical trivia, as well as state flags, seals, animals, birds, rocks, trees, mottoes, and songs. Puzzles of the United States, world, solar system, Civil

Some of the "Puzzlin' World" jigsaw puzzles from Puzzles 'N Such, Inc.

"Land Ho!" a game celebrating Christopher Columbus' voyage, from Aristoplay.

longitude, types of maps, and "our map address." Activities and tests are reproducible by photocopier for classroom use. The $45 set is intended for basic-beginners. (The company also produces a computer version; see "Software," below.) Another product, "Geography Terms" ($33), is a colorful 44" X 32" map that identifies more than 50 geographical terms. A smaller 8$\frac{1}{2}$" X 11" reproduction is priced at $14 for a set of eight.

War, and Israel, as well as the title "Stars and Stripes" (a puzzle with the history of the flag), are available. Puzzles may be ordered from Puzzles 'N Such, or may be found in a wide variety of museum shops and retail stores.

VanDam, Inc. (430 W. 14th St., New York, NY 10014, 212-929-0416; 212-929-0416) publishes a series called The Cosmos Unfolds that includes "EcoGuides" to the ocean, desert, rain forest, the moon, Mars, and the universe. These whimsical, brightly colored guides, which are valuable as educational tools, feature pop-up maps ($9.95 each).

MAP SKILLS

Modern School (1609 E. Kercher Rd., Goshen, IN 46526; 219-533-3111; 800-431-5929) publishes Map & Globe Skills, a 10-course unit centered on 14 large color charts, 24" X 17" and 17" X 12". The units cover map definition, symbols, direction, distance, scale, earth-globe relationship, projections, latitude-

National Geographic Society (17th & M sts. NW, Washington, DC 20036; 301-921-1330) offers a filmstrip, "Maps and What We Learn From Them" ($97), intended for grades 3 through 6. The filmstrip (running time: 12-15 minutes) and accompanying cassettes reveal what maps reflect about the face of the Earth, and discuss the various types of maps.

Nystrom (3333 N. Elston Ave., Chicago, IL 60618; 312-463-1144; 800-621-8086) offers products for several levels. Its Primary Social Studies Skills come in three levels, designed to teach key concepts to early elementary school students ($210 to $235 for a class of 30). For older students, Nystrom offers six Map and Globe Skills Programs that include books, maps, marking pens, and teachers' guides ($110 to $345 for a class of 30).

Pendergrass Publishing Co. (P.O. Box 66, Phoenix, NY 13135; 315-695-7261) publishes Learning to Use Maps ($4.25; teacher's key $1), an 80-page, low-reading-level book demonstrating basic map directions, map legends, abbreviations, scales, symbols, topography, and other features.

Social Studies School Service (10200 Jefferson Blvd., Rm. 1, P.O. Box 802, Culver City, CA 90232; 310-839-2436; 800-421-4246) distributes a wide variety of map- and geography-skill products from a variety of publishers. Included are maps, globes, games, books, atlases, posters, reproducible masters, charts, photo aids, and software. The materials are selected for use in schools, K-12. A catalog is available.

J. Weston Walch (321 Valley St., P.O. Box 658, Portland, ME 04104; 207-772-2846, 800-341-6094) offers several items, including: "Crossword Puzzle Maps in U.S. History" (grade 7 and up), offering a comprehensive review of U.S. history ($21.95 for 50 masters); *Where on Earth: Understanding Latitude and Longitude* (grade 7 and up), a 93-page reproducible book ($16.95); "Geography Skills Activity Pack" (grade 6 and up), a complete teaching unit including 64 masters and 18 colorful posters ($43.95); *Discovering America Through Map Activities* (grade 8

and up), a 76-page reproducible teacher book ($16.95) and student book ($8.95); Geography Teacher's Success Kit (grades 7-12), a 148-page reproducible book that contains "everything you need for success in teaching world geography" ($17.95); *Geographic Literacy: Maps for Memorization* (grades 6-12), a 137-page reproducible book to teach locations of countries, capitals, and important physical features of the world ($20.95); *World Place Geography Masters* (for middle school and up), 50 masters to "learn and remember the essential geography of the globe, to be used with an atlas" ($21.95); and Map Activities for U.S. Geography Classes (grades 6-10), 52 masters including 13 maps to complete, self-checking puzzles, and four tests ($21.95).

SOFTWARE

Broderbund Software, Inc. (500 Redwood Blvd., P.O. Box 6121, Novato, CA 94948; 415-382-4400) publishes a popular series that includes "Where in the World Is Carmen Sandiego?," "Where in the USA Is Carmen Sandiego?," "Where in Europe Is Carmen Sandiego?," "Where in Time Is Carmen Sandiego?," and "Where in America's Past Is Carmen Sandiego?"—a series of secret-agent adventure games that teach geography, research, and reasoning skills. In the programs, recommended for ages 12 and up,

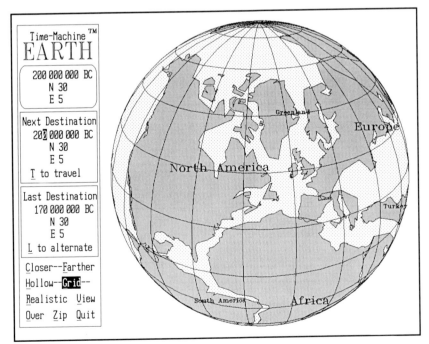

Sample Screen from Time-Machine Earth, *which demonstrates the effects of continental drift from 500 million years in the past to far in the future, from Sageware Corp.*

Carmen and her gang of thieves steal the world's priceless treasures and landmarks. The player's task is to capture her and her crooked cronies. To track them down, players begin at the scene of the crime and follow endless clues, including topography, cities, flags, currency, languages, historical events, and other facts. Programs are available for Apple II/IIe/IIc/IIgs, IBM PC and compatibles, Tandy and compatibles, Macintosh, Amiga 500/1000/2000, and Commodore 64/128 computers. Prices range from $34.95 to $44.95, depending on the edition. School editions, with teacher's guides and additional disks, are $44.95 to $54.95. A new version of "Where in the World Is Carmen Sandiego?" is available for CD-ROM.

CompuTeach (78 Olive St., New Haven, CT 06511; 203-777-7738; 800-448-3224) publishes "See the U.S.A." ($59.95), which lets users take any of a series of imaginary drives across America. On the trip, users learn about states, capitals, famous places, and state facts, such as flowers, birds, and mottoes. Intended for ages eight and up, it operates on Apple II or IBM PC and compatible computers.

Great Wave Software (5353 Scotts Valley Dr., Scotts Valley, CA 95066; 408-438-1990) publishes "American Discovery," an interactive geography and history program for the Macintosh. The program includes several activities that challenge players to find the states, click "in" the states, spell state names, find capitals, identify neighboring states, or identify prominent rivers and lakes. Other options allow players to look at state facts, or give answers to questions about historical facts and trivia, derived from 17 different fact files. The program also includes Discovery Maker, an option for creating your own questions and fact files.

Maxis Software (953 Mountain View Dr., Ste. 113, Lafayette, CA 94549; 415-376-6434) publishes "SimCity," an urban simulation game created for young people but one that has captured the eye of planning professionals and architects. The program—intended for those

age 12 and up—offers an interactive graphic representation of the dynamics of urban life. By clicking on icons, users can—budget permitting—build roads and transit lines, power plants (coal or nuclear), parks, police stations, airports, and many other urban features. As the city grows, the program calculates the impact of each new development on population, pollution, traffic, crime, and other variables. To liven things up, random-occurring events—nuclear meltdowns and airline crashes, for example—emulate real life (or some dramatic variation thereof). Prices are $49.95 for the Macintosh version, $44.95 for the Amiga version, and $29.95 for the Commodore 64/128 version. Also available: "SimEarth—The Living Planet," which gives players control over the evolution of a planet, from the origin of life to the development of civilization and interplanetary travel.

Mindscape, Inc. (Educational Div., Dept. D, 3444 Dundee Rd., Northbrook, IL 60062; 708-480-1948; 800-221-9884), as part of its Social Studies Explorer Set, produces a four-disk "World Geography Set." The disks cover "Asia and Australia," "Central United States," "Eastern United States," and "Western Europe." The program allows students to identify the state or country they're "visiting" and answer questions about the locale. Price is $39.95 per disk. Another program, "America Coast to Coast" ($49.95), is described as a "high-resolution color, animated map" that illustrates the relative sizes and locations of the 50 states. Students select a state, then learn its location, capital, shape, motto, and other facts. Both programs are available for Apple IIe/IIc, Apple II+, and IBM-compatible computers.

MLT Software (P.O. Box 98041, 6325 SW Capitol Hwy., Portland, OR 97201; 503-245-7093) publishes "Sun Clock," an inexpensive desk accessory that graphically displays where the sun is shining (and where it isn't) on a map of the world. "Sun Clock" displays the areas of day and night for the current date and time. The shape dividing day from night changes with the seasons. Viewing "Sun Clock" you can actually see the days lengthen and shorten as the year progresses. Price is $15 plus $2 shipping.

Modern School (1609 E. Kercher Rd., Goshen, IN 46526; 219-533-3111, 800-431-5929) publishes "Computer Map Skills" for all Apple II computer models. The colorful screen images teach skills similar to "Map & Globe Skills I" and comes on two disks: "Beginner (Readiness)" and "Basic." Price is $99.

PC Globe, Inc. (4440 S. Rural Rd., Tempe, AZ 85282; 602-730-9000) publishes "PC Globe" and "MacGlobe," which allows users to examine country maps as well as the full spectrum of demographic data. Maps can be printed, or exported into other programs for use with other programs. The PC version is $69.95; the Macintosh version is $79.95. Also available: "PC USA" ($49.95), which provides maps and demographic information for the 50 states and Puerto Rico; "Bush Buck" ($39.95), a PC-based treasure hunt that promotes a greater understanding of world geography; "Geo Jigsaw" ($39.95), a computerized collection of musical and animated geography jigsaw puzzles; and "GeoPuzzle USA" ($39.95), a challenging and entertaining computerized puzzle of the United States that promotes geography awareness.

Sageware Corp. (1282 Garner Ave., Schenectady, NY 12309; 518-377-1052) is creator of "Time-Machine Earth," a fascinating program that allows you to view the globe as it would appear at virtually any time since animal life first appeared in the oceans, from 500,000,000 B.C. to 20,000,000 A.D. By entering the specific year, and by "spinning" the globe to show a specific viewing point, you can watch continental shift take place. Any view may be printed on a dot-matrix printer. The "Personal Edition" of the program is $69.95; "Time-Machine Earth Professional Edition," with higher-resolution graphics, laser printer output, and presentation control, is $245. Runs on IBM PCs and compatibles and requires a graphics card.

Soft Horizon (P.O. Box 2115, Harker Heights, TX 76543; 817-699-0493) publishes "Know Your World," which teaches countries, capitals, and major cities of the world using maps and challenging learning activities. The program ($39.95), for Macintosh and IBM PC and compatibles, teaches and then quizzes users, scoring on correct answers and correct spelling.

Springboard Software Inc. (7808 Creekridge Cir., Minneapolis, MN 55435; 612-944-3915) publishes "Atlas Explorer," a world geography program that displays maps of states and countries along with general facts about the locations. Moreover, the program tests users on any location—a continent, country, state, province, or city—scoring on both accuracy and speed of answers. The program ($49.95) is intended for users ages 8 to 18 and runs on Apple IIe/IIc/IIgs, IBM PC and compatibles, Tandy and compatibles, and Macintosh Plus/SE/II computers. Also available is an Educator's Lab Pack ($100) consisting of five disks and a manual, for Apple and IBM versions only.

■ **See also: "Atlases and Globes," "Map Software," and "Map Stuff."**

Map Accessories

Having a map is a good first step toward finding your way, but sometimes even the best map isn't quite enough. Here are some accessories that may help you plot your route or reach your destination. Many of these (or similar) products are readily available in map, travel, and camping-supply stores; or you may contact the manufacturers directly. Prices shown are suggested retail prices; many retailers and mail-order houses discount these items. Be aware that there may be shipping and handling charges added for mail orders.

Magnifiers

These come in several shapes, sizes, and materials, depending on whether they will be used in a library or must be sufficiently compact to fit in a pocket or knapsack.

■ **Tasco Sales, Inc.** (7600 NW 26th St., Miami, FL 33122; 305-591-3670) carries several sizes of pocket loupes, compact powerful foldout magnifiers designed to slip into a pocket or purse. Price range is $4.95 to $29.95.
■ **Bausch & Lomb** (P.O. Box 22810, Rochester, NY 14692; 716-338-6000; 800-452-6789) manufactures a wide array of magnifiers—compact, lighted, lightweight, for all needs. Prices range from about $8 to $42.

Map Cases

A good map gets a lot of use—and abuse. It gets folded and refolded, usually not back to its original form. Used on a hike or a boat, it gets dirty or wet. Map cases provide protection, letting you study the map while it remains safe and dry. There are several varieties of map cases (not all of them watertight). For example:

■ **Omniseal** (83 S. King St., Seattle, WA 98104; 206-587-3755) produces Omniseal Waterproof

Pouches of varying sizes ($1.45 to $5.95), some designed specifically for maps. Also available are Omniseal Courier tubes, ideal for carrying rolled maps ($2.35 to $4.15).
■ **The Outsiders** (Box 626, North Salt Lake, UT 84054; 801-292-7354) manufactures clear Show-It map cases, available in many stores for about $4.

Map Preservers

One alternative to a map case is a map preserver—basically, a liquid or spray applied to maps that renders them waterproof and increases their durability.

■ **Adventure 16** (4620 Alvarado Canyon Rd., San Diego, CA 92120; 619-283-6314; 800-854-2672) distributes Map Life, a map-treatment liquid that also permits writing on a map with a grease pencil, and a similar product called Map Shield; Chart Slicker, a resealable, clear plastic envelope designed to protect maps and charts; and the OmniSeal Map/Document Holder (6" X 11") and Omniseal Map/Chart Holder (11" X 14"), both designed to provide waterproof protection.
■ **Martensen Co.** (P.O. Box 261, Williamsburg, VA 23187; 804-565-1760) manufactures Stormproof, a clear penetrating liquid treatment that impregnates paper maps. An eight-ounce can will treat about a dozen topographic maps or four large nautical charts. Available in many map and camping stores in 8-ounce ($5.95) and 16-ounce ($8.95) sizes.
■ **Tamerica Products, Inc.** (20722 Currier Rd., Walnut, CA 91789; 714-594-3888; 800-822-6555) produces but does not retail Print Protectors, plastic sleeves that can be used in place of lamination or glass or acrylic framing. They are available in a variety of sizes, including 30" X 31" and 42" X 41". Custom-order sizes are also available.

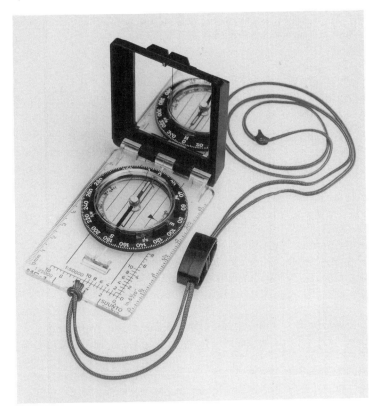

Suunto MC-1D compass, from Suunto USA.

MAP MEASURERS

These help you obtain accurate measurements of distance from maps, whether measuring hikes, highways, or the high seas. Most models measure both miles and kilometers; some also measure nautical miles.

■ **Johnson Camping, Inc.** (P.O. Box 2050, Binghamton, NY 13902; 607-779-2200) distributes through retailers compasses for use on topographic maps and the Silva Map Measure Type 40, which is calibrated to read topo maps in scales of 1:24,000, 1:62,500, and 1:250,000 ($19.35).

MAP DISPLAYS

■ **Versa-Lite Systems, Inc.** (5834 Kirby Rd., Clinton, MD 20735; 301-297-7710; 800-638-0982) produces Versa-Lite Display System, display boards with thumbtack-like lights that automatically go on or blink when placed anywhere on the board. Prices range from $395 to $3,000, depending on board size and other features.

COMPASSES

When hiking, a compass can help you orient yourself with landmarks on a map, keeping you on track. Compasses are sold by dozens of companies, including several listed above. While there are a seemingly endless number of compass "bells and whistles"—sizes, mountings, magnifiers, wrist attachments, luminescence, mirrors, and on and on— almost any compass will do. To function properly, it need only be capable of pointing toward magnetic North and have some direction and degree markings around its perimeter.

■ **Suunto USA** (2151 Las Palmas Dr., Carlsbad, CA 92009; 619-931-6788) distributes a variety of Suunto compasses, among them the A-Series compasses, which include the competitive orienteering range and can fit into the hand of a child; a Geologist's Compass, complete with a protractor, level, and clinometer; the M-Series, designed for scouting and orienteering under the most difficult conditions; and "thumb compasses," small compasses with a strap designed to fit on the thumb. A number of marine compasses are also available. Suunto also offers compass accessories, such as compass cases, pouches, and rubber covers. A free catalog is available.

Map Organizations

American Association of Petroleum Geologists (AAPG, P.O. Box 979, Tulsa, OK 74101; 918-584-2555) is a membership organization of geoscientists dedicated to encouraging scientific research and advancing the science of geology, particularly as it relates to petroleum and energy minerals. AAPG publishes and distributes to the public many geologic and energy-related maps; it holds an annual meeting and regional meetings throughout the year. Annual membership dues vary from $10 to $58, and entitle members to receive AAPG's two publications: *The Explorer*, a monthly magazine, and *The Bulletin*, a monthly technical journal. In addition, AAPG publishes *Geobyte*, a bimonthly magazine addressing computer usage in geology.

American Congress on Surveying and Mapping (ACSM, 5410 Grosvenor Ln., Ste. 100, Bethesda, MD 20814; 301-493-0200) is a nonprofit national association dedicated to serving the public interest and advancing the professions of surveying and mapping. ACSM's more than 9,000 individual members are surveyors, cartographers, geodesists, and related professionals from private industry, government, and academia. Membership benefits include professional periodicals, discounts on publications, education and certification programs, fellowships and scholarships, legislative-affairs action, annual conferences, and more. Membership is based on concurrent membership in ACSM and a member organization; dues vary. ACSM is the umbrella organization for the American Association for Geodetic Surveyors, the American Cartographic Association, and the National Society for Professional Surveyors. Information on ACSM and a catalog of publications are available by contacting ACSM.

American Geographical Society (AGS, 156 Fifth Ave., Ste. 600, New York, NY 10010; 212-242-0214) is an independent, nonprofit corporation founded in 1851 to gather and disseminate geographical information. AGS sponsors expeditions, lectures, conferences, and symposiums; conducts research on geographical topics; and publishes educational and scientific periodicals, books, maps, and atlases. Individual membership ($24 annually) includes receipt of the AGS *Newsletter* and discounts on the *Geographical Review*, *Focus*, and other AGS publications and activities. Corporate and student membership rates are also available. AGS publications are available to nonmembers; a list is furnished upon request.

American Library Association, Map and Geography Roundtable (ALA, MAGERT) (50 E. Huron St., Chicago, IL 60611; 312-944-6780; 800-545-2433) is committed to the exchange of ideas between persons working with or interested in map and geography collections; to improving communication and cooperation between map and geography libraries; and to encouraging the improvement of education and training of map and geography information specialists. The Roundtable meets twice a year, in conjunction with the ALA Midwinter Meetings. MAGERT publications include *base line*, a bimonthly newsletter; *Meridian*, a semi-annual, refereed journal, including articles on maps, the history of cartography, and computerized mapping; "Open File Reports," working documents for cartographic professionals; "Occasional Papers," a series of monographs on mapping and map librarianship, of interest to a wider audience (e.g., Occasional Paper #3: *Mapping the Transmission West, 1540-1861: An Index to the Cartobibliography*); "Circulars," a series of monographs that address specific areas of interest (e.g., Circular #1: *Cartographic Citations: A Style Manual*); and the second edition of its *Guide to U.S. Map Resources* (1990), a directory of 975 map collections in the United States. The organization is open to anyone who is a member of ALA; annual Roundtable dues are $15.

American Society for Photogrammetry and Remote Sensing (ASPRS, 5410 Grosvenor Ln., Ste. 210, Bethesda, MD 20814; 301-493-0290) is a nonprofit scientific and technical association founded in 1934 and dedicated to advancing knowledge in, and encouraging use of, photogrammetry, geographic information systems, and remote sensing. ASPRS membership includes more than 8,000 people involved in or studying photogrammetry, remote sensing, geographic information systems, and related sciences. ASPRS sponsors annual conventions and workshops and maintains an extensive publications program. Membership ($25 to $160) includes a subscription to ASPRS's monthly journal, *Photogrammetric Engineering and Remote Sensing*; invitations to local regional meetings, seminars, field trips, continuing-education workshops and symposiums; and special rates for life and accident insurance.

Association of American Geographers (AAG, 1710 16th St. NW, Washington, DC 20009; 202-234-1450) is a nonprofit group founded in 1904 with the goals of advancing professional studies in geography and encouraging the application of geographic research in education, government, and business. AAG boasts a membership of 6,300 students and professionals from around the world. The organization's activities include sponsoring research projects that apply a geographic perspective to national issues; furthering geographic education through Geography Education National Implementation Project; supporting symposiums; and producing a number of publications. Through its 40 "Specialty Groups" (which range from "Biogeography" to "Microcomputers" to "Socialist Geography"), members can meet and work with others who share their interests. Membership ($37.50 to $95) includes receipt of the monthly AAG *Newsletter*, and entitles members to receive two quarterly scholarly journals, *Annals of the Association of American Geographers* (featuring scholarly articles,

commentaries, and book reviews) and *The Professional Geographer* (including research articles, technical reports, and book and software reviews), as well as many other benefits.

Association of Map Memorabilia Collectors (AMMC, c/o Siegfried Feller, 8 Amherst Rd., Pelham, MA 01002; 413-253-3115) is a small association (membership approximately 350) founded to provide and exchange information and news between collectors of maps and maps appearing in other forms (postcards, stamps, envelopes, etc.). The primary focus of AMMC is the publication of the quarterly *Cartomania*, a chatty newsletter full of information, illustrations, and member news. Membership, open to anyone, is $12.50 annually in the U.S. and Canada; $17 elsewhere. Single issues of *Cartomania* are available for $4.

Carto-Philatelists (c/o Miklos Pinther, President, 206 Grayson Pl., Teaneck, NJ 07666) is a society of map-stamp enthusiasts, founded in 1955, which promotes cartophilately. Through the society, members are able to exchange information, trade ideas on collecting and mounting their miniature maps, and, occasionally, meet one another. *The Carto-Philatelist*, an illustrated quarterly publication, features various background articles, listings of new issues, and member news. Membership is open to anyone; dues are $15.

Chicago Map Society (c/o Secty./Treas., 60 W. Walton St., Chicago, IL 60610; 312-943-9090), claiming to be the oldest map society in North America, was founded to bring together people interested in all aspects of maps and mapping. The society holds monthly meetings (September through May) at Chicago's Newberry Library, featuring speakers, field trips, and other events. Membership is open to anyone; annual dues are $15 and include a subscription to *Mapline*, the quarterly newsletter of the Hermon Dunlap Smith Center for the History of Cartography at the Newberry Library. The society welcomes guests at its meetings.

Comité Européen des Responsables de la Cartographie Officielle (CERCO, Institut für Angewandte Geodäsie, Richard-Strauss-Allee 11, D-6000 Frankfurt am Main 70, Germany) is an organization promoting mutual information, consultation, and cooperation in cartography among the official mapping agencies of European countries. The committee meets once a year to discuss developments in cartography and related fields and to share ideas.

Geography Education National Implementation Project (GENIP, 1710 16th St. NW, Washington, DC 20009; 202-234-1450) is a joint project of the National Council for Geographic Education, the Association of American Geographers, the American Geographical Society, and the National Geographic Society. GENIP was formed in 1984 to improve the status and quality of geographic education in grades K-12 in the United States. GENIP produces various publications designed to aid geography educators and is active in many aspects of geography education, including teacher training, developing new learning materials, providing curriculum development guidelines, developing state and national networks to support geographic education, monitoring the definition of teacher certification and competency standards, and establishing links for funding to public and private agencies. GENIP publishes a thrice-yearly newsletter, GENIP *News*, available at no cost.

Geological Society of America (GSA, P.O. Box 9140, Boulder, CO 80301; 303-447-2020; 800-472-1988), a membership organization of 16,000 geoscientists worldwide, was founded in 1888 to publish scientific literature and organize scientific meetings. It holds an annual fall meeting; regional sections hold spring meetings. Members receive GSA *Today*, the society's newsletter. Members are entitled to discounts on GSA publications and maps, and to participate in GSA's specialized divisions and receive their newsletters; discounts on insurance and subscriptions to geologic magazines also come with membership. Annual member dues vary.

International Cartographic Association (ICA, c/o Jean-Philippe Grelot, Secty.-General, Institut Géographique National, 136 bis rue de Grenelle, 75007 Paris, France; [33-1] 43-98-82-95) is an international society aimed at advancing the study of cartographic problems; the coordination of cartographic research between different nations; and the organization of conferences, meetings, and exhibitions. ICA works through four standing commissions on advanced technology, education, history of cartography, and map-production technology, as well as 12 other commissions and working groups established during a four-year term. Many of these commissions and working groups publish the results of their research and seminar papers; these publications are available through Elsevier Science Publishing Co., Inc. (P.O. Box 882, Madison Square Station, New York, NY 10159; outside U.S. and Canada: Kim Miller, Elsevier Science Publishers Ltd., Crown House, Linton Rd., Barking, Essex 1G11 8JU, England). ICA is also pledged to assist with cartographic growth in developing countries and to promote cooperation with sister organizations, such as the ISPRS. Membership in ICA is limited to one organization for each nation; the American Cartographic Association is the official U.S. representative to ICA.

International Map Dealers Association (IMDA, P.O. Box 1789, Kankakee, IL 60901; 815-939-4627) is a membership organization founded in 1982 to bring together map sellers, publishers, and others related to the field of map publishing and retailing. It holds an annual conference and trade show where its members share ideas and attend workshops and meetings. Membership ($125 annually) includes subscription to *The Map Report*, a monthly newsletter containing industry and member news and feature articles.

International Society for Photogrammetry and Remote Sensing (ISPRS, c/o Shunji Murai, ISPRS Secretary General, Institute of Industrial Science, University of Tokyo, 7-22 Roppongi, Minato-ku, Tokyo, Japan; 011-813-3402-6231, ext. 2560) is an international association founded in 1910 to encourage cooperation and exchange of information among the various national societies of photogrammetry and/or remote sensing. ISPRS holds quadrennial congresses, where members report, review, and discuss developments in photogrammetry and remote sensing, as well as attending social events, technical and scientific tours, and excursions. Membership is available only to national societies.

Michigan Map Society (Clements Library, University of Michigan, Ann Arbor, MI 48109; 313-764-2347) is a 50-member society addressing the history of cartography, mapping, and mapping technology. Monthly meetings are held at the library September through May. Annual dues of $15 entitle members to attend meetings and receive *Mapline*, the quarterly newsletter of the Chicago-based Hermon Dunlap Smith Center for the History of Cartography.

National Council for Geographic Education (NCGE, Leonard 16A, Indiana Univ. of Pennsylvania, Indiana, PA 15705; 412-357-6290) was chartered in 1915 to promote geographic education at all levels of instruction. NCGE has directed its efforts to encouraging teacher training, providing active leadership in formulating geographic-education policies, developing effective geographic-education programs in schools and colleges, stimulating the production and use of geographic teaching materials and media, and enhancing public awareness of and appreciation for geography and geographers. NCGE members receive subscriptions to the following publications: *The Journal of Geography*, a bimonthly journal, and *Perspective*, a newsletter that appears five times a year. It also holds annual meetings, which provide members an opportunity to meet, and hosts a number of other activities. Membership is divided into eight categories, with fees corresponding.

National Council for the Social Studies (NCSS, 3501 Newark St. NW, Washington, DC 20016; 202-966-7840) is the largest association in the U.S. devoted solely to social studies. NCSS membership includes 25,000 members in all 50 states and in 69 foreign countries. NCSS is formed of three subgroups: The Council of State Social Studies Specialists (CS4); the Social Studies Supervisors Association (SSSA); and the College and University Faculty Assembly (CUFA). Membership dues vary.

National Geographic Society (NGS, 17th & M sts. NW, Washington, DC 20036; 202-857-7000), one of the best-known geographic organizations, was founded in 1888 as a nonprofit scientific and educational organization "for the increase and diffusion of geographic knowledge." The society supports exploration and research projects and publishes *National Geographic*, an illustrated monthly magazine featuring articles on geographic and cultural topics. Membership dues are $21 per year, most of it designated for subscription to *National Geographic*. NGS is a major organizer of "Geography Awareness Week" activities (usually held in November or December).

In 1985, realizing the lack of geography education in American schools, NGS created the "Geography Education Program," dedicated to encouraging geography education in school curriculums and to promoting public awareness of the need for geography education. The program sponsors the annual "National Geography Bee" for students (see "Geography Education Materials") and also coordinates state "alliances," funded by the NGS Education Foundation. The alliances, usually based in state universities, conduct "summer institutes" for teachers to learn how to teach geography; a more in-depth, four-week national summer institute is held annually in Washington, D.C. The Geography Education Program produces *Update*, a thrice-yearly newsletter featuring geography news and lesson plans. Subscription is free and available to anyone.

New York Map Society (c/o Map Div., New York Public Library, Fifth Ave. and 42nd St., New York, NY 10018; 212-930-0587) was founded in 1978 to support and encourage the study and preservation of maps and related materials, especially antique maps. The society holds monthly meetings (September through May) at the Museum of Natural History in New York City, featuring guest speakers and field trips. Membership ($20 annually) includes receipt of *Rhumb Line*, the society's monthly newsletter.

North American Cartographic Information Society (NACIS, AGS Collection, University of Wisconsin-Milwaukee, P.O. Box 399, Milwaukee, WI 53201; 800-558-8993) is a professional society founded in 1980 to facilitate the exchange of information in the map community. NACIS membership consists of map-makers, collectors, libraries, users, educators, and distributors. Annual dues range from $5 to $35, and entitle members to receive *Cartographic Perspective*, a quarterly journal. NACIS holds an annual meeting, where members attend seminars and workshops, as well as smaller technical meetings throughout the year.

Special Libraries Association, Geography and Map Division (1700 18th St. NW, Washington, DC 20009; 202-234-4700) is the oldest geography and map librarians' association in the U.S.

The group promotes the exchange of information in geography, map librarianship, and cartography. Division membership entitles one to attend and participate in annual conferences and quarterly meetings, as well as receive a subscription to the quarterly journal, *Bulletin*. The Division produces various publications, including *Map Collections in the United States and Canada: A Directory*. Annual SLA dues are based on five classes, ranging from student/retired ($15) to sustaining ($300).

Urban and Regional Information Systems Association (900 2nd St. NE, Ste. 304, Washington, DC 20002; 202-289-1685) works with state and local governments on a number of issues that include geographic information systems (GIS). For more information, contact the special-interest group leader for GIS. URISA has more than 3,600 members, and puts on workshops and conferences related to GIS. Individual memberships are $75 per year and include a membership directory; proceedings of the association's annual conferences; and subscriptions to *Marketplace*, a monthly job-service publication, URISA *News*, published 10 times a year, and the *Journal*, published twice a year. Institutional and corporate memberships cost more and include more benefits.

Map Software

It was inevitable: the marriage of cartography and computers. Maps, after all, represent an efficient organization of information, a method of bringing together sometimes widely disparate data about a geographical entity. Computers, for their part, are the world's information machines. They enable us to organize, store, and manipulate vast quantities of data in ways never previously imagined. And so it follows that computers would become an efficient means for organizing, storing, and manipulating the information contained on maps. It was a match made in heaven.

As computer graphics have made great strides, computerized mapping has become one of the fastest-growing areas of computer software. Coupled with the growth of "personal" desktop computers, it has created the ability for just about anyone to engage in what has come to be called "desktop mapping." There are now dozens of computer programs related to maps and mapping, some containing just a few simple black-and-white outline maps that you can insert into other documents, others containing highly sophisticated geographical data bases that, combined with cartographic software, enable you to produce sophisticated full-color maps in a few hours or even a few minutes. While such programs are not about to put government or commercial map-makers out of business—there will always be the need for the cartographer's keen eye and a geographer's intelligence and intuition—the technology is enabling more and more people to become instant map-makers, for business or pleasure.

The more sophisticated programs are finding their way into a variety of businesses, in both the public and private sectors. In Syracuse, New York, for example, the police department has used a relatively inexpensive program called MapInfo to track all "part one" crimes—homicide, rape, robbery, larceny, car theft, and

arson. The city's Crime Analysis Unit enters information on victims and suspects into a computer and produces weekly and monthly maps summarizing crime patterns. The maps are distributed to the police on the street, allowing them to stake out areas of heavy activity. The department has estimated that the system has solved or stopped dozens of crimes.

GEOGRAPHIC INFORMATION SYSTEMS

Imagine the ultimate computerized map of a city. First it shows you the whole city. By pointing or typing, you can zero in on specific buildings, streets, and even things under the street—sewer lines, subways, and all the rest—from metro areas to manhole covers.

Such a system already exists. It is called a geographic information system, or GIS, the marriage of the data base and the map. Simply put, a GIS is a map with a potentially unlimited amount of information available at every point.

As GIS becomes more widespread, so, too, do its applications: utility repair, engineering studies, environmental protection, market analysis, facilities management, route planning, advertising, oil and gas exploration. A GIS system is only limited by the amount of data you put into it. GIS systems have the potential to let you explore an entire sewer system from a computer terminal, or show a real estate client what different offices might look like. When the power goes out, an electric utility can generate a map of where the outage occurred, based on where customer calls are coming from. A city sewer repair crew can have maps of where the breaks are. Many emergency services, such as those staffed by "911" telephone operators, use GIS to plan routes and dispatch vehicles.

"Once you dive into the GIS realm, you can swim in any direction you want. It's pretty vast," says William Benz, a GIS consultant in Port-

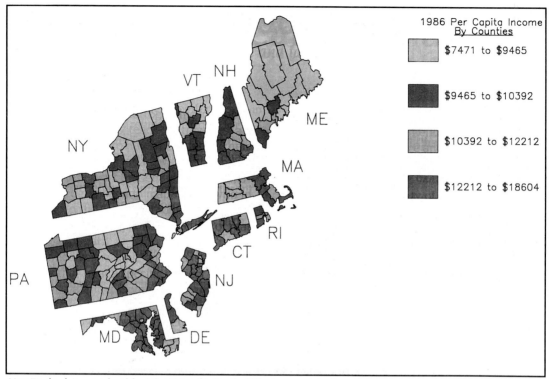

New England map produced by Atlas*Map Maker for Windows *(original in color), an* IBM-PC *program from Strategic Mapping, Inc.*

land, Oregon. "GIS is a very large field and a very complex field. There's a lot of discussion as to what it really is. It's basically an information system, a skeleton upon which attribute information that is relevant to the user is hung. It's a visual representation of the data base. You can do a visual 'what-if' by doing an analysis of the data and displaying it on a map. It allows you to test your data."

Benz cited an example of a GIS application in which planners take information about a floodplain and superimpose on it population data, thereby producing a new map that shows the possible flood danger to homes. "By putting together the two data sets," he says, "you see where one set of data is compromised by the other."

Mike Forrester, exhibits coordinator for the Urban and Regional Information Systems Association, says, "It enables you to get a graphic picture of your city. You can use it to have more accurate tax records. You can use it

to keep track of your infrastructure, your water pipes, and when they were last replaced."

Here are just a few of the many ways GIS systems are being used by companies:

■ Coca-Cola uses GIS to help analyze the "cola wars" and assess how various products are doing in different markets.
■ An A&P grocery chain in Canada uses GIS to analyze shopper buying patterns and the market share of each store, as well as to plan new store locations.
■ Traveler's Insurance uses GIS to market its insurance and physicians' networks by relating doctors to a business's employees.

Government agencies are another big user of GIS systems. For example, during the Persian Gulf War, the Defense Department used GIS to support the mapping needs of Operation Desert Storm. GIS technology is now being used to reconstruct war-torn Kuwait City.

The Digital Chart of the World

Since 1988, the Defense Mapping Agency, in cooperation with the governments of Canada, Australia, and the United Kingdom, has been working toward an ambitious goal: to provide a worldwide GIS data base, with every point and nearly every feature digitized and cataloged. That dream is becoming reality with the nearly complete development of the Digital Chart of the World (DCW).

When completed, the DCW will provide on compact disk data to create 1:1,000,000- scale maps of any point on earth. Its design will accommodate use on nearly any PC (with the right software), enabling users to import the data into GIS programs and integrate it with additional data to create customized and highly accurate maps. The finished product is expected to fit on four CDs, containing two gigabytes of data.

For more information on the DCW project, contact the Defense Mapping Agency, Combat Support Center, 6001 MacArthur Blvd., Bethesda, MD 20816; 800-826-0342.

According to GIS *World*, the Bureau of Land Management is using GIS to modernize the U.S. public-land data base, and the U.S. Forest Service is using it to keep track of forests. On the local level, the Indianapolis Public Works Department used GIS to construct a data base to manage the city's infrastructure. The data base supports the needs of the city's Public Works Department, Metropolitan Development Department, and Transportation Department, as well as the Indianapolis Water Company, Indiana Bell, Citizens Gas & Coke Utility, and 12 Marion County government agencies.

While GIS systems used to cost tens to hundreds of thousands of dollars, their prices have dropped considerably; it still depends on what you want and what you're doing. If you already have a computer and a laser printer, there are systems available for $3,000 or less; some simple ones cost as little as $750.

The greatest stimulus for making GIS data and software accessible to map-makers and others came with publication of the 1990 U.S. census. The Census Bureau publishes the information in a computer format known as TIGER (for "topologically integrated geographic encoding and referencing"), a standardized format for GIS information. That made census data easily formatted into an almost infinite number of highly specialized maps. For the first time, all the minutiae of Americans' life-styles could be easily placed in a visual format—state by state, city by city, or even block by block. (See Census Maps for additional information.)

Additional information about GIS is available from several map organizations (see page 286), including the American Congress on Surveying and Mapping, the American Society for Photogrammetry and Remote Sensing, and the Urban and Regional Information Systems Association.

In addition, here are some additional information sources about GIS and its applications:

■ *Geographic Information Systems: A Guide to the Technology*, by John C. Antenucci and PlanGraphics staff ($47.96 postpaid; 25% off if you pay in advance from PlanGraphics, Inc. 202 W. Main St., Ste. 200, Frankfort, KY 40601; 502-223-1501) is, as the title suggests, a fairly comprehensive guide to the subject.

■ *Sources for Digital Spatial Data* ($22 from USGS, Reston ESIC, 507 National Center, Reston, VA 22092; 703-860-6045) describes more than 500 data sets containing spatially referenced base or thematic categories of data, from federal, state, and local government agencies and the private sector.

■ GIS/CAD *Mapping Solutions* (Venture Communications, Box 02332, Portland, OR 97202; 503-236-5810), a monthly newsletter; $99 per year.

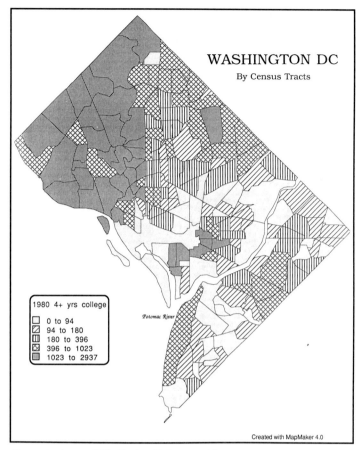

WASHINGTON DC
By Census Tracts

Potomac River

1980 4+ yrs college

☐ 0 to 94
▨ 94 to 180
▥ 180 to 396
▧ 396 to 1023
▨ 1023 to 2937

Created with MapMaker 4.0

Census tract map of Washington, D.C., created by
Atlas*Pro for Macintosh, *from Strategic Mapping, Inc.*

■ GIS World (155 E. Boardwalk Dr., Ste. 250, Ft. Collins, CO 80205; 303-223-4848), a magazine. $60 a year for 10 issues. The publisher also sponsors annual GIS conferences.

■ *Geo Info Systems* (Aster Publishing Corp., P.O. Box 10460, Eugene, OR 97440; 503-343-1200); $59 a year for 10 issues. The company also publishes GPS *World*, a magazine about global positioning satellite systems and their applications. Ten yearly issues are $59.

Maps on CD-ROM

The ability to use GIS on low-cost personal computer systems has been enhanced by the growth of compact discs, known as CD-ROMs, which can hold incredible amounts of data on a

thin removable platter identical to those that offer superior audio reproductions of music. A single compact disc can hold the equivalent of 250,000 printed pages of information; previously, such data would require more than 1,600 floppy disks. The capacity and speed of CD-ROMs make them ideal for holding geographic information. The potential created by CDs is truly astounding. Already, there are entire atlases on a single compact disc. What used to take several pounds of paper can now fit on a single ounce of plastic. (It is this same CD-ROM technology that will bring sophisticated navigational systems to the dashboards of our cars. See "Mapping the Future" for more on this coming technology.)

As most audiophiles already know, compact discs can also hold high-quality sound. Indeed, the new generation of compact discs—known as CDI, for "compact disc interactive"—feature both pictures and sound. Phillips has arranged to produce, under a special licensing agreement, a CDI edition *Rand McNally's America*, which will feature maps, statistics, and points of interest adapted from the book.

Here is a summary of popular commercial software that contains map-making capabilities. As you will see, the programs range widely in price and capabilities, from less than $100 well into the thousands. (Map-related programs intended primarily for teaching geography skills can be found in "Geography Education Materials.")

At the low end are programs that contain ready-made maps. Some of these programs allow you to customize boilerplate maps, but they are not intended for map-making. They are primarily for reviewing; some can be printed or "exported" into other programs so that maps can be incorporated in reports and other documents.

In the mid range are graphics packages, intended for drawing maps or customizing maps included with the program. Many of these programs offer sophisticated computer drawing techniques, enabling the creation of very high-quality finished products. But these programs, like the low-end programs, are not linked to data bases.

The most sophisticated programs are geographic information systems, which allow spatial and data analysis, and the interrelationships of the two. With these programs, you can structure simple or sophisticated queries—the number of people over age 50 living within 10 miles of a given point, for example—and have the answer plotted on a map. The plotted information will be keyed to a specific latitude and longitude.

Some of these programs listed here require that you use other "shell" programs. A few require your computer to be equipped with a compact-disc reader, which run from about $250 on up, as well as with appropriate cables, circuit boards, and software to connect it to your computer. Most of these packages work on either IBM-compatible or Macintosh computers, but not both. Some programs are sold on both floppy disk and CD-ROM. However, a growing number are being published in both Macintosh and IBM PC formats. If a program in which you are interested isn't listed in the computer format you use, check with the publisher to see if newer releases are available (or planned) that will work on your system.

Keep in mind that the publishers of these programs frequently issue updated versions, often containing impressive enhancements. Because it isn't possible to fully list these programs' capabilities (or limitations) in the space below, you are encouraged to contact the publishers directly to obtain their current literature, sample disks, sample printed maps, and price information. Also be aware that many programs are available through discount mail-order retailers, often at substantial discounts.

PROGRAMS FOR IBM PCs AND COMPATIBLES

Atlas*GIS (Strategic Mapping, Inc., 4030 Moorpark Ave., Ste. 250, San Jose, CA 95117; 408-985-7400) is a geographic information system capable of linking up to 250 map layers to an internal data base management system, making possible sophisticated geographic analysis. Other features include: map import, export, creation, and editing; built-in custom report writer; geographic and data base queries; street-level data; full-featured address matching; thematic mapping; rich graphics toolset; extensive input and output device support; and network ready. The program, which was selected Corporate Product of the Year by the Association of American Geographers, requires 2 MB RAM and costs $2,595. Also available from Strategic Mapping are two map-making programs: "Atlas*Pro for DOS" ($795) and "Atlas*MapMaker for Windows" ($395).

Automap (Automap Inc., 9831 S. 51st St., Ste. C-113, Phoenix, AZ 85044; 800-545-6626) is a computerized road atlas of the United States that can help plan efficient routes for business or vacations. The on-screen maps feature more than 50,000 cities and more than 350,000 miles of freeways, tollways, and state and county roads. However, it does not show city streets. Besides cities, you can locate parks, lakes and rivers, historic sites and monuments, military installations, Indian reservations, game reserves, and other features. There is also demographic information about most areas. The program retails for $99.95 and requires 4 MB RAM, graphics capabilities, and a mouse. Also available: "Automap Europe," priced at $149.95.

Censational Mapper (Geo Demographics, Ltd., 69 Arch St., Johnson City, NY 13790; 607-729-5220) allows you to generate a wide range of thematic maps based on 1990 census data. The basic program ($1,295) includes one U.S. county and its street base map, census tracts, and a data module that includes total population, number of households, voting age population, race/ethnicity, and housing units. Other modules ($100 to $175 per county) are available containing additional data. The data come premapped as an electronic atlas, so you do not have to learn mapping techniques or computer GIS functions.

GeoFinder (Thomas Bros. Maps, 17731 Cowan, Irvine, CA 92714; 714-863-1984, 800-899-6277) represents a computerized version of Thomas' highly regarded street maps of Los Angeles and Orange County, California. Using "GeoFinder" you can view or customize maps of a given area showing street-level data. The system is aimed primarily at business users, especially those that rely on delivery vehicles and must locate addresses and create efficient routes. A database component lets you plot customer information and create customized marketing maps. Another feature allows you to calculate distances between any two points on a map. The program, which includes both counties, retails for $195.

GisPlus (Caliper Corp., 1172 Beacon St., Newton, MA 02161; 617-527-4700) is designed to solve a wide range of geographic management needs, including access to demographic data, locating the shortest paths between many points, locating streets, and creating maps of cities or regions. The program, which requires 8 MB of hard-disk space and a math coprocessor, accepts information from many other sources, including Census Bureau TIGER files and popular spreadsheet programs. Included with the program are data bases for U.S. highways and major roads, cities, and places; zip codes; and state and county boundaries. The base package sells for $2,995. In 1992, "GisPlus" was named Outstanding Commercial Software Product by the American Association of Geographers.

Harvard GeoGraphics (Software Publishing Corp., 3165 Kifer Rd., P.O. Box 54983, Santa Clara, CA 95056; 408-988-7518) was designed for those who need to create custom maps for inclusion in presentations and reports. It

allows users to analyze data throughout the world by creating custom maps from a data base that includes 192 countries and territories, the 50 U.S. states, 3,141 U.S. counties, and more than 900 sectional center facilities (aggregate three-digit zip codes); in addition, users can pinpoint city locations from a data base that includes over 60,000 U.S. cities and more than 3,000 international cities. The program does not have street-level data. The program, which is IBM PC-compatible, requires a minimum 512K memory and hard disk and a CGA, VGA, or EGA graphics board. Price is $395.

MapInfo (MapInfo Corp., 200 Broadway, Troy, NY 12180; 518-274-6000, 800-327-8627) is a multiplatform desktop mapping software package that integrates mapping and data base management capabilities. Combined with files (purchased separately) containing a range of geographic data such as country, state, county, zip-code and postal-code boundaries; census tracts; street-level maps; highways; waterways and a variety of demographic information, "MapInfo" gives desktop computer users the ability to visualize and analyze data and see the patterns, relationships, and trends that would otherwise be overlooked. It works directly with data stored in popular data bases and spreadsheets. In one example, sales and marketing professionals start by displaying a territory on "MapInfo," then overlaying data bases of prospects and market demographics for that territory to analyze the new business potential and allocate resources accordingly. The range and scope of applications for geographic data analysis is virtually unlimited. "MapInfo" requires Windows on PC-compatibles ($995); it is also available for Macintosh ($995). Hewlett-Packard and Sun workstations ($1,795) share the same interface and can be used in a multiplatform environment. Custom applications can be developed with the MapBasic programming language. A PC version is also available using the MapCode programming language for custom applications.

MapVision (Polestar, Inc., 1716 Tipton Dr., Crofton, MD 21114; 410-261-3529) is an easy-to-use and relatively inexpensive GIS program using TIGER data. The basic program ($295) comes loaded with data for one geographic region, which you specify when ordering the program. Additional counties ($125) may be ordered separately.

MicroCAM (freeware distributed by several sources, including Microcomputer Specialty Group [MSG] of the Association of American Geographers, c/o Dept. of Geography, IUP, Indiana, PA 15705) is an extremely powerful program written and placed in the public domain for noncommercial purposes by Dr. Scott A. Loomer. "MicroCAM" produces excellent outline maps with the user specifying 27 projections, any scale, geographic features (coasts, rivers, country boundaries of the world, plus states and counties for the U.S.), line types and thicknesses, choropleth maps, and more. A user-friendly Interface helps "MicroCAM" serve as an educational tool for teaching cartography and map use. The Interface plus suggested exercises has versions in English and Portuguese and can have versions in other languages (contact Paul S. Anderson, Geography, ISU, Normal, IL 61761). The software and documentation can be freely copied. Anyone needing to purchase a copy of the software ($9) or printed documentation ($10) should contact the MSG at the above address.

MicroStation (Intergraph, Huntsville, AL; 205-730-2000; 800-345-4856) is a computer-aided design program that allows users to associate cartographic features with data in relational data bases. "MicroStation" has data base capabilities that allow users to access landbase information, perform geographical analyses, and create customized reports. Or build a world of specialized mapping applications accessible within a single environment with "MicroStation Development Language." Reference files allow multiple users—on different platforms—to work concurrently on a project. Updates are

viewed as they happen. "MicroStation" features an OSF Motif graphic user interface for easy map creation, manipulation, and editing. Build layer upon layer of geographic data in fast, full 3-D. "Microstation" also displays vector data simultaneously so users can use aerial photographs as background reference for heads-up digitizing. "MicroStation" runs on PCs and compatibles, Intergraph workstations, Sun SPARCstations, and Hewlett-Packard Series 700 workstations. Price: $3,450.

PC Arc/Info (Environmental Systems Research Institute, 380 New York St., Redlands, CA 92373; 714-793-2853) is a GIS program that runs on IBM and compatible computers. The basic starter kit costs $1,495, and there are five add-on modules costing $1,000 each. The program is available for larger computer systems. The company also makes "Arc/View," a program that provides a graphic interface for geographic data bases, which costs $495 for IBM-compatible and Macintosh versions and $995 for larger systems; and "Arc/CAD," a program that links GIS software with computer-assisted drafting systems. The initial version, for IBM compatibles, costs $3,995.

PC Globe (PC Globe Inc., 4400 S. Rural Rd., Tempe, AZ 85282; 602-730-9000) is an inexpensive ($69.95) and relatively powerful program that provides a comprehensive data base for 208 countries—including population statistics, political information, demographic information, and currency conversion—and the ability to generate what the publisher calls "geographic graphics" for slide presentations or desktop publishing. The program does not include street-level data. The graphics and text from the program can be exported to other PC-based programs, including WordPerfect, Ventura, and Lotus 1-2-3. The program requires 640K memory and a Hercules monochrome or CGA, EGA, or VGA color-graphics board.

PC USA (PC Globe Inc., 4400 S. Rural Rd., Tempe, AZ 85282; 602-730-9000) is a single-country version of "PC Globe" (see above), offering more in-depth information on the country and its individual cities and states, but not streets within cities. The $49.95 program requires 684K memory and a Hercules monochrome or CGA, EGA, or VGA color-graphics board. Also available: **MacUSA** for Macintosh computers.

StatMap III (Geovision, Inc., 5680 Peachtree Pkwy., Ste. B, Norcross, GA 30092; 404-448-8224) is a Windows-based statistical mapping program that provides the capability to match demographic data to geographic coordinate files to create maps for analysis or presentation. The program allows direct access to Census Bureau TIGER base map files and the demographic data bases collected in the 1990 census. The program links with popular spreadsheet and presentation programs. Price is $595.

Street Atlas USA (DeLorme Mapping, P.O. Box 298, Freeport, ME 04032; 207-865-4171) is a Windows-based program that puts a street map for the entire United States on a single CD-ROM. By simply typing in a zip code, phone number, or the name of a city, users may call up a map for virtually any area. The map includes such details as city and town names, highway symbols, railroads, mountains, rivers, streams, main streets, and back roads. Major metropolitan areas also include address ranges. Price is $169.

StreetSmart (Street Map Software, 1014 Boston Cir., Schaumburg, IL 60193; 708-529-4044) is designed to create street maps and generate detailed directions to specific locations. Intended for those who must navigate their way around cities and counties—fire fighters, police, delivery companies, and salespeople, for example—it allows you to design maps one intersection at a time, using on-screen commands. Also available are separate files containing computerized map files created by the Census Bureau for the 1990 census. Those files, which vary in price according to county size, cover virtually all streets in

the U.S. With "StreetSmart," users can edit the files to generate custom maps. The program is $995 and requires 640K of memory, a hard disk, 2 MB RAM, and a graphics display.

Streets on a Disk (Klynas Engineering, P.O. Box 499, Simi Valley, CA 93062; 805-529-1717) can display your mailing lists or other data base information in map form. Intended for salespeople, dispatchers, fire departments, and motorists, the program will help plot a route between two or more points, including detailed directions ("Turn left on Beverly Blvd. and go west 0.115 miles...") as well as travel distance, estimated travel time, even fuel usage. Price is $169, which includes a detailed sample TIGER file of the Hollywood, Calif., area. Additional county files are available for $225 each.

Tactician (Tactics International, Ltd., 16 Haverhill St., Andover, MA 01801; 508-475-4475) uses GIS data to facilitate marketing, sales management, advertising, and other promotional campaigns. The system enables users to locate an address anywhere in the U.S. and display nearby streets with their names. It permits a vast range of data analysis, integrating sales information with TIGER census data and other demographics, all of which can be displayed and printed as maps, tables, and charts. The basic program is $2,495, with additional packages required for zip code information and other detailed data. Runs on Mac II series (requires math coprocessor) as well as on PC compatibles (286 machines and higher, running under Windows).

U.S. Atlas (The Software Toolworks, Inc., 60 Leveroni Ct., Novato, CA 94949; 800-231-3000) contains topographic, statistical, county boundary, and highway maps for all the states. The maps are linked to a data base of information for every state on such things as government, travel, economy, crime, transportation, health, agriculture, and education. The program is updated annually, and is available in a variety of formats and operating systems.

Vistapro (Virtual Reality Laboratories, Inc., 2341 Ganador Ct., San Luis Obispo, CA 93401; 805-545-8515) can render images from simple geographic data files mixed with sophisticated rules from the world of artificial intelligence. Using USGS data files, the $130 program allows you to produce customized topographic maps, albeit with less detail found in USGS versions. From there, you can tinker with the map, adding trees, snow, weather conditions, and other aspects of the landscape. You can add rivers, lakes, and other features wherever you want. However, only a handful of locations is included with the program.

Window on the World (Geovision, Inc., 5680 Peachtree Pkwy., Ste. B, Norcross, GA 30092; 404-448-8224) is an IBM-compatible software program for Windows that utilizes geographic data bases on CD-ROM. Each disc has a capacity of 550 MB of information containing highways, roads, boundaries, bodies of water, topographic detail, land use, and landmarks, among other things. Users can create, display, and modify overlays and store composites of graphics, text, and symbols on a hard disk. The program includes a built-in "surveyor" that provides distance, bearing, and position information. Price of the basic program is $495, plus $495 for the National Series data base, based on the USGS 1:2,000,000 Scale Digital Line Graph National Atlas "Geodisc U.S. Atlas"; purchased together, the price is $595.

World Atlas (The Software Toolworks, 60 Leveroni Ct., Novato, CA 94949; 415-883-3000) is similar to "U.S. Atlas" above, except it covers the entire world.

PROGRAMS FOR MACINTOSH

Atlas*Pro (Strategic Mapping, Inc., 4030 Moorpark Ave., Ste. 250, San Jose, CA 95117; 408-985-7400) is a geographic data analysis and presentation program. Its built-in spreadsheet links data-base files to maps and includes query features that allow you to ask questions—and get answers—related to data-base or map information. It also gives you the ability to create a wide variety of presentation maps that reveal important geographic relationships and bring out the meaning in your data. The program is compatible with both System 6 and 7. Other features include street-based mapping and thematic mapping. Cost is $795.

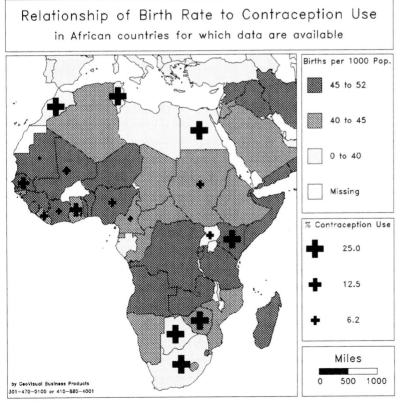

Relationship of Birth Rate to Contraception Use in African countries for which data are available

Births per 1000 Pop.
45 to 52
40 to 45
0 to 40
Missing

% Contraception Use
25.0
12.5
6.2

Miles
0   500   1000

by GeoVisual Business Products
301-470-0100 or 410-880-4001

Sample output from Atlas*GIS, produced by GeoVisual Business Products, Betlsville, MD 301-470-0100.

Azimuth (Graphsoft, 8370 Court Ave., Ste. 202, Ellicott City, MD 21043; 410-461-9488) lets you create maps of the Earth in 3-D perspective from any point in space. You can view the globe as if you were hovering above it, gazing down. The program comes with a set of six disks containing outlines of the world (by country) and the United States (by state). The program features drawing tools to allow you to customize and save any of these maps in PICT format. Price is $399.

Bytes of the Big Apple (Dept. of City Planning, 22 Reade St., New York, NY 10007; 212-720-3551) includes 15 disks full of maps of New York City, created in the Adobe Illustrator 88 format by the New York City Department of City Planning. The disks include block outlines and street names for 35 of the city's 59 community districts, plus tax block outlines for the six districts covering Manhattan below 59th Street. The disks, which come with a 12-page guide, cost $50 each.

Electronic Map Cabinet (Highlighted Data, 4350 N. Fairfax Dr., Ste. 450, Arlington, VA 22203; 703-516-9211) is a Macintosh-based CD-ROM package that includes data for most of the U.S. The program does not store maps, but generates them on request from a geographical data base containing more than 400 million bits of information. The maps range from the complete continental U.S. down to areas encompassing only a few square blocks. Maps can show political boundaries, coastlines, bodies of water, public facilities, and, for the 300 largest metropolitan areas, highways down to the local street level. Maps can be enhanced with standard drawing and text tools. Completed images can be imported as PICT files into other programs. The disk sells for $199.95.

GAIA—Geographic Access Image and Analysis (GAIA Software, 235 W. 56th St., Ste. 20-N, New York, NY 10019; 212-246-6074) allows you to display, analyze, and manipulate color satellite images of Earth. The program uses digital data collected and distributed by

---

Travel Report

Start: 5822 Grosvenor Lane
To north 0.005 mile(s). (10.00 mph)
Turn left on Grosvenor Lane and go west
    0.120 mile(s). (30.00 mph)
Turn left on Hurst St. and go south 0.261
    mile(s). (30.00 mph)
Turn right on Kingsweed Road and go west
    0.124 mile(s). (30.00 mph)
Hard left on Old Georgetown Road and go
    southeast 0.182 mile(s). (45.00 mph)
Hard right on I-495 and go west 0.793
    mile(s). (55 mph)
Turn left on Fernwood Road and go south-
    east 0.182 mile(s). (45.00 mph)
Slight turn right on Bradley Blvd. and go
    west 0.118 mile(s). (45.00 mph)
Turn left on Burning Tree Road and go south
    0.564 mile(s). (30.00 mph)
Slight turn left on Meadowlark Lane and go
    southeast 0.258 mile(s). (30.00 mph)
Stop: 8300 Meadowlark Lane

Travel Stop Total:
Distance: 3.176 mile(s)
Time: 0 hr(s), 5.45 min. = 0.091 hrs.
Fuel Usage: 0.16 gallons = 0.60 liter(s)
Cost: $0.79

Sample "Travel Report" for map on facing page, produced by Streets on a Disk. Besides explicit directions, it shows speed limits for each street, travel distance and time, and fuel use.

commercial satellite-image services such as Landsat and Spot (see "Space Imagery," page 255, for more information). Users can view images, and magnify or shrink them to any scale between 120,000:1 and 1:120,000. The program also exports images in PICT format for further use with other programs. The program is priced at $2,500; an evaluation package is available for $500, with the price applied to subsequent purchase.

GeoQuery (GeoQuery Corp., 475 Alexis R. Shuman Blvd., Ste. 385E, Naperville, IL 60563;

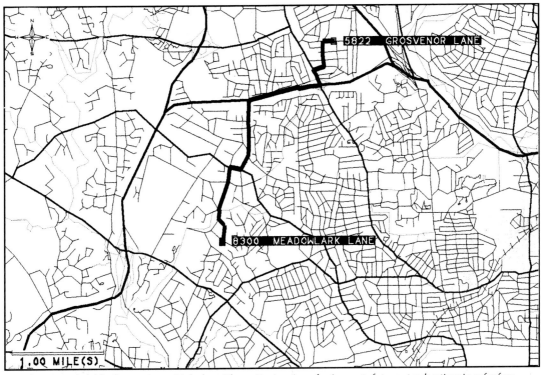

Sample map produced by Streets on a Disk, *from Klynas Engineering, showing route between two locations in suburban*
Washington, D.C. Accompanying "Travel Report," showing written directions and other data, appears on facing page.

708-357-0535; 800-541-0181) is a program for
viewing and analyzing geographic relationships
in business data and creating presentation
maps. The program's interactive maps help
business managers, particularly sales and
marketing executives, make better decisions
when location is an important consideration.
Using its built-in maps and zip code data base,
"GeoQuery" automatically classifies and locates
business data, such as customer lists and
corporate facilities. (However, it does not show
street-level data.) Also included are more than
200 demographic statistics to suport business
planning. Applications include: manipulating
sales and service territories, tracking customers
and prospects, planning business travel, and
targeting direct marketing campaigns. The
program ($395) requires 2 MB RAM and a hard
disk, and is compatible with System 6 or 7.

Global Recall (World Game Institute, 3508
Market St., Philadelphia, PA 19104; 215-387-

0220) is a Hypercard-based geographical and
statistical software product that displays more
than 200 scaled maps of the world, the continents, and 174 countries, plus key data on
each. You can locate any continent or country
simply by clicking on the location on the
screen. Price is $85.

HyperAtlas (Micromaps Software, Inc., Box
757, Lambertville, NJ 08530; 609-397-1611; 800-
334-4291) is a Hypercard stack containing
information about countries, states, and U.S.
cities. The program includes maps and information stacks that are linked. Users can add
new cards, stacks, or buttons. Price is $99 and
requires Hypercard.

MacAtlas (Micromaps Software, Inc., Box 757,
Lambertville, NJ 08530; 609-397-1611; 800-334-
4291) includes a set of customizable maps of
the world, world regions, the U.S., and the 50
states, which can be used as they appear on

disk without modification, or enhanced with fill patterns, shadows, and colors. The program comes in several formats: PICT ($199; requires MacDraw, MacDraft, or Canvas), Encapsulated PostScript ($199; requires Adobe Illustrator or Aldus Freehand), and Paint ($99; requires MacPaint, FullPaint, or SuperPaint).

MacUSA (PC Globe Inc., 4400 S. Rural Rd., Tempe, AZ 85282; 602-730-9000) is a Macintosh version of "PC USA" (see page 297). Price is $59.95.

Map II (John Wiley & Sons, Inc., 605 Third Ave., New York, NY 10158; 212-850-6000) calls itself a "map processor." In reality, it is a geographical information system designed for map-making, viewing, marking, measuring, and transforming. Maps can be created using graphic techniques analogous to working with a map base on a

light table, or data can be imported in a variety of formats. Cartographic marking, measuring, analysis, and modeling can be accomplished by screen tools as well as by specifying text-based transformations. Maps may be printed in black-and-white or color and exported to other applications. The program ($109.95) requires 2 MB of memory and a hard disk.

MapArt (Micromaps Software, Inc., Box 757, Lambertville, NJ 08530; 609-397-1611; 800-334-4291) is a collection of presentation-quality maps that can be manipulated using graphics programs. Included are four world maps (two with country outlines and two with coastal outlines), 12 regional maps with major city locations, and 25 country maps showing states or provinces. The maps are available in three formats: EPS files ($179), MacDraw II files ($179), or Paint files ($79).

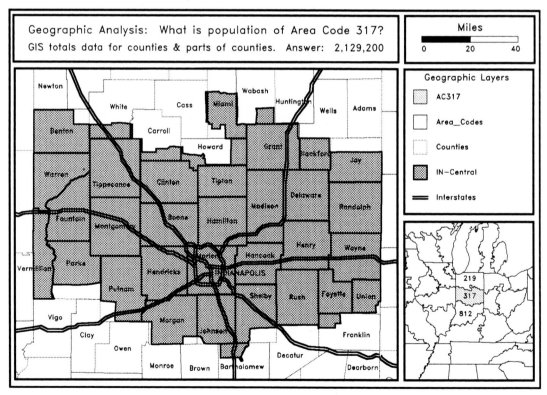

Example of query posed to a geographic information system, in this case using Atlas*GIS from Strategic Mapping, Inc. Map courtesy GeoVisual Business Systems, Beltsville, MD, 301-470-0100.

MapGrafix (ComGrafix, Inc., 620 E St., Clearwater, FL 34616; 813-443-6807, 800-448-6277) is a sophisticated geographical information system. Data base capabilities provide for the association of descriptive attribute data with map features. The software allows you to utilize data from any ASCII text file whether in a flat file, spreadsheet, or relational format. "MapGrafix" simplifies the access and use of spatial data for improved decision-making in areas of land-use planning and analysis, transportation planning, environmental studies, demographic and impact analysis, zoning enforcement, and more, but does not include street-level data. Requires coprocessor and 2 MB RAM. Most applications also require a digitizer, plotter or printer, and relational data base program. Retail price is $4,995. Among the modules available are "MapLink" ($995), which facilitates conversion of maps and drawings that already exist in a standard digital format to MapGrafix map files and vice versa; and "MapView" ($495), which provides the capability of transforming digital maps from one cartographic projection or standard coordinate system to another.

MapMaker (Select Micro Systems, Inc., 322 Underhill Ave., Yorktown Heights, NY 10598; 914-245-4670) is intended for custom map drawing. It can store and retrieve maps as files containing boundary and point information as well as in graphic formats. The program includes a large library of boundary and data files, with additional files available separately. You can also create custom boundary files. The program offers flexibility in font styles and sizes. Price is $395.

MapPack Global Perspectives (Micromaps Software Inc., Box 757, Lambertville, NJ 08530; 609-397-1611; 800-334-4291) includes 18 views of the Earth as seen from about 100,000 miles in space. These images—available as Postscript or MacDraw II files—are useful for showing relative positions of locations on different continents, or on opposite sides of continents or oceans. Price is $49. Also available:

"MapPack US by County" ($49), which includes each of the 50 states divided into counties; and "MapPack Metro Areas" ($49), a collection of 25 major U.S. cities, designed to be used as is or modified using Adobe Illustrator of Aldus Freehand.

QuickMap (Micromaps Software, Inc., Box 757, Lambertville, NJ 08530; 609-397-1611; 800-334-4291) is a geographic analysis tool that allows you to represent data on a map. You may import data sets from spreadsheets and data bases, or enter data directly into the program. Data can be analyzed by calculating ratios, sums, differences, and percentages. Completed maps can be pasted into other programs, including desktop publishing applications. Price is $99 and requires Hypercard.

State-Smart (Platypus Software, P.O. Box 1591, Corvallis, OR 97339; 503-758-3429) is a Hypercard stack that contains outline maps of each state, contour and topographical maps of U.S. regions, and maps showing state facts. By clicking on icons, you can view population information, elevations, zip codes, and other information.

Tactician (Tactics International, Ltd., 16 Haverhill St., Andover, MA 01801; 508-475-4475), described under PC section, also runs on Mac II series (requires math coprocessor).

CHARTING AND NAVIGATION SYSTEMS

ComECDIS (ComGrafix, Inc., 620 E St., Clearwater, FL 34616; 813-443-6807, 800-448-6277) is a charting and navigation system for Macintosh computers that combines Loran or GPS positioning, detailed charts, and many navigational functions, including course planning, automatic logging, vector-based NOAA charts, and real-time tracking. The program sells for $599.95, including one charting area. It's also available for the Powerbook.

Navigate! (Fair Tide Technologies, Inc., 18 Ray Ave., Burlington, MA 01803; 617-229-6409, 800-

732-3284) is a digital-chart navigation system for either Macintosh or IBM-compatible computers. The program provides full-color nautical charts, including depth-contour lines to warn sailors of shallow waters and other hazards. You can plot a course by pointing at various locations along the route and clicking on the mouse. The program automatically calculates the latitude and longitude of each point and its range and bearing from the previous point. There are two versions: one in black-and-white ($395 for Macintosh) and one in color ($695 for Macintosh, $595 for IBM). Each comes with one free chart of your choice; additional charts are $95. There are nearly 200 charts available (examples: "Cape Canaveral to Key West" or "Monterey Bay to Coos Bay"). Also available are packages of five to eight maps of a given region (e.g., northern New England, from Boston to the Canadian border) for $395.

GIS Data Bases

Geographic Data Technology, Inc. (13 Dartmouth College Hwy., Lyme, NH 03768; 603-795-2183) sells TIGER files for $225 for the first county in a state, $25 for each subsequent county in that state. The data is available on 9-track tape or floppy disks. The firm also sells an enhanced version of the census data with missing street names and corrections called "Dynamap/2000." For one to five users, the nationwide version costs $100,000; California, Florida, New Jersey, and New York go for $30,000 all together; Illinois, Ohio, Pennsylvania, and Texas cost $20,000; and all other states are $10,000 each. Any county is $800. Prices are higher for multiple users.

U.S. Geological Survey's Earth Science Information Center offers inventories of digital spatial data bases—collections of computerized data that have some coordinate system that can be used by cartographic software. The publication *Sources for Digital Spatial Data* describes more than 500 such data sets containing spatially referenced base or thematic categories of data, from federal, state, and local government agencies and the private sector. Examples include "Natural Resource Digital Data Base for Death Valley National Monument and Surrounding Region," produced by the National Park Service; "Sanitary Sewers Data Base," produced by the City of San Jose (California) Planning Department; and "Larimer County Area Soil Survey, Colorado," produced by the U.S. Soil Conservation Service. The complete survey, updated and printed on a weekly basis, is $22 from USGS-ESIC, 507 National Center, Reston, VA 22092; 703-860-6045.

■ **See also: "Census Maps," Geography Education Materials."**

Map Stuff

It used to be that maps appeared only on flat or folded sheets of paper and on globes. But no more. Today, you can find maps printed on just about everything—from scratch pads to shower curtains, wastebaskets to basketballs. Not all of these are suitable for getting from here to there, or even for locating the world's capital cities. But no matter: these maps are more for entertainment than enlightenment.

The proliferation of map images on everyday products isn't surprising. After all, it's a big, beautiful world—why not display it proudly? Thanks to a growing collection of map "stuff," you can.

Here is a representative sampling of what's out there:

CALENDARS

Prices indicated are for 1990 calendars. You are advised to inquire about price and availability of calendars for subsequent years.

Pomegranate Publications (Box 808022, Petaluma, CA 94975; 707-765-2005; 800-227-1428) publishes a colorful 16" X 14" "Masters of Cartography" calendar ($13.95), featuring maps of 15th-, 16th-, and 17th-century European cartographers. A "Masters of Cartography" address book ($16.95) is also available, with colorful illustrated maps from the Huntington Library reproduced.

CLOCKS

Geochron Enterprises, Inc. (899 Arguello St., Redwood City, CA 94063; 415-361-1771; 800-342-1661) manufactures the "Geochron World Time Indicator," a back-lighted, electrome-chanical map/clock of the world. Its Mercator projection (updated and available each year) displays all the legal time zones in the world. The map moves at a rate of one inch per hour,

reflecting the Earth's rotation, while a station-ary time scale at the top of the map displays the correct time for each zone. In conjunction with the time, Geochron accurately depicts the moment of sunrise and sunset anywhere in the world; the duration of sunlight changes auto-matically with the seasons. Four models are available, with prices ranging from $1,265 to $2,465.

Wuersch Time, Inc. (1273 Robeson St., Fall River, MA 02720; 508-672-8018) produces a variety of clocks with topographic maps and nautical charts on the face. Clocks available range from a 6" X 8" nautical chart wall clock with a teak frame ($45) to a $12^1/_2$-inch topo-graphic map wall clock framed in brass ($74). Call or write for brochure.

CLOTHING

The Cockpit (33-00 47th Ave., Long Island City, NY 11101; 718-482-1860; 800-272-9464) sells several items, including an "Allied Pilot's Cloth Invasion/Escape Map," an 18-inch-square reproduction ($14); "A.A.F. Air Bases T-Shirts," featuring maps of England noting airfields used by the 8th and 9th A.A.F. during World War II ($17.50); "14th Air Force 'Briefing Map' Under-wear" ($14.50), boxer shorts made from repro-ductions of Flying Tigers World War II maps; and "Original World War II Cloth Escape Maps" ($50), pilot's A.A.F. cloth charts printed by the Army Map Service in May 1945 for the Allied invasion of the Japanese mainland. One side shows the East China Sea and Japanese mainland; the other portrays Japan and the South China seas.

Buckminster Fuller Institute (1743 S. La Cienega Blvd., Los Angeles, CA 90035; 310-837-7710) sells the "Dymaxion Map T-Shirt" ($9.95), a 100-percent cotton T-shirt with Buckminster

A selection of "Map Stuff" from several companies.

Fuller's Dymaxion world map printed on the front and the caption "A One World Island in a One World Ocean."

Interarts, Ltd. (15 Mt. Auburn St., Cambridge, MA 02138; 617-354-4655) sells unique and colorful "Wearin' the World" map jackets made of lightweight Tyvek, featuring Sweden's attractive GLA Kartor (formerly Esselte) map graphics ($49.95). Also available are "World Map Tote Bag" ($13.95), "World Map Baseball Cap" ($14.95), "United States 'Wearin' the States' Map Jacket" ($49.95), and "United States Tote Bag" ($13.95). Laminated world map desk blotter ($14.95) is also available.

Michael Poisson Associates (P.O. Box 84, Boulder Creek, CA 95006; 408-338-2984) sells nature and science products wholesale to dealers only. Products include inflatable globes, including Earthball, Animal Globe, and geopolitical, constellation, dinosaurs, environmental, glow-in-the-dark; geosphere posters, including the Earth from space; puzzles, including Celestial Planisphere and Travel

America; galactic posters, including the universe, solar systems, space stations, lunar views, lunar phases, and Aztec cosmos; and Earth jewelry, including earrings, pendants, ornaments, and key chains, Also markets planispheres, star globes, and satellite-image T-shirts.

POSTCARDS AND STATIONERY

CTM/Zia Maps (P.O. Box 4982, Boulder, CO 80306; 303-444-1670) produces the *Book of Postcards—The Colorado Series*, an assortment of 3-D images showing the state of Colorado and detailing 12 specific regions, including the state's ski areas. Each map shows towns, roads, political boundaries, and geographic features. The image surfaces—highlighted to show shaded relief and coupled with color elevation tinting—are the latest in computer terrain mapping. There are sixteen 7" X 9" images ($12). In conjunction with the *Book of Postcards*, CTM/Zia is offering the same 2-D and 3-D images as digital clip art for Macintosh and PC desktop publishing. They're available on high-density 3.5-inch disks in compressed file formats.

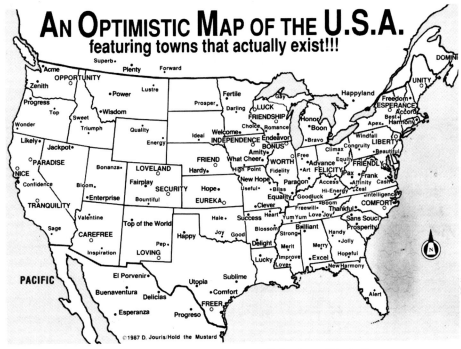

AN OPTIMISTIC MAP OF THE U.S.A.
featuring towns that actually exist!!!

"An Optimistic Map of the U.S.A.," ©1987 David Jouris/Hold the Mustard Productions

Hold the Mustard Productions (P.O. Box 822, Berkeley, CA 94701; 415-549-9444) produces humorous postcards including 16 thematic maps ($11 for the set) featuring names of towns that actually exist. Titles include: "An Optimistic Map of the U.S.A.," "A Pessimistic Map of the U.S.A.," "An Animal Map of the U.S.A.," "An Exotic Map of the U.S.A.," "A Confusing Map of the U.S.A.," "A Lovers' Map of the U.S.A.," "An Eccentric Map of the U.S.A.," "An Artists' Map of the U.S.A.," "A Curiously Juxtaposed Map of the U.S.A.," "A Saints' Map of the U.S.A.," "A Literary Map of the U.S.A.," "A Professional Map of the U.S.A.," "A Heavenly Map of the U.S.A.," "A Musical Map of the U.S.A.," "A Numerical Map of the U.S.A.," and "An Eccentric Map of Great Britain." A catalog is available.

Magna Carta (4608 Davenport St. NW, Washington, DC 20016; 202-244-0506) offers a set of world map antique-reproduction notecards from images in the Geography and Map Division of the Library of Congress. The six images trace the world view from before the voyages of Colum-

bus to the incorporation of knowledge of the New World. The cards come as a boxed set with envelopes.

New England Cartographics (P.O. Box 369, Amherst, MA 01004; 413-253-7415) produces "Topolopes," envelopes made from U.S. and Canadian government-surplus topographic maps. These novel envelopes require only an address label to meet U.S. postal regulations. They cost $.10 to $.20 each, and are available in map stores.

PUZZLES AND GAMES

Better Boating Association (295 Reservoir St., Needham, MA 02194; 617-449-3314) produces "Chart Kit Puzzles" ($8.95 each), full-color, 550-piece puzzles of nautical charts. The 18" X 22" puzzles are available for Annapolis/St. Michaels, Maryland; Fisher's Island Sound, Connecticut; Martha's Vineyard, Massachusetts; Mt. Desert/ Frenchman's Bay, Maine; Newport, Rhode Island; and Sanibel/Captiva, Florida.

Coburn Designs (P.O. Box 331, Nashua, NH 03061; 603-889-2070) sells jigsaw puzzles of U.S. national parks ($11 each, suggested retail). The full-color, 500-piece puzzles, reproduced from U.S. Geological Survey maps, show scenic routes, trails, elevations, contour lines, and points of interest. Puzzles are available for

Acadia National Park, Grand Canyon National Park, Great Smoky Mountains National Park, Mount McKinley/Denali National Park, Mount Rainier National Park, Rocky Mountain National Park, White Mountain National Forest, Yellowstone National Park, Yosemite National Park, and Washington, D.C.

Buckminster Fuller Institute (1743 S. La Cienega Blvd., Los Angeles, CA 90035; 310-837-7710) sells copies of the Dymaxion map in several forms, among them, "Dymaxion Sky-Ocean World Map" ($5), a 22" X 14$\frac{1}{2}$" map on heavy stock that folds into a 5$\frac{1}{2}$-inch icosahedron; and postcards ($1.95 each).

GeoLearning Corp. (555 Absaraka St., Sheridan, WY 82801; 307-674-6436; 800-843-6436) produces many interesting things, among them:

■ "The Spilhaus GeoGlyph" ($24.95), a puzzle showing the continuous surface of the world. More than 100 maps can be created from the pieces.
■ "GeOdyssey—The World Game" ($14.95), in which players compete to build a world map, tile by tile, testing their geography knowledge by identifying continents, coastlines, and other geographical features.
■ "GeOdyssey Deluxe" ($29.95), a version of GeOdyssey featuring larger nine-color playing tiles and labeled oceans.
■ "GeoCards" ($7.95), a colorful game that features a deck of 48 cards, with each card representing a different geographical location.
■ "Tectonic Cube" ($4.50), a fascinating seven-sided geometric form showing how the Earth's tectonic plates fit together. The cube illustrates the plates' various ridges, boundaries, zones, and faults.
■ "Tectonocycle" ($3), which the company describes as "a type of hexaflexagon or kaleidocycle." By assembling and rotating this ingenious cardboard model, the Tectonocycle demonstrates the breakup of the continent Pangea in four stages.
■ "Flight Lines" ($5.95), an educational puzzle

"Wearin' the World" jacket, distributed by Interarts, Ltd.

game featuring "Geography-Triangles," such as Los Angeles to Sydney, Paris to Rio, Tokyo to Chicago, and many more.

National Geographic Society (17th & M sts. NW, Washington, DC 20036; 202-921-1200) sells "Global Pursuit" ($21.95), with nearly 1,000 geography questions to test the global knowledge of students and adults alike. Comes with a world map.

Omni Resources (1238 Anthony Rd., P.O. Box 2096, Burlington, NC 27216; 919-227-8300) distributes jigsaw puzzles of U.S. national parks, made from USGS topographic maps ($12.95 each), available for six national parks.

Optimago (43 Perrymead St., London SW6 3SN, England; 071-736-2380) produces wooden jigsaw puzzles of several interesting maps. Among the puzzles available are the 1750 "Nouvelle Mappe Monde" by Bailleul le Jeune, a 1574 map of London, a celestial chart from the *Folio Atlas of the Heavens* by Andreas Cellarius in 1600, a map of Japan by Adrian Reland, and a circa 1507 world map by Martin

Waldseenmuller that first bestowed the name "America."

Pacific Puzzle Co. (378 Guemes Island Rd., Anacortes, WA 98221; 206-293-7034) offers colorful, hand-cut hardwood puzzles, including three maps of the U.S. ($24 to $70), a political world map ($16), a Dymaxion world map ($22), and five continent puzzles ($16 to $19 each). Shipping is extra; write for catalog.

Puzzles 'N Such, Inc. (19 Prairie Dunes, Hutchinson, KS 67502; 316-663-4192) produces the colorful, information-packed Puzzlin' World series of jigsaw puzzles. The puzzle of each U.S. state features county boundaries, county seats, rivers, lakes, points of interest, and historical trivia, as well as state flags, seals, animals, birds, rocks, trees, mottoes, and songs. Other puzzles depict the United States, the world, the solar system, the Civil War, Israel, and "Stars and Stripes," describing the history of the American flag. Puzzles may be ordered from Puzzles 'N Such, or may be found in a wide variety of museum shops and retail stores.

World Impressions, Inc. (P.O. Box 460, Tracyton, WA 98393; 800-255-3627) produces colorfully illustrated sports and travel jigsaw puzzles, based on their popular ArtMap products. The 550-piece puzzles—"Baseball," "Football," "Basketball," "Skiing," "Golf," "Raceways," and "Endangered Species"—are $12.95 each. "San Francisco" is a complex 1,200-piece "expert" puzzle ($15.95). A limited number of the ArtMaps—including "San Francisco," "Endangered Species," "Yosemite," "Baseball," and "Football"—are available as black-and-white Coloring ArtMaps, excellent gifts for the younger set ($10.95 each in an attractive gift box with 10 pens). The other ArtMap products are available as postcards ($.50 each, 10 minimum), paper ArtMaps ($11.95 each), laminated in flexible polyvinyl ($19.95 each), and ready-to-hang wall plaques ($59.95 each).

Worldsat International, Inc. (1495 Bonhill Rd., Unit 10, Mississauga, Ontario, Canada L5T 1M2; 416-795-0110) produces the GeoSphere jigsaw puzzles that reproduce the company's spectacular satellite views of the planet. "Earth From Space" (24" X 36") is available as a 216-piece ($14.95) or a 1,000-piece ($17.95) puzzle. Two 60-piece, $8^1/_2$" X 11" puzzles—"Earth Robinson" and "Earth Pacific"—are also available ($4.45).

ET CETERA

Baden Sports, Inc. (1120 SW 16th, Reton, WA 98055; 206-235-1830) produces "World Ball," a basketball with a seven-color world map printed on it. The ball is available in a regulation National Basketball Association size ($29^1/_2$ inches), $29.95; and in a "mini-star" size ($22^1/_2$ inches), $19.95.

Era-Maptec, Ltd. (5 S. Leinster St., Dublin 2, Ireland; 353-1-766266) produces posters, T-shirts, calendars, and jigsaw puzzles from its satellite images of U.S. and foreign metropolitan areas, including Hong Kong, San Diego, and San Francisco.

Fantasy Productions (2124 Westlake Ave., Seattle, WA 98121; 206-343-0903; 800-678-8697) produces but does not retail inflatable globes. The "Dinosaur Globe" features major fossil finds marked with descriptions of prehistoric creatures; the "Star System Globe" illustrates the constellations and planets; there are also a "Blue World Globe" and a "Clear World Globe."

Gabelli U.S. (1228 West Ave. #711, Miami Beach, FL 33139; 305-532-6956) distributes brightly colored map clipboards, briefcases, duffel bags, pencil cases, rucksacks, and wallets. The company also distributes a new line of clothing and accessories, featuring the "Montiscolor World Map"; these cotton caps and jackets present a perfect 3-D effect of relief and depth.

Hugg-a-Planet (XTC Products, Inc., 247 Rockingstone Ave., Larchmont, NY 10538; 914-833-0200; 800-332-7840) sells "Political Hugg-a-

Planet Earth" ($20), a soft, colorful fabric globe with more than 600 places labeled that was a Parents' Choice Classic Award Winner. It's also available as the "Geophysical Hugg-a-Planet Earth" ($20), with natural features, mountain ranges, rivers, lakes, and population densities; the six-inch "Baby Hugg-a-Planet Earth" ($10); and "Super Hugg-a-Planet Earth" ($90). "Hugg America" ($15) is the only soft map in the shape of the United States; it features Alaska to scale with the rest of the country and more than 400 places labeled, including all national parks. "Hugg-a-Planet Mars" ($15) is a colorful soft form with more than 450 places labeled, while "Hugg-a-Star" shows all 88 major constellations.

Mino Publications (9009 Paddock Ln., Potomac, MD 20854; 301-294-9514) produces a four-color laminated place-mat map of downtown Washington, D.C., with subway and Capital Beltway maps on the reverse ($3.50).

Parkwest Publications, Inc. (238 W. 72nd St., Ste. 2F, New York, NY 10023; 212-222-6100)

distributes "The Tarquin Globe" ($7.95), a full-color, paper build-it-yourself globe, illustrating all countries and more than 1,000 major cities, seas, rivers, and other features. The kit comes with a 24-page booklet full of facts and ideas. A similar product, "The Tarquin Star Globe" ($7.95), is for constructing a three-dimensional globe of the night sky.

Wings Over the World (225 5th Ave., New York, NY 10010; 212-683-3244) produces but does not retail several fun map products, including a colorful "World Shower Curtain" ($35); "Star Gazer Shower Curtain" ($35), showing the night sky; a handy-size "World Umbrella" ($16); inflatable globes, available in clear or blue (four sizes: 9, 12, 16, and 27 inches, with prices ranging from $4 to $28), a "World Poncho" ($25), and a "Star Gazer Umbrella" ($16). Also available is the "Global Yo-Yo" ($4), a globe on a string.

■ **See also: "Geography Education Materials."**

APPENDIXES

APPENDIX A
State Map Agencies

TRANSPORTATION/HIGHWAY OFFICES

Alabama
Alabama Highway Dept.
State Map Room
1409 Coliseum Blvd.
Montgomery, AL 36130
205-242-6071

Alaska
Div. of Design & Construction
Alaska Dept. of Transportation & Public Facilities
P.O. Box Z
Juneau, AK 99811
907-465-3900

Arizona
Arizona Dept. of Transportation
Highway Div.
206 S. 17th Ave.
Phoenix, AZ 85007
602-255-7391

Arkansas
Arkansas State Highway & Transportation Dept.
P.O. Box 2261
Little Rock, AR 72203
501-569-2444

California
California Dept. of Transportation
Highways Div.
1120 N St.
Sacramento, CA 95814
916-654-5267

Colorado
Colorado Dept. of Highways
4201 E. Arkansas Ave.
Denver, CO 80222
303-757-9011

Connecticut
Connecticut Dept. of Transportation
P.O. Drawer A
Wethersfield, CT 06109
203-566-3010

Delaware
Delaware Dept. of Transportation
P.O. Box 778
Trans. Admin. Bldg.
Dover, DE 19903
302-739-4323

Florida
Dept. of Transportation
605 Suwannee St.
Tallahassee, FL 32399
904-488-6721

Georgia
Georgia Dept. of Transportation
2 Capitol Sq.
Atlanta, GA 30334
404-656-5267

Hawaii
Hawaii Dept. of Transportation
869 Punchbowl St.
Honolulu, HI 96813
808-587-2150

Idaho
Idaho Transportation Dept.
State Highway Administrator
P.O. Box 7129
Boise, ID 83707
208-334-8802

Illinois
Illinois Dept. of Transportation
Highways Div.
2300 S. Dirksen Pkwy.
Springfield, IL 62764
217-782-6953

Indiana
Indiana Transportation Dept.
100 N. Senate Ave.
Indianapolis, IN 46204
317-232-5518

Iowa
Iowa Dept. of Transportation
Highways Div.
800 Lincoln Way
Ames, IA 50010
515-239-1124

Kansas
Kansas Dept. of Transportation
Public Information Office
Docking State Office Bldg.
Topeka, KS 66612
913-296-3585

Kentucky
Kentucky Transportation Cabinet
Office of Public Relations
State Office Bldg.
Frankfort, KY 40622
502-564-4980

Louisiana
Dept. of Transportation & Development
P.O. Box 94245
Baton Rouge, LA 70804
504-379-1200

Maryland
Maryland State Highway Admin.
707 N. Calvert St.
Baltimore, MD 21202
301-333-1111

Massachusetts
Executive Office of Transportation & Construction
10 Park Plaza
Boston, MA 02116
617-973-7000

Michigan
Michigan Dept. of Transportation
425 W. Ottawa
P.O. Box 30050
Lansing, MI 48909
517-373-2090

Minnesota
Minnesota Dept. of Transportation
395 John Ireland Blvd.
St. Paul, MN 55155
612-297-4532

Mississippi
Mississippi Highway Dept.
P.O. Box 1850
Jackson, MS 39215
601-359-1217

Missouri
Highway & Transportation Dept.
P.O. Box 270
Jefferson City, MO 65102
314-751-2840

Montana
Montana Dept. of Highways
2701 Prospect Ave.
Helena, MT 59620
406-444-6200

Nebraska
Nebraska Dept. of Roads
P.O. Box 94759
Lincoln, NE 68509
402-479-4671

Nevada
Nevada Dept. of Transportation
1263 S. Stewart St.
Carson City, NV 89712
702-885-4322

New Hampshire
Dept. of Transportation
Hazen Dr.
Concord, NH 03301
603-271-3731

New Jersey
New Jersey Dept. of Transportation
1035 Parkway Ave., CN600
Trenton, NJ 08625
609-292-3105

New Mexico
New Mexico State Highway Dept.
1120 Cerrillos Rd.
Santa Fe, NM 87503
505-983-0452

New York
Mapping Services Bureau
Dept. of Transportation
State Campus, Bldg. 5
Albany, NY 12232
518-457-3555

North Carolina
North Carolina Dept. of Transportation
P.O. Box 25201
Raleigh, NC 27611
919-733-4713

Ohio
Map Sales
Ohio Dept. of Transportation
25 S. Front St., Rm. B100
Columbus, OH 43215
614-446-7170

Oklahoma
Reproduction Branch
Oklahoma Dept. of Transportation
200 NE 21st St.
Oklahoma City, OK 73105
405-521-2586

Pennsylvania
Pennsylvania Dept. of Transportation
1200 Transportation & Safety Bldg.
Harrisburg, PA 17120
717-783-8800

Rhode Island
Planning Div.
Rhode Island Dept. of Transportation
210 State Office Bldg.
Providence, RI 02903
401-277-2694

South Carolina
Map Sales, Traffic Engineering Div.
Dept. of Highways & Public Transportation
P.O. Box 191
Columbia, SC 29202
803-737-1270

South Dakota
South Dakota Dept. of Transportation
700 Broadway Ave. E.
Pierre, SD 57501
605-773-3265

Tennessee
Information Office
Tennessee Dept. of Transportation
700 James K. Polk Bldg.
Nashville, TN 37243
615-741-2331

Texas
Texas Highways Dept.
P.O. Box 5064
Austin, TX 78763
512-483-3705

Utah
Office of Community Relations
Utah Dept. of Transportation
4501 South 2700 West
Salt Lake City, UT 84119
801-965-4104

Vermont
Transportation Agency
133 State St.
Montpelier, VT 05602
802-828-2657

Virginia
Transportation Dept.
1041 E. Broad St.
Richmond, VA 23219
804-786-2715

Washington
Public Affairs Office
Washington Dept. of Transportation
Transportation Bldg., KF-01
Olympia, WA 98504
206-753-2150

West Virginia
Statewide Planning Div.
West Virginia Dept. of Highways
Charleston, WV 25305
304-348-2868

Wisconsin
Wisconsin Dept. of Transportation
P.O. Box 7910
Madison, WI 53707
608-266-7744

Wyoming
Wyoming Dept. of Transportation
P.O. Box 1708
Cheyenne, WY 82002
307-777-4010

TOURISM OFFICES

Alabama
Alabama Bureau of Tourism and Travel
532 S. Perry St.
Montgomery, AL 36104
205-261-4169; 800-ALA-BAMA

Alaska
Div. of Tourism
Dept. of Commerce & Economic Development
P.O. Box E
Juneau, AK 99811
907-465-2010

Arizona
Arizona Office of Tourism
1100 W. Washington St.
Phoenix, AZ 85007
602-542-3618

Arkansas
Arkansas Dept. of Parks and Tourism
1 Capitol Mall
Little Rock, AR 72201
501-682-1765

California
California Office of Tourism
State Dept. of Commerce
1121 L St.
Sacramento, CA 95814
916-322-2881

Colorado
Colorado Tourism Board
P.O. Box 38700
Denver, CO 80202
303-592-5410

Connecticut
Connecticut Dept. of Economic Development
Div. of Tourism
210 Washington St.
Hartford, CT 06106
203-566-3385

Delaware
Delaware Development Office
Tourism Office
P.O. Box 1401
99 Kings Hwy.
Dover, DE 19903
302-736-4271

District of Columbia
D.C. Convention and Visitors Bureau
1212 New York Ave. NW
Washington, DC 20005
202-789-7000

Florida
Florida Dept. of Commerce
Div. of Tourism
Collins Bldg., Ste. 530
Tallahassee, FL 32399
904-488-7300

Georgia
Industry, Trade and Tourism Dept.
P.O. Box 1776
Atlanta, GA 30301
404-656-3590

Guam
Guam Visitors Bureau
1220 Pale San Vitores Rd.
P.O. Box 3520
Tamuning, Guam 96911
671-646-5278

Hawaii
Hawaii Visitors Bureau
2270 Kalakaua Ave., Ste. 801
Honolulu, HI 96815
808-923-1811

Idaho
Idaho Department of Commerce
Div. of Travel Promotion
700 State Street
Boise, ID 83720
208-334-2470

Illinois
Illinois Dept. of Commerce & Community Affairs
Div. of Tourism
620 E. Adams
Springfield, IL 62701
217-782-7139

Indiana
Indiana Div. of Tourism
1 N. Capitol, Ste. 700
Indianapolis, IN 46205
317-232-8860

Iowa
Iowa Department of Economic Development
Division of Tourism & Visitors
200 E. Grand Ave.
Des Moines, IA 50309
515-281-3100

Kansas
Kansas Dept. of Commerce
Div. of Tourism & Travel
400 SW 8th St., #500
Topeka, KS 66603
913-296-2009

Kentucky
Kentucky Tourism Cabinet
Capitol Plaza Tower, 24th Fl.
Frankfort, KY 40601
502-564-4270

Louisiana
Louisiana Office of Tourism
P.O. Box 94291
99 Riverside N.
Baton Rouge, LA 70804
504-342-7800

Maine
Maine Office of Tourism
189 State St.
State House Station 59
Augusta, ME 04333
207-298-5710

Maryland
Maryland Office of Tourism
45 Calvert St.
Baltimore, MD 21401
301-974-2686

Massachusetts
Massachusetts Dept. of Commerce
Division of Tourism
Leverett H. Saltonstall Bldg., 13th Fl.
Boston, MA 02202
617-723-7800

Michigan
Michigan Dept. of Commerce
Travel Bureau
P.O. Box 30226
Lansing, MI 48909
517-373-0670

Minnesota
Minnesota Office of Tourism
375 Jackson St.
250 Skyway Level
St. Paul, MN 55101
612-297-2333; 800-652-9747 (in Minn.); 800-328-1461
   (out of state)

Mississippi
Dept. of Economic Development
Div. of Tourism
P.O. Box 849
Jackson, MS 39205
601-359-3297; 800-647-2290

Missouri
Missouri Div. of Tourism
P.O. Box 1055
Truman State Office Bldg.
301 W. High St.
Jefferson City, MO 65102
314-751-4133

Montana
Travel Montana
Dept. of Commerce
1424 9th Ave.
Helena, MT 59620
406-444-2654; 800-584-3390

Nebraska
Travel & Tourism Div.
Nebraska Dept. of Economic Development
P.O. Box 94666
301 Centennial Mall S.
Lincoln, NE 68509
402-471-3111; 800-742-7595 (in Neb.); 800-228-4307
   (out of state)

Nevada
Nevada Commission on Tourism
State Capitol Complex
Carson City, NV 89710
702-885-4322; 800-237-0774

New Hampshire
Office of Vacation Travel
Dept. of Resources & Economic Development
P.O. Box 856
105 Loudon Rd.
Concord, NH 03301
603-271-2666; 800-258-3608

New Jersey
New Jersey Div. of Travel & Tourism
20 W. State St. CN826
Trenton, NJ 08625
609-292-2470; 800-537-7397

New Mexico
New Mexico Economic Development Dept.
Tourism Div.
1100 St. Francis Dr., Rm. 8900
Santa Fe, NM 87503
505-827-0291

New York
Div. of Tourism
New York State Dept. of Economic Development
One Commerce Plaza
Albany, NY 12245
518-474-4116

North Carolina
North Carolina Dept. of Commerce
Div. of Travel & Tourism
P.O. Box 25249
430 N. Salisbury St.
Raleigh, NC 27603
919-733-4171

North Dakota
North Dakota Tourism Promotion
Liberty Memorial Bldg.
600 East Boulevard
Bismarck, ND 58505
701-224-2525; 800-472-2100 (in N.D.); 800-437-2077
   (out of state)

Ohio
Div. of Travel & Tourism
Ohio Dept. of Development
P.O. Box 1001
77 High St., 29th Fl.
Columbus, OH 43266
614-466-8844; 800-282-5393

Oklahoma
Oklahoma Tourism & Recreation Dept.
500 Will Rogers Bldg.
Oklahoma City, OK 73105
405-521-2406; 800-652-6552

Oregon
Div. of Tourism
Economic Development Dept.
775 Summer St. NE
Salem, OR 97310
503-378-3451; 800-547-7842 (out of state)

Pennsylvania
Bureau of Travel Development
Pennsylvania Dept. of Commerce
453 Forum Bldg.
Harrisburg, PA 17120
717-787-5453; 800-847-4872

Rhode Island
Tourism Div.
Dept. of Economic Development
7 Jackson Walkway
Providence, RI 02903
401-277-2601; 800-556-2484 (out of state)

South Carolina
Dept. of Parks, Recreation & Tourism
South Carolina Div. of Tourism
1205 Pendleton St.
Columbia, SC 29201
803-734-0133

Tennessee
Tennessee Dept. of Tourism Development
P.O. Box 23170
Nashville, TN 37202
615-741-2158

Texas
Div. of Tourism
P.O. Box 12728
First City Centre
Austin, TX 78711
512-462-9191

Utah
Utah Travel Council
Council Hall, Capitol Hill
300 N. State St.
Salt Lake City, UT 84114
801-538-1030

Vermont
Vermont Travel Div.
134 State St.
Montpelier, VT 05602
802-828-3236

Virginia
Virginia Div. of Tourism
202 N. 9th St., Ste. 500
Richmond, VA 23219
804-786-2051

Washington
Dept. of Trade & Economic Development
Tourism Promotion & Development Div.
101 General Administration Bldg.
Olympia, WA 98504
206-753-5600

West Virginia
West Virginia Dept. of Commerce
Travel Development Div.
2101 Washington St., E.
Charleston, WV 25305
304-348-2286

Wisconsin
Wisconsin Tourism Development
P.O. Box 7970
123 W. Washington Ave.
Madison, WI 53707
608-266-1018

Wyoming
Wyoming Travel Commission
I-25 at College Dr.
Cheyenne, WY 82002
307-777-7777

NATURAL RESOURCES OFFICES

Alabama
Div. of State Parks
Alabama Dept. of Conservation & Natural Resources
64 N. Union St.
Montgomery, AL 36130
205-242-3334

Alaska
Dept. of Natural Resources
400 Willoughby Ave.
Juneau, AK 99801
907-465-2400

Mines Information Office
794 University Ave., Basement
Fairbanks, AK 99701
907-474-7062

Div. of Technical Services
Dept. of Natural Resources
Pouch 7035
Anchorage, AK 99510
907-786-2291

Div. of Land & Water Management
Dept. of Natural Resources, Pouch 7-005
Anchorage, AK 99510
907-265-4355

Arizona
Natural Resources Div.
1616 W. Adams
Phoenix, AZ 85007
602-542-4626

California
California Resources Agency
1416 9th St., Rm. 1311
Sacramento, CA 95814
916-653-5656

Colorado
Colorado Dept. of Natural Resources
1313 Sherman St., Rm. 718
Denver, CO 80203
303-866-3311

Connecticut
Dept. of Environmental Protection
165 Capitol Ave.
Hartford, CT 06106
203-566-5599

Florida
Department of Natural Resources
MS 10, 3900 Commonwealth Blvd.
Tallahassee, FL 32399
904-488-7326

Georgia
Georgia Natural Resources Dept.
205 Butler St. SE, Ste. 1252
Atlanta, GA 30328
404-656-3214

Hawaii
Dept. of Land & Natural Resources
P.O. Box 621
Honolulu, HI 96809
808-587-0401

Idaho
Idaho Lands Dept.
1215 W. State St.
Boise, ID 83720
208-334-0200

Illinois
Illinois Dept. of Conservation
524 S. 2nd St.
Springfield, IL 62706
217-785-8287

Indiana
Div. of State Parks
402 W. Washington St.
Indianapolis, IN 46204
317-232-4124

Iowa
Iowa Natural Resources Dept.
Information and Education Bur.
Wallace State Office Bldg.
Des Moines, IA 50319
515-281-5973

Kansas
Kansas Wildlife and Parks Dept.
Landon State Office Bldg.
900 Jackson St., Ste. 502
Topeka, KS 66612
913-296-2281

Louisiana
Office of State Parks
P.O. Drawer 1111
Baton Rouge, LA 70821
504-925-3830

Maine
Dept. of Conservation
State House Station #22
Augusta, ME 04333
207-289-3821

Maryland
Dept. of Natural Resources
Tawes State Office Bldg.
Annapolis, MD 21401
301-768-0895

Massachusetts
Div. of Forests & Parks
100 Cambridge St.
Boston, MA 02202
617-727-3180

Michigan
Public Information Office
Michigan Dept. of Natural Resources
P.O. Box 30028
Lansing, MI 48909
517-373-1214

Minnesota
Bureau of Information
Minnesota Dept. of Natural Resources
350 Centennial Office Bldg.
St. Paul, MN 55101
612-296-3336

Mississippi
Bureau of Geology
Dept. of Map Sales
P.O. Box 5348
Jackson, MS 39216
601-354-6228

Missouri
Park, Recreation & Historical Preservation Div.
Missouri Dept. of Natural Resources
P.O. Box 176
Rolla, MO 65102
314-751-2479

Montana
Cartographic Bureau
Natural Resource & Conservation Dept.
1520 E. 6th Ave.
Butte, MT 59620
406-444-6739

Nebraska
Information & Education Div.
State Game & Parks Commission
P.O. Box 30370
Lincoln, NE 68503
402-471-5481

Nevada
Minerals Dept.
400 W. King St., Rm. 106
Carson City, NV 89710
702-687-5050

New Hampshire
Parks & Recreation Div.
Dept. of Resources & Economic Dev.
P.O. Box 856
Concord, NH 03301
603-271-2214

New Jersey
Dept. of Environmental Protection
Div. of Parks & Forestry
501 E. State St.
Trenton, NJ 08625
609-292-7794

New Mexico
New Mexico State Parks & Recreation Comm.
141 E. de Vargas, #35
Santa Fe, NM 87503
505-827-7465

New York
Lands & Forests Div.
Dept. of Environmental Conservation
50 Wolf Rd.
Albany, NY 12223
518-427-2475

North Carolina
Parks & Recreation Div.
Dept. of Environment, Health & Natural Resources
P.O. Box 27687
Raleigh, NC 27611
919-733-4181

North Dakota
North Dakota Parks & Recreation Dept.
1424 W. Century Ave.
209 E. Boulevard Ave.
Bismarck, ND 58501
701-224-4887

Ohio
Public Information & Education Office
Ohio Dept. of Natural Resources
Fountain Square
Columbus, OH 43224
614-265-6791

Oregon
Oregon Dept. of Geology & Mineral Industries
910 State Office Bldg.
Portland, OR 97201
503-229-5580

Pennsylvania
Dept. of Environmental Resources
P.O. Box 2063
Harrisburg, PA 17120
717-787-5338

Rhode Island
Rhode Island Dept. of Environmental Management
Div. of Parks & Recreation
Providence, RI 02903
401-277-2632

South Carolina
South Carolina Land Resources
Conservation Commission
2221 Devine St., Ste. 222
Columbia, SC 29205
803-734-9100

South Dakota
Parks & Recreation Div.
South Dakota Dept. of Game, Fish, & Parks
445 E. Capitol
Pierre, SD 57501
605-773-3392

Tennessee
Information Dept.
Dept. of Conservation
701 Broadway
Nashville, TN 37243
615-742-6738

Texas
Parks & Wildlife Dept.
4200 Smith School Rd.
Austin, TX 78744
512-389-4992

Utah
Div. of Parks & Recreation
1596 W. North Temple
Salt Lake City, UT 84116
801-533-6012

Vermont
Natural Resources Agency
103 S. Main St.
Waterbury, VT 05676
802-244-8711

Virginia
Virginia Resources Authority
909 E. Main St.
Richmond, VA 23219
804-644-3100

Washington
Dept. of Natural Resources
201 John A. Cherberg Bldg.
MSQW-21
Olympia, WA 98504
206-459-6372

West Virginia
Public Relations Office
Natural Resources Div.
Capitol Complex, Bldg. 3
Charleston, WV 25304
304-348-3381

AVIATION/AERONAUTICAL OFFICES

Alabama
Alabama Dept. of Air Transportation
4545 Hangar Ct.
Montgomery, AL 36108
205-242-4051

Alaska
International Airport System
P.O. Box 190649
Anchorage, AK 99519
907-266-2525

Arizona
Arizona Dept. of Transportation
Aeronautics Div.
1801 W. Jefferson
Phoenix, AZ 85007
602-255-7691

Arkansas
Arkansas Dept. of Aeronautics
1 Airport Rd., 3rd Fl.
Little Rock, AR 72202
501-376-6781

California
California Dept. of Transportation
Aeronautics Div.
1120 N St.
Sacramento, CA 95814
916-654-5627

Connecticut
Connecticut Dept. of Transportation
Bureau of Aviation and Ports
P.O. Drawer A
Wethersfield, CT 06109
203-566-4417

Delaware
Delaware Transportation Authority
Aeronautics Administration
P.O. Box 778
Transportation Bldg.
Dover, DE 19903
302-739-3264

Georgia
Georgia Transportation Dept.
Aeronautics Bur.
2 Capitol Sq.
Atlanta, GA 30334
404-986-1350

Idaho
Idaho Transportation Dept.
Aeronautics Bur.
Box 7129
Boise, ID 83707
208-334-8786

Illinois
Illinois Div. of Aeronautics
1 Langhorn Bond Dr.
Springfield, IL 62707
217-785-8515

Indiana
Indiana Transportation Dept.
Aeronautics Div.
100 N. Senate Ave.
Indianapolis, IN 46204
317-232-1477

Iowa
Iowa Transportation Dept.
Air and Transit Div.
800 Lincoln Way
Ames, IA 50313
515-287-2802

Kansas
Aviation Div.
Docking State Office Bldg.
Topeka, KS 66612
913-296-2553

Kentucky
Aeronautics Ofc.
State Office Bldg.
Frankfort, KY 40622
502-564-4780

Maine
Air Transportation Div.
Transportation Dept.
State House Station 16
Augusta, ME 04333
207-289-3185

Maryland
Maryland Aviation Admin.
P.O. Box 8766
BWI Airport
Baltimore, MD 21240
301-859-7060

Massachusetts
Massachusetts Aeronautics Commission
10 Park Plaza, Rm. 6620
Boston, MA 02116
617-973-7350

Michigan
Aeronautics Bureau
Michigan Transportation Dept.
Box 30050
Lansing, MI 48909
517-373-1834

Minnesota
Aeronautics Div.
Transportation Bldg., Rm. 417
John Ireland Blvd.
St. Paul, MN 55155
612-296-8046

Mississippi
Mississippi Aeronautics Commission
P.O. Box 5
Jackson, MS 39205
601-359-1270

Missouri
Aviation Div.
Missouri Highway & Transportation Dept.
P.O. Box 270
Jefferson City, MO 65102
314-751-2840

Montana
Montana Aeronautics Div.
Transportation Dept.
2701 Prospect Ave.
Helena, MT 59620
406-444-2506

Nebraska
Nebraska Dept. of Aeronautics
P.O. Box 82088
Lincoln, NE 68501
402-471-2371

New Hampshire
New Hampshire Aeronautics Commission
Concord Airport
Concord, NH 03301
603-271-2551

New Jersey
Aeronautics Div.
Dept. of Transportation
CN600, 1035 Parkway Ave.
Trenton, NJ 08625
609-530-2900

New Mexico
Aircraft Unit
New Mexico Highway & Transportation Dept.
P.O. Box 1149
Santa Fe, NM 87504
505-471-8919

New York
Aviation Div.
Dept. of Transportation
State Campus, Bldg. 5
Albany, NY 12232
518-457-2820

North Carolina
Aviation
Dept. of Transportation
P.O. Box 25201
Raleigh, NC 27611
919-787-9616

North Dakota
Aeronautics Commission
Box 5020
Bismarck, ND 58502
701-224-2748

Oklahoma
Oklahoma Aeronautics Commission
200 NE 21st St.
Oklahoma City, OK 73105
405-521-2377

Pennsylvania
Pennsylvania Bureau of Aviation
Transportation Dept.
1200 Transportation & Safety Bldg.
Harrisburg, PA 17120
717-783-2282

South Carolina
South Carolina Aeronautics Commission
P.O. Box 280068
Columbia, SC 29228
803-822-5400

Tennessee
Aeronautics Office
Dept. of Transportation
700 James K. Polk Bldg.
Nashville, TN 37243
615-741-3208

Texas
Aviation Dept.
Capitol Station
Box 12607
Austin, TX 78711
512-476-9262

Utah
Div. of Aeronautical Operations
Dept. of Transportation
4501 S. 2700 West
Salt Lake City, UT 84119
801-533-5057

Virginia
Aviation Dept.
Commonwealth of Virginia
4508 S. Laburnmer, Box 7716
Richmond, VA 23231
804-786-1364

Wyoming
Aeronautics Commission
State of Wyoming
Cheyenne, WY 82002
307-777-7481

GEOLOGICAL SURVEYS

Alabama
Geological Survey of Alabama
P.O. Box O
Tuscaloosa, AL 35486
205-349-2852

Alaska
Division of Geological and Geophysical Surveys
3700 Airport Way
Fairbanks, AK 99709
907-474-7147

Arkansas
Arkansas Geology Commission
3815 W. Roosevelt Rd.
Little Rock, AR 72204
501-371-1488

Colorado
Colorado Dept. of Natural Resources
Geological Survey Div.
1313 Sherman St., Rm. 718
Denver, CO 80203
303-866-2611

Delaware
Delaware Geological Survey
University of Delaware
DGS Bldg.
Newark, DE 19716
302-451-2833

Idaho
Idaho Geological Survey
Univ. of Idaho
332 Morrill Hall
Moscow, ID 83843
208-885-7991

Illinois
Illinois Geological Survey
615 E. Peabody Dr.
Champaign, IL 61820
217-333-4747

Indiana
Indiana Dept. of Natural Resources
Geological Survey Div.
611 N. Walnut Grove
Bloomington, IN 47405
812-855-9350

Iowa
Iowa Geological Survey Bureau
123 N. Capitol St.
Iowa City, IA 52242
319-335-1575

Kansas
Kansas Geological Survey
1930 Constant Ave.
Campus West
Topeka, KS 66047
913-864-3965

Kentucky
Kentucky Geological Survey
228 Mining and Resources Bldg.
University of Kentucky
Lexington, KY 40506
606-257-5863

Louisiana
Louisiana Geological Survey
Box G, University Station
Baton Rouge, LA 70893
504-388-5320

Maryland
Maryland Geological Survey
2300 St. Paul St.
Baltimore, MD 21218
301-554-5503

Michigan
Natural Resources Dept.
Geological Survey Div.
Box 30028
Lansing, MI 48909
517-334-6907

Minnesota
Minnesota Geological Survey
2642 University Ave.
St. Paul, MN 55114
612-627-4780

Missouri
Geological Survey
Geology & Land Survey Div.
P.O. Box 250
111 Fairgrounds Rd.
Rolla, MO 65401
314-364-1752

Ohio
Div. of Geological Survey
Ohio Dept. of Natural Resources
Fountain Square, Bldg. B
Columbus, OH 43224
614-265-6605

Pennsylvania
Pennsylvania Geologic Survey
P.O. Box 2357
Harrisburg, PA 17120
717-787-2169

South Dakota
Geological Survey Div.
Environment & Natural Resources Dept.
Joe Foss Bldg.
523 E. Capitol Ave.
Pierre, SD 57501
605-624-4471

Tennessee
Tennessee State Geologist
Conservation Dept.
701 Broadway
Nashville, TN 37243
615-742-6691

Utah
Geological & Mineral Survey Div.
606 Black Hawk Way
Salt Lake City, UT 84108
801-581-6831

Vermont
State Geologist Div.
Natural Resources Agency
103 S. Main St.
Waterbury, VT 05676
802-244-5164

West Virginia
West Virginia Geological & Economic Survey
P.O. Box 879
Morgantown, WV 26507
304-594-2331

Wisconsin
Wisconsin Geological Survey
University of Wisconsin
1815 University Ave.
Madison, WI 53705
608-263-7389

Wyoming
Geological Survey of Wyoming
Box 3008
University Station
Laramie, WY 82071
307-766-2286

Federal Map Agencies

AGRICULTURAL STABILIZATION AND CONSERVATION SERVICE (ASCS)

2222 W. 2300 S., P.O. Box 30010, Salt Lake City, UT 84130; 801-524-5856.

The U.S. Department of Agriculture's ASCS distributes aerial photographs produced by it and other branches of the USDA. Payment should be in the form of a money order or check, drawn from a U.S. or Canadian bank in U.S. dollars, made payable to ASCS.

ASCS's Aerial Photography Field Office will provide Photo Indexes ($5 each) of specific areas in aerial photographic form. Photo Indexes of Forest Service and Soil Conservation Service aerial photographs, as well as those by the ASCS, are available. A price list, order form, and descriptive pamphlet, "ASCS Aerial Photography," will be sent upon request.

ARMY CORPS OF ENGINEERS

Public Affairs, Army Corps of Engineers, Dept. of the Army, Dept. of Defense, 20 Massachusetts Ave. NW, Rm. 1101, Washington, DC 20314; 202-272-0011.

The corps produces and distributes inland waterway charts and maps of federal water-recreation lands within its regional districts. Write to the district nearest the areas for which you need maps. Some maps are free, while others are offered for a minimal fee. For a listing of Corps of Engineers districts and publications, write the Office of Public Affairs.

BUREAU OF THE CENSUS

Customer Services Branch, Data User Services, Bureau of the Census, Washington, DC 20233; 301-763-4100.

The Customer Services Branch will accept Visa, MasterCard, personal checks, and money orders made payable to the "Commerce/ Census" for census publications. A four-page "Geographic Products for the 1990 Decennial Census" that describes both hard copy and machine-readable products is available free upon request.

Certain census map products are available from the Government Printing Office (Superintendent of Documents, U.S. Government Printing Office, Washington, DC 20402; 202-783-3238), rather than from the Bureau of the Census, including the *Congressional District Atlas*. The free GPO subject index "Maps and Atlases" describes some Census Bureau products available from GPO.

BUREAU OF LAND MANAGEMENT

USGS is the distributor for BLM Surface Management and Minerals Management maps, published as 30-minute X 60-minute maps at a scale of 1:100,000 ($4). Map coverage is shown on the USGS "Index to Intermediate Scale Mapping," available from Map Distribution Centers in Denver, Colorado, and Fairbanks, Alaska, as well as from ESIC offices. Copies can be secured by mail from the Distribution Centers.

Plats of townships and mineral surveys are available for public distribution, as follows:

■ For Illinois, Indiana, Iowa, Kansas, Missouri, and Ohio, plats may be ordered from:

National Archives and Record Administration
Cartographic Archives Div.
Pennsylvania Ave. at 8th St. NW
Washington, DC 20408

■ For all other public-land states, plats may be ordered from:

Bureau of Land Management
Eastern States Office
350 S. Pickett St.
Alexandria, VA 22304

CENTRAL INTELLIGENCE AGENCY

CIA maps are available from several sources. The National Technical Information Service distributes most CIA maps published since 1980. Orders should be directed to:

National Technical Information Service (NTIS)
U.S. Dept. of Commerce
5285 Port Royal Rd.
Springfield, VA 22161
703-487-4650

Use the NTIS document number (PB number) when ordering. NTIS accepts personal checks and money orders drawn on U.S. or Canadian banks and made payable to NTIS.

Maps and other CIA publications produced before 1980 are available from:

Library of Congress
Photoduplication Service
Washington, DC 20504
202-707-5650

Staff in the Library's Geography and Map Division can help locate CIA maps in its collection.

A free catalog listing CIA maps and where to obtain them, "CIA Maps and Publications Released to the Public," is available from:

Central Intelligence Agency
Public Affairs Office
Washington, DC 20505
703-351-2053.

DEFENSE MAPPING AGENCY

DMA Combat Support Center, Attn.: PMSD16, Washington, DC 20315; 301-227-2495; 800-826-0342.

The Defense Mapping Agency is the central map-producing branch of the Department of Defense. Products may be purchased with a check or money order in U.S. dollars, drawn from a U.S. or Canadian bank and made payable to "Treasurer of the United States."

Catalogs of DMA products are available from the Combat Support Center or authorized DMA map dealers for $2.50 each. The "Department of Defense/Defense Mapping Agency Catalog of Maps, Charts and Related Products" is divided into the following public sales catalogs: *Aerospace Products* (free; CATP6V03); *Hydrographic Products* (CATP2V01 uniform, $10.50); and *Topographic Products* (free; CATP6V01). Product prices and listings of authorized DMA map dealers are listed in the catalogs.

EARTH SCIENCE INFORMATION OFFICE

The Earth Science Information Office operates a nationwide information and sales service for the results of Earth science research, maps, and related products and publications. A network of Earth Science Information Centers (ESIC) provides information on geologic, hydrologic, topographic, and land-use maps, books, and reports; aerial, satellite, and radar images and related products; Earth science and map data in digital form and related applications software; and geodetic data. ESIC offices can take orders for such customized products as digital cartographic data, and geographic names gazeteers.

ESIC OFFICES

Alaska
4230 University Dr., Rm. 101
Anchorage, AK 99508
907-786-7011

Rm. G-84
605 W. 4th Ave.
Anchorage, AK 99501
907-271-2754

California
Federal Bldg., Rm. 7638
300 N. Los Angeles St.
Los Angeles, CA 90012
213-894-2850

Bldg. 3, Rm. 3128 (MS 532)
345 Middlefield Rd.
Menlo Park, CA 94025
415-329-4309

504 Custom House
555 Battery St.
San Francisco, CA 94111
415-705-1010

Colorado
169 Federal Bldg.
1961 Stout St.
Denver, CO 80294
303-844-4169

Box 25046 (MS 504)
Denver Federal Center
Denver, CO 80225
303-236-5829

District of Columbia
Dept. of the Interior Bldg., Rm. 2650
1849 C St. NW
Washington, DC 20240
202-208-4047

Mississippi
Bldg. 3101
Stennis Space Center
Bay St. Louis, MS 39529
601-688-3544

Missouri
1400 Independence Rd. (MS 231)
Rolla, MO 65401
314-341-0851

South Dakota
EROS Data Center
Sioux Falls, SD 57198
605-594-6151

Utah
8105 Federal Bldg.
125 S. State St.
Salt Lake City, UT 84138
801-524-5652

Virginia
507 National Center, Rm. 1C402
12201 Sunrise Valley Dr.
Reston, VA 22092
703-648-6045

Washington
678 U.S. Courthouse
W. 920 Riverside Ave.
Spokane, WA 99201
509-353-2524

ESIC STATE AFFILIATES

Alabama
Geological Survey of Alabama
420 Hackberry Ln.
P.O. Box O, Univ. Station
Tuscaloosa, AL 35486
205-349-2852

Alaska
Geophysical Institute
Univ. of Alaska-Fairbanks
Fairbanks, AK 99775
907-474-7487

Arizona
Arizona State Land Dept., Resource Analysis Div.
1616 W. Adams
Phoenix, AZ 85007
602-542-4061

Arkansas
Arkansas Geological Commission
Vardelle Parham Geology Center
3815 W. Roosevelt Rd.
Little Rock, AR 72204
501-371-1488

California
California Dept. of Conservation
Div. of Mines and Geology, Info. Office
660 Bercut Dr.
Sacramento, CA 95814
916-324-7380

San Diego State University
Library, Map Collection
San Diego, CA 92812
619-594-5650

Map and Imagery Laboratory
Library, University of California
Santa Barbara, CA 93106
805-893-2779

Connecticut
Natural Resources Center
Dept. of Environmental Protection
165 Capitol Ave.
State Office Bldg., Rm. 553
Hartford, CT 06106
203-566-3540

University of Connecticut
Map Library, Level 4
Storrs, CT 06268
203-486-4589

Delaware
Delaware Geological Survey
Cartographic Information Center
University of Delaware
101 Penny Hall
Newark, DE 19716
302-451-8262

Florida
Florida Resources and Environmental Analysis
  Center
361 Bellamy Bldg.
Florida State University
Tallahassee, FL 32306
904-644-2883

Georgia
Office of Research and Information
Dept. of Community Affairs
1200 Equitable Bldg.
100 Peachtree St.
Atlanta, GA 30303
404-656-5526

Hawaii
Dept. of Business and Economic Development
Kamamalu Bldg.
P.O. Box 2359
Honolulu, HI 96804
808-548-3047

University of Hawaii at Manoa
Thomas Hale Hamilton Library
2550 The Mall
Honolulu, HI 96822
808-956-6199

Idaho
Idaho State Historical Library
610 N. Julia Davis Dr.
Boise, ID 83702
208-334-3356

University of Idaho Library
Map Collection
Moscow, ID 83843
208-885-6344

Illinois
University of Illinois, Urbana-Champaign
Map and Geography Library
1408 W. Gregory Dr.
Urbana, IL 61801
217-333-0827

Illinois State Geological Survey
615 E. Peabody Dr.
Champaign, IL 61820
217-244-0933

Indiana
Purdue University
Entomology Bldg., Rm. 214
West Lafayette, IN 47907
317-494-6305

Iowa
Iowa Geological Survey
123 N. Capitol St.
Iowa City, IA 52242
319-335-1575

Kansas
Kansas Geological Survey
University of Kansas
1930 Constant Ave., Campus West
Lawrence, KS 66046
913-864-3965

Kansas Applied Remote Sensing Program
Space Technology Center
University of Kansas
2291 Irving Hill Dr.
Lawrence, KS 66045
913-864-7720

Kentucky
Kentucky Geological Survey
228 Mining & Mineral Resources Bldg.
University of Kentucky
Lexington, KY 40506
606-257-5500

Louisiana
Office of Public Works
Dept. of Transportation and Development
P.O. Box 94245 Capitol Station
Baton Rouge, LA 70804
504-379-1473

Maine
Maine Geological Survey
State House Station, #22
Augusta, ME 04333
207-289-2801

University of Maine
College of Forest Resources
The Map Store
130 Nutting Hall
Orono, ME 04469
207-581-6277

Maryland
Maryland Geological Survey
2300 St. Paul St.
Baltimore, MD 21218
301-554-5524

Massachusetts
University of Massachusetts
Cartographic Information Research Services
102D Hasbrouck Laboratory
Amherst, MA 01003
413-545-0359

Michigan
Land and Water Management
Michigan Dept. of Natural Resources
Steven T. Mason Bldg., Box 30028
Lansing, MI 48909
517-373-9123

Minnesota
Minnesota State Planning Agency
Land Management Information Center
300 Centennial Office Bldg.
658 Cedar St.
St. Paul, MN 55155
612-297-2490

University of Minnesota
S76 Wilson Library
John R. Borchert Map Library
Minneapolis, MN 55455
612-624-4549

Mississippi
Mississippi Institutions of Higher Learning
MARIS
3825 Ridgewood Rd.
Jackson, MS 39211
601-982-6354

Missouri
Missouri Dept. of Natural Resources
Div. of Geology and Land Survey
P.O. Box 250
Rolla, MO 65401
314-364-1752

Montana
Montana Bureau of Mines and Geology
Montana Tech
Main Hall, Rm. 200
Butte, MT 59701
406-496-4167

Nebraska
Conservation and Survey Div.
University of Nebraska-Lincoln
901 N. 17th St.
Lincoln, NE 68508
402-472-2567

Nevada
Government Documents Dept. Library
Univ. of Nevada-Las Vegas
4505 Maryland Pkwy.
Las Vegas, NV 89154
702-739-3409

Nevada Bureau of Mines and Geology
University of Nevada-Reno, MS 178
Reno, NV 89557
702-784-6691

New Hampshire
Documents Dept.
Dimond Library
University of New Hampshire
Durham, NH 03824
603-862-1777

New Jersey
Dept. of Environmental Protection
New Jersey Geological Survey
CN-029
Trenton, NJ 08625
609-292-2576

New Mexico
University of New Mexico
Technology Applications Center
2808 Central Ave., SE
Albuquerque, NM 87131
505-277-3622

New York
Map Information Unit
New York Dept. of Transportation
Albany, NY 12232
518-457-3555

North Carolina
North Carolina Geological Survey
Dept. of Environment, Health & Natural Resources
P.O. Box 27687
Raleigh, NC 27611
919-733-2423

North Carolina Geological Survey
Dept. of Environment, Health & Natural Resources
59 Woodfin Pl.
Asheville, NC 28801
704-251-6208

North Dakota
North Dakota Geological Survey
600 East Boulevard Ave.
Bismark, ND 58505
701-224-4109

Ohio
Ohio Dept. of Natural Resources
Div. of Soil and Water Conservation
Remote Sensing Section - ESIC
Fountain Square, Bldg. E2
Columbus, OH 43224
614-265-6770

Oklahoma
Geology Library
University of Oklahoma
100 East Boyd, Rm. R-220
Norman, OK 73019
405-325-3031

Oregon
Oregon State Library
State Library Bldg.
Salem, OR 97301
503-378-4368

University of Oregon Library
Map Library
165 Condon Hall
Eugene, OR 97403
503-346-3051

Dept. of Geology and Mineral Industries (DOGAMI)
1400 S.W. 5th Ave.
State Office Bldg., Rm. 910
Portland, OR 97201
503-229-5580

Pennsylvania
Dept. of Environmental Resources
Bureau of Topographic and Geological Survey
P.O. Box 2357
Harrisburg, PA 17120
717-787-2169

South Carolina
South Carolina Land Resources Conservation
    Commission
2221 Devine St., Ste. 222
Columbia, SC 29205
803-734-9100

South Dakota
South Dakota Geological Survey
Science Center
University of South Dakota
Vermillion, SD 57069
605-677-5227

Tennessee
Map Library
Rm. 15 Hoskins
The University of Tennessee
Knoxville, TN 37997
615-974-4315

Texas
Texas Natural Resources Information System
P.O. Box 13231
Austin, TX 78711
512-463-8406

Utah
Utah Geological and Mineral Survey
606 Black Hawk Way
Research Park
Salt Lake City, UT 84108
801-581-6831

Vermont
University of Vermont
Documents/Map Dept.
Bailey/Howe Library
Burlington, VT 05405
802-656-2503

Virginia
Dept. of Mines, Minerals and Energy
Div. of Mineral Resources
Natural Resources Bldg.
Box 3667
Charlottesville, VA 22903
804-293-5121

Washington
Washington State Library
Information Services Div.
Olympia, WA 98504
206-753-4027

University of Washington
Map Collection & Cartographic Information Center
University of Washington-Libraries
FM-25
Seattle, WA 98195
206-543-9392

West Virginia
West Virginia Geological and Economic Survey
West Virginia Cartographic Center
Box 879
Morgantown, WV 26507
304-594-2331

Wisconsin
State Cartographer's Office
155 Science Hall
550 N. Park St.
Madison, WI 53706
608-262-6850

Wyoming
State Engineer
Herschler Bldg.
Cheyenne, WY 82002
307-777-7354

EROS Data Center

User Services Section, EROS Data Center, U.S. Geological Survey, Sioux Falls, SD 57198; 605-594-6151.

EROS is the clearinghouse for aerial photographs and satellite and space imagery created by the federal government. EROS (like all USGS branches) accepts checks or money orders in U.S. dollars made payable to the Department of the Interior/USGS, for the exact amount of the order. Order forms for products can be obtained from either EROS or the Earth Science Information Center (507 National Center, 12201 Sunrise Valley Dr., Reston, VA 22092; 703-648-6045) and affiliated offices (see ESIC listing for addresses).

Order forms are available for "Aerial Mapping Photography," "NASA Aircraft Photography," "Inquiry for Geographic Search for Aircraft Data," "NHAP: National High Altitude Photography Program/NAPP: National Aerial Photography Program," "Land Satellite Images," "Manned Spacecraft Photographs & Major Metropolitan Area Photographs and Images," "Understanding Color-Infrared Photographs and False Color Composites," and "Catalog of Cartographic Data." EROS will supply price lists upon request and USGS produces a series of free pamphlets that explain products and ordering procedures. Pamphlet titles include "How to Order Landsat Images," "Looking for an Old Aerial Photograph," "EROS: A Space Program for Earth Resources," "The Aerial Photography Summary Record System," "Manned Spacecraft Photographs & Major Metropolitan Area Photographs and Images," "Understanding Color-Infrared Photographs and False Color Composites," "Catalog of Cartographic Data," and "How to Obtain Aerial Photographs."

Federal Emergency Management Agency

Attn.: Publications, 500 C St. SW, Washington, DC 20472; 202-646-4600.

FEMA runs the National Flood Insurance program, which creates and distributes "Flood Hazard Boundary Maps" and "Flood Insurance Rate Maps." A free "Guide to Flood Insurance Rate Maps" is available by writing to FEMA

Publications at the above address; maps may be ordered by calling 800-333-1363.

FEDERAL ENERGY REGULATORY COMMISSION

Div. of Public Affairs, Federal Energy Regulatory Commission, 825 N. Capitol St. NE, Washington, DC 20426; 202-208-0055.

FERC produces an energy map relating to interstate gas pipelines. The map is available from GPO and the FERC Public Reference Branch. The map is in the free index, "Maps and Atlases," available at GPO bookstores.

FISH AND WILDLIFE SERVICE

Div. of Realty, Fish and Wildlife Service, Washington, DC 20240; 703-358-1713.

The Fish and Wildlife Service provides free maps and brochures for its protected lands. There is no catalog, but the maps can be obtained either at the sites themselves or from the Division of Realty. Address lists of FWS hatcheries can be obtained free from the Division of Hatcheries, and lists of refuges can be obtained free from the Division of Refuges, both located at the above address. Information about FWS's "National Wetlands Inventory" can be obtained from FWS offices; maps produced as part of NWI are available through USGS ESIC offices. Information on ordering NWI maps may be obtained by calling 800-USA-MAPS (in Virginia, 703-648-6045).

GOVERNMENT PRINTING OFFICE

Superintendent of Documents, U.S. Government Printing Office, Washington, DC 20402; 202-275-3050.

GPO accepts Visa, MasterCard, and money orders or personal checks in U.S. dollars drawn on U.S. and Canadian banks and made payable to the "Superintendent of Documents." Mail orders should be placed by writing Superintendent of Documents, P.O. Box 371954, Pitts-

burgh, PA 15250; phone orders may be placed by calling 202-783-3238 between 8 a.m. and 4 p.m. Eastern time, while fax orders may be placed 24 hours a day, seven days a week, by calling 202-275-2529 for publications and 202-275-0019 for subscriptions. There are more than 100 free subject indexes available at most GPO stores, listing products by category, including "Maps and Atlases"; other subject indexes cover areas such as "Farms and Farming," "Oceanography," and "Public and Private Utilities." A free catalog, "U.S. Government Books," lists numerous GPO books, including atlases and other map-filled volumes. Although few GPO bookstores carry the full catalog of available maps, most have certain Census Bureau and CIA maps in stock. There are GPO bookstores around the country:

Alabama
O'Neill Bldg.
2021 Third Ave., North
Birmingham, AL 35203
205-731-1056
205-731-3444 (FAX)

California
ARCO Plaza, C-Level
505 S. Flower St.
Los Angeles, CA 90071
213-239-9844
213-239-9848 (FAX)

Rm. 1023, Federal Bldg.
450 Golden Gate Ave.
San Francisco, CA 94102
415-252-5334
415-252-5339 (FAX)

Colorado
Rm. 117, Federal Bldg.
1961 Stout St.
Denver, CO 80294
303-844-3964
303-844-4000 (FAX)

Worth Savings Bldg.
720 N. Main St.
Pueblo, CO 81003
719-544-3142
719-544-6719 (FAX)

District of Columbia
U.S. Government Printing Office
710 N. Capitol St. NW
Washington, DC 20401
202-512-0133

1510 H St. NW
Washington, DC 20005
202-653-5075
202-376-5055 (FAX)

Florida
Rm. 158, Federal Bldg.
400 W. Bay St.
Jacksonville, FL 32202
904-353-0569
904-353-1280 (FAX)

Georgia
Rm. 100, Federal Bldg.
275 Peachtree St. NE
Atlanta, GA 30303
404-331-6947
404-331-1787 (FAX)

Illinois
Rm. 1365, Federal Bldg.
219 S. Dearborn St.
Chicago, IL 60604
312-353-5133
312-353-1590 (FAX)

Maryland
Warehouse Sales Outlet
8660 Cherry Ln.
Laurel, MD 20707
301-953-7974
301-498-9107 (FAX)

Massachusetts
Thomas P. O'Neill Bldg.
Rm. 179
10 Causeway St.
Boston, MA 02222
617-720-4180
617-720-5753 (FAX)

Michigan
Ste. 160, Federal Bldg.
477 Michigan Ave.
Detroit, MI 48226
313-226-7816
313-226-4698 (FAX)

Missouri
12 Bannister Mall
5600 E. Bannister Rd.
Kansas City, MO 64137
816-765-2256
816-767-8233 (FAX)

New York
Rm. 110
26 Federal Plaza
New York, NY 10278
212-264-3825
212-264-9318 (FAX)

Ohio
Rm. 1365, Federal Bldg.
1240 E. 9th St.
Cleveland, OH 44199
216-522-4922
216-522-4714 (FAX)

Rm. 207, Federal Bldg.
200 N. High St.
Columbus, OH 43215
614-469-6956
614-469-5374 (FAX)

Oregon
1305 SW First Ave.
Portland, OR 97201
503-221-6217
503-225-0563 (FAX)

Pennsylvania
Robert Morris Bldg.
100 N. 17th St.
Philadelphia, PA 19103
215-597-0677
215-597-4548 (FAX)

Rm. 118, Federal Bldg.
1000 Liberty Ave.
Pittsburgh, PA 15222
412-644-2721
412-644-4547 (FAX)

Texas
Rm. 1C46, Federal Bldg.
1100 Commerce St.
Dallas, TX 75242
214-767-0076
214-767-3239 (FAX)

Ste. 120, Texas Crude Bldg.
801 Travis St.
Houston, TX 77002
713-228-1187
713-228-1186 (FAX)

Washington
Rm. 194, Federal Bldg.
915 Second Ave.
Seattle, WA 98174
206-553-4271
206-553-6717 (FAX)

Wisconsin
Rm. 190, Federal Bldg.
517 E. Wisconsin Ave.
Milwaukee, WI 53202
414-297-1304
414-297-1300 (FAX)

INTERNATIONAL BOUNDARY AND WATER COMMISSION, U.S. AND MEXICO

The Commons, Bldg. C, Ste. 310, 4171 N. Mesa, El Paso, TX 79902; 915-534-6700.

The International Boundary and Water Commission produces several maps of the region in and around the United States-Mexico border. Map prices vary; a complete listing of maps available to the public will be sent upon request.

INTERNATIONAL BOUNDARY COMMISSION, U.S. AND CANADA

1250 23rd St. NW, Ste. 405, Washington, DC 20037; 202-736-9100.

IBC sells maps of the U.S.-Canadian borders for $3 each. A listing that details available maps will be sent upon request.

LIBRARY OF CONGRESS

Geography and Map Div., Library of Congress, Washington, DC 20540; 202-707-6277.

The Geography and Map Division's Reading Room (located in the James Madison Memorial Building, Rm. LM-B01, 101 Independence Ave. SE, Washington, DC 20540) is open to the general public. Maps may not be taken from the room, but reproduction services are available. Two free pamphlets, available in the Reading Room or through the mail, "Geography and Map Division, Library of Congress," and "Publications of the Geography and Map Division," provide information about the division, and its services and products.

Complete price and reproduction information can be obtained from the Library's Photoduplication Service (202-707-5640) at the above address.

NATIONAL AERONAUTIC AND SPACE ADMINISTRATION

NASA aircraft photography is available from the EROS Data Center (User Services Section, U.S. Geological Survey, Sioux Falls, SD 57198; 605-594-6151). NASA space imagery is distributed through Bara-King Photographic Inc., 4805 Frolich Ln., Hyattsville, MD 20781; 301-322-7900.

A complete price list and information on ordering available NASA space imagery can be obtained from Bara-King Photographic Inc. or NASA's Audiovisual Department (National Aeronautics & Space Admin., Rm. 6035, 400 Maryland Ave. SW, Washington, DC 20546; 202-453-8375).

NATIONAL ARCHIVES CARTOGRAPHIC AND ARCHITECTURAL BRANCH

Washington, DC 20408; 703-756-6700.

You must have a researcher's card to use the Archives, which can be obtained at the front desk of the Archives map headquarters (located at 841 S. Pickett St., Alexandria, VA 22304) to use the reading room of the Archives Cartographic and Architectural collection. A price list for reproduction services is available upon request, or can be quoted over the telephone. (Photocopy facilities are located on the premises; higher-quality reproduction work generally takes six to eight weeks.) It helps to know the file number of the maps you need reproduced, but the staff can sometimes help locate this information. Free inventories and catalogs of various parts of the Archives collection are listed in the free pamphlet "Cartographic and Architectural Branch," available both at the branch location and from the above mailing address. Among the inventories available are "Cartographic Records of the Bureau of the Census," "Cartographic Records of the Forest Service," and "Cartographic Records of the United States Marine Corps."

NATIONAL CLIMATIC DATA CENTER

Federal Bldg., Asheville, NC 28801; 704-259-0682.

The National Climatic Data Center, part of the National Oceanic and Atmospheric Administration, has a Historical Climatology Series that includes several long-term weather records, maps, and atlases. A free catalog of the series, as well as a price list, are available upon request. Payment can be made with American Express, Visa, and MasterCard, or check and money order drawn on U.S. funds and made payable to "Commerce-NOAA-NCDC."

NATIONAL GEOPHYSICAL DATA CENTER

Code E/GC4, Dept. ORD, 325 Broadway, Boulder, CO 80303; 303-497-6423.

The National Geophysical Data Center, part of the National Oceanic and Atmospheric Administration, compiles data on various seismic and natural resource subjects for domestic and foreign areas. Many maps are produced from this data; a publications catalog is available. Prepayment is required on all nonfederal orders; make checks and money orders payable to "Commerce/NOAA/NGDC." NGDC accepts payments made with American Express, MasterCard, and Visa. A $10 handling fee is charged for each order; there is an additional $10 charge for non-U.S. orders.

NATIONAL OCEAN SERVICE

Distribution Branch, N/CG33, National Ocean Service, Riverdale, MD 20737; 301-436-6990.

NOS, a branch of the National Oceanic and Atmospheric Administration, distributes nautical and aeronautical charts of the U.S. created by NOAA. The products may be purchased with Visa and MasterCard or with a check or money order made payable to "NOS, Department of Commerce." Five catalogs of available nautical charts and tables—"Atlantic and Gulf Coasts," "Pacific Coast," "Alaska," "Great Lakes," and "Bathymetric and Fishing Maps"—are free upon request, as is the "Catalog of Aeronautical Charts and Related Publications."

Maps and charts can also be purchased from:

National Ocean Service
Counter Sales
6501 Lafayette Ave.
Riverdale, MD 20737
301-436-6990

FAX orders may be placed by calling 3-1-436-6829. National Ocean Service maps can also be obtained at hundreds of authorized dealers around the country (most are map, sports equipment, boating and tackle, and aviation equipment stores). The dealers are listed in the free catalogs.

Nautical and aeronautical maps of foreign countries are distributed through the Defense Mapping Agency.

NATIONAL PARK SERVICE

Office of Public Inquiries, National Park Service, Rm. 1013, Washington, DC 20240; 202-208-4747.

The National Park Service supplies the visitor-information centers of its national parks, forests, seashores, and historical sites with maps and information folders, most of which are free to the public. The maps and folders can also be obtained through the Office of Public Inquiries. The Government Printing Office is the distributor for all Park Service publications, including booklets or studies of parks and historic sites, many of which also contain maps and guides.

Tennessee Valley Authority

Maps and Surveys Branch, Map Information and Records Unit, 100 Haney Bldg., Chattanooga, TN 37401; 615-751-6277.

TVA produces a wide variety of maps related to its region. Maps may be purchased with a check or money order in U.S. dollars, drawn on a U.S. or Canadian account, and made payable to the Tennessee Valley Authority.

A "TVA Maps Price Catalog," as well as indexes of TVA nautical and topographic maps, will be sent free upon request. More information on TVA's mapping program can be obtained by writing to the above address.

U.S. Forest Service

Public Affairs Office, U.S. Forest Service, 2nd Fl., Auditors Bldg., 14th & Independence Ave. SW, Washington, DC 20250; 202-205-1760.

There are maps available for each of the U.S. Forest Service's 155 National Forests. They are available either at each forest visitor center or from regional offices of the Forest Service. Most maps cost from $1.00 to $3.50 and may be purchased with checks or money orders drawn on U.S. dollars and made payable to USFS. A national map with an address list of National Forests will be sent free upon request.

U.S. Geological Survey

USGS Map Sales, Box 25286, Denver, CO 80225; 303-236-7477.

USGS accepts money orders and personal checks made payable to the "Department of the Interior-USGS." State-by-state indexes of topographic, geologic, and general maps, as well as listings of maps by category (land use, *National Atlas*, etc.); indexes by map scale; price lists; and order forms are available free upon request from either the map distribution center or from regional Earth Science Information Centers. Call 800-USA-MAPS to receive an order form and current list of USGS maps.

Alaska residents may purchase geologic, hydrologic, and topographic maps of Alaska from USGS Map Sales-Alaska, 101 12th Ave., Fairbanks, AK 99701; 907-456-7535.

EROS Data Center is the USGS distributor of images produced from Landsat imagery, aerial photographs and photomaps. Hundreds of map and travel stores, as well as state offices, are authorized dealers of USGS products. Names and addresses of USGS map dealers are listed on the state indexes already mentioned. The maps may also be purchased over the counter at the USGS's Reston, Va., location.

APPENDIX C
Selected Map Stores

The list of map stores is constantly growing. The **International Map Dealers Association**, a trade association for retail map dealers, distributors, and manufacturers of maps and related products, can provide names and addresses of map dealers in your area. IMDA is located at P.O. Box 1789, Kankakee, IL 60901; 815-939-4627.

Alabama
Carto-Craft Maps, Inc.
738 Shades Mountain Plaza
Birmingham, AL 35226
205-822-2103

Re-Print Corp.
2025 First Ave. N.
Birmingham, AL 32202
205-251-9171

Alaska
The Maps Place
3545 Artic Blvd., Olympic Center
Anchorage, AK 99503
907-562-6277

Arizona
Arizona Hiking Shack
11645 N. Cave Creek Rd.
Phoenix, AZ 85020
602-943-2722

Desert Mountain Sports
2824 E. Indian School Rd. #4
Phoenix, AZ 85016
602-955-2875

Earth Tracks Recreational Maps
3644 E. McDowell Rd.
Phoenix, AZ 85008
602-224-9578

Tucson Map & Flag Center
2590 N. First Ave.
Tucson, AZ 85719
602-623-1104; 800-473-1204; FAX 602-798-1641

Wide World of Maps
2626 W. Indian School Rd.
Phoenix, AZ 85017
602-279-2323; FAX 602-279-2350

Wide World of Maps
1526 N. Scottsdale Rd.
Tempe, AZ 85281
602-949-1012; FAX 602-279-2350

Wide World of Maps
1440 S. Country Club Dr.
Mesa, AZ 85210
602-844-1134

Arkansas
AAA Map Company
3520 W. 69th St., Ste. 106
Little Rock, AR 72209
501-562-6219

Accurate Mapping Company
903-A W. Johnson Ave., P.O. Box 1729
Springdale, AR 72765
501-751-1402

Shepherd's, Inc.
603 W. Markham St.
Little Rock, AR 72205
501-375-6937

California
Allied Services
966 N. Main St.
Orange, CA 92667
714-532-4300

A.L.S. Maps
610 N. Azusa Ave.
West Covina, CA 91791
818-915-5165

Bookends Bookstore
1014 Coombs St.
Napa, CA 94559
707-224-7455

Bucksport Sporting Goods
3650 Broadway
Eureka, CA 95501
707-442-1832

Cal-Gold
2569 E. Colorado Blvd.
Pasadena, CA 91107
818-792-6161; FAX 818-792-1226

California Map & Travel Center
3211 Pico Blvd.
Santa Monica, CA 90405
310-829-6277; FAX 310-829-2316

California Survey & Drafting Supply
4733 Auburn Blvd.
Sacramento, CA 95841
916-344-0232; FAX 916-344-2998

Compass Maps
1172 Kansas Ave.
Modesto, CA 95351
209-529-5017

Dustbooks and Fulton's Bookstore
P.O. Box 100
Paradise, CA 95967
916-877-6110; 800-477-6110; FAX 916-877-0222

Easy Going Travel
1385 Shattuck Ave.
Berkeley, CA 94709
510-843-3533; 800-233-3533

Geographia
4000 Riverside Dr.
Burbank, CA 91505
818-848-1414

Geographic Maps & Travel Books
4000 Riverside Dr.
Burbank, CA 91505
818-848-1414

Global Graphics
2819 Greentop St.
Lakewood, CA 90712
310-429-8880

Global Map Store
735 N. Fulton
Fresno, CA 93728
209-266-9831

The Map Center
2440 Bancroft Way
Berkeley, CA 94704
510-843-8080

Map Centre
2611 University Ave.
San Diego, CA 92104
619-291-3830

Map Link
25 E. Mason St.
Santa Barbara, CA 93101
805-965-4402; FAX 805-962-0884

Map Shop
12112 W. Washington Blvd.
Los Angeles, CA 90066
310-391-1848

MAPS etc.
21919 Sherman Way
Canoga Park, CA 91303
818-347-9160

Maps & Travel
112 S. El Camino Real
Encinitas, CA 92024
619-942-9642

Maps Unlimited
2005 Crow Canyon Pl #138
San Ramon, CA 94583
415-277-1885; FAX 415-277-9611

Mountain Sports
176 E. 3rd St.
Chico, CA 95928
916-345-5011

Natural Wonders
30031 Ahern St.
Union City, CA 94587
510-429-9900; FAX 510-429-8428

Pacific Coast Map Service
12021 Long Beach Blvd.
Lynwood, CA 90262
213-636-6657

Pasadena Map Co.
1778 E. Colorado Blvd.
Pasadena, CA 91106
818-795-3626

Rand McNally Retail Store
595 Market St.
San Francisco, CA 94105
415-777-3131

Thomas Bros. Map Store
603 W. 7th St.
Los Angeles, CA 90017
213-627-4018

Thomas Bros. Map Store
550 Jackson St.
San Francisco, CA 94133
415-981-7520

Travel Gallery
1007 Manhattan Ave.
Manhattan Beach, CA 90266
310-379-9199

Maps by Mail

Here are six one-stop-shopping sources for both foreign and domestic maps of all types. Each of the companies offers mail-order services. Contact each to obtain a current catalog and ordering information.

Access Maps & Gear (321 S. Guadalupe, #M3, Santa Fe, NM 87501; 505-982-3330) offers "The Catalog for Map Lovers" featuring a diverse but select line of unique maps and related products from around the world. Products include travel maps and guides, astronomical charts, globes, map display and storage items, map wraps and stationery, tools for map use, map clothing, puzzles, and games. Access seeks out innovative and hard-to-find gear. Mail and phone orders are welcome. The Access Map & Gear catalog is free.

Forsyth Travel Library (9154 W. 57th St., P.O. Box 2975, Shawnee Mission, KS 66201; 913-384-3440) is a specialist in travel books and maps, offering mail-order service as

well as a warehouse open to the public. Forsyth Travel Library carries a wide range of guidebooks and maps for travel destinations all over the world.

Geoscience Resources (2990 Anthony Rd., P.O. Box 2096, Burlington, NC 27216; 919-227-8300; 800-742-2677) distributes thousands of maps from more than 80 foreign map companies and more than 75 foreign government surveys. Well-known maps, such as Kümmerly & Frey and Recta Foldex, are represented by Geoscience Resources, as well as maps from smaller publishers, such as the Automóvil Club of Argentina and P.T. Pembina of Indonesia. City maps, road maps, topographic maps, and recreation maps are among the offerings.

ITMB Publishing Ltd. (736A Granville St., Vancouver, BC, Canada V6Z 1G3; 604-687-3320) distributes more than 50 cartographic publishers worldwide, from the U.S.'s Rand McNally and Prentice Hall to Chile's

Travel Market
130 Pacific Avenue Mall
San Francisco, CA 94111
415-421-4080

Traveller's Bookcase
8375 W. 3rd St.
Los Angeles, CA 90048
213-655-0575

USA Maps
2974 First St., Ste. 1
La Verne, CA 91750
714-593-3601

Westwind & Mountain Bookshop
17247 Mt. Everest Ct.
Sonora, CA 95370
209-532-6117

Word Journeys
667 San Rodolfo Dr., Ste. 131
Solana Beach, CA 92075
619-481-4158

World of Maps
607 Mission Ave.
Oceanside, CA 92049
619-967-7141

Colorado
Boulder Map Gallery
1708 13th St.
Boulder, CO 80302
303-444-1406

Chinook Bookshop Inc.
210 N. Tejon St.
Colorado Springs, CO 80903
719-635-1195

Motouiti to Germany's Falk Verlag to Iran's Sahab Publishing. ITMB carries a wide range of tourist maps and road atlases for countries, regions, cities, and towns in virtually every area of the world. ITMB also distributes guidebooks from nearly 40 international publishers, including many small publishing houses, such as Corax Press (Canada), Inca Press (U.S.), Progress Press (U.S.S.R.), and TT Publications (India). ITMB offers a selection of more than 200 guidebooks, from general guides to more specialized hiking guides, nature guides, ethnology guides, architecture guides, and boating guides, for travel destinations in Asia, Africa, Europe, the Pacific and the Americas.

Map Link (25 E. Main St., Santa Barbara, CA 93101; 805-965-4402) is a map wholesaler and retailer, stocking more than 85,000 titles representing every region of the world. It distributes topographic, city, regional, and wall maps. Map Link is a good resource for otherwise hard-to-find maps. A catalog is available upon request. Map Link has also compiled *The World Map*

Directory, a guide to its extensive map inventory ($29.95). Map Link can provide a list of local map stores that distribute their maps and can also help in finding appropriate map collections.

The Map Store (5821 Karric Sq. Dr., Dublin, OH 43017; 800-332-7885) carries maps from more than 100 U.S. publishers and imports maps from 75 foreign publishers, and boasts of one of the largest selections of U.S. maps in the country. Its computerized data base contains detailed listings of nearly every U.S. map in print, including measurements, coverage, scale, format, and other data. All of this has been compiled into its U.S. *Map Directory* ($49.95).

McCarthy Geographic (404 Bloomfield, Montclair, NJ 07042; 201-316-5494) specializes in business-related products, although its product line includes a few less-than-serious items, too. Among products featured in McCarthy's catalog are maps for sales analysis and market planning, business travel maps and road atlases, and zip code maps.

Crossroads Map Co.
2717 E. Louisiana Ave.
Denver, CO 80210
303-733-2131

International Map Service
12211 W. Alameda Pkwy.
Lakewood, CO 80228
303-987-2747

Mac Van Productions, Inc.
308J S. 8th St., Ste. J
Colorado Springs, CO 80905
719-633-5757

Maps Unlimited
899 Broadway
Denver, CO 80203
303-623-4299

Mountain Maps
7595 W. Hwy. 50, P.O. Box 387
Salida, CO 81201
719-539-4334

Pierson Graphics
899 Broadway
Denver, CO 80203
303-623-4299

Tattered Cover Bookstore
1536 Wynkoop
Denver, CO 80202
303-322-7727; FAX 303-399-2279

Wilderness Society
7475 Dakin St.
Denver, CO 80221
303-650-5818

Connecticut
Huntington's Book Stores
65 Asylum
Hartford, CT 06103
203-527-1835

Map House
1520 Rhey Ave.
Wallingford, CT 06492
203-269-0685

The Melko Corp.
620 Villa Ave.
Fairfield, CT 06430
203-367-8327

Whitlock's, Inc.
17 Broadway
New Haven, CT 06511
203-562-9841

Delaware
First State Map & Globe Co.
12 Mary Ella Dr.
Wilmington, DE 19805
302-998-6009; FAX 302-999-7618

Newark Newsstand
70 E. Main St.
Newark, DE 19711
302-368-8770

Ninth Street Book Shop
110 W. 9th St.
Wilmington, DE 19801
302-652-3315

Nor-Mar
1624 Delaware Ave., C.M.S. Bldg.
Wilmington, DE 19806
302-655-2861

District of Columbia
Hudson Trail Outfitters
4437 Wisconsin Ave. NW
Washington, DC 20015
202-393-1244

Lloyd Books
3145 Dumbarton
Washington, DC 20007
202-333-8989

The Map Store
1636 Eye St. NW
Washington, DC 20006
202-628-2608; 800-544-2659

National Geographic Bookstore
17th & M Sts. NW
Washington, DC 20036
202-857-7000

National Map Gallery & Travel Center
Union Station, 50 Massachusetts Ave. NE
Washington, DC 20002
202-789-0100

Florida
Breslin Reproduction Service Inc.
919 N. Beach St.
Daytona Beach, FL 32117
904-257-1277; FAX 904-257-1512

Central Florida Map Company
2216 Vincent Rd.
Orlando, FL 32867
407-277-4408

Champion Map Corporation
200 Fentress Blvd.
Daytona Beach, FL 32114
800-438-7406; 800-444-1072

Map and Globe Store
1920 E. Colonial Dr.
Orlando, FL 32803
407-898-0757; FAX 407-898-5872

The Map Shop
2161 McGregor Blvd., Ste. C
Fort Myers, FL 33901
813-337-1949; FAX 813-337-4964

Travel Books Plus
340 Huntington Dr., P.O. Box 966
DeLand, FL 32724
904-736-8190

The World
3520 E. 10th Ave.
Hialeah, FL 33013
305-835-7139

Georgia
Borders Book Shop
3655 Roswell Rd. NE
Atlanta, GA 30342
404-237-0707

Bradford Map Co.
1873 Lawrenceville Hwy.
Decatur, GA 30033
404-633-7562

Latitudes
Lenox Square Mall, 3393 Peachtree Rd.
Atlanta, GA 30326
404-237-6144

Latitudes
2246 Perimeter Mall, P.O. Box 467518
Atlanta, GA 30346
404-394-2772

Map Solutions International
1615 Peachtree St. NE
Atlanta, GA 30367
404-876-9977

Oxford Book Store
360 Pharr Rd. NE
Atlanta, GA 30305
404-262-3333

Review Office Products
9 W. Henry, P.O. Box 1736
Savannah, GA 31402
912-236-4417; FAX 912-236-0450

Travel Source
2550 Heritage Ct., Ste. 202
Atlanta, GA 30339
404-955-1358

Hawaii
Basically Books
169 Keawe St.
Hilo, HI 96720
808-961-0144

Pacific Map Center
647 Auahi St.
Honolulu, HI 96813
808-531-3800

Idaho
Hunt Enterprises
6208 Cassia St.
Boise, ID 83709
208-375-4200

Illinois
Rand McNally Retail Store
444 N. Michigan Ave.
Chicago, IL 60611
312-332-4628

The Savvy Traveller
50 E. Washington
Chicago, IL 60602
312-263-2100

Suburban Map Store
1041 S. Rd. 83
Elmhurst, IL 60126
708-941-7978

World Image
6348 W. 95th St., Ste. 104
Oak Lawn, IL 60453
708-233-0208

Indiana
Cram Co., Inc.
301 S. LaSalle, P.O. Box 426
Indianapolis, IN 46201
317-635-5564; 800-227-4199; FAX 317-635-2720

Odyssey Map Store
148 N. Delaware St.
Indianapolis, IN 46204
317-635-3837

Print Graphics
9900 Westpoint Dr.
Indianapolis, IN 46256
317-577-6385

Riegel's
624 S. Calhoun St.
Ft. Wayne, IN 46802
219-424-1429

Iowa
Haunted Bookshop
520 Washington St.
Iowa City, IA 52240
319-337-2996

Oak Ridge Sports, Inc.
450 Central Ave.
Dubuque, IA 52001
319-556-0861

Roberts' Maps
2911 Ingersoll Ave.
Des Moines, IA 50312
515-274-5010; 800-397-9617

Travel Genie
620 W. Lincolnway
Ames, IA 50010
515-292-1070

Kansas
Forsyth Travel Library, Inc.
9154 W. 57th St., P.O. Box 2975
Shawnee Mission, KS 66201
913-384-3440; 800-Forsyth; FAX 913-384-3553

McLeod's
506 S. Edgemoor
Wichita, KS 67218
316-683-5400

Rector's Bookstore
206 E. Douglas Ave.
Wichita, KS 67202
316-265-0611

Sportsmen's Maps Headquarters
333 E. English St., Ste. 280
Wichita, KS 67202
316-262-2192

Superior School Supply Center
241 N. Hydraulic
Wichita, KS 67214
316-265-7683

Kentucky
La Belle Gallery
741 E. Chestnut
Louisville, KY 40202
502-589-0621

Owl and Pussycat
316 S. Ashland Ave.
Lexington, KY 40502
606-266-7121

Louisiana
Beaucoup Books
5414 Magazine
New Orleans, LA 70115
504-895-2663

Globe Map Company
206 Milam St.
Shreveport, LA 71101
318-222-7453

McCurnin Nautical Charts
2318 Woodlawn Ave.
Metairie, LA 70001
504-888-4500; 800-638-4544; FAX 504-888-7850

New Orleans Map Co.
3130 Paris Ave.
New Orleans, LA 70119
504-943-0878

Vidrine Office Supply
7730 W. Main, P.O. Box 7
Galliano, LA 70354
504-632-2163; 504-632-2527

Maine
Books-N-Things
Oxford Plaza
Oxford, ME 04270
207-743-7197

DeLorme Map Store
Lower Main St., P.O. Box 298
Freeport, ME 04032
207-865-4171; 800-227-1656; FAX 207-865-9628

Kennebec Books
82 Western Ave.
Augusta, ME 04330
207-622-7843

Maryland
Bookstall
10144 River Rd.
Potomac, MD 20854
301-469-7800

First Frame Graphics
P.O. Box 2179
Easton, MD 21601
410-820-5095 (Mail-order)

Greetings and Readings
809 Taylor Ave.
Towson, MD 21204
301-825-4225

Travel Books & Language Center
4931 Cordell Ave.
Bethesda, MD 20814
301-951-8533, FAX 301-951-8546

Massachusetts
A2Z Science and Nature Store
150 Main St.
Northampton, MA 01060
413-586-1611

Arts & Cards Inc.
374 Boylston St.
Brookline, MA 02146
617-566-4984

Baldwin Map Corp.
18 Elm St.
Woburn, MA 01801
617-935-5599

Eastern Mountain Sports
1041 Commonwealth Ave.
Boston, MA 02115
617-254-4250

Globe Corner Bookstore
1 School St.
Boston, MA 02108
617-523-6658; FAX 617-227-5594

Globe Corner Bookstore
49 Palmer St.
Cambridge, MA 02138
617-497-6277

The Harvard Square Map Store
49 Palmer St.
Cambridge, MA 02138
617-497-6277

The Reference House
550 Rogers Ave., P.O. Box 918
West Springfield, MA 01090
413-788-4733

Michigan
Delta Maps
5800 12 Mile Rd.
Warren, MI 48092
313-573-9273; FAX 313-573-8965

Geography Ltd.
912 Fountain St.
Ann Arbor, MI 48103
313-769-5152

Swann Corporation
2517 Robinson Rd. SE
Grand Rapids, MI 49506
616-949-1363

Universal Map
795 Progress Court, P.O. Box 15
Williamston, MI 48895
517-655-5641

Minnesota
Hudson Map Company
2510 Nicollet Ave.
Minneapolis, MN 55404
612-872-8818

Latitudes
3001 Hennepin Ave. S.
Minneapolis, MN 55408
612-823-3742

The Map Store
348 N. Robert St.
St. Paul, MN 55101
612-227-6277, FAX 612-224-4742

The Map Store
120 S. 6th St., 211 Skyway
Minneapolis, MN 55402
612-339-4117, FAX 612-339-2767

Mississippi
George's Map Service
133 Country Band Pl.
Jackson, MS 39212
601-371-3875

Missouri
Gallup Map Co.
1733 Main
Kansas City, MO 64108
816-842-1994

Montana
Trail Head
110 East Pine St.
Missoula, MT 59802
406-543-6966

Nebraska
Stephenson School Supply
1112 O St.
Lincoln, NE 68508
402-476-7663

Nevada
Bob Coffin Books
1139 Fifth Pl.
Las Vegas, NV 89104
702-384-9501; FAX 702-384-9629

Front Boy Service Co.
3340 Sirius Ave.
Las Vegas, NV 89102
702-876-7822

New Hampshire
Action Map Company
P.O. Box 15
Seabrook, NH 03874
508-462-3810

Globe Corner Bookstore
Settlers Green, Route 16, P.O. Box 1756
North Conway, NH 03860
603-356-7063

Goodman's
383 Chestnut St.
Manchester, NH 03101
603-622-2153

New Jersey
Ardic Book Distributors Inc.
74 Route 206 S.
Somerville, NJ 08876
201-359-2828

Geo Graphics, Inc.
208 Glenridge Ave., P.O. Box 183
Montclair, NJ 07042
201-744-7873

Geostat Map & Travel Center
Montgomery Shopping Center, Rte. 206 and 518
Skillman, NJ 08558
609-924-2121

International Map Company
547 Shaler Blvd.
Ridgefield, NJ 07657
201-943-5550; FAX 201-943-6566

McCarthy Geographics
404 Bloomfield Ave.
Montclair, NJ 07042
201-744-7873; FAX 201-744-4052

Universal Success Corp.
550 Cookman Ave.
Asbury Park, NJ 07712
201-774-2020

New Mexico
Access Maps & Gear
321 S. Guadalupe
Santa Fe, NM 87501
505-988-2442; FAX 505-988-2920

Base Camp
121 W. San Francisco St.
Santa Fe, NM 87501
505-982-9707

Holman's, Inc.
401 Wyoming Blvd. NE
Albuquerque, NM 87123
505-265-7981

Page One Newsstand & Bookstore
11200 Montgomery Blvd. NE
Albuquerque, NM 87111
505-294-3054

New York
Book House of Stuyvesant Plaza, Inc.
Stuyvesant Plaza
Albany, NY 12203
518-489-4761

Complete Traveller Bookstore
199 Madison Ave.
New York, NY 10016
212-679-4339

Hagstrom Map & Travel Center
57 W. 43rd St.
New York, NY 10036
212-398-1222

JIMAPCO
P.O. Box 1137
Clifton Park, NY 12065
518-899-5091; 800-MAPS123; FAX 518-899-5093

Map Man
120 Bethpage Rd.
Hicksville, NY 11801
516-931-8404

The Map Shop
1820 Lake Rd.
Webster, NY 14580
716-265-0566

Marshall-Penn-York Co., Inc
538 Erie Blvd. W.
Syracuse, NY 13204
315-422-2162; FAX 315-422-2181

New York Map & Travel Center
150 E. 52nd St.
New York, NY 10022
212-758-7488

New York Nautical
140 W. Broadway
New York, NY 10013
212-962-4522

Rand McNally Map Store
150 East 52nd St.
New York, NY 10022
212-758-7488

Sanborn Map Co.
629 5th St.
Pelham, NY 10801
914-738-1649

Timesavers
One N. Transit, P.O. Box 229
Lockport, NY 14094
716-434-1234

North Carolina
Carolina Maps, Inc.
210 W. Fourth St., P.O. Box 8026
Greenville, NC 27834
919-757-0279

Geoscience Resources
2990 Anthony Rd., P.O. Box 2096
Burlington, NC 27216
919-227-8300; 800-742-2677; FAX 919-227-3748

The Map Shop
5033-C South Blvd.
Charlotte, NC 28217
704-523-6277

Treasure Hutch
6490 Shallowford Rd.
Lewisville, NC 27040
919-945-3831

North Dakota
Book Fair
212 DeMers Ave.
Grand Forks, ND 58201
701-775-6491

Ohio
Commercial Survey Company
812 Hurron Rd. #203 Caxton Bldg.
Cleveland, OH 44115
216-771-3995

Duttenhofer's Map Store
210 W. McMillan St.
Cincinnati, OH 45219
513-381-0007

4 Corners Map & Travel Shop
2747 Crawfish Blvd. #101
Fairlawn, OH 44333
216-869-6277

Leo's Book Shop
330 N. Superior
Toledo, OH 43604
419-255-5506

The Map Store
5821 Karric Square Dr.
Dublin, OH 43017
614-792-6277; 800-332-7885; FAX 614-848-5045

Ohio Canoe Adventures, Inc.
Backpackers Shop, 5128 Colorado Ave.
Sheffield Village, OH 44054
216-934-5345

Oklahoma
Mosher-Adams Maps
400 West Commerce St.
Oklahoma City, OK 73109
405-632-3321

Topographic Mapping Co.
6709 N. Classen
Oklahoma City, OK 73116
405-843-4847

Traveler's Pack, Ltd.
9427 N. May
Oklahoma City, OK 73120
405-755-2924

Oregon
Captain's Nautical Supplies
138 NW 10th
Portland, OR 97209
503-227-1648

Libra Books, Inc.
856 Olive St.
Eugene, OR 97401
503-484-0512

Pittmon Map Co.
732 SE Hawthorne Blvd.
Portland, OR 97214
503-232-1161; 215-336-6415

Powell's Travel Store
Pioneer Courthouse Square, 701 SW 6th Ave.
Portland, OR 97204
503-228-1108

Pennsylvania
Book Swap
316 Horsham Rd.
Horsham, PA 19044
215-674-3919

Franklin Maps
333 S. Henderson Rd.
King of Prussia, PA 19406
215-265-6277; FAX 215-337-1575

Alfred B. Patton, Inc.
Swamp Rd. & Center St., P.O. Box 857
Doylestown, PA 18901
215-345-0700

Pilothouse
1100 S. Delaware Ave.
Philadelphia, PA 19147
215-336-6414; FAX 215-336-6415

J. R. Wedlin Co.
415 Wood St.
Pittsburgh, PA 15222
412-281-0123

University of Pennsylvania Bookstore
3729 Locust Walk
Philadelphia, PA 19104
215-898-7595

Way to Go
4228 Main St.
Philadelphia, PA 19127
215-483-7387

Rhode Island
Armchair Sailor Bookstore
543 Thames St.
Newport, RI 02840
401-847-4252

The Map Center, Inc.
671 N. Main St.
Providence, RI 02904
401-421-2184; FAX 401-454-8058

Outdoorsman
357 S. Main St.
Providence, RI 02903
401-274-6770

South Carolina
Capitol Map Supplies
601 12th St.
W. Columbia, SC 29169
803-796-3399

Luden Marine Supplies
360 Concord St.
Charleston, SC 29401
803-723-7829

The Map Shop
5-B E. Coffee St., P.O. Box 1602
Greenville, SC 29602
803-271-6277

Tennessee
The Map Source
41 Federal Dr., Ste. 3
Jackson, TN 38305
901-664-8676; FAX 901-668-8110

Texas
ABC Blueprints
906 S. Tyler, P.O. Box 15145
Amarillo, Texas 79101
800-288-1841; FAX 806-376-6523

Allstate Map Co.
1201 Henderson St.
Ft. Worth, TX 76102
817-332-1111

Apache Trading Post
P.O. Drawer 929
Alpine, TX 79830
915-837-5149

Ferguson Map & Travel
8131 IH 10 West
San Antonio, TX 78230
512-341-6277

Key Maps, Inc.
1411 W. Alabama St.
Houston, TX 77006
713-522-7949

MAPSCO
5308 Maple Ave.
Dallas, TX 75235
812-283-6277, 800-950-5308; FAX 214-559-0081

One Map Place
212 Webb Chapel Village
Dallas, TX 75229
214-241-2680

Southwest Map
2406 S. Juniper Rd., Ste. 5
Garland, TX 75041
214-494-4443; 800-633-1723

Venture Map & Globe Co., Inc.
2130 Highland Mall
Austin, TX 78752
512-452-2326

Zdansky Map Store
5230 Kostoryz #16
Corpus Christi, TX 78415
512-855-9226

Utah
Map World Services
6550 S. State St.
Salt Lake City, UT 84107
801-262-1814; FAX 801-262-0450

Vermont
Woodknot Bookshop
68 Main St.
Newport, VT 05855
802-334-6720

Virginia
Globe and Map Technik, Inc.
11634 Busy St., Ste. A
Richmond, VA 23236
804-320-0719

Hudson Trail Outfitters
9683 Lee Hwy.
Fairfax, VA 22030
703-591-2950

Hudson Trail Outfitters
11750 Fair Oaks Mall
Fairfax, VA 22030
703-385-3907

Washington
Arnold Map Service
119 W. 24th St.
Vancouver, WA 98660
206-695-7897

Metsker Maps of Seattle
702 First Ave.
Seattle, WA 98104
206-623-8747

Metsker Maps of Tacoma
6249 Tacoma Mall Blvd.
Tacoma, WA 98409
206-474-6277

Northwest Map Service
W. 713 Spokane Falls Blvd.
Spokane, WA 99201
509-455-6981

Pacific Northwest National Parks Assn.
Mount Rainer Branch
Longmier, WA 98397
206-569-2211

Pioneer Maps
1645 140th Ave., NE
Bellevue, WA 98007
206-746-3200

West Virginia
H. T. Hall Co.
3624 MacCorkle Ave. SE
Charleston, WV 25304
304-925-1117

Highway Maps, Inc.
4838 MacCorkle Ave. SW
S. Charleston, WV 25309
304-768-0441

Wisconsin
Clarkson Map Company
1225 Delanglade St., P.O. Box 218
Kaukauna, WI 54130
414-766-3000

Dover Flag & Map
300 Main St.
Racine, WI 53403
414-632-3133

Laub Specialty Maps
P.O. Box 634
Minocqua, WI 54548
715-356-6851

Milwaukee Map Service
959 N. Mayfair Rd.
Wauwatosa, WI 53226
414-774-1300; FAX 414-774-3181

Maps For You
711 S. Fisk
Green Bay, WI 54303
414-494-4904

Wyoming
Mountain Sports
543 S. Center St.
Casper, WY 82601
307-266-1136

Teton Mountaineering
86 E. Broadway
Jackson, WY 83001
307-733-3595

CANADA
Alberta
Carter Mapping, Ltd.
1223 31st Ave. NE
Calgary, Alberta T2E 7W1
403-264-1230

Map World Services, Inc.
209 6th Ave. SW
Calgary, Alberta T2P OR2
403-294-0393

Map Town, Ltd.
640 6th Ave. SW
Calgary, Alberta T2P 0S4
403-266-2241

British Columbia
Earth Quest Books
1286 Broad St.
Victoria, BC V8W 2A5
604-361-4533

Travel Bug
2667 W. Broadway
Vancouver, BC V6K 2G2
604-737-1122

World Wide Books and Maps
736A Granville St.
Vancouver, BC V6Z 1G3
604-687-3320

Manitoba
Global Village Map & Travel Store
736 Osborne St.
Winnipeg, Manitoba R3L 2C2
204-453-7081

Ontario
A-1 Maps
1623 Bloor St. W.
Toronto, Ontario M6P 1A6
416-531-4108

A-1 Maps Main Branch
1325 Eglinton Ave. E., Ste. 213
Mississauga, Ontario L4W 4L9
416-602-0844; FAX 416-588-6431

Allmaps Canada, Ltd.
390 Steelcase Rd. E.
Markham, Ontario L3R 1G2
416-477-8480; FAX 416-477-7408

Canada Map Co.
211 Yonge St.
Toronto, Ontario M5B 1M4
416-362-9297; FAX 416-362-9381

Gulliver's Travel Bookstore
609 Bloor St. W.
Toronto, Ontario M6G 1K5
416-537-7700

H. M. Dignam Corp., Ltd.
370 Dunlop St. W., Unit 807
Barrie, Ontario L4N 5R7
705-721-1515

Open Air Books and Maps
25 Toronto St.
Toronto, Ontario M5C 2R1
416-363-0719

Oxford Books & Stationery
740 Richmond St.
London, Ontario N6A 1L6
519-438-8336; FAX 519-667-0865

Pathfinder Map, Inc.
RR 2 Carp
Ottawa, Ontario K0A 1L0
613-836-7832; FAX 613-836-5223

Perly's Maps
345 Adelaide St. W., Ste. 400
Toronto, Ontario M5V 1R5
416-593-6277; FAX 416-593-6204

Place Bell Bookstore
175 Metcalfe St.
Ottawa, Ontario K2P 2E9
613-233-3821

Pro-Lam
160 Manhood-Johnston Dr.
Kincardine, Ontario N2Z 3A2
519-396-4430; FAX 519-396-9492

Technicom Consultants
115 Randall Dr., Unit 5
Waterloo, Ontario N2V 1C5
519-747-1779

Worldwide Maps and Guides
Box 374 Station A
Ottawa, Ontario K1N 8V4
613-562-1342; FAX 613-562-1343

Quebec
Aux Quatre Points Cardinaux (AQPC)
551 Ontario E.
Montreal, Quebec H2L 1N8
514-843-8116

Conexfor, Inc.
CP 697 Succ Desjardins
Montreal, Quebec H5B 1B8
514-849-5741

Dougherty Maps
762 Millington Ave.
Greenfield Park, Quebec J4V 1R7
514-672-5348

Distribution Ulysse
4176 rue St. Denis
Montreal, Quebec H2W 2M5
514-843-9447

ENGLAND
Bellows & Bown
7 Commercial Rd.
Gloucester GL1 1NW
011-44-452-21206

Cook, Hammond & Kell, Ltd.
35 Eveline Rd.
Mitcham, Surrey CR4 3XR
011-081-648-9262

Eland
22 Bedford St.
St. Exeter, Devon EX1 1LE
011-443-925-5788; FAX 011-03-924-13121

Heffers Map Shop
19 Sidney St.
Cambridge CB2 3HL
011-02-233-58241; FAX 011-02-233-23926

AUSTRALIA
Australian Mineral Foundation, Inc.
63 Conyngham St., Glenside 5065
South Australia
08-379-0444

Cartotech Services Pty., Ltd.
51 John St., 1st Fl.
Salisbury 5108
South Australia
618-221-2461

Hema Maps
24 Allgas St, Slacks Creek
P.O. Box 724 Springwood
Brisbane, Qld 4127
07-29-00-322; FAX 07-290-0478

Rex Map Centres
9 Huntingdon St.
Crows Nest, NSW 2065
61-2-906-6058; FAX 61-2-906-3667

MEXICO
Guia Roji
Jose Moran #31
Miguel Hidalgo, Mexico DF 11850
905-515-0384; 905-515-7963; FAX 905-702-0886

NETHERLANDS
De Wandelwinkel Maps & Guides
Bergkerkplein 5
EN Deventer NL-7411
011-315-700-15077

Geographic Bookshop Van Wyngaarden
Overtoom 136
Amsterdam, Holland 1054HN
011-31-206-121901; FAX 31-206-892666

JAPAN
Map House Co., Ltd.
5th Fl., Taiyodo Bldg., 1-10 Jimbocho, Kanda
Chiyoda-ku, Tokyo 101
03-3295-1555; FAX 03-3925-1686

Teikoku-Shoin Co., Ltd.
29, Jimbocho 3-chome, Kanda
Chiyoda-ku, Tokyo 101
03-3262-5039; FAX 03-3234-7965

SCOTLAND
Aberdeen Map Shop
74 Skene St.
Aberdeen AB1 1QE
011-44-22-463-7999

Thomas Nelson & Sons
51 York Pl.
Edinburgh EH1 1JD
011-44-31-557-3011; FAX 031-557-8195

Selected Map Libraries

GENERAL LIBRARIES

Alabama
Auburn University
Ralph B. Draughon Library
Special Collections Dept.
Auburn, AL 36841
205-844-1700

University of Alabama
Map Library, Dept. of Geography
Box 870322
Tuscaloosa, AL 35487
205-348-5047

Arizona
Arizona State University
Noble Science & Engineering Library
Map Collection
Tempe, AZ 85287
602-965-3582

University of Arizona
Main Library, Map Collection
Tucson, AZ 85721
602-621-2596

Arkansas
University of Central Arkansas
Dept. of Geography, Map Library
Old Main
Conway, AR 72035
501-450-3164

University of Arkansas
University Libraries
Reference & Govt. Documents
Map Library
Fayetteville, AR 72701
501-575-4101

California
University of California, Berkeley
Earth Sciences Library
230 Earth Sciences Bldg.
Dept. of Geology & Geophysics
Berkeley, CA 94720
510-642-2997

University of California, Berkeley
General Library, Map Rm.
Berkeley, CA 94720
510-642-4940

California State University, Chico
Meriam Library-Maps
Chico, CA 95929
916-898-4003

University of California, Davis
Shields Library
Govt. Documents Dept., Map Section
Davis, CA 95616
916-752-1624

California State University, Fresno
Henry Madden Library, Map Library
5200 N. Barton Ave.
Fresno, CA 93740
209-278-2405

California State University, Los Angeles
Geography and Map Library
Geography & Urban Studies Dept.
5151 State University Dr.
Los Angeles, CA 90032
213-343-2220

Los Angeles Public Library
Mary Helen Peterson Map Rm.
630 W. 5th St.
Los Angeles, CA 90071
213-612-3314

University of California, Los Angeles
Map Library
Bunche Hall A-253
Los Angeles, CA 90024
310-825-3526

University of California, Los Angeles
Wm. C. Putnam Map Rm.
4697 Geology Bldg.
405 Hilgard
Los Angeles, CA 90024
310-825-1055

Oakland Public Library
125 14th St.
Oakland, CA 94612
510-238-3136

San Diego State University
University Library, Map Collection
San Diego, CA 92182
619-594-5650

University of California, San Diego
Map Section 0175P, University Library
9500 Gilman Dr.
La Jolla, CA 92093
619-534-1248

San Jose State University
Dept. of Geology, Map Rm.
San Jose, CA 95192
408-277-2387

University of California, Santa Cruz
Map Collection, University Library
Santa Cruz, CA 95064
408-429-2364

Colorado
University of Colorado
University Libraries, Map Library
Campus Box 184
Boulder, CO 80309
303-492-7578

Denver Public Library
Map Collection
Govt. Publications Dept.
1357 Broadway
Denver, CO 80203
303-640-8846

Colorado School of Mines
Arthur Lakes Library, Map Rm.
Golden, CO 80402
303-273-3697

Connecticut
Wesleyan University
Science Library
Middletown, CT 06459
203-347-9411

Yale University Library
Map Collection
Box 1603A, Yale Station
New Haven, CT 06520
203-432-1867

Yale University
Geology Library
210 Whitney Ave.
P.O. Box 6666
New Haven, CT 06511
203-432-3157

University of Connecticut
University Library
Map Library U-5M
19 Fairfield Rd.
Stoors, CT 06268
203-486-4589

District of Columbia
Defense Mapping Agency
Hydrographic/Topographic Ctr.
Scientific Data Dept., Support Div.
4600 Sangamore Rd.
Bethesda, MD 20816
301-227-2375

Library of Congress
Geography & Map Div.
Washington, DC 20540
202-707-5522

National Geographic Society
Map Library
1146 16th St. NW
Washington, DC 20036
202-857-7000

Florida
Florida State University
R. M. Strozier Library
Maps Dept.
Documents-Maps-Micromaterials Dept.
Tallahassee, FL 32306
904-644-6061

Georgia
Georgia Institute of Technology
Price Gilbert Memorial Library
Dept. of Govt. Documents & Maps
225 North Ave.
Atlanta, GA 30332
404-894-4538

Hawaii
University of Hawaii, Manoa
Hamilton Library, Map Collection
2550 The Mall
Honolulu, HI 96822
808-956-6199

Idaho
Boise State University, Library
Map Dept.
1910 University Dr.
Boise, ID 83725
208-385-3958

University of Idaho Library
Map Section
Moscow, ID 83843
208-885-6344

Illinois
Southern Illinois University
Science Div., Map Library
Morris Library
Carbondale, IL 62901
618-453-2705

Rand McNally & Co.
Map Library
8255 N. Central Park
Skokie, Il 60076
708-673-9100

University of Chicago Library
Map Collection
1100 E. 57th St.
Chicago, IL 60637
312-702-8740

University of Illinois, Chicago
Main Library, MC-234
Documents/Map Section
P.O. Box 8198, 801 S. Morgan St.
Chicago, IL 60680
312-996-5277

Northern Illinois University
Map Library
Davis Hall 222
DeKalb, IL 60115
815-753-1813

Southern Illinois University, Edwardsville
Lovejoy Library, Map Library
Box 1063
Edwardsville, IL 62025
618-692-2422

Northwestern University
University Library, Map Collection
1935 Sheridan Rd.
Evanston, IL 60208
708-491-7603

Western Illinois University
University Map Library
Tillman Hall Rm 016
Macomb, IL 61455
309-298-1171

Illinois State University
Map Rm., Milner Library
Normal, IL 61761
309-438-3486

Illinois State Library
300 S. 2nd St., 3rd Fl.
Springfield, IL 62701
217-782-5823

Indiana
Indiana University
Geography & Map Library
Student Bldg. 015
Bloomington, IN 47405
812-855-1108

Indiana University
Geology Library
Geology Bldg., Rm. 601
1005 E. 10th St.
Bloomington, IN 47405
812-855-7170/812-855-1338

DePaul University
Roy O. West Library
Box 137, 400 S. College Ave.
Greencastle, IN 46135
317-658-4434

Indiana State Library
Serials/Documents Section
140 N. Senate Ave.
Indianapolis, IN 46204
317-232-3686

Ball State University
Dept. of Library Science
Map Collection
Muncie, IN 47306
317-285-1097

University of Notre Dame
Memorial Library
Microtext Reading Rm.
Notre Dame, IN 46556
219-239-6450

Indiana State University
Dept. of Geography & Geology, Map Library
Terre Haute, IN 47809
812-237-2444

Valparaiso University
Moellering Memorial Library, Map Library
Valparaiso, IN 46383
219-464-5364

Purdue University Libraries
Earth, Atmosphere and Science Library
Civil Engineering Library 2215
Map Collection
Stewart Ctr., Rm. 279
West Lafayette, IN 47907
317-494-3264

Iowa
Iowa State University
Parks Library 152, Map Rm.
Ames, IA 50011
515-294-3956

Kansas
University of Kansas
Govt. Documents and Maps Library
KU Map Library
6001 Malott Hall
Lawrence, KS 66045
913-864-4420

Kansas State University Library
Map & Atlas Unit/Govt. Documents
Manhattan, KS 66502
913-532-7449

Louisiana
Louisiana State University
Dept. of Georgraphy and Anthropology
Attn.: Cartographic Information Ctr.
Baton Rouge, LA 70893
504-388-2354

Maryland
Enoch Pratt Free Library
Attn.: Map Collection
400 Cathedral St.
Baltimore, MD 21201
301-396-5472

Johns Hopkins University
Milton S. Eisenhower Library
Govt. Publications/Maps/Law Dept.
Baltimore, MD 21218
301-516-8360

University of Maryland
Hornbake Library
Documents/Maps Unit
College Park, MD 20742
301-405-9165

Massachusetts
University of Massachusetts
Morrill Biological Sciences Library, Map Collection
Amherst, MA 01003
413-545-2397

Harvard College Library
Pusey Library
Harvard Map Collection
Cambridge, MA 02138
617-495-2417

Massachusetts Institute of Technology
Sciences Library
Stein Club Map Rm.
14S-134
Cambridge, MA 02139
617-253-5651

Tufts University
Wessell Library
Govt. Publications, Microforms & Maps Dept.
Medford, MA 02155
617-628-3930

Smith College Map Library
Clark Science Ctr.
Dept. of Geology
Burton Hall
Northampton, MA 01063
413-584-2700

Clark University
Geography Dept., Map Library
Guy H. Burnham Map & Aerial Photograph Library
Worcester, MA 01610
508-793-7322

Michigan
University of Michigan
Hatcher Graduate Library, Map Rm.
Ann Arbor, MI 48109
313-764-0407

Detroit Public Library
History & Travel Dept., Map Rm.
5201 Woodward Ave.
Detroit, MI 48202
313-833-1445

Michigan State University
Map Library, Libraries 310
East Lansing, MI 48824
517-353-4737

Michigan Technological University
Map Library
Govt. Documents Dept.
Houghton, MI 49931
906-487-2506

Western Michigan University
Map Library, Waldo Library
Kalamazoo, MI 49008
616-387-5046

Minnesota
Mankato State University
Memorial Library, Map Collection
Mankato, MN 56001
507-389-1288

Carleton College
Geology Map Library
Northfield, MN 55057
507-663-4401

St. Cloud State University
Learning Resources
Govt. Documents/Maps
St. Cloud, MN 56301
612-255-2022

Missouri
University of Missouri
Geology Library
201 Geology Bldg.
Columbia, MO 65211
314-882-4860

Southwest Missouri State University
Duane G. Meyer Library, Map Collection
901 S. National
Springfield, MO 65804
417-836-4534

Saint Louis University
Pius XII Memorial Library
Govt. Documents
3650 Lyndell Blvd.
St. Louis, MO 63108
314-658-3105

St. Louis Public Library
1301 Olive St.
St. Louis, MO 63103
314-241-2288

Washington University
Earth & Planetary Sciences Library
Box 1169
1 Brookings Dr.
St. Louis, MO 63130
314-889-5406

Montana
Montana Tech. Library
Documents Div.
West Park St.
Butte, MT 59701
406-496-4286

University of Montana
Map Collection, Documents Div.
Maureen & Mike Mansfield Library
Missoula, MT 59812
406-243-4564

Nebraska
University of Nebraska, Lincoln
Geology Library
303 Morrill Hall
Lincoln, NE 68588
402-472-3628

New Hampshire
Dartmouth College
Library Map Rm., Baker Library
Hanover, NH 03755
603-646-2579

New Jersey
Hammond, Inc.
Editorial Dept. Library
515 Valley St.
Maplewood, NJ 07040
201-763-6000

Rutgers University
Library of Science & Medicine
Piscataway, NJ 08854
908-932-2895

Princeton University Library
Richard Halliburton Map Collection
1 Washington Rd.
Princeton, NJ 08544
609-258-3214

Princeton University
Geology Library, Map Collection
Guyot Hall
Princeton, NJ 08544
609-258-3267

New Mexico
University of New Mexico
Engineering Library
Map and Geographic Information Ctr.
Albuquerque, NM 87131
505-277-5738

New York
New York State Library
Manuscripts & Special Collections
Cultural Education Ctr.
Albany, NY 12230
518-474-4461

Brooklyn Public Library
History Div., Map Collection
Grand Army Plaza
Brooklyn, NY 11238
718-780-7700

Buffalo & Erie County Public Library
Map Collection
Lafayette Sq.
Buffalo, NY 14203
716-858-7103

State University of New York, Buffalo
University Libraries
Capen Hall
Science & Engineering Library Map Collection
Buffalo, NY 14260
716-636-2946

Cornell University
016 John M. Olin Library
Dept. of Maps, Microtexts, Newspapers
Ithaca, NY 14853
607-255-9566

Columbia University Libraries
Lehman Library, Map Rm. 327
420 W. 118th St.
New York, NY 10027
212-854-5002

New York Public Library
Map Div., Rm 117
Fifth Ave. & 42nd St.
New York, NY 10018
212-930-0587

United Nations Map Collection
Dag Hammarskjold Library
Rm L-282
New York, NY 10017
212-963-7425

State University of New York, Stony Brook
Melville Library, Map Collection
Stony Brook, NY 11794
516-632-7110

Syracuse University Libraries
Map Collection
E. S. Bird Library
222 Waverly Ave
Syracuse, NY 13244
315-443-4196

North Carolina
Appalachian State University Map Library
Dept. of Geography and Planning
Boone, NC 28608
704-262-3000

University of North Carolina, Chapel Hill
Wilson Library, Maps Collection
3B#3928
Chapel Hill, NC 27599
919-962-3028

University of North Carolina, Chapel Hill
Geology Library
3B#3315
Mitchell Hall
Chapel Hill, NC 27599
919-962-2386

Duke University
Perkins Library
Public Documents & Maps Dept.
Durham, NC 27706
919-684-2380

North Dakota
North Dakota State University Library
Fargo, ND 58105
701-237-8886

University of North Dakota
Dept. of Geology and Geological Engineering
Geology Library
8068 University Station
Grand Forks, ND 58202
701-777-3221

Ohio
Ohio University
Alden Library
Map Collection
Athens, OH 45701-2978
614-593-2658

Public Library of Cincinnati & Hamilton County
Map Collection, History Dept.
800 Vine St.
Cincinnati, OH 45202
513-369-6909

University of Cincinnati Library
227 Braustein
Cincinnati, OH 45221
513-556-1867

Cleveland Public Library Map Collection
325 Superior Ave.
Cleveland, OH 44114
216-623-2880

Ohio State University
Main Library, Rm. 226
1858 Neil Ave. Mall
Columbus, OH 43210
614-292-2393

Kent State University
Map Library
410 McGilvrey Hall
Kent, OH 44242-0001
216-672-2017

University of Toledo
William S. Carlson Library Map Collection
2801 W. Bancroft St.
Toledo, OH 43606
419-537-2865

Oklahoma
University of Oklahoma Geology Library
100 E. Boyd, Rm. R220
Norman, OK 73019
405-325-6451

Oklahoma State University
Edmon Lowe Library, Map Rm.
Box 12927, Capitol Station
Stillwater, OK 74078
405-744-9731

Oregon
Oregon State University
William Jasper Kerr Library, Map Rm. 121
Corvallis, OR 97333
503-737-2971

Library Association of Portland
Literature & History Dept., Map Collection
801 SW 10th
Portland, OR 97205
503-248-5123

Pennsylvania
Bryn Mawr College
Dept. of Geology
New Gulph Rd.
Bryn Mawr, PA 19010
215-526-5111

Free Library of Philadelphia
Map Collection
1901 Vine St.
Philadelphia, PA 19103
215-686-5397

Temple University
Samuel Paley Library, Map Reference
Philadelphia, PA 19122
215-787-8213

University of Pennsylvania
Geology Map Library
Hayden Hall
Philadelphia, PA 19104
215-898-5724

Carnegie Library of Pittsburgh
Science & Technology Dept.
4400 Forbes Ave.
Pittsburgh, PA 15213
412-622-3138

University of Pittsburgh
G-8 Hillman Library, Map Collection
Pittsburgh, PA 15260
412-648-3330

Pennsylvania State University
Pattee Library, Maps Collection
University Park, PA 16802
814-863-0094

Rhode Island
Brown University
201 Thayer St.
Map Collection, Sciences Library, Box 1
Providence, RI 02912
401-863-3333

South Carolina
South Carolina Dept. of Archives & History
P.O. Box 11 669
Columbia, SC 29211
803-734-8577

University of South Carolina
Map Library
Columbia, SC 29208
803-777-2802

South Dakota
South Dakota State University
H. M. Briggs Library, Documents Dept.
Box 211
Brookings, SD 57007
605-688-5576

Tennessee
University of Tennessee
Dept. of Geography, Map Library
401 G&S Bldg.
Knoxville, TN 37996-1420
615-974-2418

Vanderbilt University Library
Science Library Map Rm.
Gene and Alexander Heard Library
Nashville, TN 37240-0007
615-322-2775

Texas
University of Texas, Austin
Map Collection, PCL 1306
Austin, TX 78713
512-495-4275

Texas A & M University
Sterling C. Evans Library, Map Dept.
College Station, TX 77843
409-845-1024

Southern Methodist University
Science Engineering Library/Map Library
Dallas, TX 75275
214-692-2285

University of Texas, El Paso
Library/Govt. Documents
El Paso, TX 79968
915-747-5685

Utah
Brigham Young University
Geography Dept., Map Collection
690 SWKT
Provo, UT 84602
801-378-3851

Brigham Young University
Harold B. Lee Library, Map Collection
1354 HBLL
Provo, UT 84602
801-378-4482

University of Utah
Science & Engineering Library
Map Collection
158 Marriott Library
Salt Lake City, UT 84112
801-581-7533

Vermont
University of Vermont
Bailey/Howe Library, Map Rm.
Burlington, VT 05405
802-656-2588

Middlebury College
Dept. of Geography
Science Ctr. 402
Middlebury, VT 05753
802-388-5562

Virginia
Virginia Tech
Newman Library, Map Collection
Blacksburg, VA 24061
703-231-6181

George Mason University
Fenwick Library, Audiovisual Library
4400 University Dr.
Fairfax, VA 22030
703-323-2605

U.S. Army Corps of Engineers
Norfolk District
803 Front St.
Norfolk, VA 23510
804-441-7575

U.S. Geological Survey Library, Reston
12201 Sunrise Valley Dr.
Reston, VA 22092
703-648-4302

Virginia State Library
Archives Branch Map Collection
11th & Capitol Sts.
Richmond, VA 23219
804-786-2306

Washington
Western Washington University
Dept. of Geography & Regional Planning
Map Library
Bellingham, WA 98247
206-676-3272

Seattle Public Library
History Dept., Map Collection
1000 4th Ave.
Seattle, WA 98104
206-386-4625

University of Washington Libraries
Map Collection FM-25
Seattle, WA 98195
206-543-9392

West Virginia
West Virginia University Library
Map Collection
P.O. Box 6069
Morgantown, WV 26506
304-293-3640

Wisconsin
University of Wisconsin, Eau Claire
Simpson Geographic Research Ctr.
Dept. of Geography
Eau Claire, WI 54701
715-836-3244

University of Wisconsin, Milwaukee
American Geographical Society Collection
P.O. Box 399
Milwaukee, WI 53201
414-229-6282

University of Wisconsin, Stevens Point
Map Library
Geography-Geology Dept.
Stevens Point, WI 54481
715-346-2629

Wyoming
University of Wyoming
Map Collection, Coe Library
University Station, Box 3334
Laramie, WY 82071
307-766-2174

AERIAL PHOTOGRAPHY COLLECTIONS

California
University of California, Berkeley
Dept. of Geography Library
501 Earth Science Bldg.
Berkeley, CA 94720
510-642-3903

U.S. Geological Survey Library, Menlo Park
345 Middlefield Rd., MS 55
Menlo Park, CA 94025
415-853-8300

University of California, Santa Barbara
Map & Imagery Laboratory
Santa Barbara, CA 93106
805-893-2779

Florida
Map Library
University of Florida
MSL-110
Gainesville, FL 32611
904-392-2825

Georgia
University of Georgia Libraries
Science Library, Map Collection
Athens, GA 30602
404-542-0690

Hawaii
Bernice P. Bishop Museum Library
Geography & Map Div.
P.O. Box 19000-A
Honolulu, HI 96819
808-847-3511

Iowa
University of Iowa Libraries
Map Collection
311 Main Library
Iowa City, IA 52242
319-335-5920

Kansas
Kansas Dept. of Transportation
Bureau of Transportation Planning
State Office Bldg.
Topeka, KS 66612
913-296-3841

Minnesota
Bemidji State University
Geography Dept. Map Library
Roy P. Meyer Memorial Map Library
Bemidji, MN 56601
218-755-2878

University of Minnesota
Wilson Library, Map Library S-76
309 19th Ave. S.
Minneapolis, MN 55455
612-624-4549

Nebraska
Kearney State College
Geography Map Library
Kearney, NE 68849
308-234-8356

Nevada
Nevada Bureau of Mines & Geology
Open Files Section
Mail Stop 178, University of Nevada
Reno, NV 89557
702-784-6691

New York
New York State Dept. of Transportation
Map Information Unit
State Campus Bldg., Rm. 105
Albany, NY 12232
518-457-3555

Oregon
University of Oregon
Map Library
165 Condon Hall
Eugene, OR 97403
503-346-3051

South Dakota
EROS Data Ctr.
Data Management Section
Sioux Falls, SD 57198
605-594-6594

Texas
Lunar & Planetary Institute
Planetary Image Ctr.
3600 Bay Area Blvd.
Houston, TX 77058
713-486-2172

Utah
USDA-ASCS Aerial Photography Field Office
P.O. Box 47031
Salt Lake City, UT 84119
801-524-5846

Washington
Washington Dept. of Natural Resources
Photos, Maps & Reports, QW-21
Olympia, WA 98504
206-753-5338

Wisconsin
University of Wisconsin, Madison
Arthur M. Robinson Map Library
310 Science Hall
550 N. Park St.
Madison, WI 53706
608-262-1471

University of Wisconsin
Milwaukee Library
American Geographical Society Map Collection
P.O. Box 399
Milwaukee, WI 53201
414-229-6282

SATELLITE IMAGERY COLLECTIONS

Arizona
University of Arizona
Space Imagery Ctr.
Lunar & Planetary Laboratory
Tucson, AZ 85721
602-621-4861

California
University of California, Berkeley
Dept. of Geography Library
501 Earth Science Bldg.
Berkeley, CA 94720
510-642-3903

U.S. Geological Survey Library, Menlo Park
345 Middlefield Rd., MS 55
Menlo Park, CA 94025
415-853-8300

Regional Planetary Image Facility
Jet Propulsion Laboratory
4800 Oak Grove Dr., Mail Stop 264-115
Pasadena, CA 91109
818-354-4321

University of California, Santa Barbara
Map & Imagery Laboratory
Santa Barbara, CA 93106
805-893-2779

Colorado
Colorado State University Libraries
Govt. Documents Div., Map Collection
Fort Collins, CO 80523
303-491-1882

Florida
Map Library
University of Florida
MSL-110
Gainesville, FL 32611
904-392-2825

Georgia
University of Georgia Libraries
Science Library, Map Collection
Athens, GA 30602
404-542-0690

Iowa
University of Iowa Libraries
Map Collection
311 Main Library
Iowa City, IA 52242
319-335-5920

Minnesota
University of Minnesota
Wilson Library, Map Library
309 19th Ave. S.
Minneapolis, MN 55455
612-624-4549

Missouri
Washington University
Dept. of Earth and Planetary Sciences
Regional Planetary Image Facility
1 Brookings Dr.
St. Louis, MO 63130
314-935-5679

New York
Spacecraft Planetary Imaging Facility
Cornell University
317 Space Sciences Bldg.
Ithaca, NY 14853
607-255-3833

Oregon
University of Oregon Map Library
165 Condon Hall
Eugene, OR 97403
503-346-3051

South Dakota
EROS Data Ctr.
Data Management Section
Sioux Falls, SD 57198
605-594-6594

Wisconsin
University of Wisconsin, Madison
Arthur M. Robinson Map Library
310 Science Hall, 550 N. Park St.
Madison, WI 53706
608-262-1471

University of Wisconsin
Milwaukee Library
American Geographical Society Map Collection
P.O. Box 399
Milwaukee, WI 53201
414-229-6282

SPECIAL COLLECTIONS

Arizona
Grand Canyon Study Collection
Map Library
P.O. Box 129
Grand Canyon Natl. Park, AZ 86023
602-638-7769

California
Hoover Institution on War, Revolution & Peace
Stanford University
Stanford, CA 94305
415-723-1754

District of Columbia
World Bank Cartography Library
1818 H St. NW
Washington, DC 20433
202-473-8670

Association of American Railroads
Economics & Finance Dept. Library
1920 L St. NW, Rm. 523
Washington, DC 20036
202-639-2300

Massachusetts
Woods Hole Oceanographic Institution
Data Library, McLean Laboratory
Quissett Campus
Woods Hole, MA 02543
508-548-1400

Texas
Amoco Production Co.
Library Information Ctr.
501 Westlake Park Blvd.
Houston, TX 77079
713-556-4217

Utah
Latter Day Saints Genealogical Dept. Library
Map Dept.
35 N. West Temple
Salt Lake City, UT 84150
801-240-2531

Index

A.I.D. Associates, Inc., 49
Abbeville Press, 228, 237
Access Maps & Gear, 338
Accu-Data, 246-247
ADC The Map People, 30, 49, 77
Adirondack Mountain Club, 49, 54
Adventure 16, 284
aerial photographs, 126, 250-254
aeronautical charts, 222-226, 234
        dealers of, 225-226
Agricultural Stabilization and Conservation Service,
        122, 123, 324
agriculture maps, 122-124, 133-134
Air Photographics, Inc., 251
Allmaps Canada, Ltd., 57, 96
American Association for State and Local History,
        164
American Association of Petroleum Geologists, 140,
        201-202, 214-215, 286
American Association of Weather Observers, 245-246
American Automobile Association, 14, 90, 93
American Congress on Surveying and Mapping, 20,
        286
American Geographical Society, 103-104, 133, 163,
        286
American Library Association, Map and Geography
        Roundtable, 286
American Map Corp., 56, 57, 64, 65, 72, 96-97,
        184-186, 188
American Nature Maps, 160
American Society for Photogrammetry and Remote
        Sensing, 287
American Weather Enterprises, 246
American Youth Hostels, 30
antique map dealers, 164-171
antique maps and reproductions, 125, 162-171
        reproductions versus originals, 168-169
        researching, 164
Appalachian Mountain Club, 49, 54
Appalachian Trail Conference, 54
Aristoplay, 176, 276
Army Corps of Engineers, 44, 114, 115, 122, 210,
        217-219, 324
Arrow Map, Inc., 97
Association of American Geographers, 287
Association of Map Memorabilia Collectors, 287
astronomical charts and maps, 227-228, 231, 237-241
Astronomical Society of the Pacific, 227
atlases, 260-269
        choosing, 260-263
        world, 264-265

Austin Peirce, 307
Automap, Inc., 295
Automobile Club of Southern California, 85, 87

Bade Sports, Inc., 309
Basin Street Press, 61
bathymetric maps, 213
Bausch & Lomb, 284
Better Boating Association, Inc., 210, 211, 308
Bicycle Federation of America, 30
bicycle route maps, 30-33
BikeCentennial, 30
blind persons, maps for, 15
Blue Hill Observatory, 246
Bluewater Books & Charts, 210-211
boating maps, *see* nautical charts and maps;
        recreation maps; river, lake, and waterway maps;
        tide and current maps
books on map skills, 21-22
boundary maps, 108-111
Boy Scouts of America, 21
Braille maps, 15
Broderbund Software, Inc., 281
Buckeye Trail Association, Inc., 54-55
Bureau of Land Management, 44, 114-115, 324-325
Bureau of the Census, *see* Census Bureau
bus and subway maps, 34-39
business maps, 184-188
        see also census maps
The Butterworth Co., Cape Cod, 30-31, 49, 61, 101

calendars, 305
Caliper Corp., 296
Canada Map Office, 42, 46, 86, 118-119, 133, 140,
        147, 153, 158, 160, 172-173, 180, 200-201, 205,
        219, 224, 245
Canadian Hydrographic Service, 46-47, 210, 214
Canadian Orienteering Federation, 55
Canadian Society of Petroleum Geologists, 202
Carto-Philatelists, 287
cartographers, 23-28
cartographic laboratories, 25-28
cartography, history of, 8-11
CD-ROM, 294
Celestial Arts, 87, 175, 213, 227, 231, 237
cellular telephone maps, 205, 206
Census Bureau, 76, 84, 88, 110, 184, 189-194, 204,
        324
census data files, 12
census maps, 129, 189-194
        see also software